THE QUANTUM AGE™

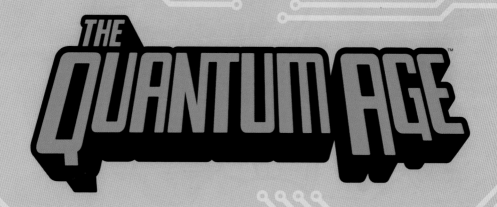

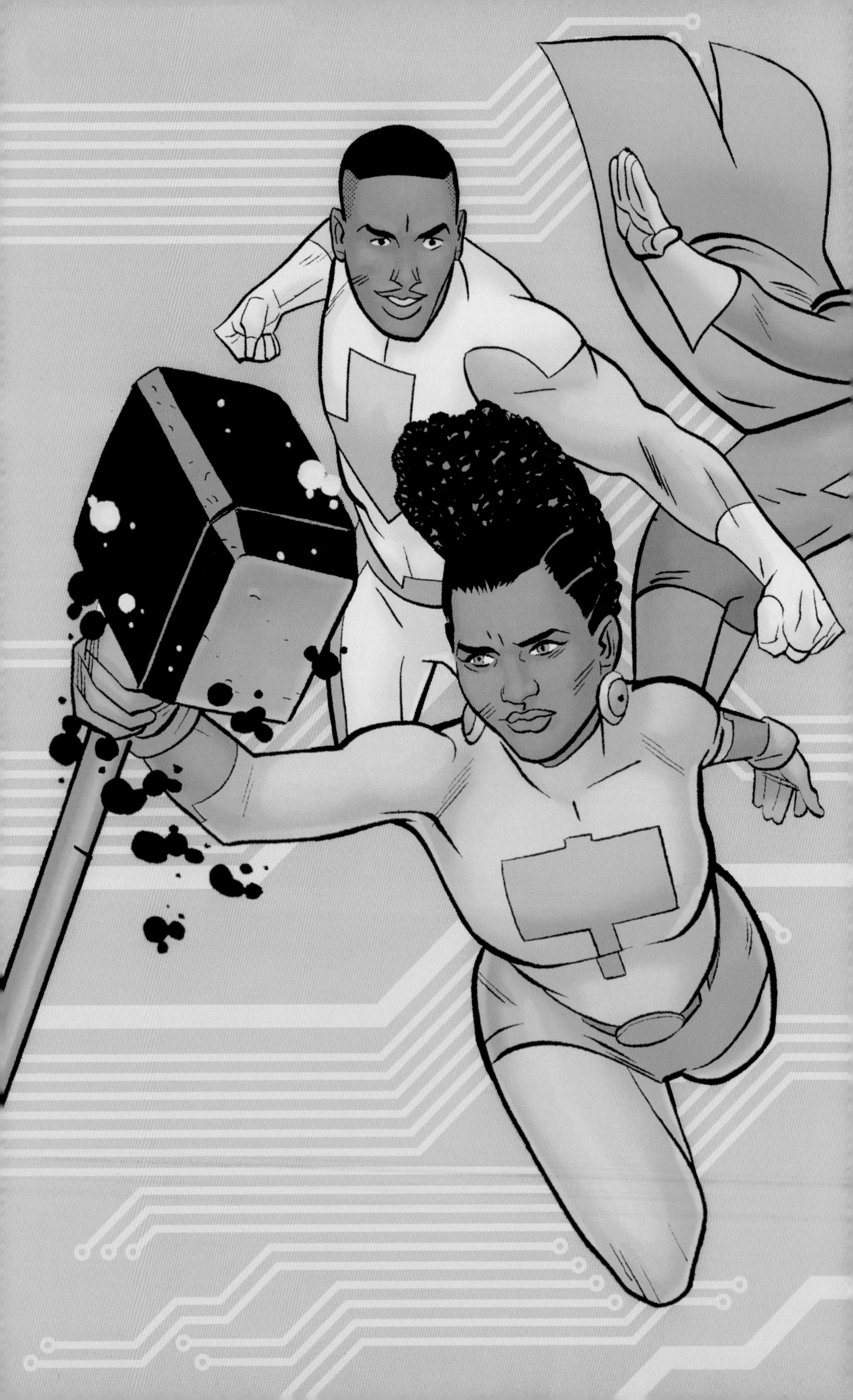

THE QUANTUM AGE

WRITER **JEFF LEMIRE**

ARTIST **WILFREDO TORRES**

COLORIST **DAVE STEWART**

LETTERER **NATE PIEKOS OF BLAMBOT®**

PROLOGUE LETTERER **TODD KLEIN**

COVER BY **WILFREDO TORRES**
AND **DAVE STEWART**

CHAPTER BREAKS BY
**WILFREDO TORRES, CHRISTIAN WARD,
ANDREW MACLEAN, MARCO RUDY, BRENDAN MCCARTHY,
TULA LOTAY, JEFF LEMIRE, AND DAVE STEWART**

CREATED BY **JEFF LEMIRE AND DEAN ORMSTON**

DARK HORSE BOOKS

PRESIDENT & PUBLISHER **MIKE RICHARDSON**

EDITOR **DANIEL CHABON**

ASSISTANT EDITORS **CHUCK HOWITT** AND **BRETT ISRAEL**

DESIGNER **ETHAN KIMBERLING**

DIGITAL ART TECHNICIAN **JOSIE CHRISTENSEN**

QUANTUM AGE
Quantum Age™ © 2018, 2019 171 Studios, Inc., and Dean Ormston. Dark Horse Books® and the Dark Horse logo are registered trademarks of Dark Horse Comics LLC. All rights reserved. No portion of this publication may be reproduced or transmitted, in any form or by any means, without the express written permission of Dark Horse Comics LLC. Names, characters, places, and incidents featured in this publication either are the product of the author's imagination or are used fictitiously. Any resemblance to actual persons (living or dead), events, institutions, or locales, without satiric intent, is coincidental.

Collects issues #1–#6 of the Dark Horse Comics series *Quantum Age*, as well as material from Free Comic Book Day 2018.

Published by
Dark Horse Books
A division of Dark Horse Comics LLC
10956 SE Main Street
Milwaukie, OR 97222

DarkHorse.com

To find a comics shop in your area,
visit comicshoplocator.com

First edition: May 2019
ISBN 978-1-50670-841-6

10 9 8 7 6 5 4 3 2 1
Printed in China

Library of Congress Cataloging-in-Publication Data

Names: Lemire, Jeff, writer. | Torres, Wilfredo (Comic book artist), artist.
 | Stewart, Dave, colourist, artist. | Piekos, Nate, letterer.
Title: Quantum age / writer, Jeff Lemire ; artist, Wilfredo Torres ;
 colorist, Dave Stewart ; letterer, Nate Piekos of Blambot ; cover by
 Wilfredo Torres and Dave Stewart.
Description: First edition. | Milwaukie, OR : Dark Horse Books, 2019- | "From
 the world of Black Hammer" | v. 1: "Collects issues #1-#6 of the Dark
 Horse Comics series Quantum Age, as well as material from Free Comic Book
 Day 2018."
Identifiers: LCCN 2018052528 | ISBN 9781506708416 (v. 1 : paperback)
Subjects: LCSH: Comic books, strips, etc. | BISAC: COMICS & GRAPHIC NOVELS /
 Horror. | COMICS & GRAPHIC NOVELS / Superheroes.
Classification: LCC PN6728.Q36 L46 2019 | DDC 741.5/973--dc23
LC record available at https://lccn.loc.gov/2018052528

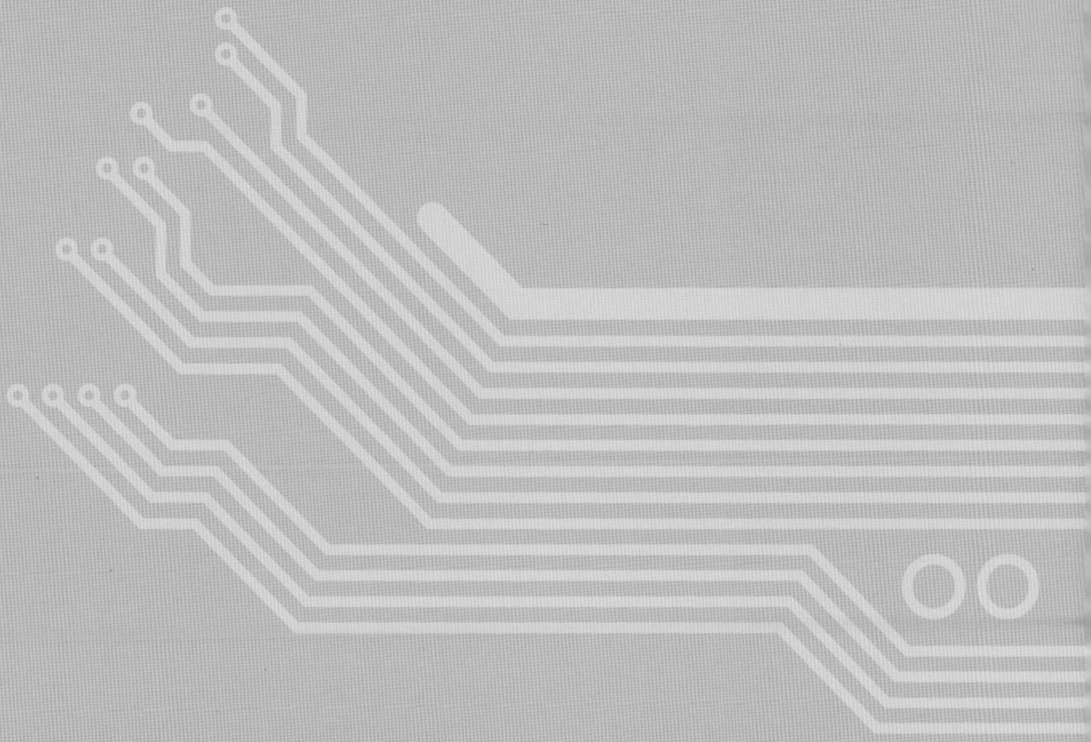

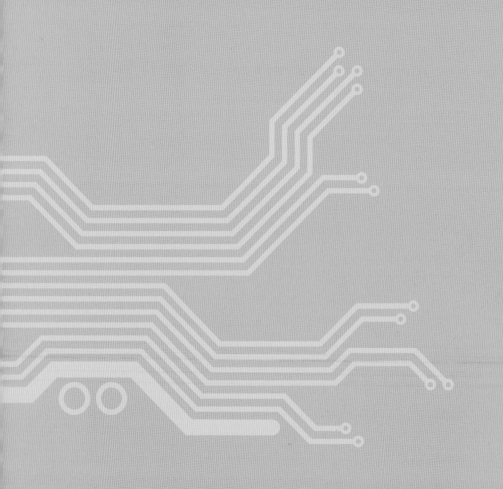

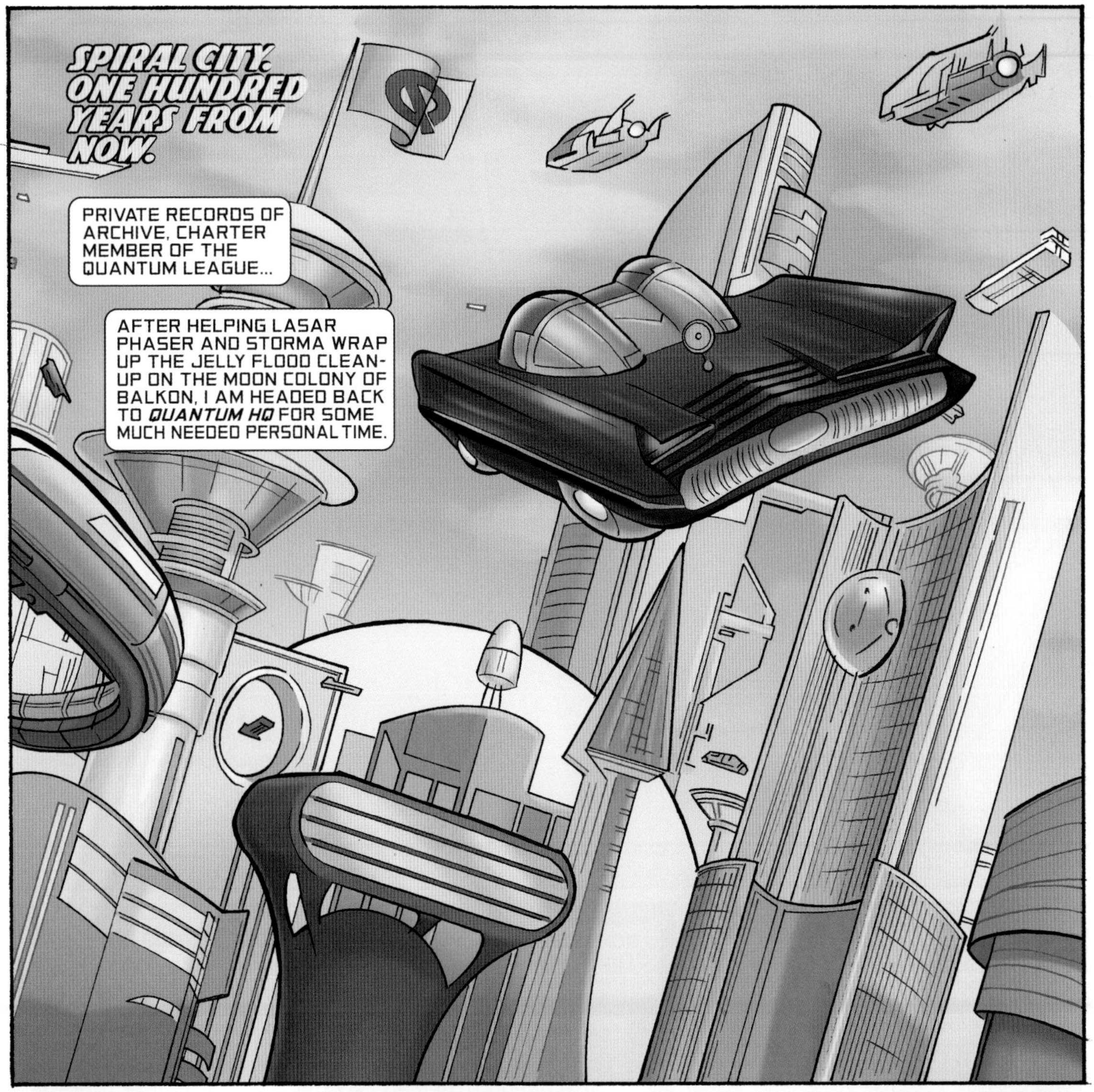
SPIRAL CITY. ONE HUNDRED YEARS FROM NOW.
PRIVATE RECORDS OF ARCHIVE, CHARTER MEMBER OF THE QUANTUM LEAGUE...
AFTER HELPING LASAR PHASER AND STORMA WRAP UP THE JELLY FLOOD CLEAN-UP ON THE MOON COLONY OF BALKON, I AM HEADED BACK TO *QUANTUM HQ* FOR SOME MUCH NEEDED PERSONAL TIME.

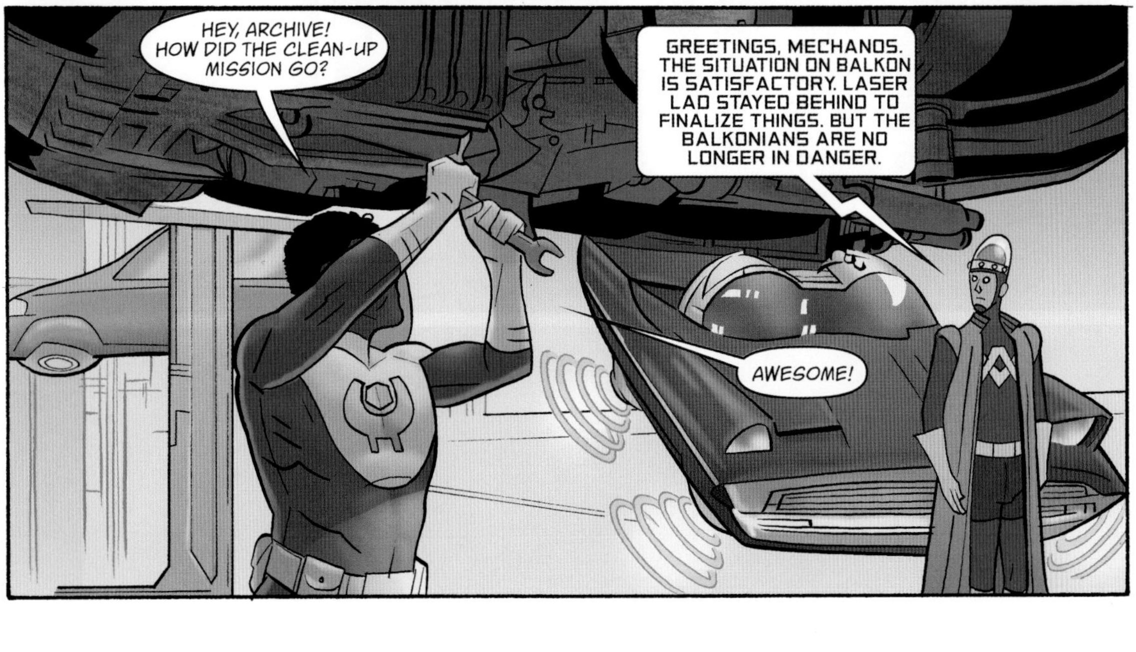
HEY, ARCHIVE! HOW DID THE CLEAN-UP MISSION GO?
GREETINGS, MECHANOS. THE SITUATION ON BALKON IS SATISFACTORY. LASER LAD STAYED BEHIND TO FINALIZE THINGS. BUT THE BALKONIANS ARE NO LONGER IN DANGER.
AWESOME!

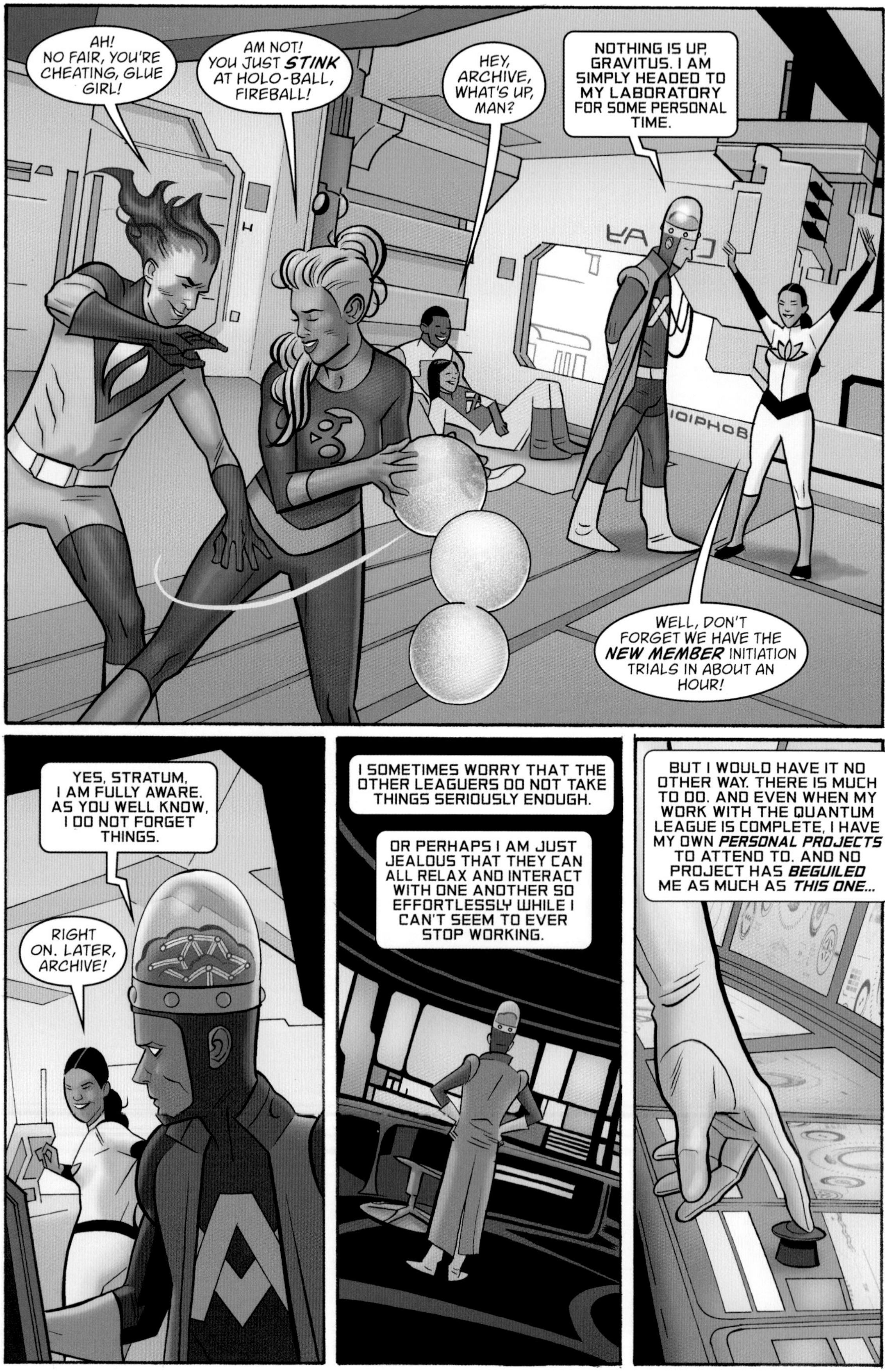
AH! NO FAIR, YOU'RE CHEATING, GLUE GIRL!
AM NOT! YOU JUST STINK AT HOLO-BALL, FIREBALL!
HEY, ARCHIVE, WHAT'S UP, MAN?
NOTHING IS UP, GRAVITUS. I AM SIMPLY HEADED TO MY LABORATORY FOR SOME PERSONAL TIME.
WELL, DON'T FORGET WE HAVE THE NEW MEMBER INITIATION TRIALS IN ABOUT AN HOUR!
YES, STRATUM, I AM FULLY AWARE. AS YOU WELL KNOW, I DO NOT FORGET THINGS.
RIGHT ON. LATER, ARCHIVE!
I SOMETIMES WORRY THAT THE OTHER LEAGUERS DO NOT TAKE THINGS SERIOUSLY ENOUGH.
OR PERHAPS I AM JUST JEALOUS THAT THEY CAN ALL RELAX AND INTERACT WITH ONE ANOTHER SO EFFORTLESSLY WHILE I CAN'T SEEM TO EVER STOP WORKING.
BUT I WOULD HAVE IT NO OTHER WAY. THERE IS MUCH TO DO. AND EVEN WHEN MY WORK WITH THE QUANTUM LEAGUE IS COMPLETE, I HAVE MY OWN PERSONAL PROJECTS TO ATTEND TO. AND NO PROJECT HAS BEGUILED ME AS MUCH AS THIS ONE...

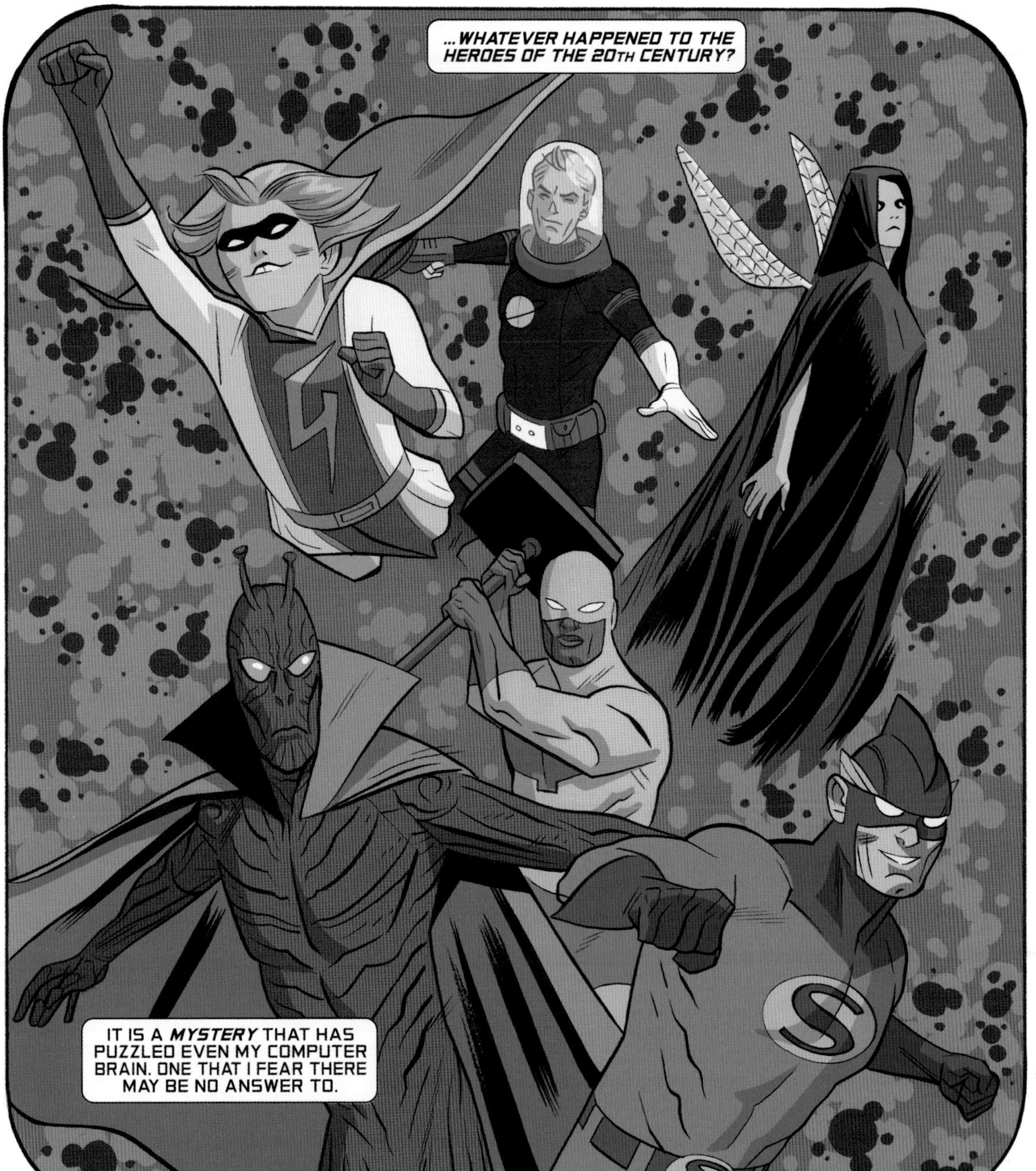
...WHATEVER HAPPENED TO THE HEROES OF THE 20TH CENTURY?
IT IS A MYSTERY THAT HAS PUZZLED EVEN MY COMPUTER BRAIN. ONE THAT I FEAR THERE MAY BE NO ANSWER TO.

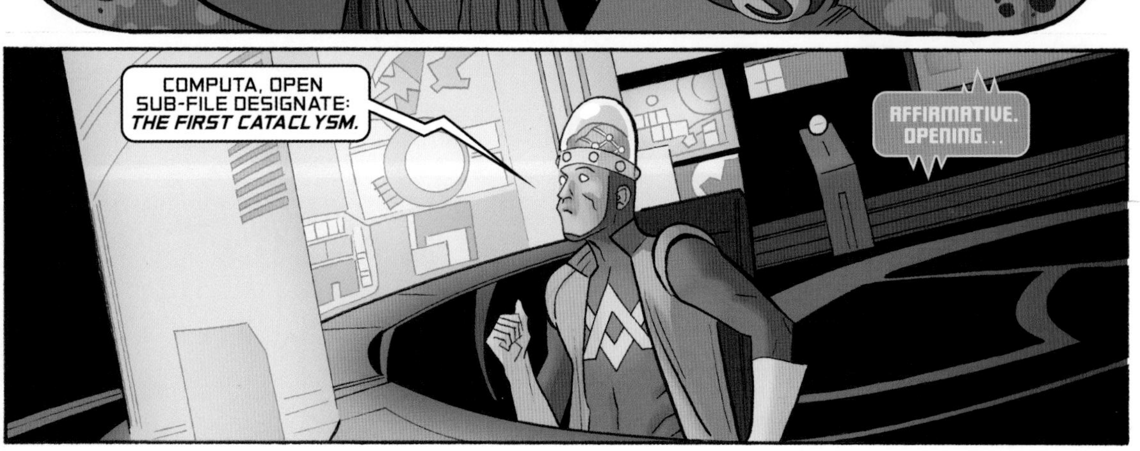
COMPUTA, OPEN SUB-FILE DESIGNATE: THE FIRST CATACLYSM.
AFFIRMATIVE. OPENING...

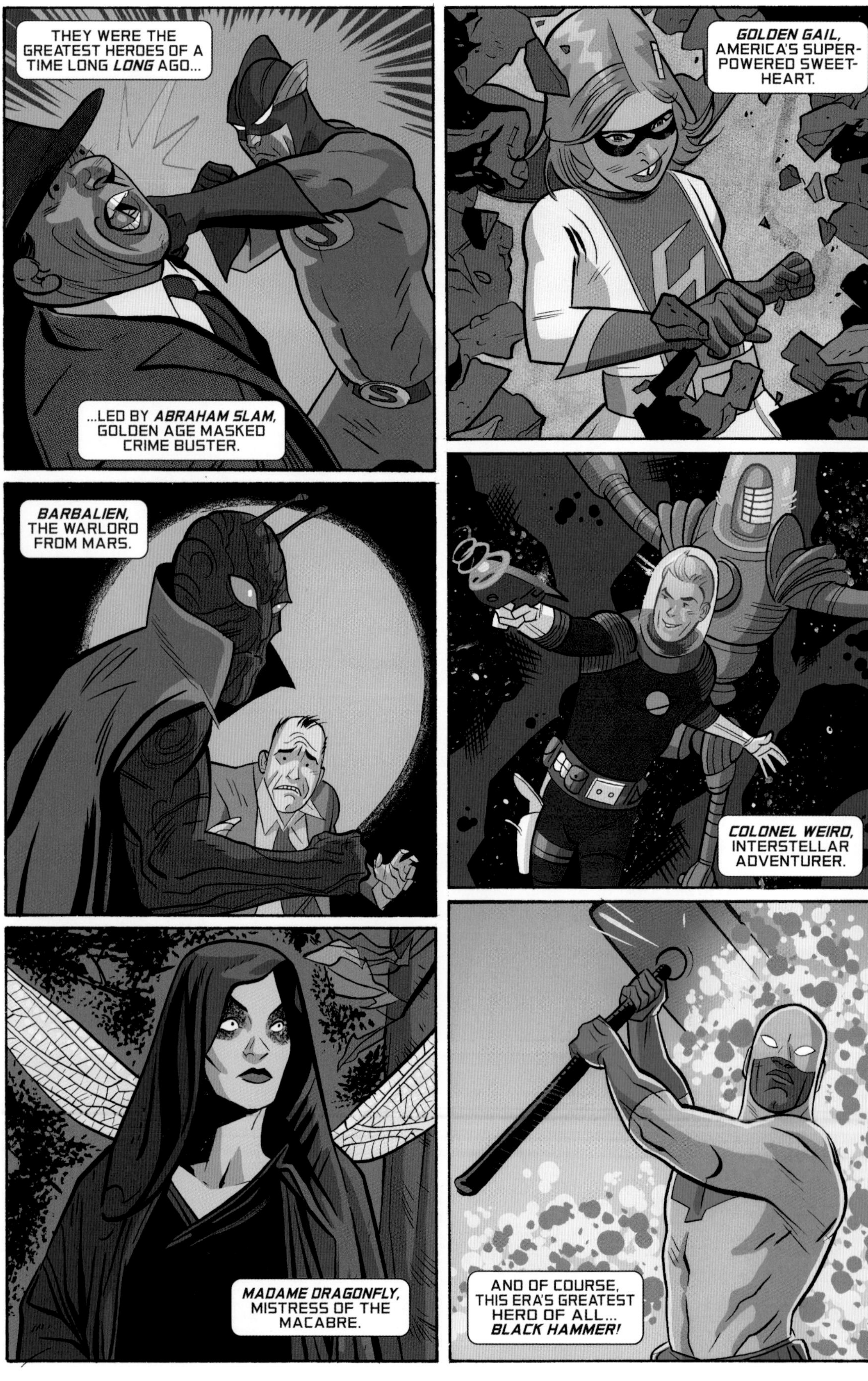
THEY WERE THE GREATEST HEROES OF A TIME LONG *LONG* AGO...
...LED BY ***ABRAHAM SLAM,*** GOLDEN AGE MASKED CRIME BUSTER.
GOLDEN GAIL, AMERICA'S SUPER-POWERED SWEET-HEART.
BARBALIEN, THE WARLORD FROM MARS.
COLONEL WEIRD, INTERSTELLAR ADVENTURER.
MADAME DRAGONFLY, MISTRESS OF THE MACABRE.
AND OF COURSE, THIS ERA'S GREATEST HERO OF ALL... ***BLACK HAMMER!***

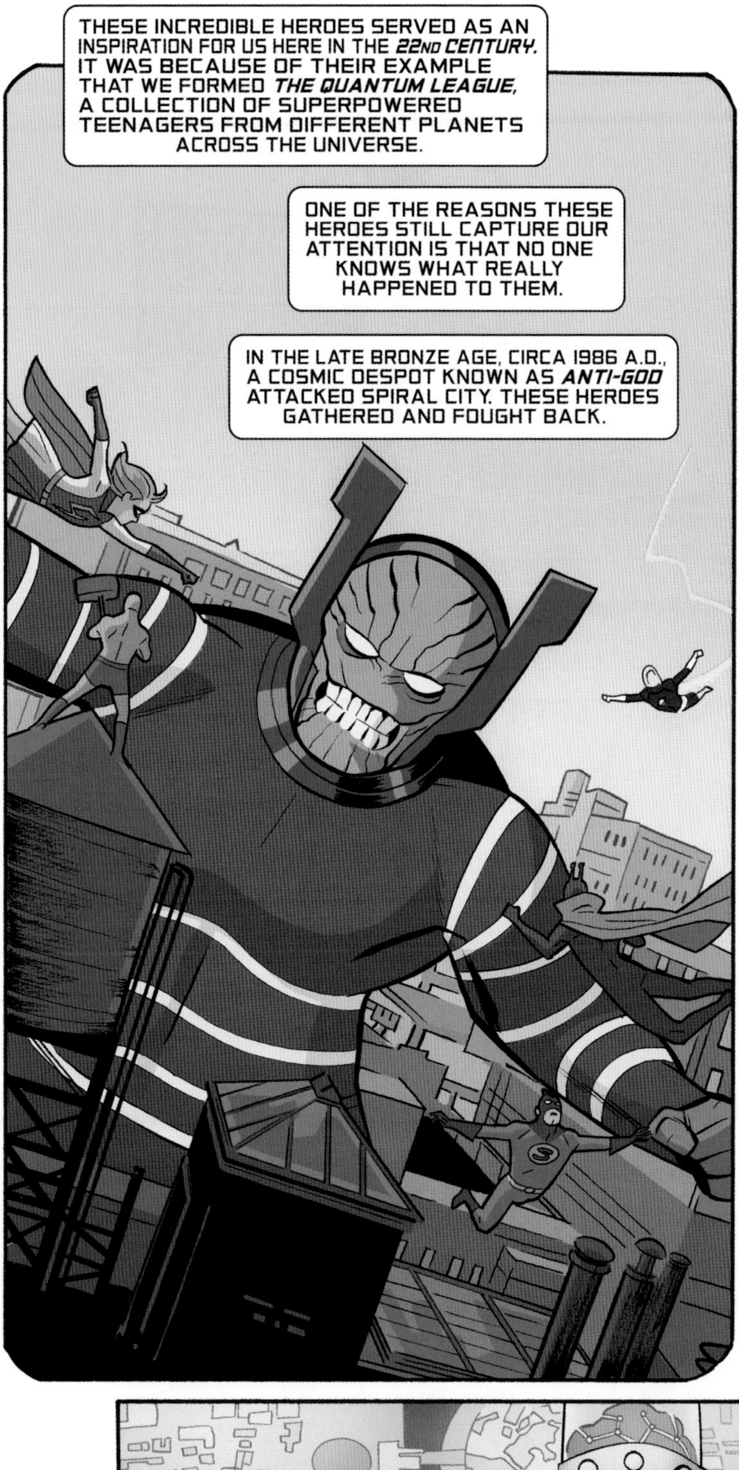
THESE INCREDIBLE HEROES SERVED AS AN INSPIRATION FOR US HERE IN THE *22ND CENTURY.* IT WAS BECAUSE OF THEIR EXAMPLE THAT WE FORMED *THE QUANTUM LEAGUE,* A COLLECTION OF SUPERPOWERED TEENAGERS FROM DIFFERENT PLANETS ACROSS THE UNIVERSE.
ONE OF THE REASONS THESE HEROES STILL CAPTURE OUR ATTENTION IS THAT NO ONE KNOWS WHAT REALLY HAPPENED TO THEM.
IN THE LATE BRONZE AGE, CIRCA 1986 A.D., A COSMIC DESPOT KNOWN AS *ANTI-GOD* ATTACKED SPIRAL CITY. THESE HEROES GATHERED AND FOUGHT BACK.

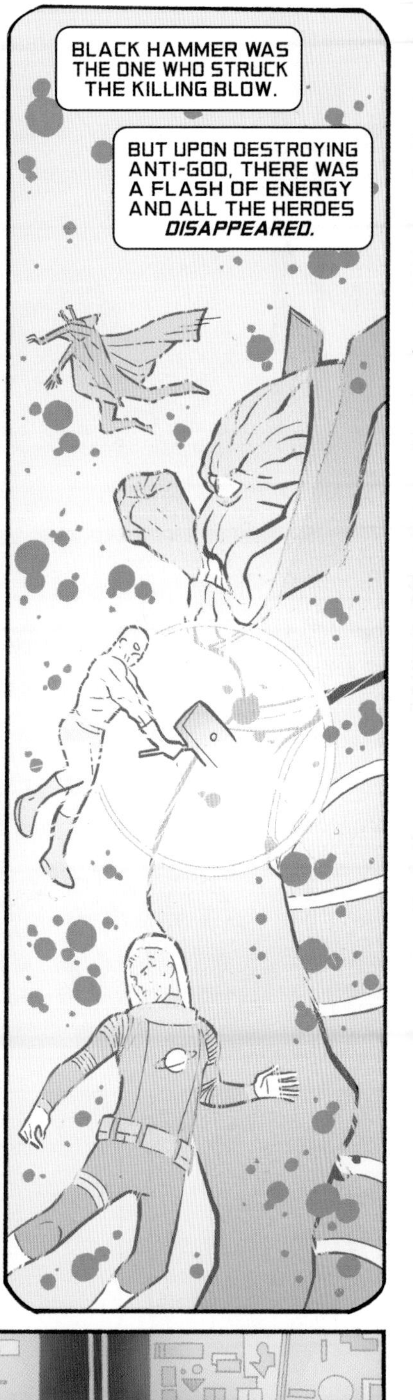
BLACK HAMMER WAS THE ONE WHO STRUCK THE KILLING BLOW.
BUT UPON DESTROYING ANTI-GOD, THERE WAS A FLASH OF ENERGY AND ALL THE HEROES *DISAPPEARED.*

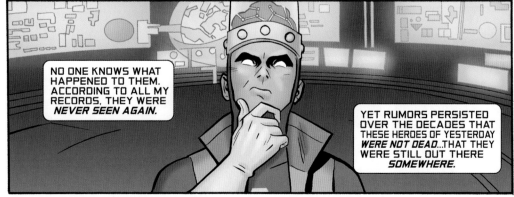

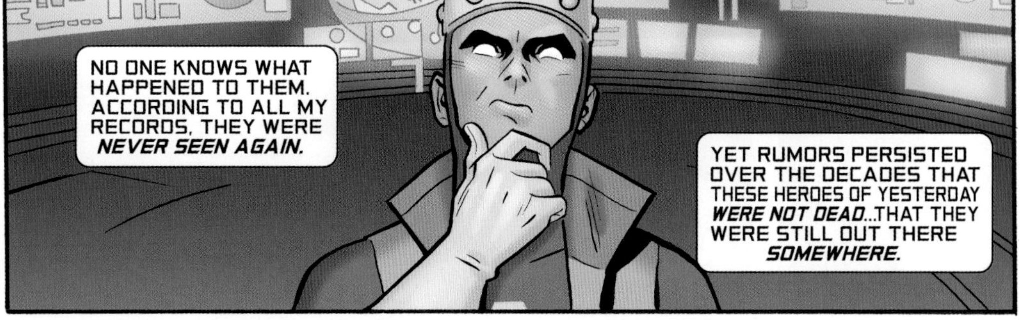
NO ONE KNOWS WHAT HAPPENED TO THEM. ACCORDING TO ALL MY RECORDS, THEY WERE *NEVER SEEN AGAIN.*
YET RUMORS PERSISTED OVER THE DECADES THAT THESE HEROES OF YESTERDAY *WERE NOT DEAD*...THAT THEY WERE STILL OUT THERE *SOMEWHERE.*

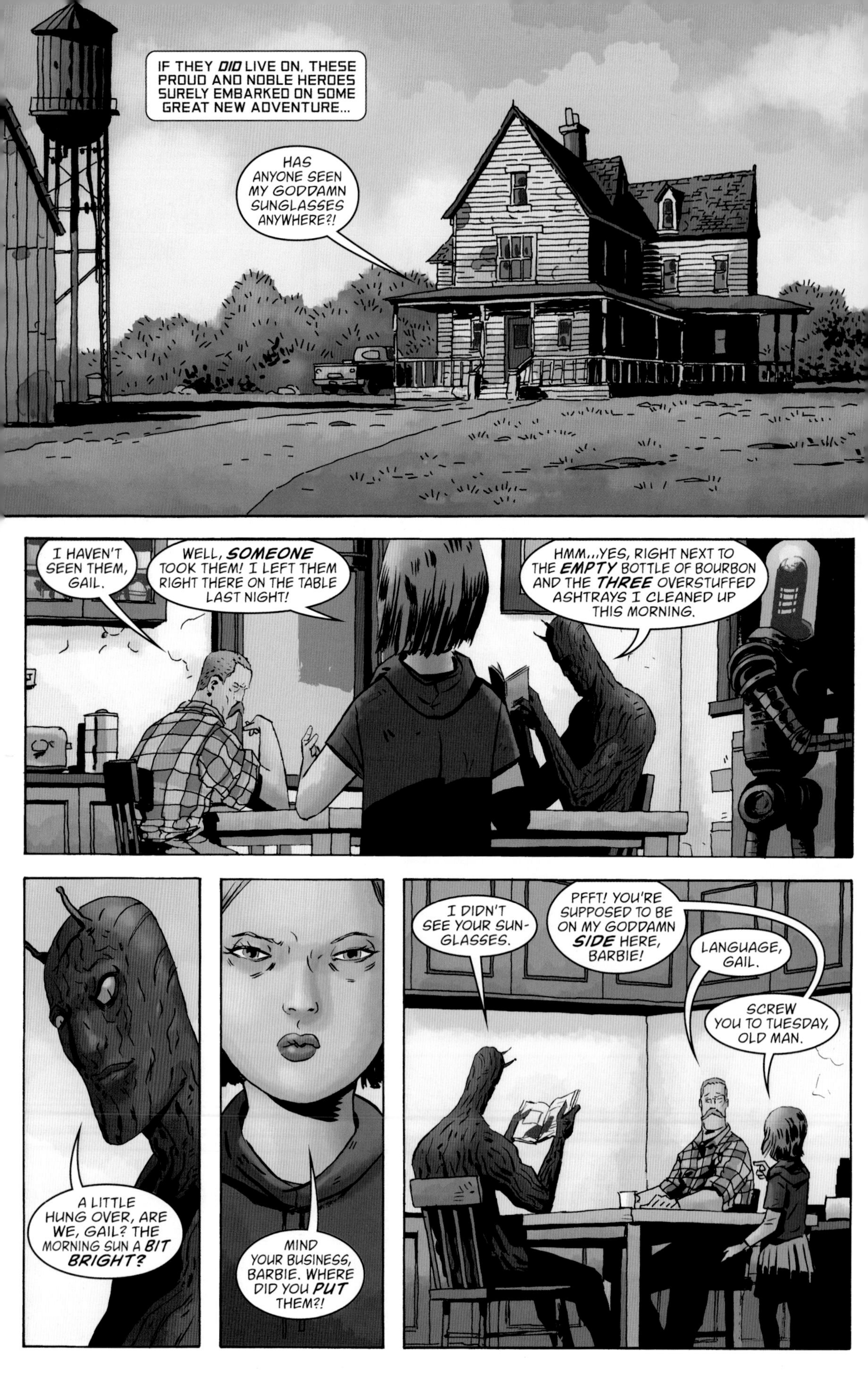
IF THEY DID LIVE ON, THESE PROUD AND NOBLE HEROES SURELY EMBARKED ON SOME GREAT NEW ADVENTURE...
HAS ANYONE SEEN MY GODDAMN SUNGLASSES ANYWHERE?!
I HAVEN'T SEEN THEM, GAIL.
WELL, SOMEONE TOOK THEM! I LEFT THEM RIGHT THERE ON THE TABLE LAST NIGHT!
HMM...YES, RIGHT NEXT TO THE EMPTY BOTTLE OF BOURBON AND THE THREE OVERSTUFFED ASHTRAYS I CLEANED UP THIS MORNING.
A LITTLE HUNG OVER, ARE WE, GAIL? THE MORNING SUN A BIT BRIGHT?
MIND YOUR BUSINESS, BARBIE. WHERE DID YOU PUT THEM?!
I DIDN'T SEE YOUR SUN-GLASSES.
PFFT! YOU'RE SUPPOSED TO BE ON MY GODDAMN SIDE HERE, BARBIE!
LANGUAGE, GAIL.
SCREW YOU TO TUESDAY, OLD MAN.

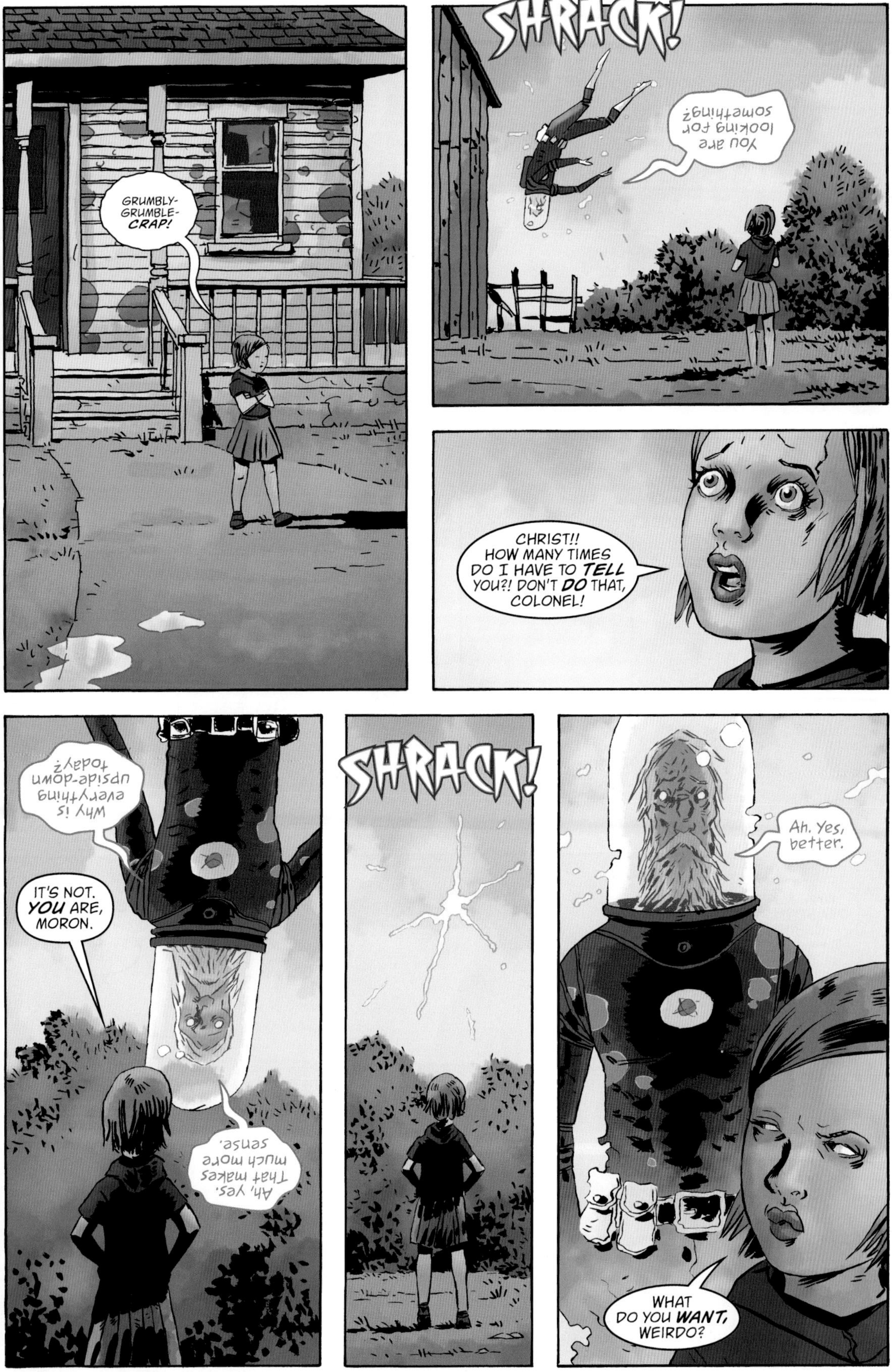
GRUMBLY-GRUMBLE-*CRAP!*
SHRACK!
You are looking for something?
CHRIST!! HOW MANY TIMES DO I HAVE TO *TELL* YOU?! DON'T *DO* THAT, COLONEL!
Why is everything upside-down today?
IT'S NOT. *YOU* ARE, MORON.
Ah, yes. That makes much more sense.
SHRACK!
Ah. Yes, better.
WHAT DO YOU *WANT,* WEIRDO?

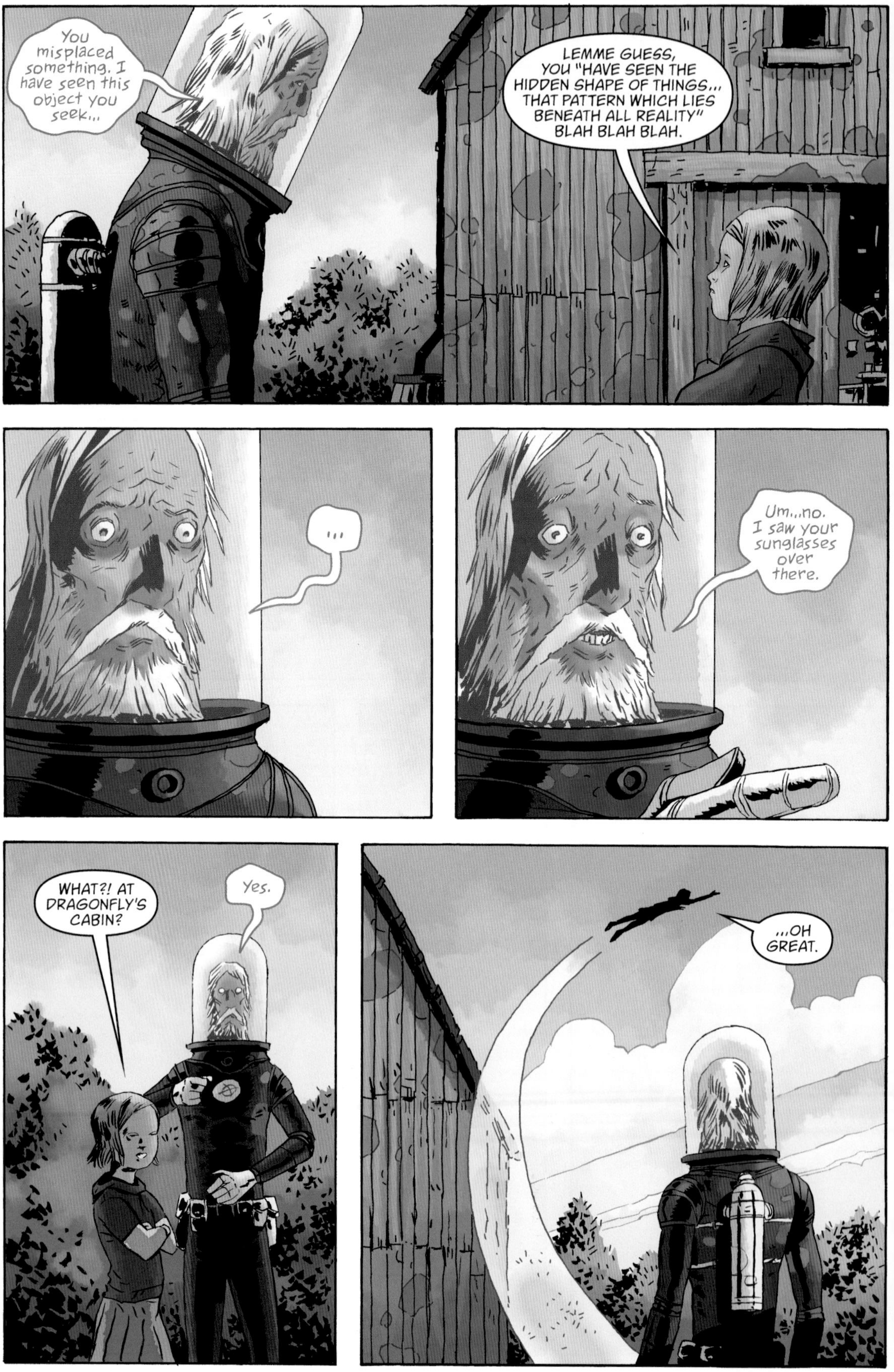
You misplaced something. I have seen this object you seek...
LEMME GUESS, YOU "HAVE SEEN THE HIDDEN SHAPE OF THINGS... THAT PATTERN WHICH LIES BENEATH ALL REALITY" BLAH BLAH BLAH.
...
Um...no. I saw your sunglasses over there.
WHAT?! AT DRAGONFLY'S CABIN?
Yes.
...OH GREAT.

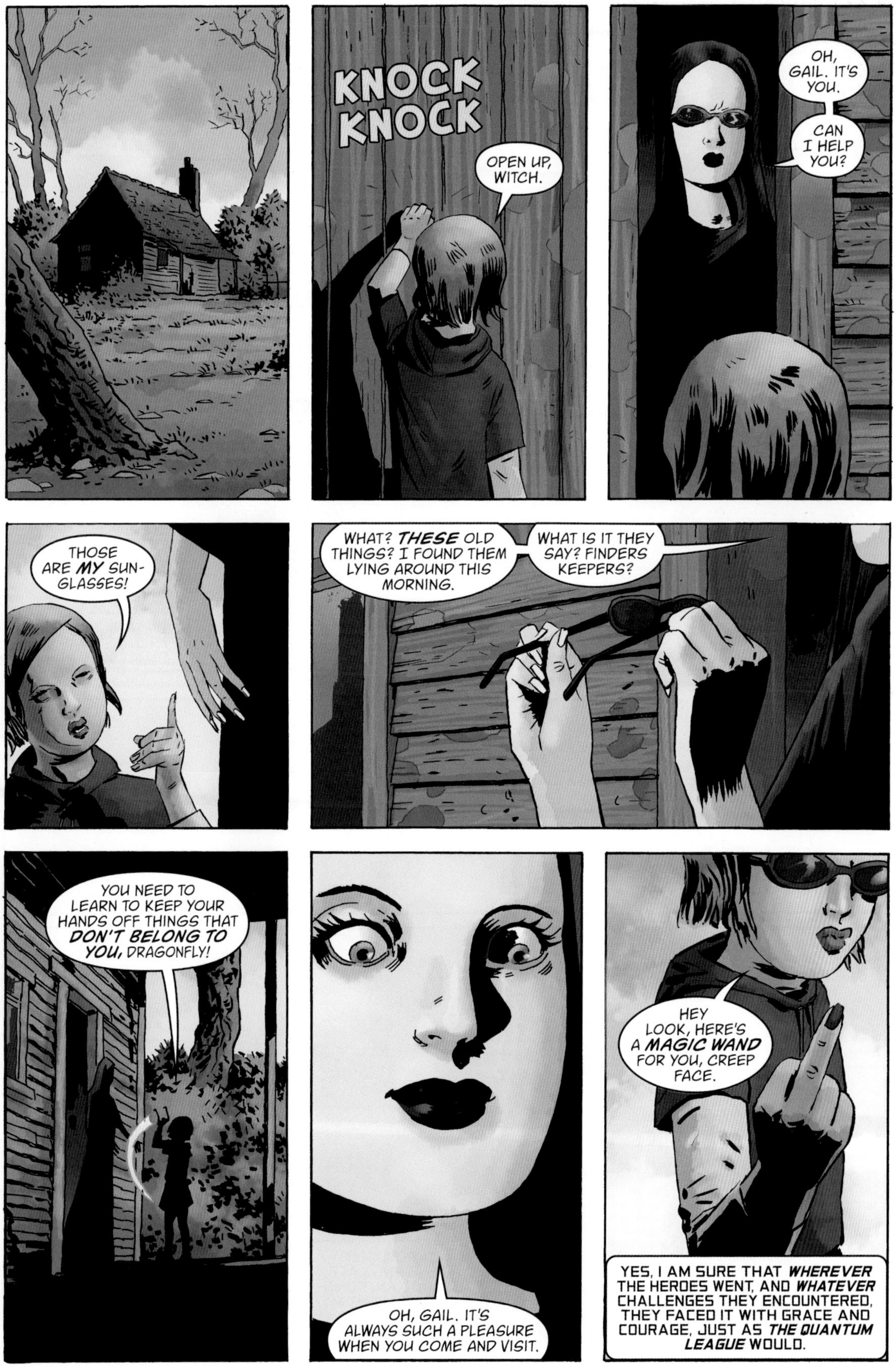
KNOCK KNOCK
OPEN UP, WITCH.
OH, GAIL. IT'S YOU.
CAN I HELP YOU?
THOSE ARE MY SUN-GLASSES!
WHAT? THESE OLD THINGS? I FOUND THEM LYING AROUND THIS MORNING.
WHAT IS IT THEY SAY? FINDERS KEEPERS?
YOU NEED TO LEARN TO KEEP YOUR HANDS OFF THINGS THAT DON'T BELONG TO YOU, DRAGONFLY!
OH, GAIL. IT'S ALWAYS SUCH A PLEASURE WHEN YOU COME AND VISIT.
HEY LOOK, HERE'S A MAGIC WAND FOR YOU, CREEP FACE.
YES, I AM SURE THAT WHEREVER THE HEROES WENT, AND WHATEVER CHALLENGES THEY ENCOUNTERED, THEY FACED IT WITH GRACE AND COURAGE, JUST AS THE QUANTUM LEAGUE WOULD.

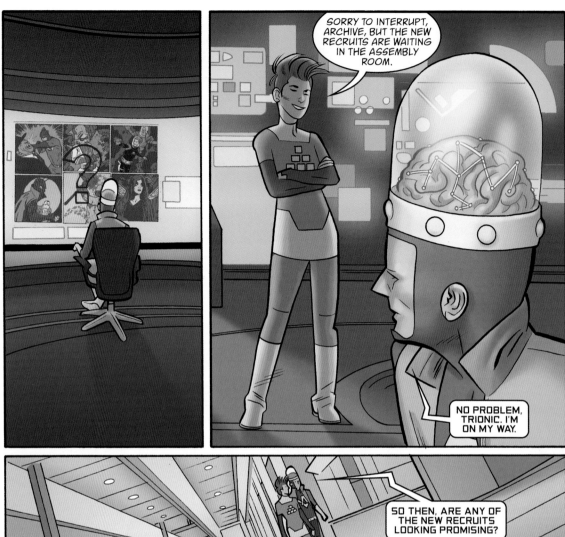

SORRY TO INTERRUPT, ARCHIVE, BUT THE NEW RECRUITS ARE WAITING IN THE ASSEMBLY ROOM.

NO PROBLEM, TRIONIC. I'M ON MY WAY.

SO THEN, ARE ANY OF THE NEW RECRUITS LOOKING PROMISING?

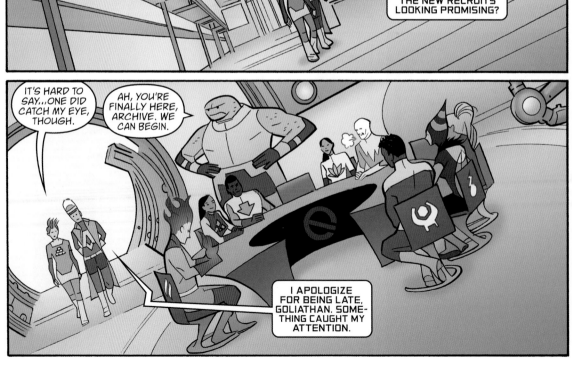

IT'S HARD TO SAY...ONE DID CATCH MY EYE, THOUGH.

AH, YOU'RE FINALLY HERE, ARCHIVE. WE CAN BEGIN.

I APOLOGIZE FOR BEING LATE, GOLIATHAN. SOME-THING CAUGHT MY ATTENTION.

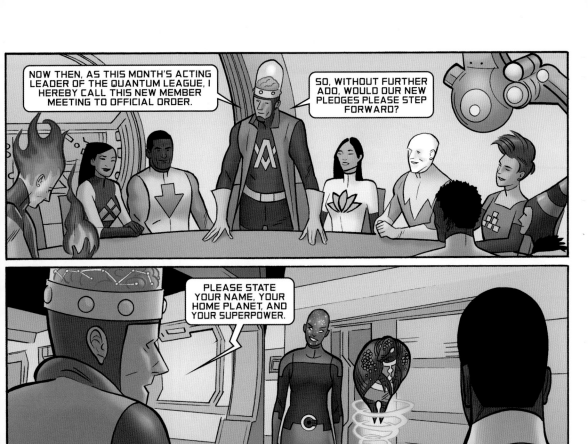

NOW THEN, AS THIS MONTH'S ACTING LEADER OF THE QUANTUM LEAGUE, I HEREBY CALL THIS NEW MEMBER MEETING TO OFFICIAL ORDER.

SO, WITHOUT FURTHER ADO, WOULD OUR NEW PLEDGES PLEASE STEP FORWARD?

PLEASE STATE YOUR NAME, YOUR HOME PLANET, AND YOUR SUPERPOWER.

I AM FELINDA TRAK FROM VWENTILLA. MY CODENAME IS *COSMO GIRL.* I CAN CREATE PORTALS AND TRANSPORT PEOPLE AND THINGS ACROSS SPACE AND TIME.

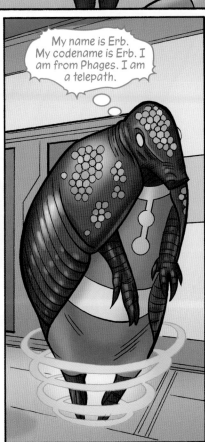

My name is Erb. My codename is Erb. I am from Phages. I am a telepath.

WAIT! I WANT TO JOIN TOO!

WHAT?! THIS IS A CLOSED MEETING! INVITATION ONLY!

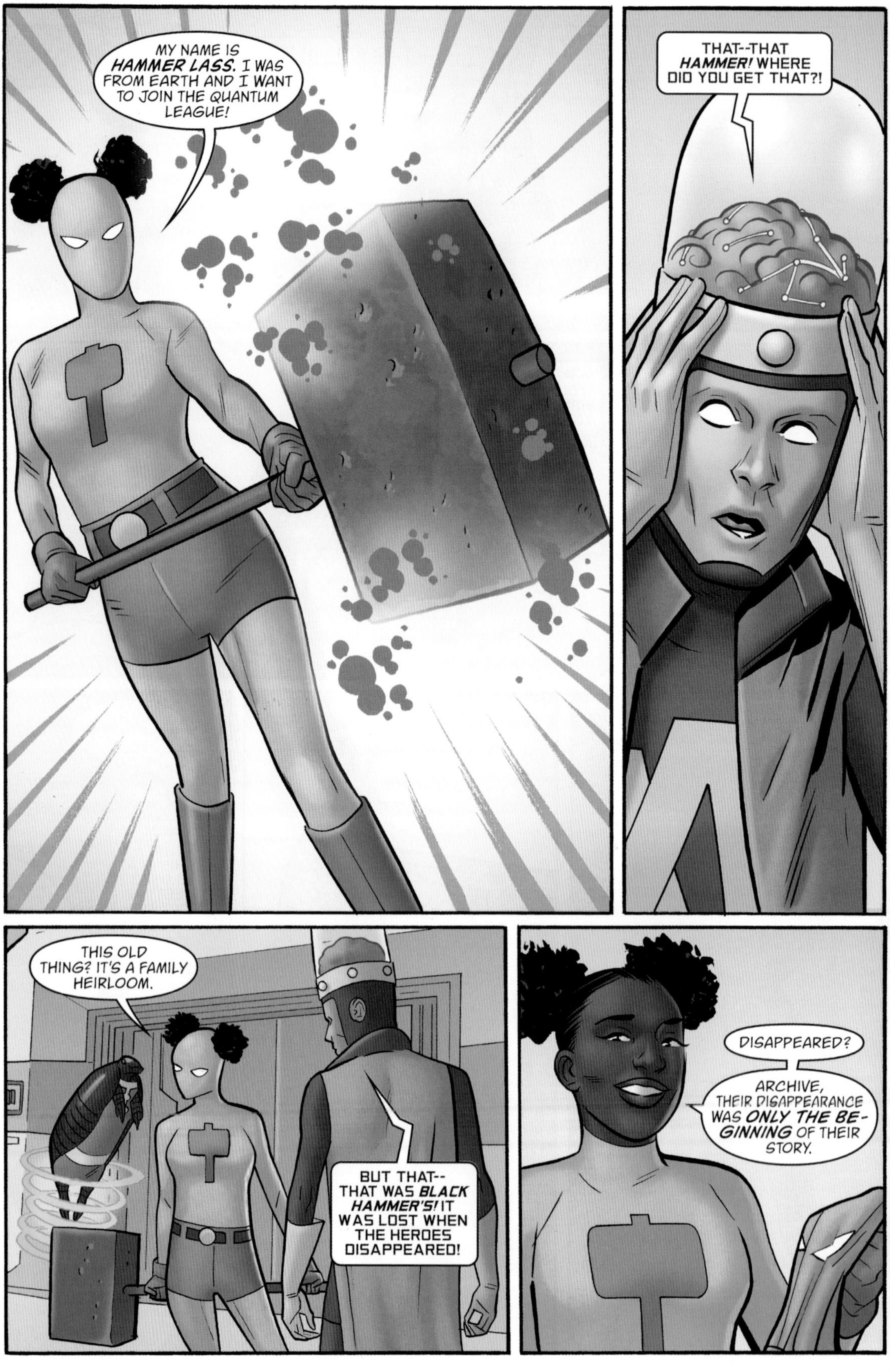
MY NAME IS HAMMER LASS. I WAS FROM EARTH AND I WANT TO JOIN THE QUANTUM LEAGUE!
THAT--THAT HAMMER! WHERE DID YOU GET THAT?!
THIS OLD THING? IT'S A FAMILY HEIRLOOM.
BUT THAT-- THAT WAS BLACK HAMMER'S! IT WAS LOST WHEN THE HEROES DISAPPEARED!
DISAPPEARED?
ARCHIVE, THEIR DISAPPEARANCE WAS ONLY THE BE-GINNING OF THEIR STORY.

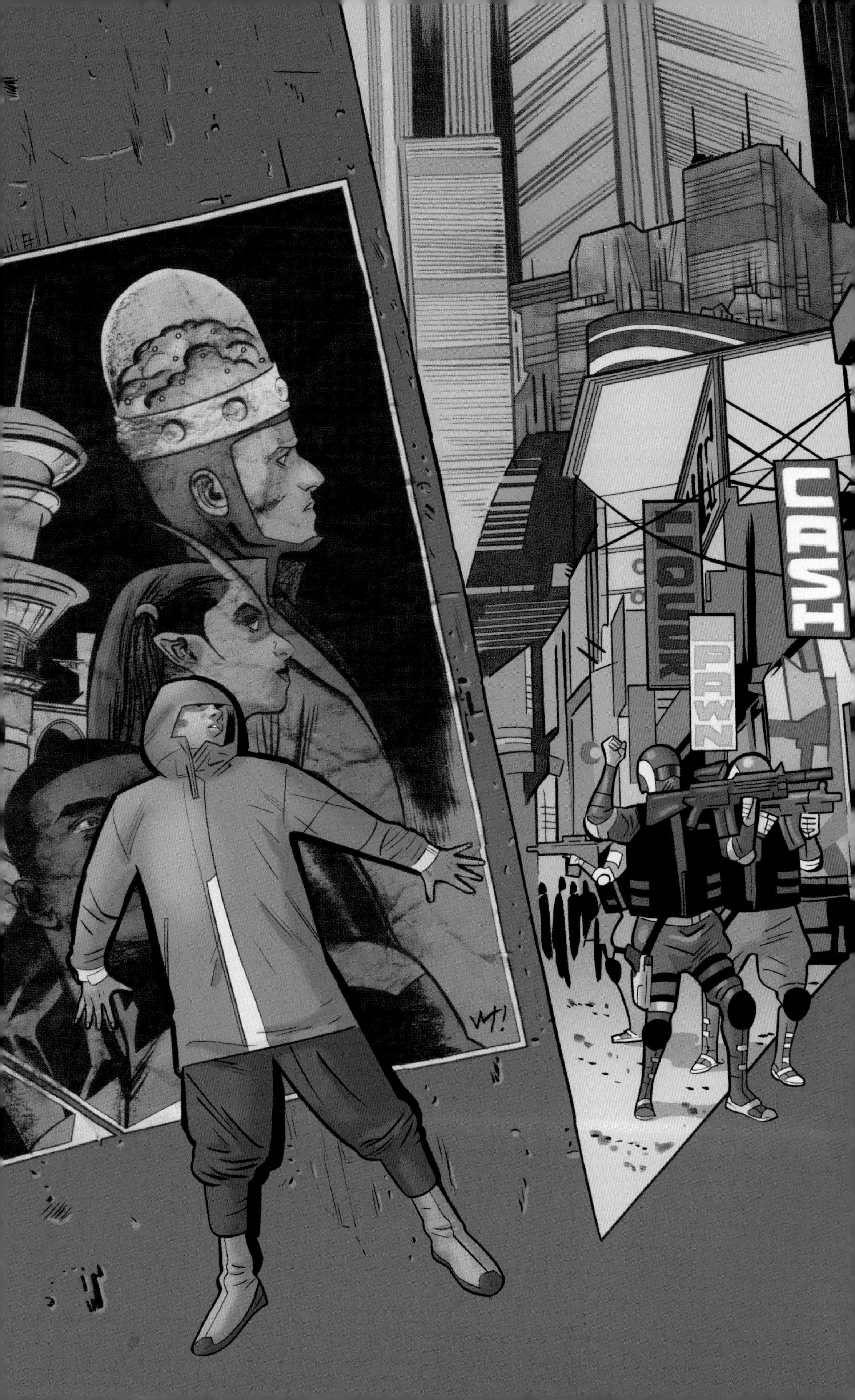
CASH
LIQUOR
PAWN

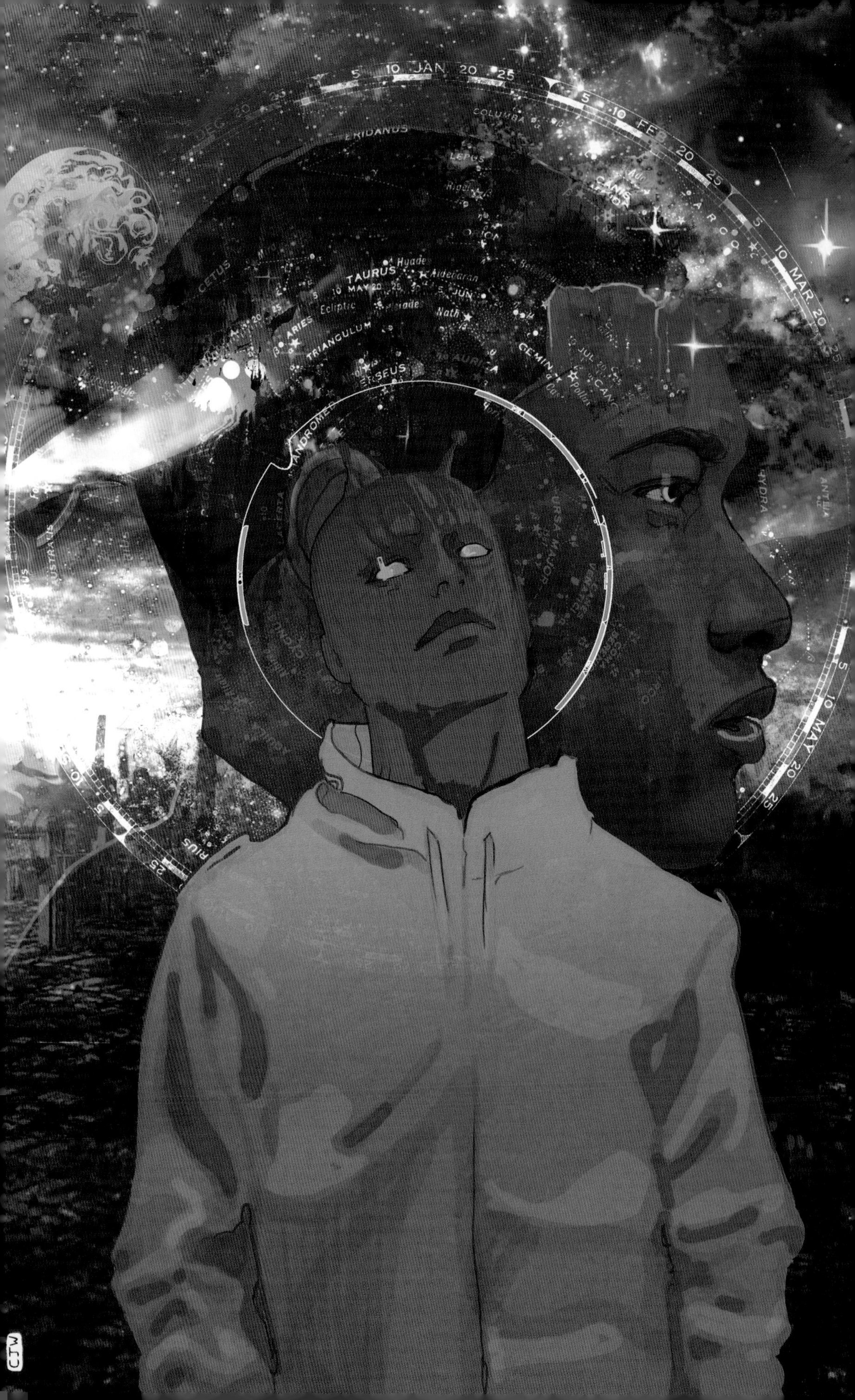
5 10 JAN 20 25
10 FEB 20 25
10 MAR 20
10 MAY 20 25
ERIDANUS
COLUMBA
LEPUS
Rigel
CETUS
TAURUS
Hyades
Aldebaran
Ecliptic
ARIES
TRIANGULUM
PERSEUS
AURIGA
Pollux
URSA MAJOR
HYDRA
CTW

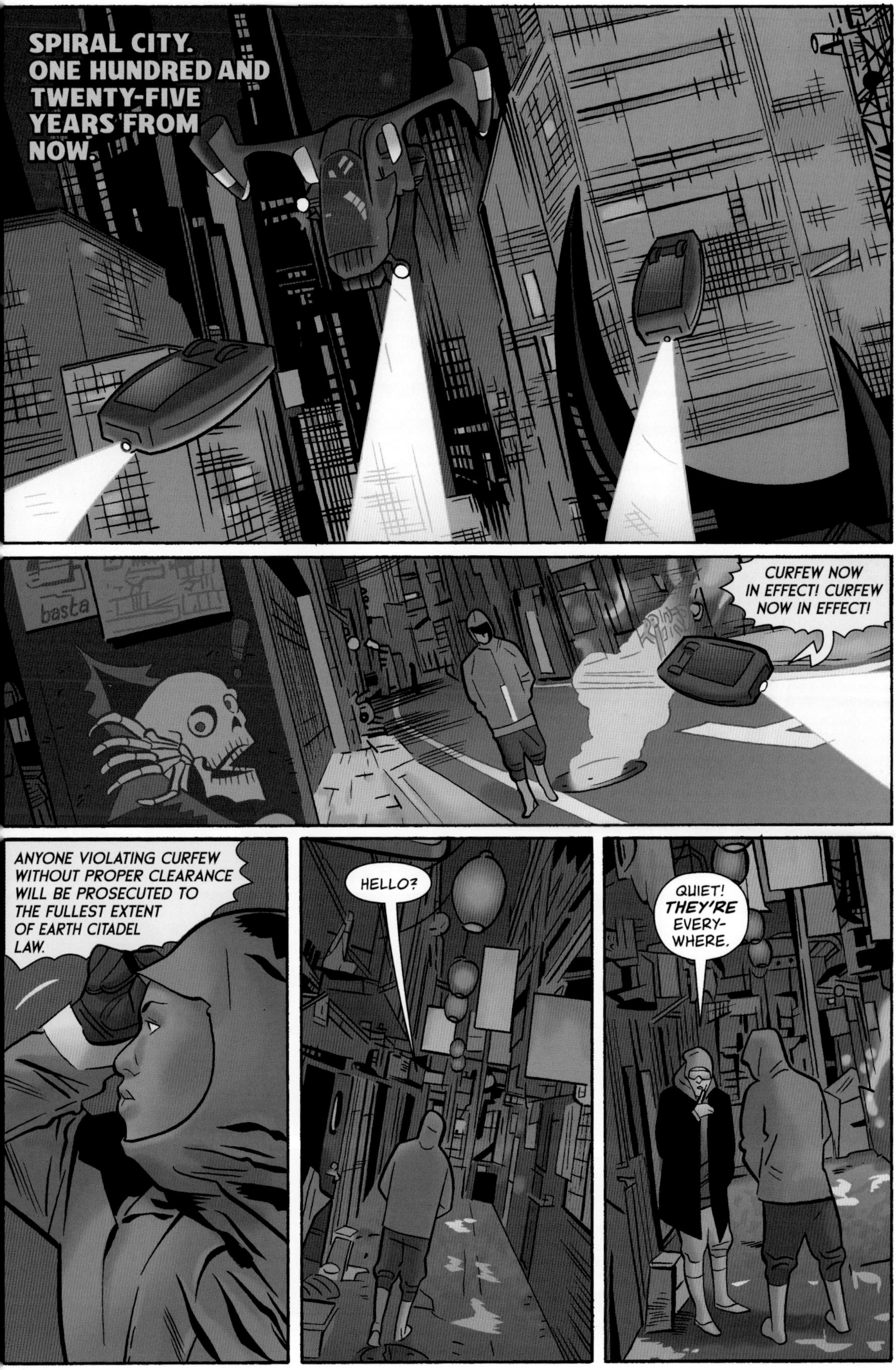
SPIRAL CITY.
ONE HUNDRED AND TWENTY-FIVE YEARS FROM NOW.
basta
CURFEW NOW IN EFFECT! CURFEW NOW IN EFFECT!
ANYONE VIOLATING CURFEW WITHOUT PROPER CLEARANCE WILL BE PROSECUTED TO THE FULLEST EXTENT OF EARTH CITADEL LAW.
HELLO?
QUIET! THEY'RE EVERY-WHERE.

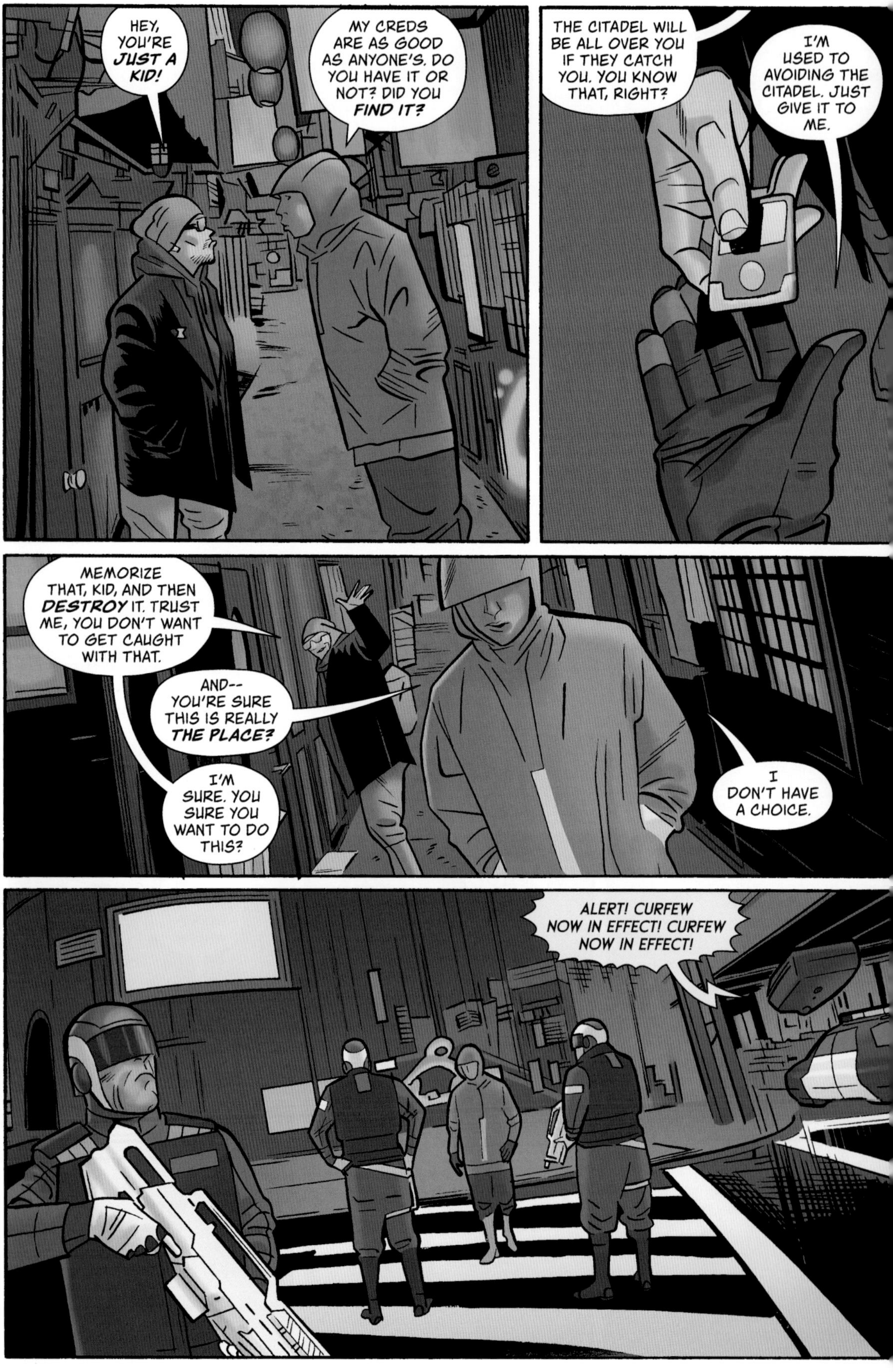
HEY, YOU'RE ***JUST A KID!***
MY CREDS ARE AS GOOD AS ANYONE'S. DO YOU HAVE IT OR NOT? DID YOU ***FIND IT?***
THE CITADEL WILL BE ALL OVER YOU IF THEY CATCH YOU. YOU KNOW THAT, RIGHT?
I'M USED TO AVOIDING THE CITADEL. JUST GIVE IT TO ME.
MEMORIZE THAT, KID, AND THEN ***DESTROY*** IT. TRUST ME, YOU DON'T WANT TO GET CAUGHT WITH THAT.
AND-- YOU'RE SURE THIS IS REALLY ***THE PLACE?***
I'M SURE. YOU SURE YOU WANT TO DO THIS?
I DON'T HAVE A CHOICE.
ALERT! CURFEW NOW IN EFFECT! CURFEW NOW IN EFFECT!

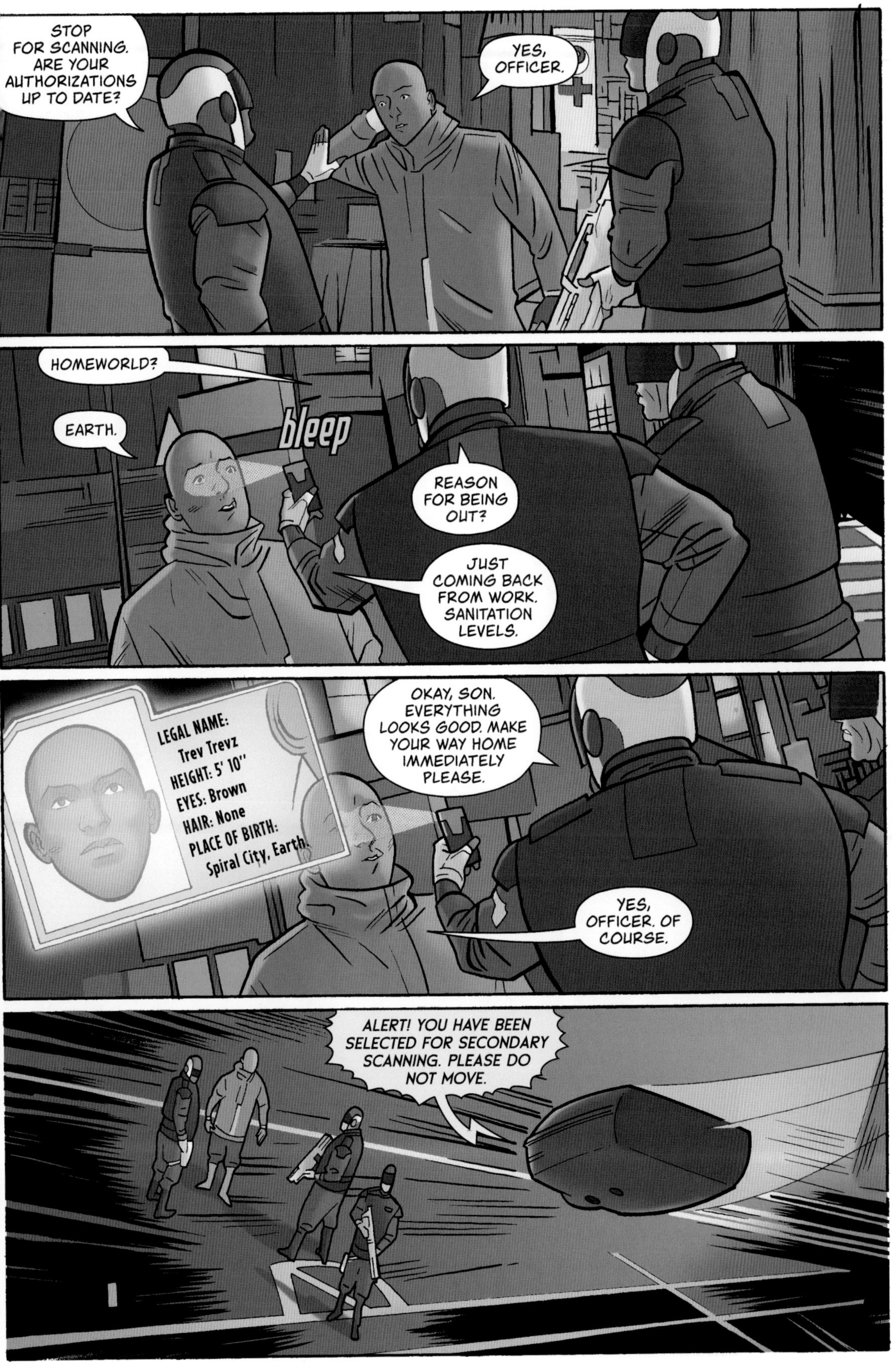
STOP FOR SCANNING. ARE YOUR AUTHORIZATIONS UP TO DATE?
YES, OFFICER.
HOMEWORLD?
EARTH.
bleep
REASON FOR BEING OUT?
JUST COMING BACK FROM WORK. SANITATION LEVELS.
LEGAL NAME: Trev Trevz
HEIGHT: 5' 10''
EYES: Brown
HAIR: None
PLACE OF BIRTH: Spiral City, Earth
OKAY, SON. EVERYTHING LOOKS GOOD. MAKE YOUR WAY HOME IMMEDIATELY PLEASE.
YES, OFFICER. OF COURSE.
ALERT! YOU HAVE BEEN SELECTED FOR SECONDARY SCANNING. PLEASE DO NOT MOVE.

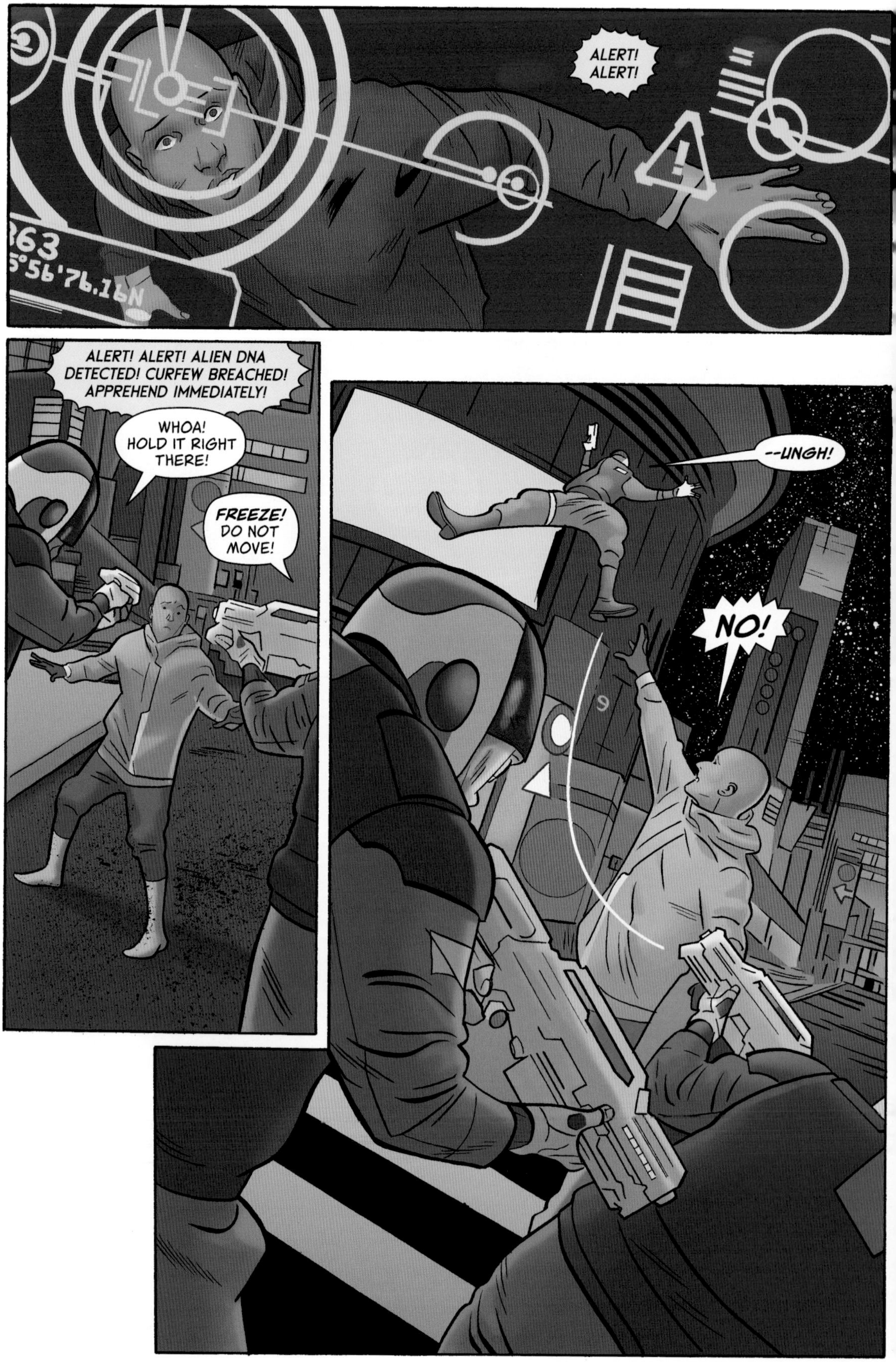
ALERT! ALERT!
ALERT! ALERT! ALIEN DNA DETECTED! CURFEW BREACHED! APPREHEND IMMEDIATELY!
WHOA! HOLD IT RIGHT THERE!
FREEZE! DO NOT MOVE!
--UNGH!
NO!

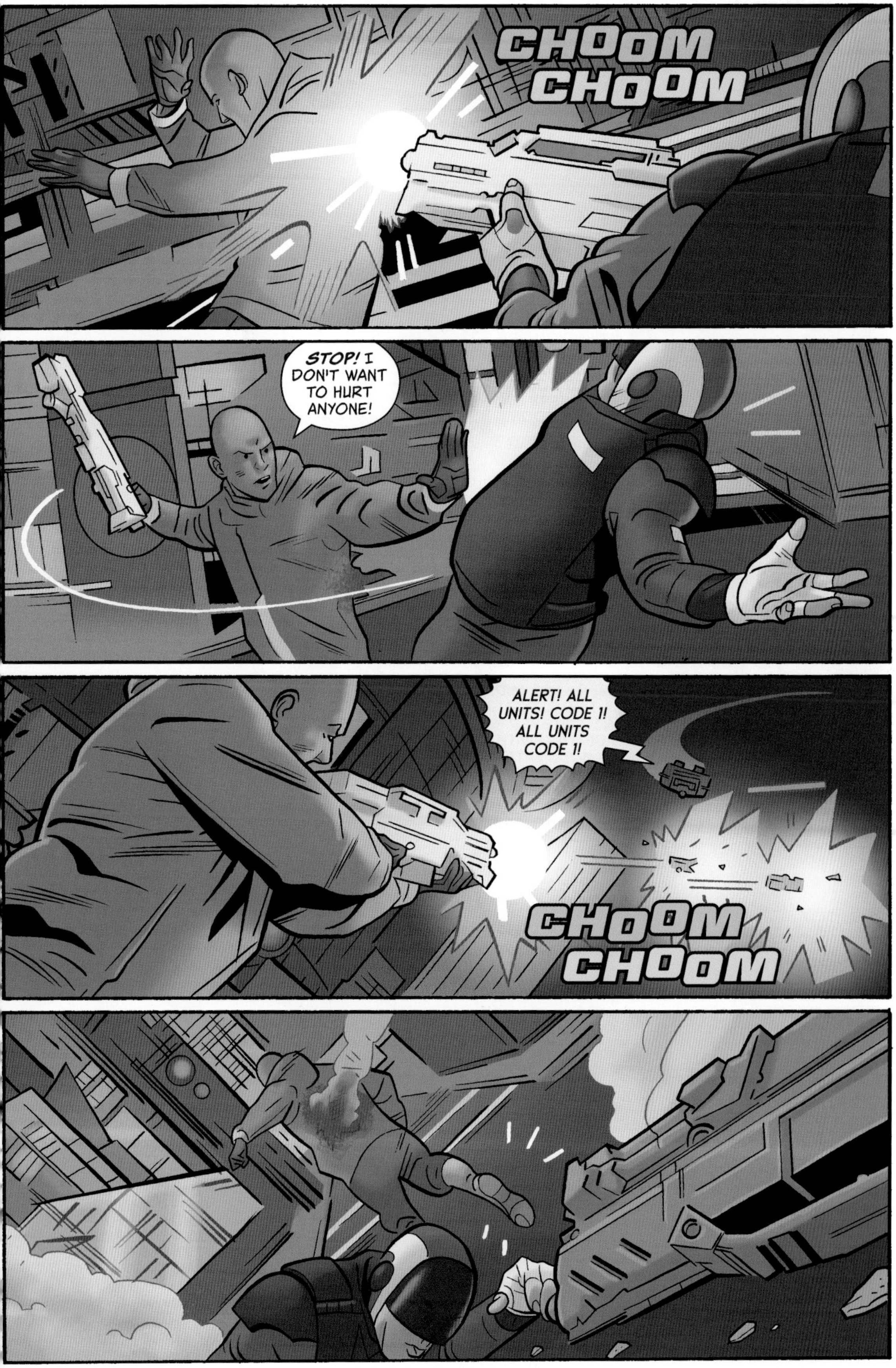
CHOOM
CHOOM
STOP! I DON'T WANT TO HURT ANYONE!
ALERT! ALL UNITS! CODE 1! ALL UNITS CODE 1!
CHOOM
CHOOM

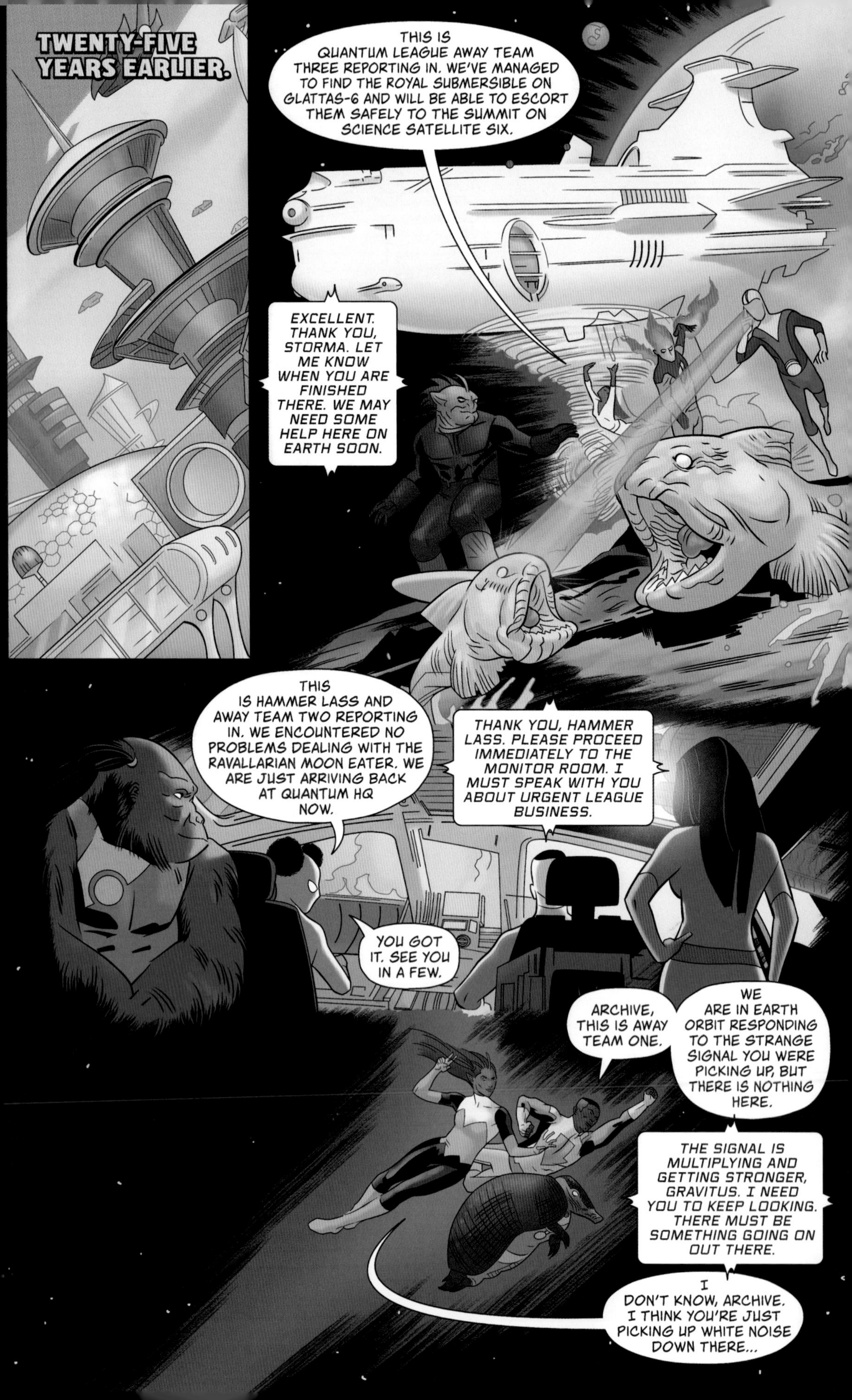
TWENTY-FIVE YEARS EARLIER.
THIS IS QUANTUM LEAGUE AWAY TEAM THREE REPORTING IN. WE'VE MANAGED TO FIND THE ROYAL SUBMERSIBLE ON GLATTAS-6 AND WILL BE ABLE TO ESCORT THEM SAFELY TO THE SUMMIT ON SCIENCE SATELLITE SIX.
EXCELLENT. THANK YOU, STORMA. LET ME KNOW WHEN YOU ARE FINISHED THERE. WE MAY NEED SOME HELP HERE ON EARTH SOON.
THIS IS HAMMER LASS AND AWAY TEAM TWO REPORTING IN. WE ENCOUNTERED NO PROBLEMS DEALING WITH THE RAVALLARIAN MOON EATER. WE ARE JUST ARRIVING BACK AT QUANTUM HQ NOW.
THANK YOU, HAMMER LASS. PLEASE PROCEED IMMEDIATELY TO THE MONITOR ROOM. I MUST SPEAK WITH YOU ABOUT URGENT LEAGUE BUSINESS.
YOU GOT IT. SEE YOU IN A FEW.
ARCHIVE, THIS IS AWAY TEAM ONE.
WE ARE IN EARTH ORBIT RESPONDING TO THE STRANGE SIGNAL YOU WERE PICKING UP, BUT THERE IS NOTHING HERE.
THE SIGNAL IS MULTIPLYING AND GETTING STRONGER, GRAVITUS. I NEED YOU TO KEEP LOOKING. THERE MUST BE SOMETHING GOING ON OUT THERE.
I DON'T KNOW, ARCHIVE. I THINK YOU'RE JUST PICKING UP WHITE NOISE DOWN THERE...

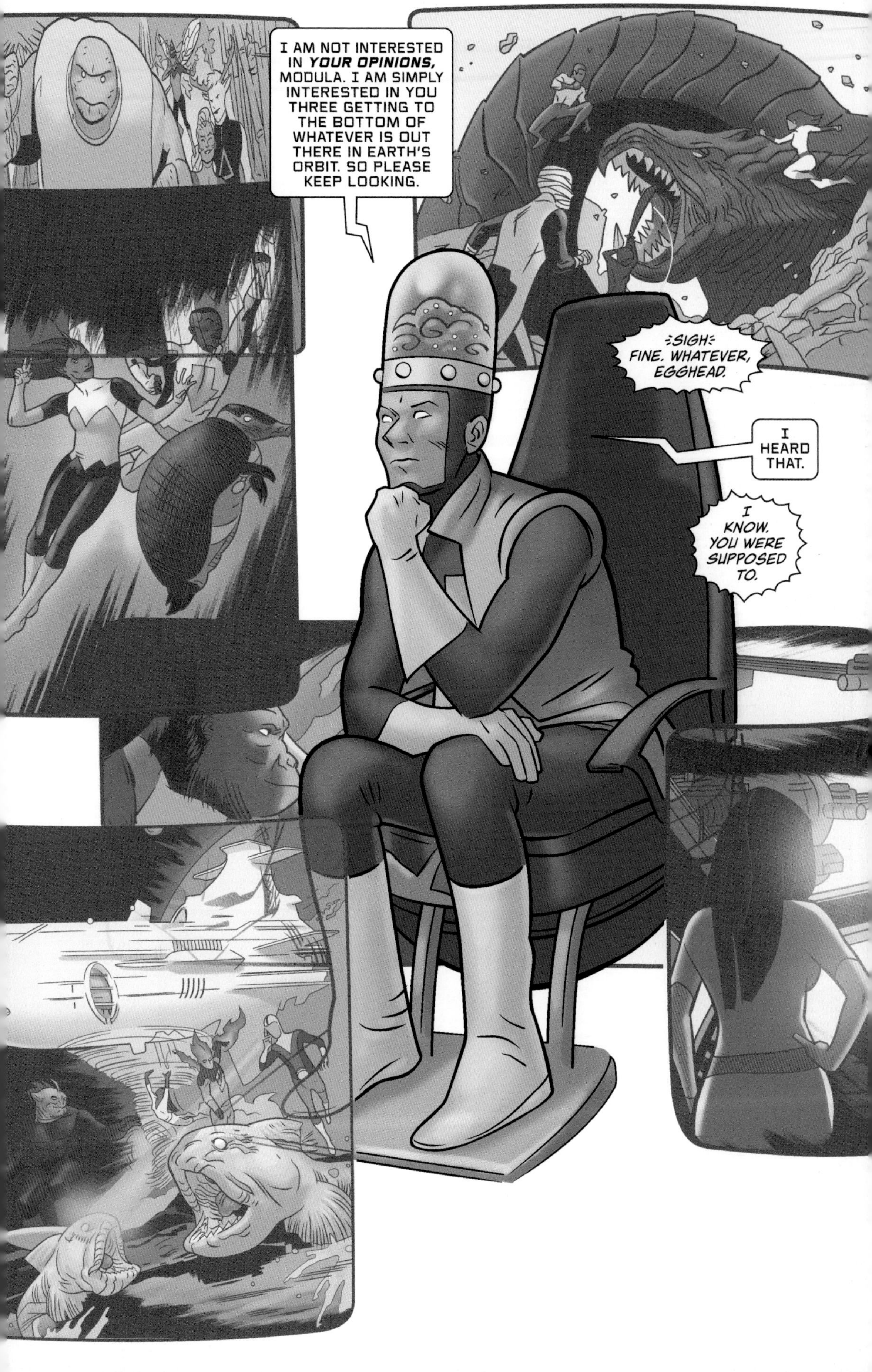
I AM NOT INTERESTED IN ***YOUR OPINIONS,*** MODULA. I AM SIMPLY INTERESTED IN YOU THREE GETTING TO THE BOTTOM OF WHATEVER IS OUT THERE IN EARTH'S ORBIT. SO PLEASE KEEP LOOKING.
SIGH FINE. WHATEVER, EGGHEAD.
I HEARD THAT.
I KNOW. YOU WERE SUPPOSED TO.

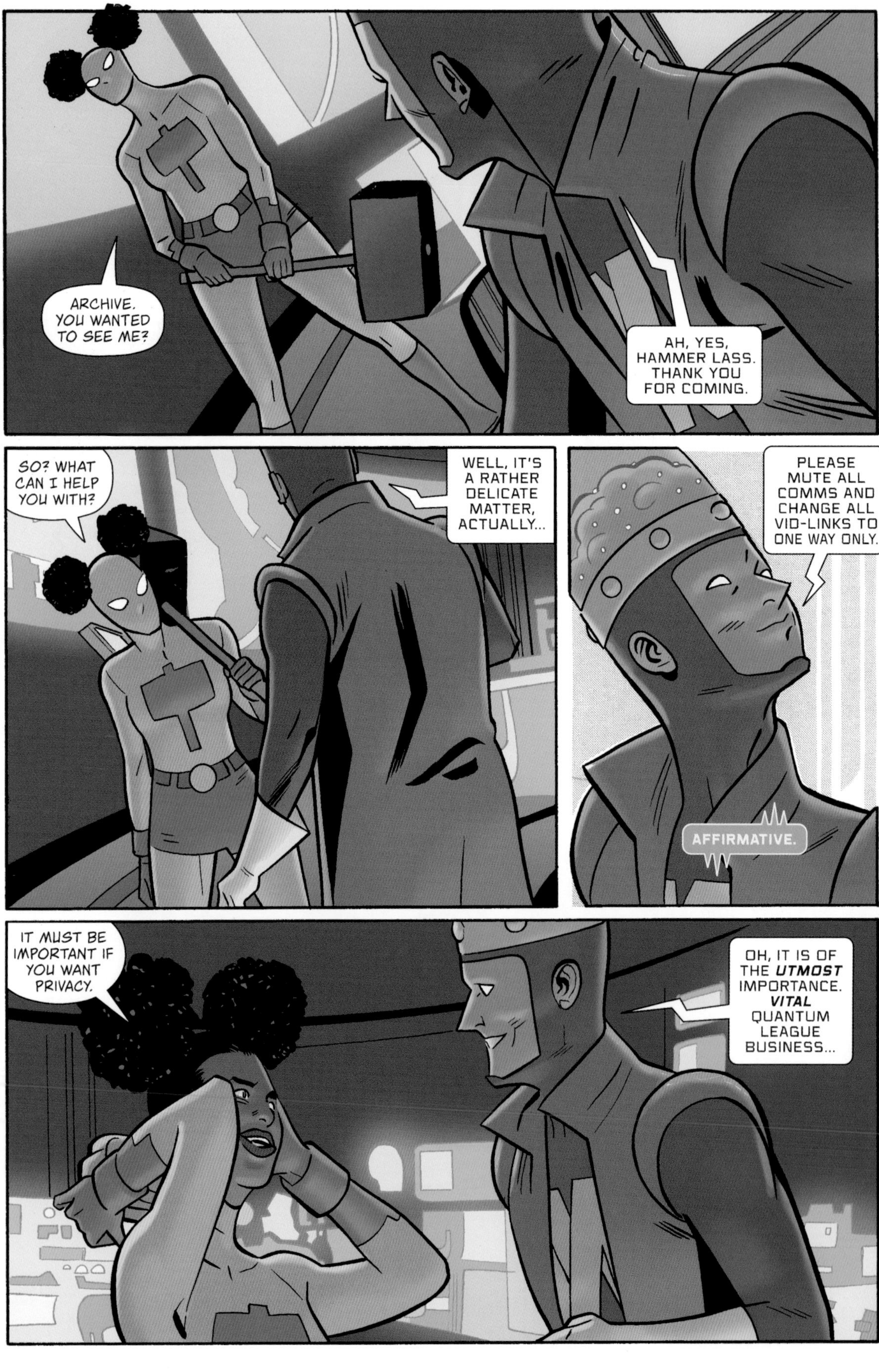
ARCHIVE. YOU WANTED TO SEE ME?
AH, YES, HAMMER LASS. THANK YOU FOR COMING.
SO? WHAT CAN I HELP YOU WITH?
WELL, IT'S A RATHER DELICATE MATTER, ACTUALLY...
PLEASE MUTE ALL COMMS AND CHANGE ALL VID-LINKS TO ONE WAY ONLY.
AFFIRMATIVE.
IT MUST BE IMPORTANT IF YOU WANT PRIVACY.
OH, IT IS OF THE *UTMOST* IMPORTANCE. *VITAL* QUANTUM LEAGUE BUSINESS...

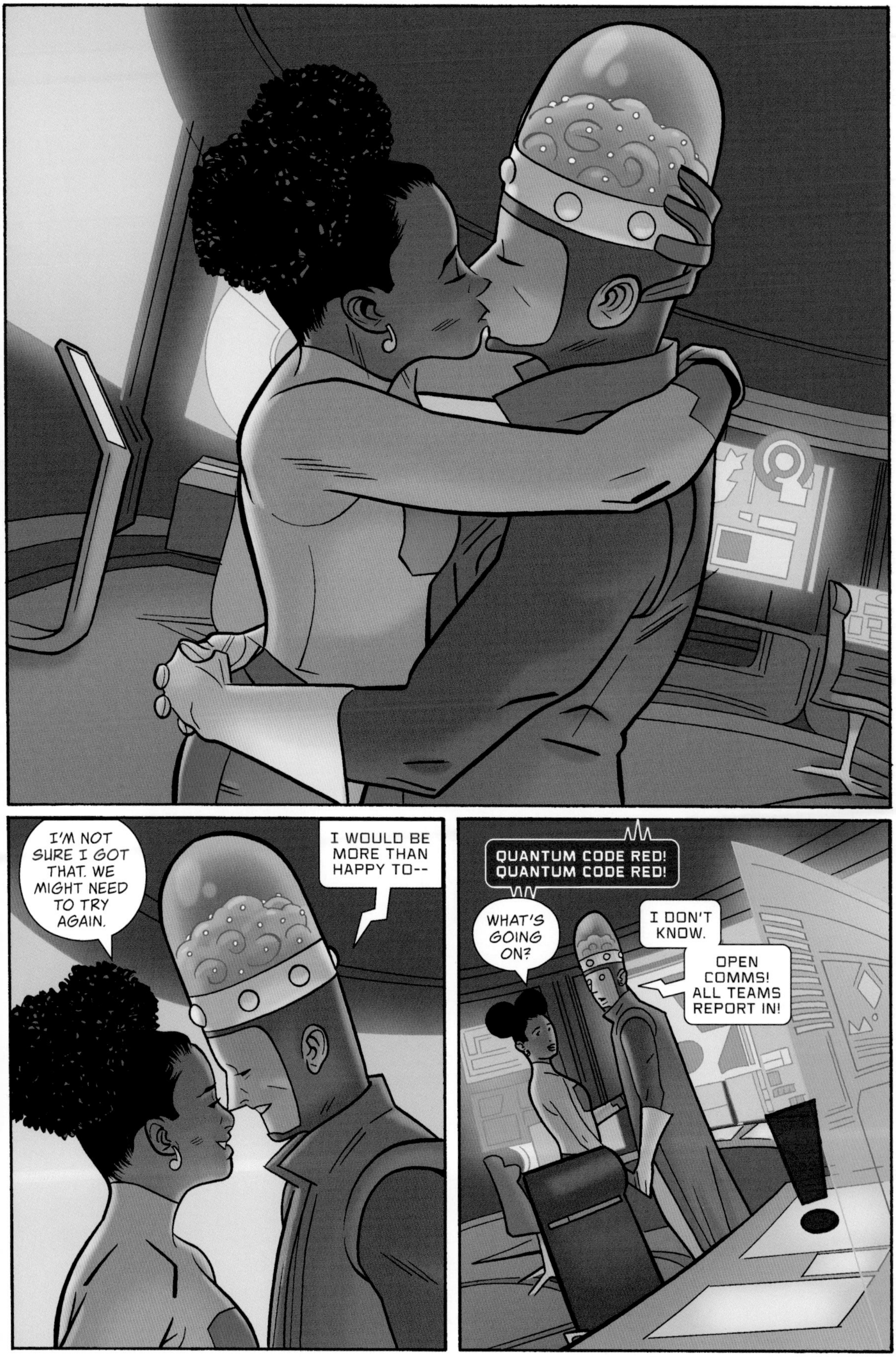
I'M NOT SURE I GOT THAT. WE MIGHT NEED TO TRY AGAIN.
I WOULD BE MORE THAN HAPPY TO--
QUANTUM CODE RED! QUANTUM CODE RED!
WHAT'S GOING ON?
I DON'T KNOW.
OPEN COMMS! ALL TEAMS REPORT IN!

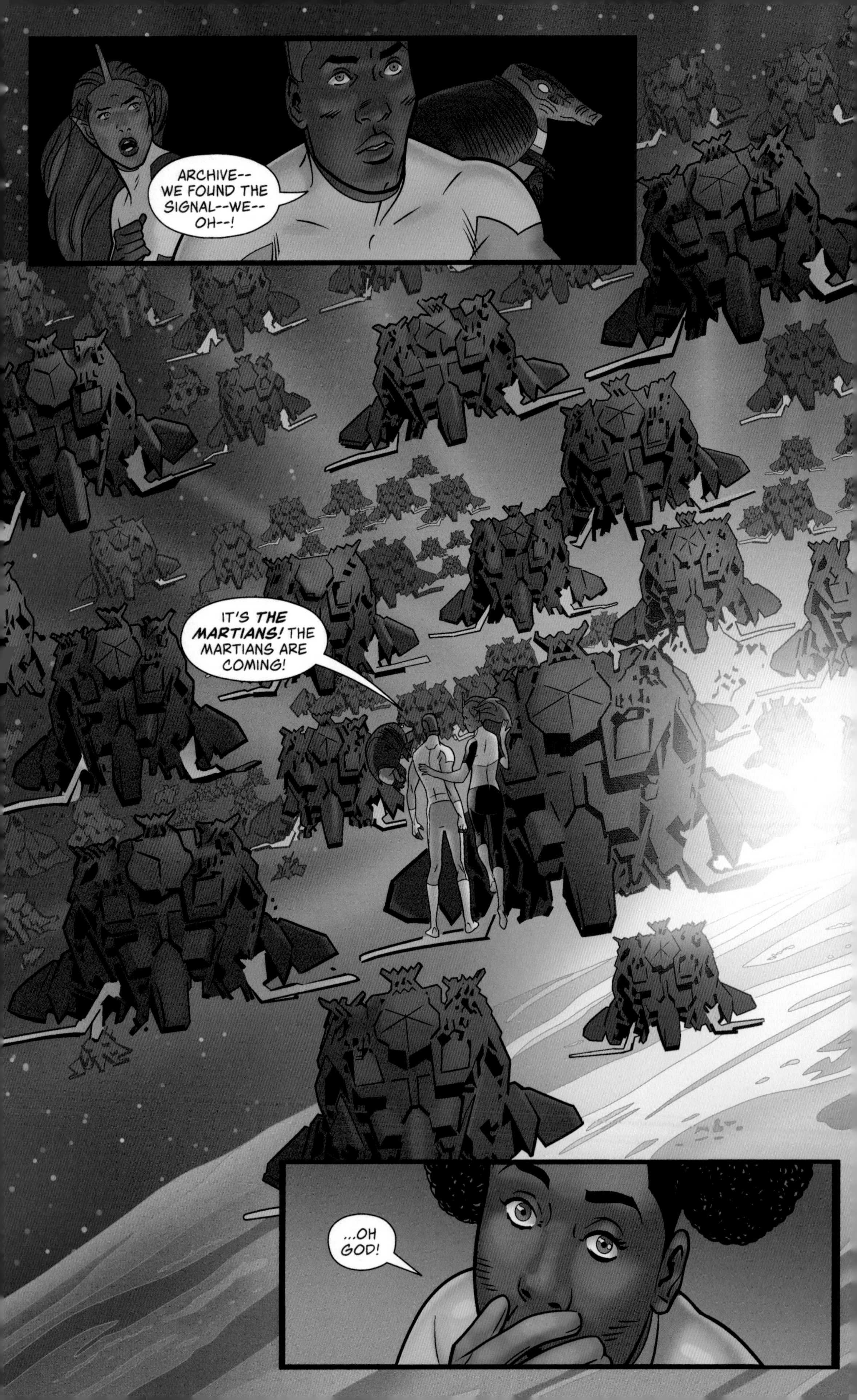
ARCHIVE--
WE FOUND THE
SIGNAL--WE--
OH--!
IT'S THE MARTIANS! THE MARTIANS ARE COMING!
...OH GOD!

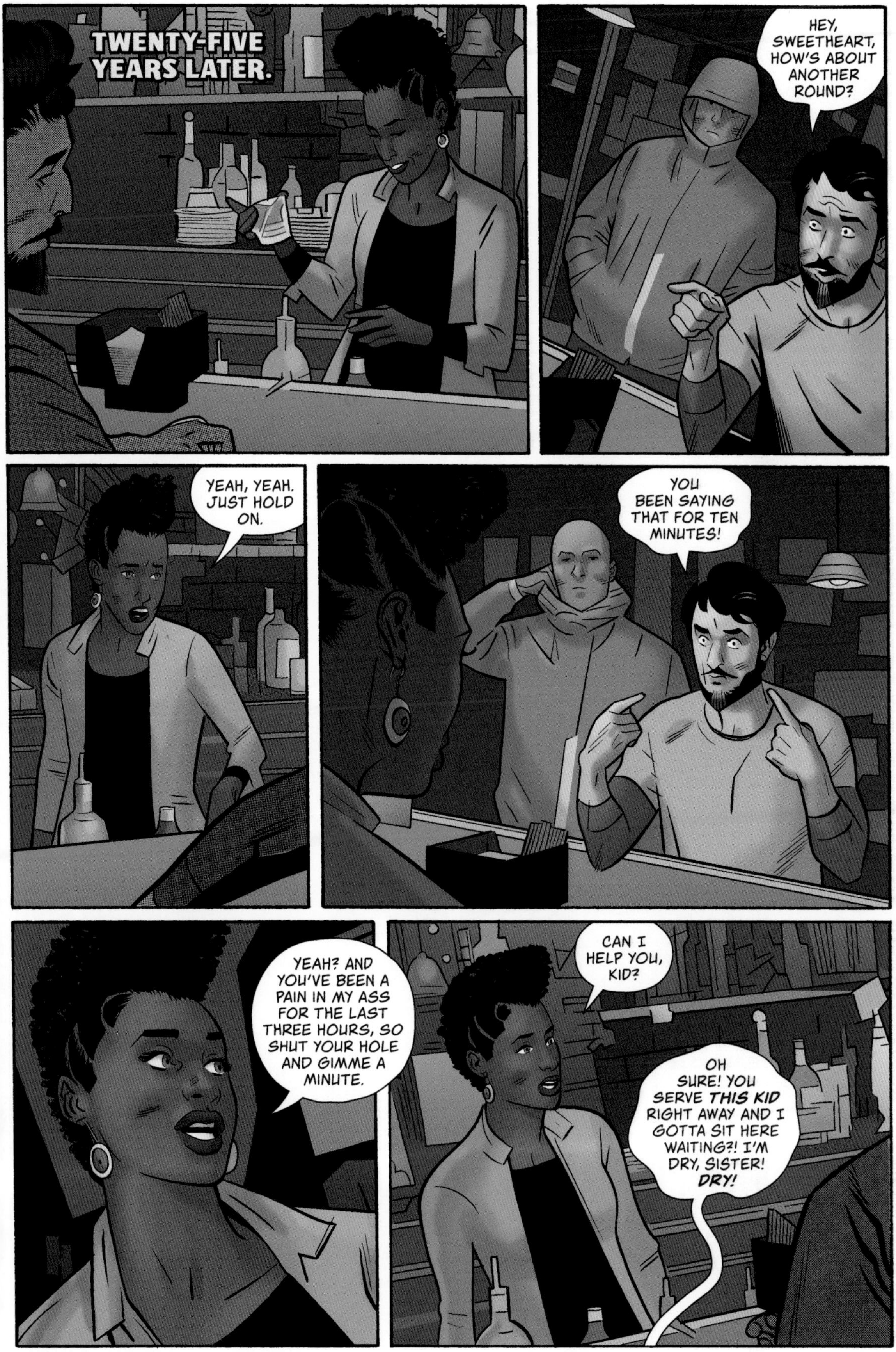
TWENTY-FIVE YEARS LATER.
HEY, SWEETHEART, HOW'S ABOUT ANOTHER ROUND?
YEAH, YEAH. JUST HOLD ON.
YOU BEEN SAYING THAT FOR TEN MINUTES!
YEAH? AND YOU'VE BEEN A PAIN IN MY ASS FOR THE LAST THREE HOURS, SO SHUT YOUR HOLE AND GIMME A MINUTE.
CAN I HELP YOU, KID?
OH SURE! YOU SERVE **THIS KID** RIGHT AWAY AND I GOTTA SIT HERE WAITING?! I'M DRY, SISTER! **DRY!**

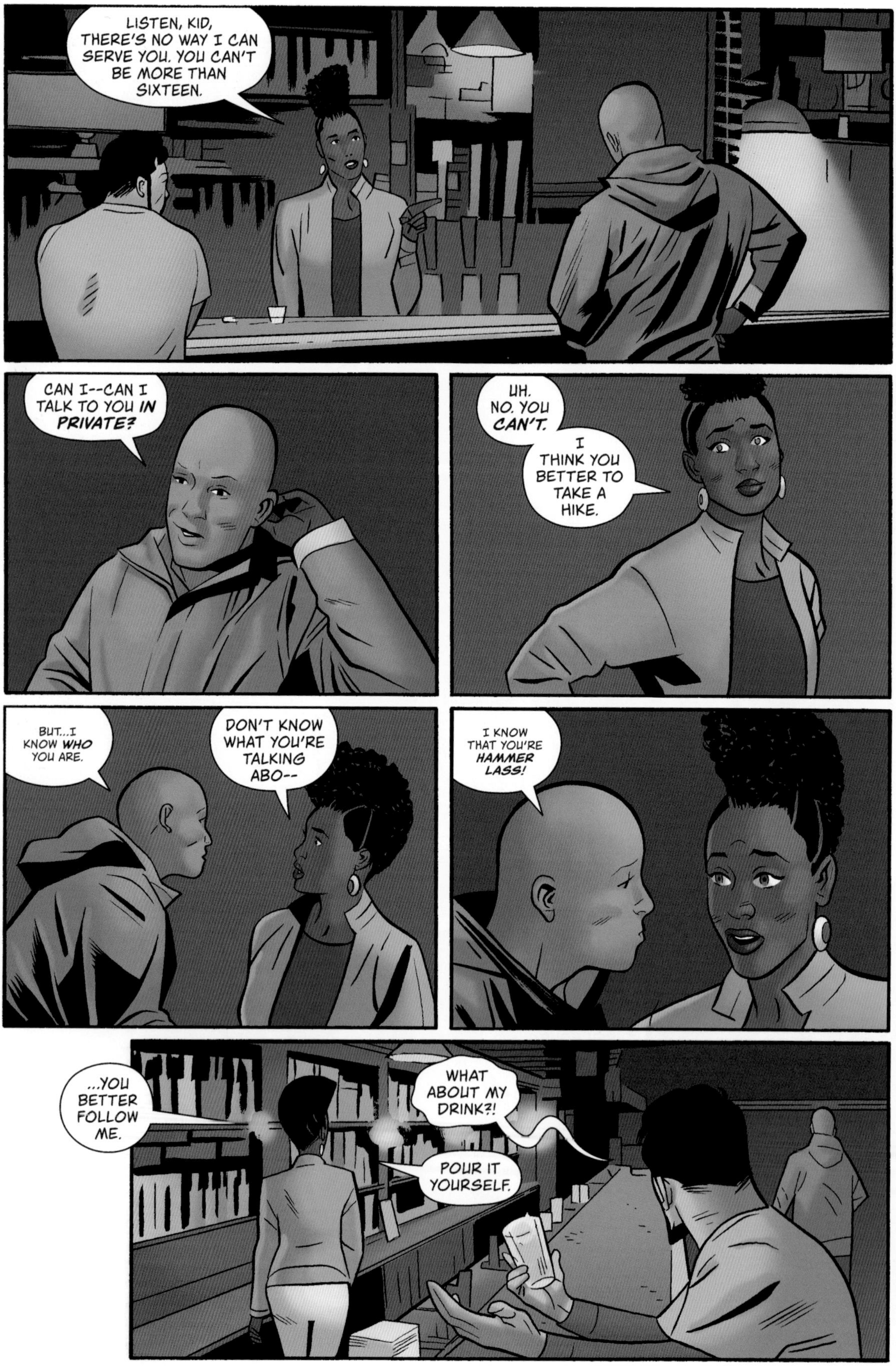
LISTEN, KID, THERE'S NO WAY I CAN SERVE YOU. YOU CAN'T BE MORE THAN SIXTEEN.
CAN I--CAN I TALK TO YOU **IN PRIVATE?**
UH. NO. YOU **CAN'T.**
I THINK YOU BETTER TO TAKE A HIKE.
BUT...I KNOW **WHO** YOU ARE.
DON'T KNOW WHAT YOU'RE TALKING ABO--
I KNOW THAT YOU'RE **HAMMER LASS!**
...YOU BETTER FOLLOW ME.
WHAT ABOUT MY DRINK?!
POUR IT YOURSELF.

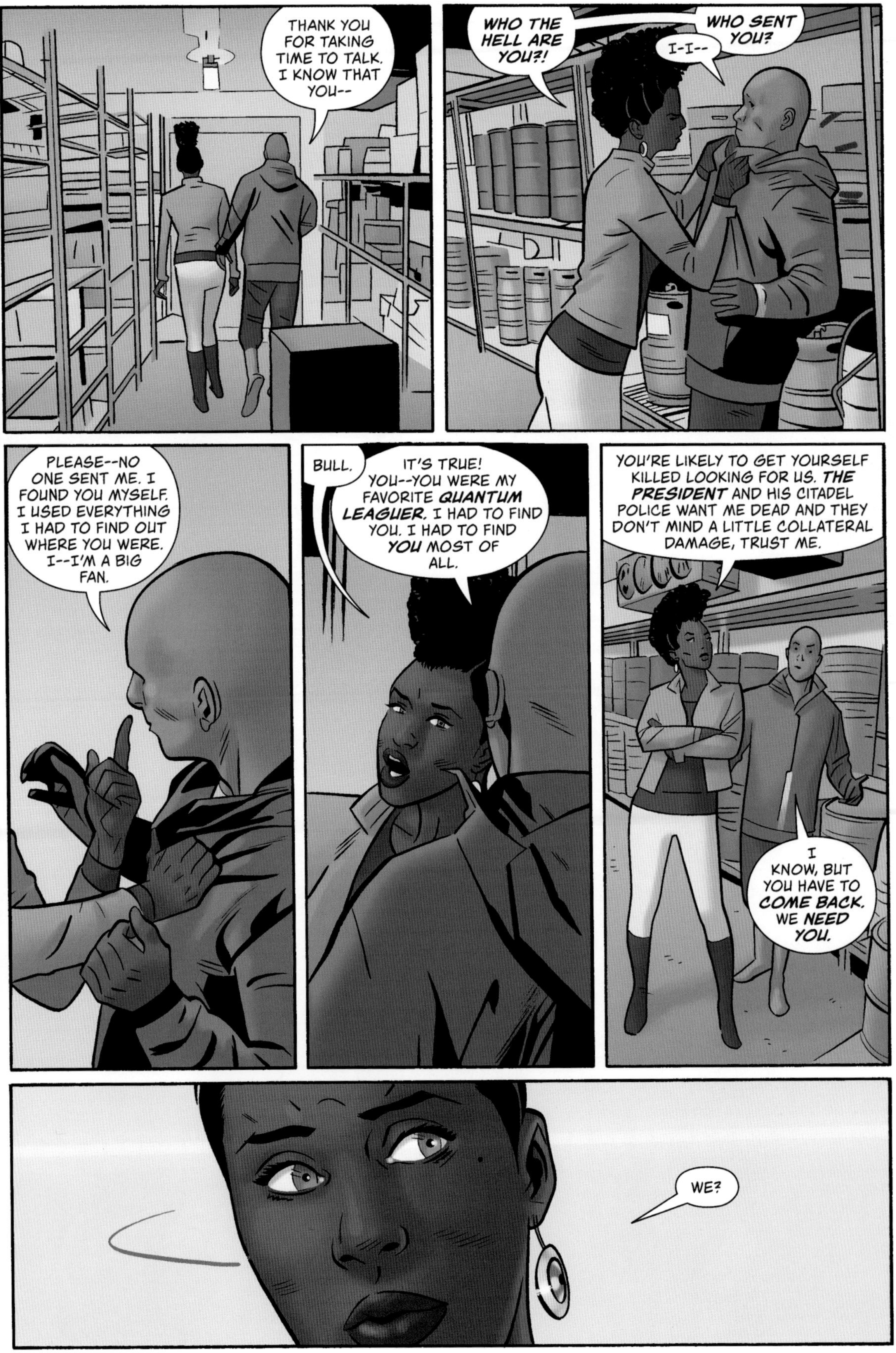
THANK YOU FOR TAKING TIME TO TALK. I KNOW THAT YOU--
WHO THE HELL ARE YOU?!
WHO SENT YOU?
I-I--
PLEASE--NO ONE SENT ME. I FOUND YOU MYSELF. I USED EVERYTHING I HAD TO FIND OUT WHERE YOU WERE. I--I'M A BIG FAN.
BULL.
IT'S TRUE! YOU--YOU WERE MY FAVORITE QUANTUM LEAGUER. I HAD TO FIND YOU. I HAD TO FIND YOU MOST OF ALL.
YOU'RE LIKELY TO GET YOURSELF KILLED LOOKING FOR US. THE PRESIDENT AND HIS CITADEL POLICE WANT ME DEAD AND THEY DON'T MIND A LITTLE COLLATERAL DAMAGE, TRUST ME.
I KNOW, BUT YOU HAVE TO COME BACK. WE NEED YOU.
WE?

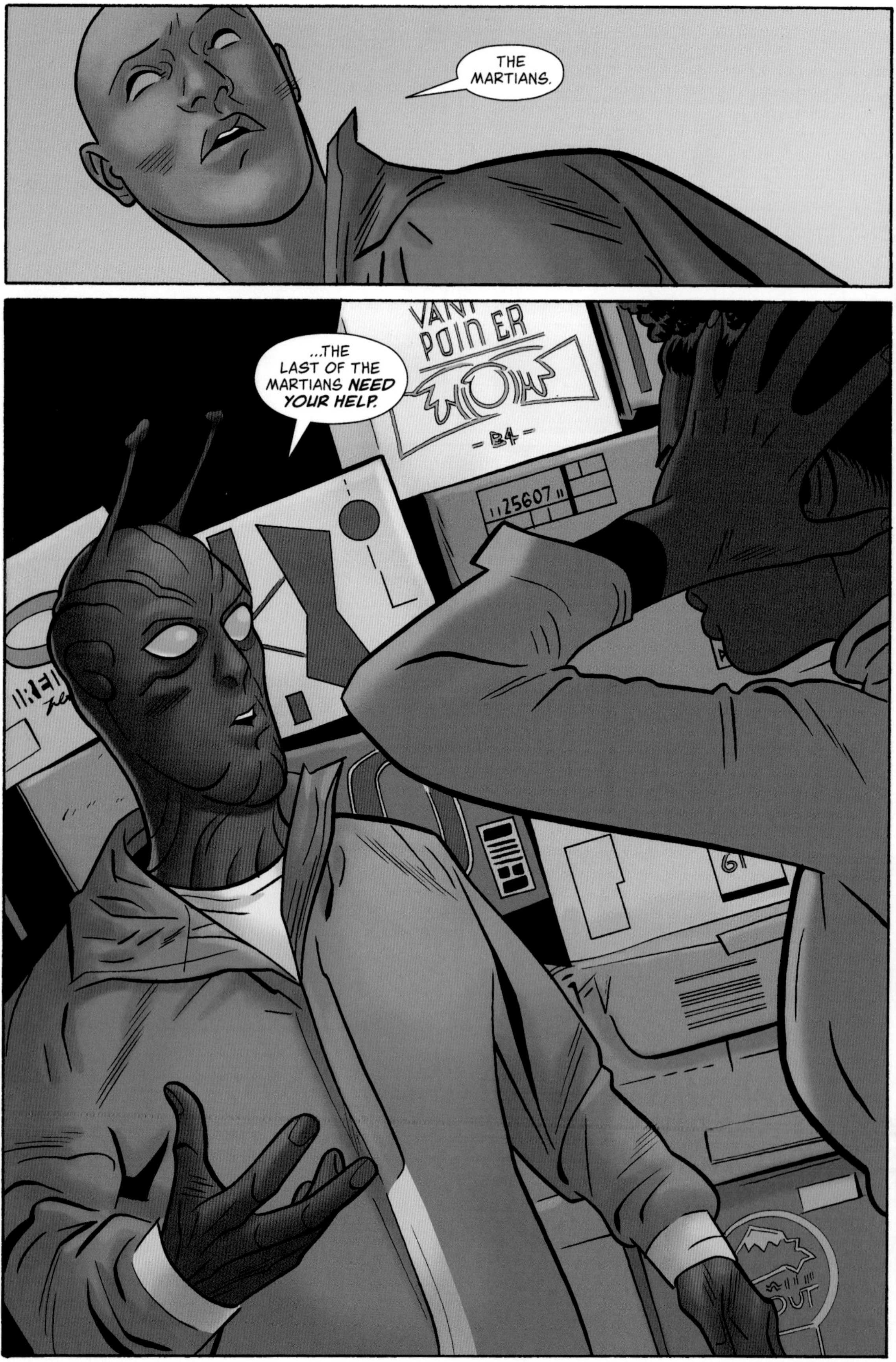
THE MARTIANS.
...THE LAST OF THE MARTIANS **NEED YOUR HELP.**

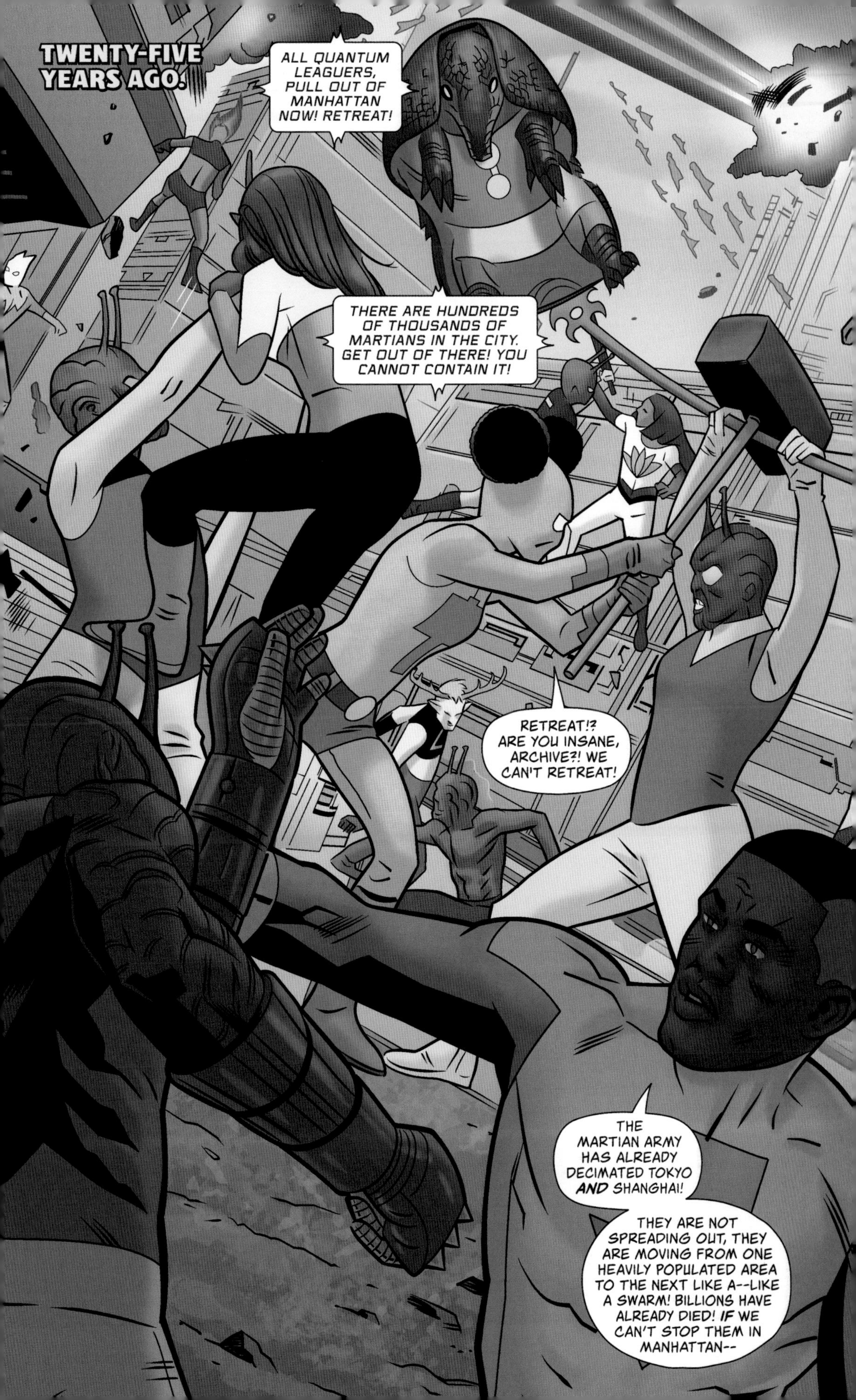
TWENTY-FIVE YEARS AGO.
ALL QUANTUM LEAGUERS, PULL OUT OF MANHATTAN NOW! RETREAT!
THERE ARE HUNDREDS OF THOUSANDS OF MARTIANS IN THE CITY. GET OUT OF THERE! YOU CANNOT CONTAIN IT!
RETREAT!? ARE YOU INSANE, ARCHIVE?! WE CAN'T RETREAT!
THE MARTIAN ARMY HAS ALREADY DECIMATED TOKYO **AND** SHANGHAI!
THEY ARE NOT SPREADING OUT, THEY ARE MOVING FROM ONE HEAVILY POPULATED AREA TO THE NEXT LIKE A--LIKE A SWARM! BILLIONS HAVE ALREADY DIED! **IF** WE CAN'T STOP THEM IN MANHATTAN--

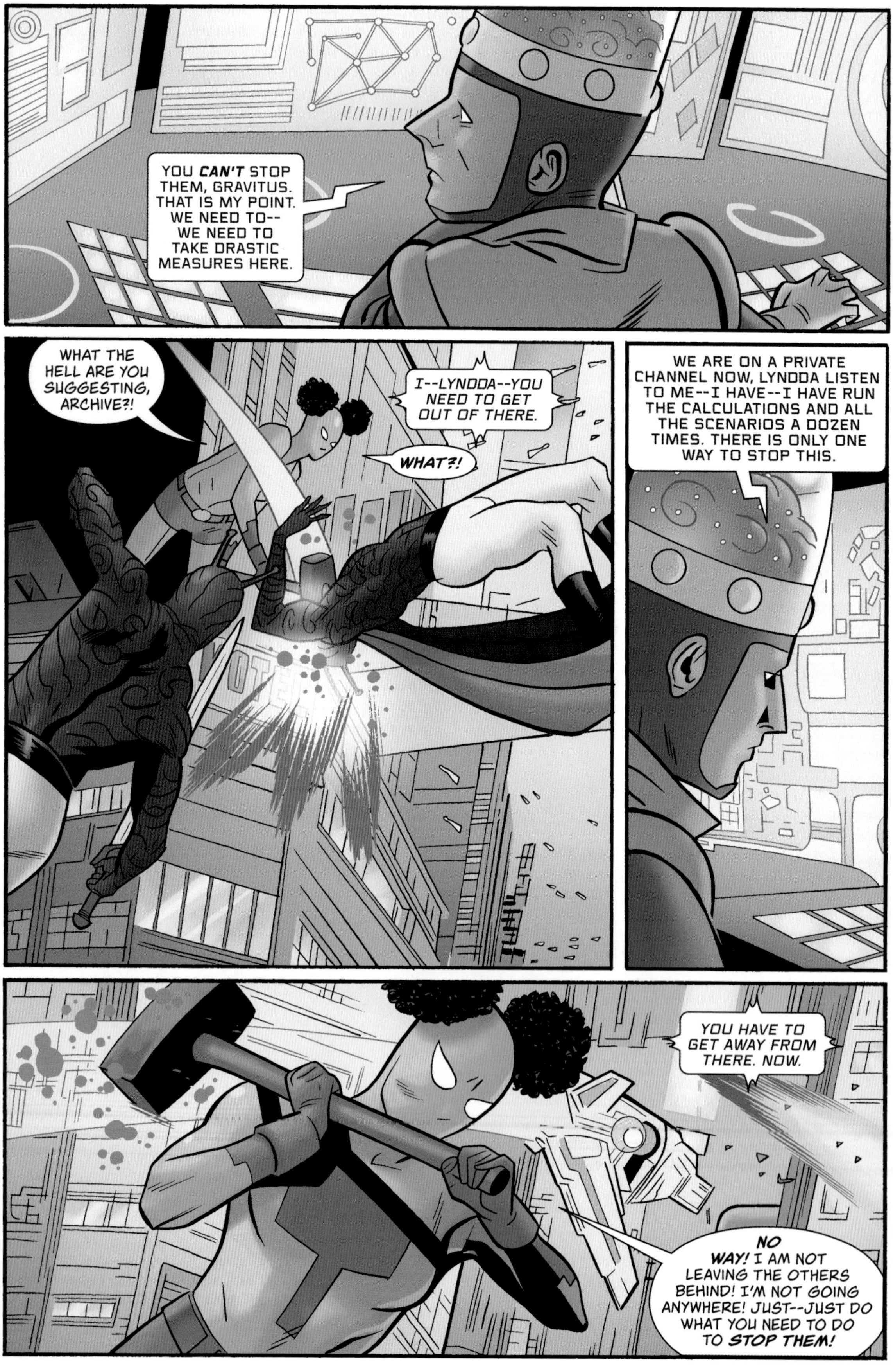
YOU CAN'T STOP THEM, GRAVITUS. THAT IS MY POINT. WE NEED TO-- WE NEED TO TAKE DRASTIC MEASURES HERE.
WHAT THE HELL ARE YOU SUGGESTING, ARCHIVE?!
I--LYNDDA--YOU NEED TO GET OUT OF THERE.
WHAT?!
WE ARE ON A PRIVATE CHANNEL NOW, LYNDDA LISTEN TO ME--I HAVE--I HAVE RUN THE CALCULATIONS AND ALL THE SCENARIOS A DOZEN TIMES. THERE IS ONLY ONE WAY TO STOP THIS.
YOU HAVE TO GET AWAY FROM THERE. NOW.
NO WAY! I AM NOT LEAVING THE OTHERS BEHIND! I'M NOT GOING ANYWHERE! JUST--JUST DO WHAT YOU NEED TO DO TO STOP THEM!

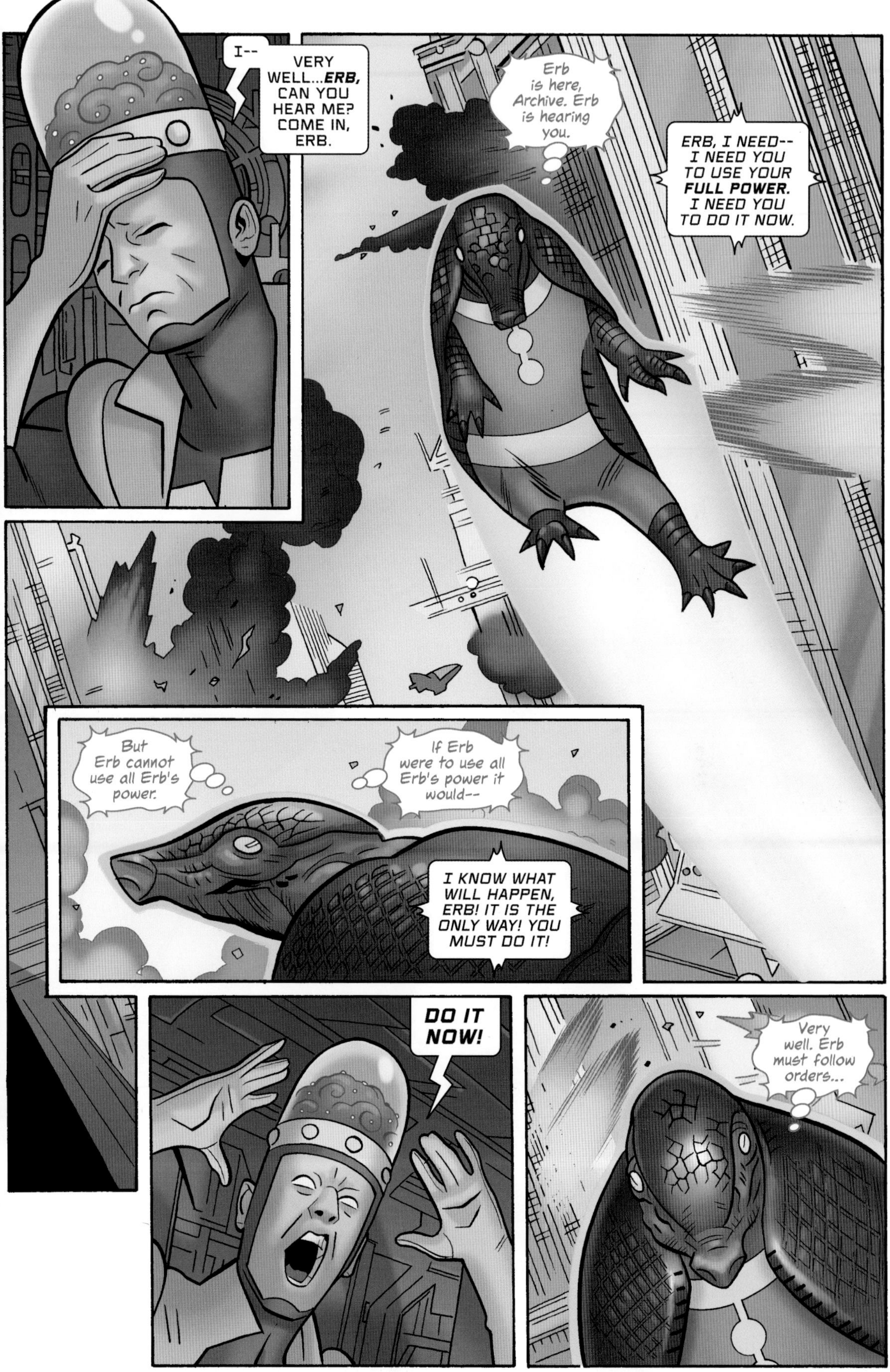
I--
VERY WELL...ERB, CAN YOU HEAR ME? COME IN, ERB.
Erb is here, Archive. Erb is hearing you.
ERB, I NEED-- I NEED YOU TO USE YOUR FULL POWER. I NEED YOU TO DO IT NOW.
But Erb cannot use all Erb's power.
If Erb were to use all Erb's power it would--
I KNOW WHAT WILL HAPPEN, ERB! IT IS THE ONLY WAY! YOU MUST DO IT!
DO IT NOW!
Very well. Erb must follow orders...

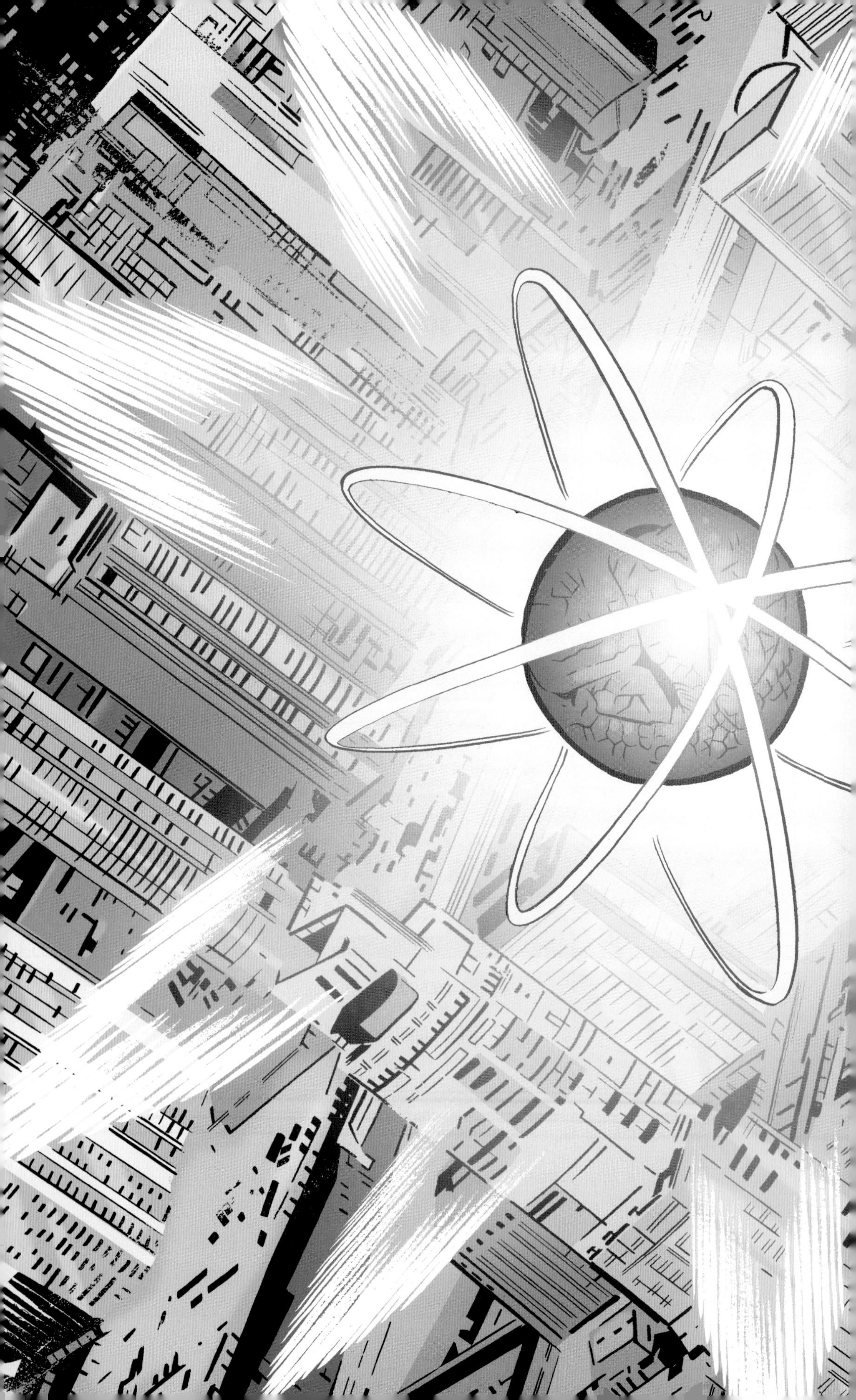

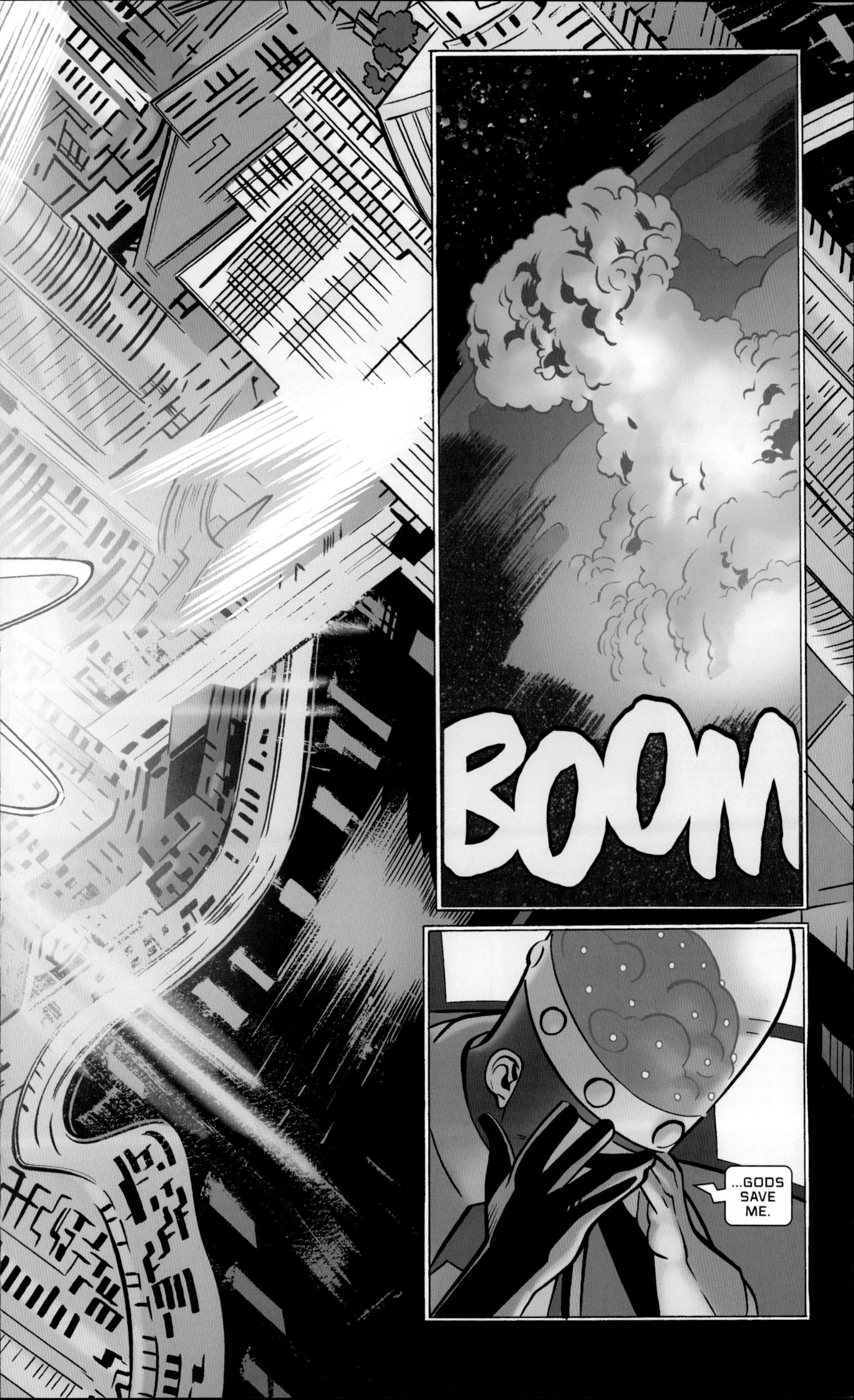
BOOM
...GODS SAVE ME.

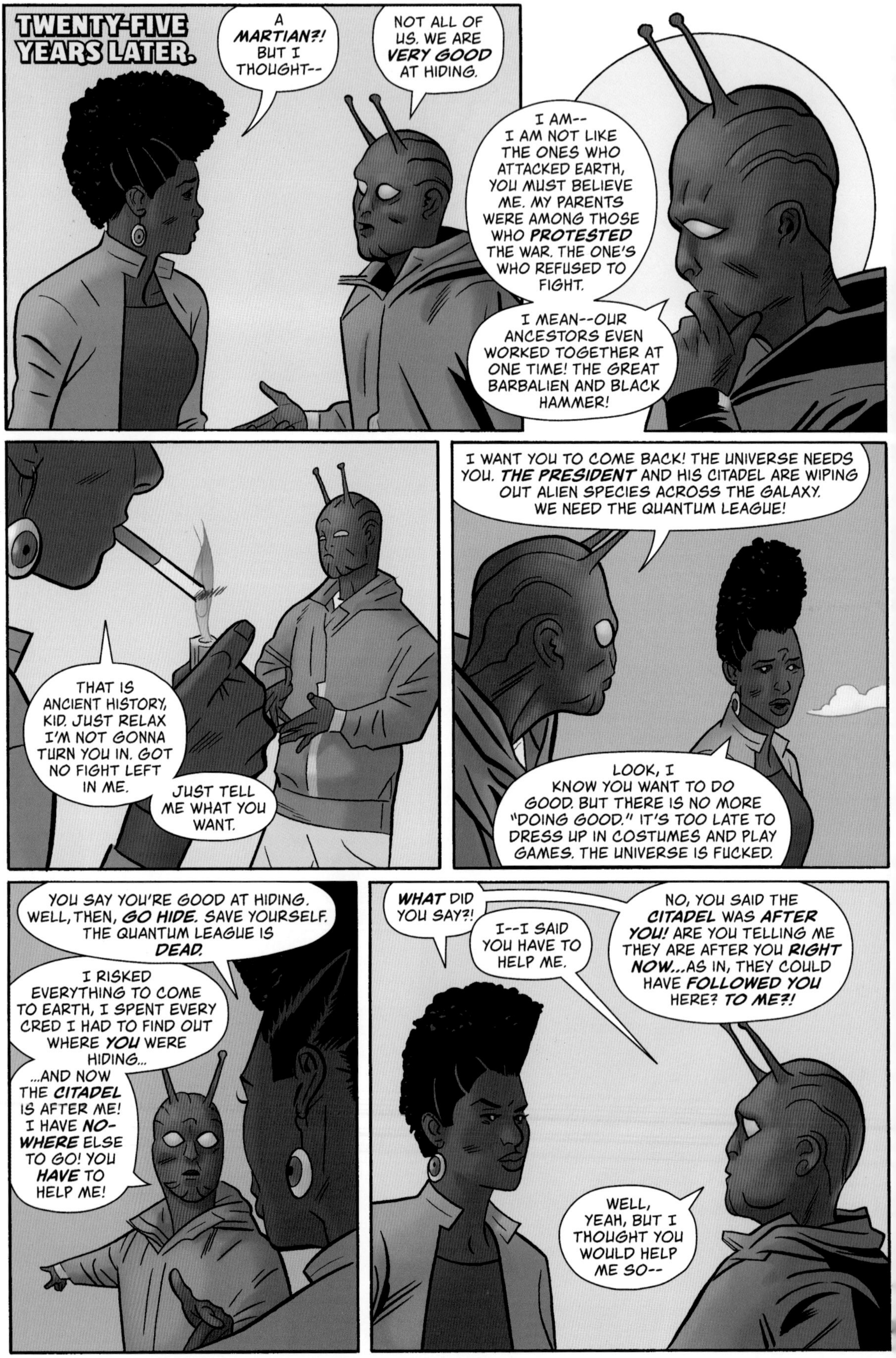

TWENTY-FIVE YEARS LATER.
A MARTIAN?! BUT I THOUGHT--
NOT ALL OF US. WE ARE VERY GOOD AT HIDING.
I AM-- I AM NOT LIKE THE ONES WHO ATTACKED EARTH, YOU MUST BELIEVE ME. MY PARENTS WERE AMONG THOSE WHO PROTESTED THE WAR. THE ONE'S WHO REFUSED TO FIGHT.
I MEAN--OUR ANCESTORS EVEN WORKED TOGETHER AT ONE TIME! THE GREAT BARBALIEN AND BLACK HAMMER!
THAT IS ANCIENT HISTORY, KID. JUST RELAX I'M NOT GONNA TURN YOU IN. GOT NO FIGHT LEFT IN ME.
JUST TELL ME WHAT YOU WANT.
I WANT YOU TO COME BACK! THE UNIVERSE NEEDS YOU. THE PRESIDENT AND HIS CITADEL ARE WIPING OUT ALIEN SPECIES ACROSS THE GALAXY. WE NEED THE QUANTUM LEAGUE!
LOOK, I KNOW YOU WANT TO DO GOOD. BUT THERE IS NO MORE "DOING GOOD." IT'S TOO LATE TO DRESS UP IN COSTUMES AND PLAY GAMES. THE UNIVERSE IS FUCKED.
YOU SAY YOU'RE GOOD AT HIDING. WELL, THEN, GO HIDE. SAVE YOURSELF. THE QUANTUM LEAGUE IS DEAD.
I RISKED EVERYTHING TO COME TO EARTH, I SPENT EVERY CRED I HAD TO FIND OUT WHERE YOU WERE HIDING...
...AND NOW THE CITADEL IS AFTER ME! I HAVE NOWHERE ELSE TO GO! YOU HAVE TO HELP ME!
WHAT DID YOU SAY?!
I--I SAID YOU HAVE TO HELP ME.
NO, YOU SAID THE CITADEL WAS AFTER YOU! ARE YOU TELLING ME THEY ARE AFTER YOU RIGHT NOW...AS IN, THEY COULD HAVE FOLLOWED YOU HERE? TO ME?!
WELL, YEAH, BUT I THOUGHT YOU WOULD HELP ME SO--

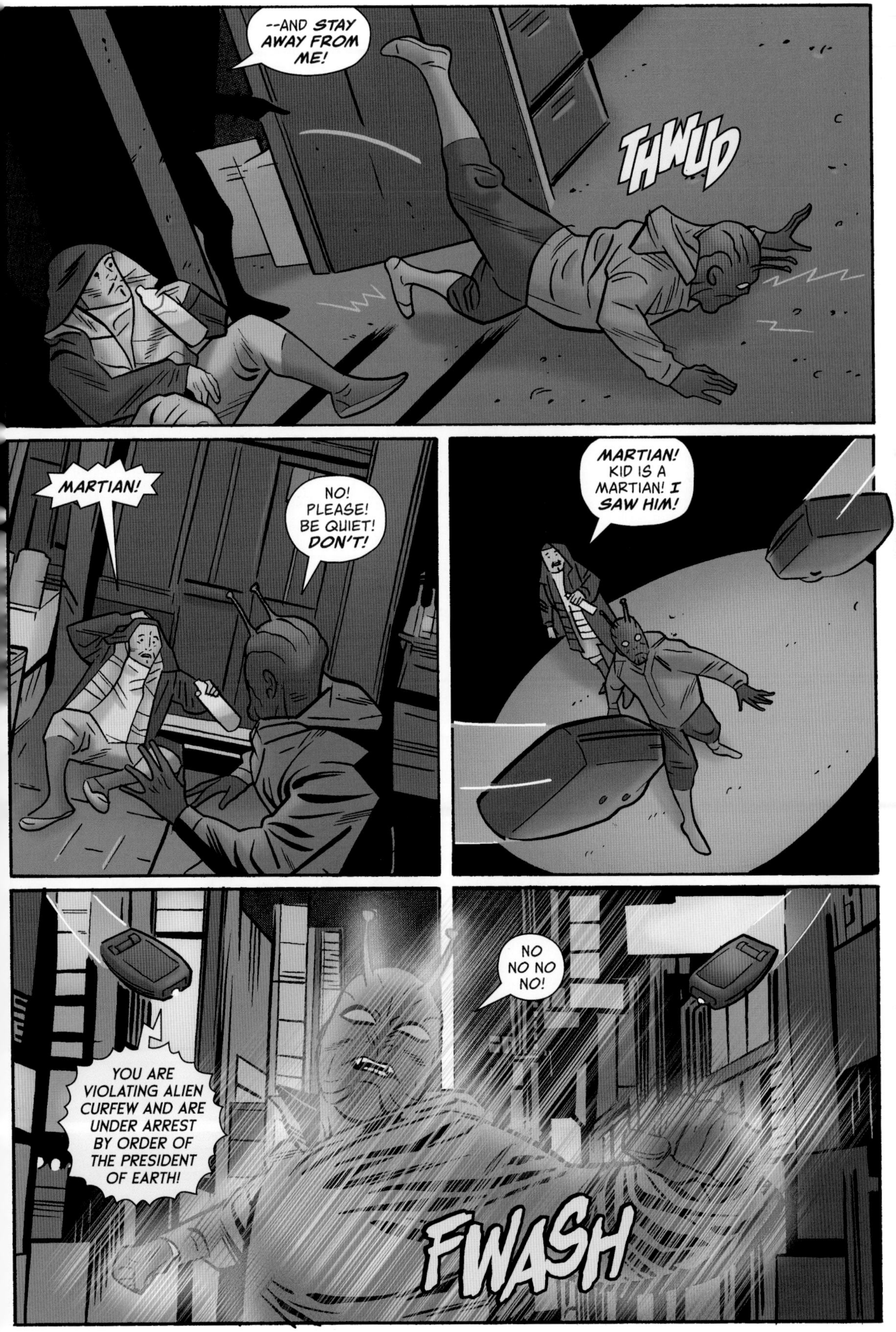
--AND STAY AWAY FROM ME!
THWUD
MARTIAN!
NO! PLEASE! BE QUIET! DON'T!
MARTIAN! KID IS A MARTIAN! I SAW HIM!
YOU ARE VIOLATING ALIEN CURFEW AND ARE UNDER ARREST BY ORDER OF THE PRESIDENT OF EARTH!
NO NO NO NO!
FWASH

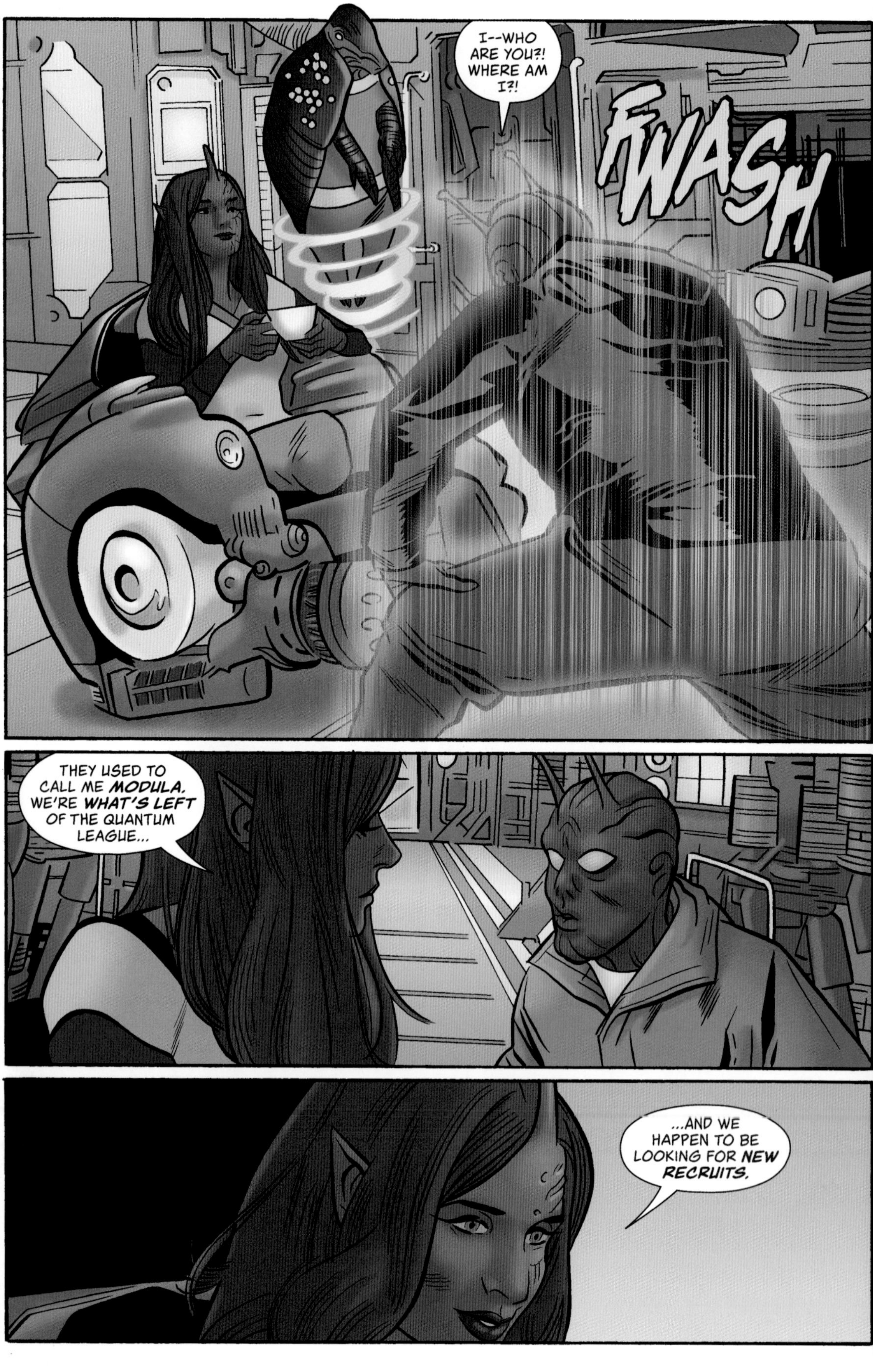
I--WHO ARE YOU?! WHERE AM I?!
FWASH
THEY USED TO CALL ME MODULA. WE'RE WHAT'S LEFT OF THE QUANTUM LEAGUE...
...AND WE HAPPEN TO BE LOOKING FOR NEW RECRUITS.

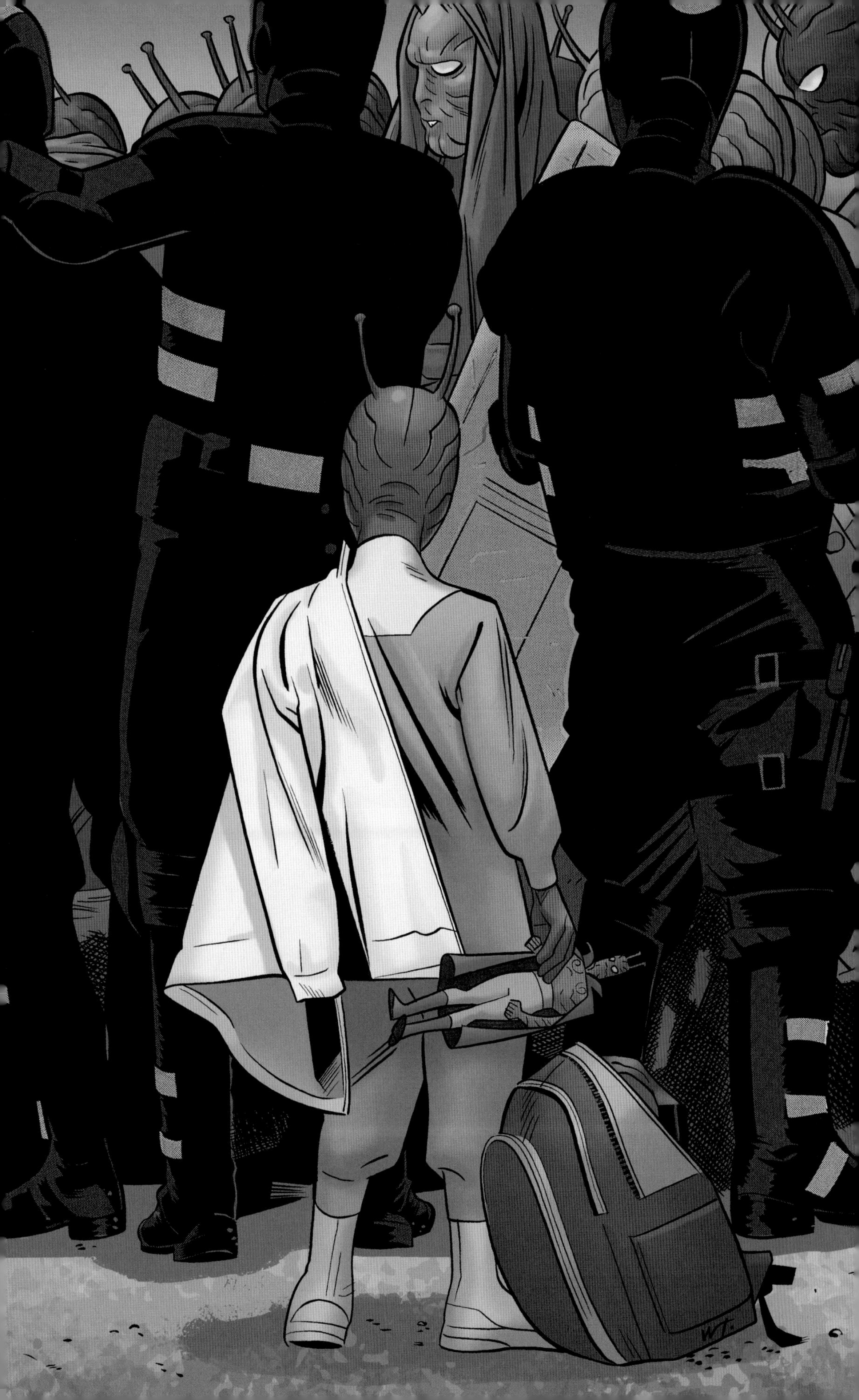

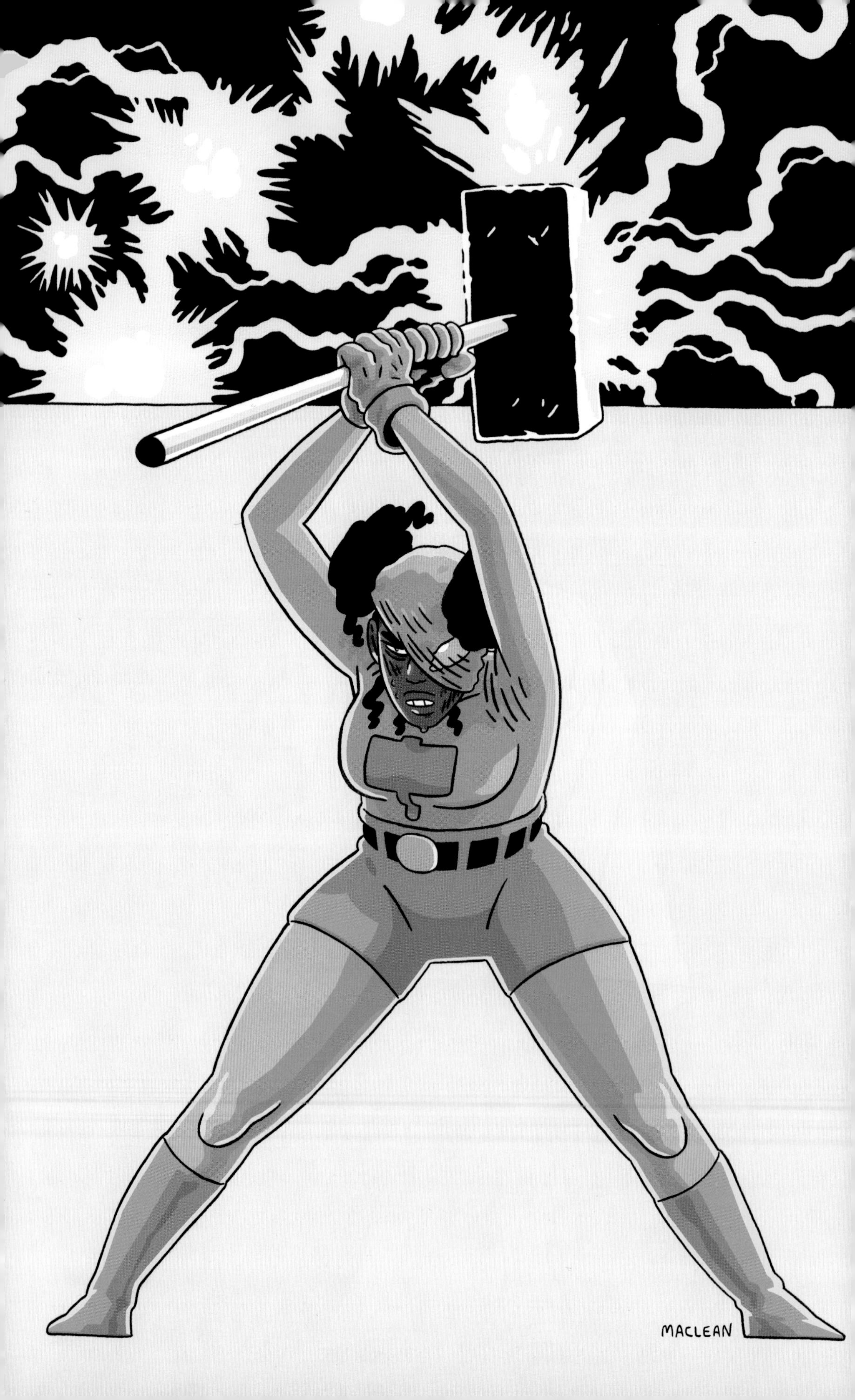
MACLEAN

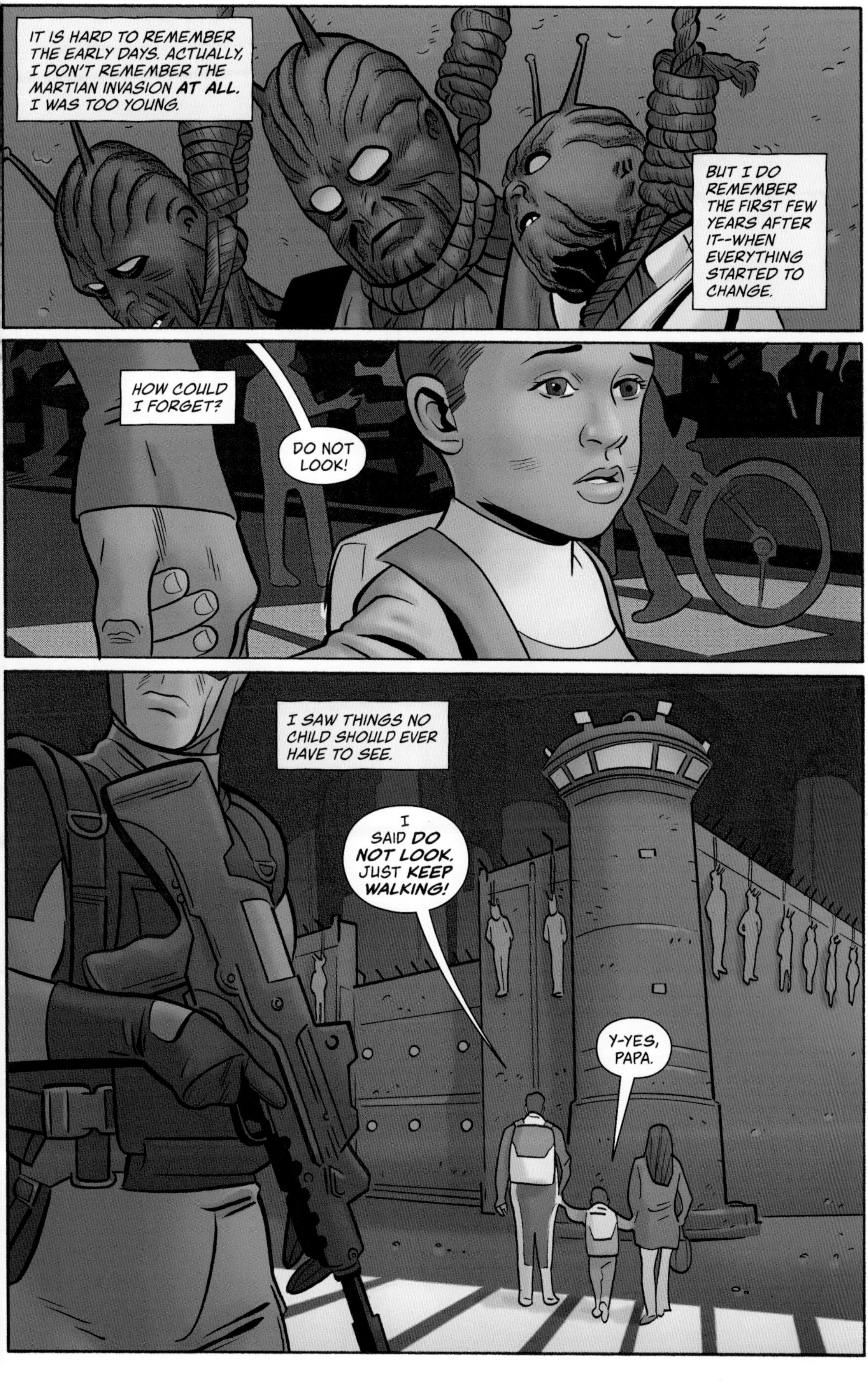
IT IS HARD TO REMEMBER THE EARLY DAYS. ACTUALLY, I DON'T REMEMBER THE MARTIAN INVASION AT ALL. I WAS TOO YOUNG.
BUT I DO REMEMBER THE FIRST FEW YEARS AFTER IT--WHEN EVERYTHING STARTED TO CHANGE.
HOW COULD I FORGET?
DO NOT LOOK!
I SAW THINGS NO CHILD SHOULD EVER HAVE TO SEE.
I SAID DO NOT LOOK. JUST KEEP WALKING!
Y-YES, PAPA.

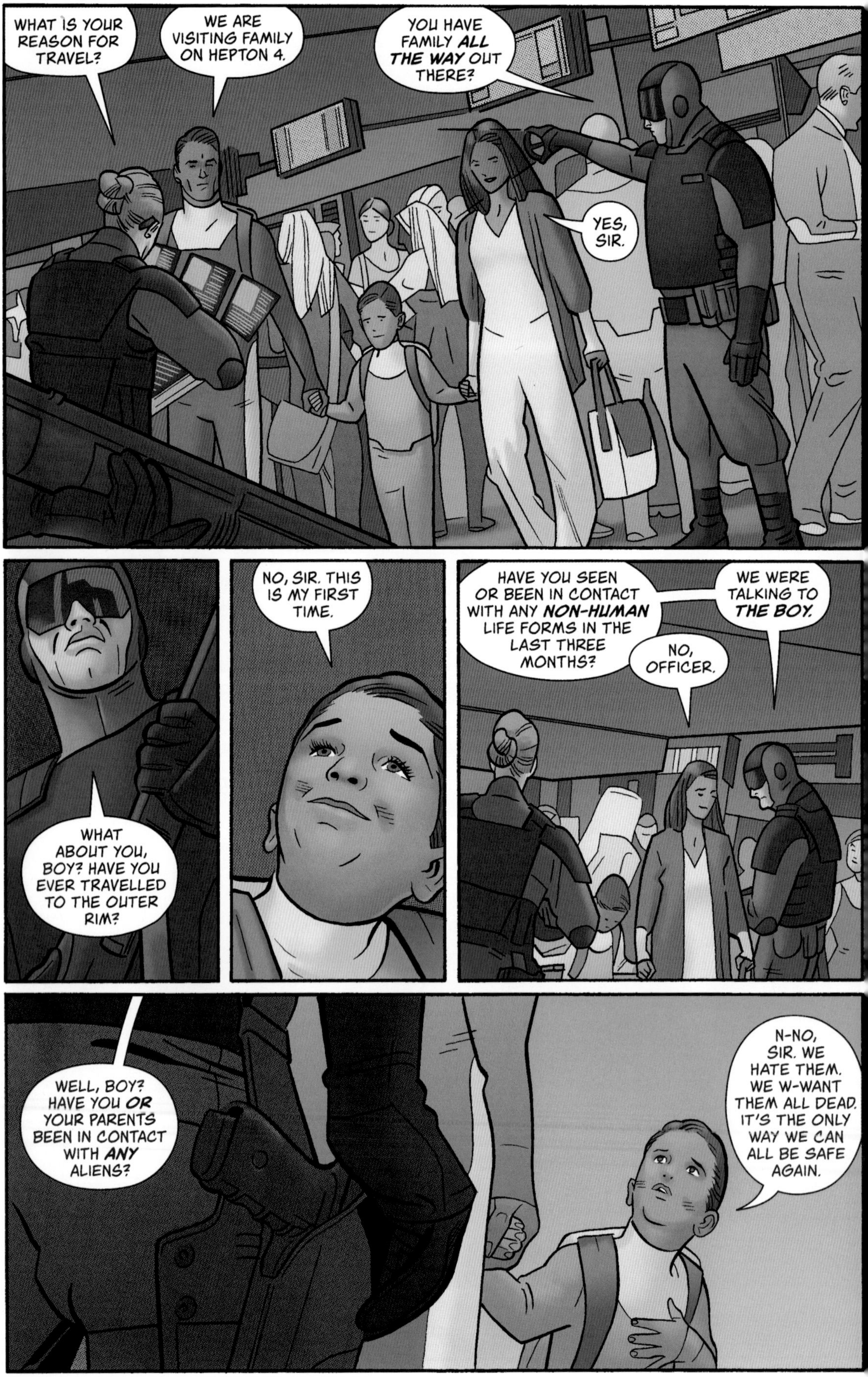
WHAT IS YOUR REASON FOR TRAVEL?
WE ARE VISITING FAMILY ON HEPTON 4.
YOU HAVE FAMILY ALL THE WAY OUT THERE?
YES, SIR.
WHAT ABOUT YOU, BOY? HAVE YOU EVER TRAVELLED TO THE OUTER RIM?
NO, SIR. THIS IS MY FIRST TIME.
HAVE YOU SEEN OR BEEN IN CONTACT WITH ANY NON-HUMAN LIFE FORMS IN THE LAST THREE MONTHS?
NO, OFFICER.
WE WERE TALKING TO THE BOY.
WELL, BOY? HAVE YOU OR YOUR PARENTS BEEN IN CONTACT WITH ANY ALIENS?
N-NO, SIR. WE HATE THEM. WE W-WANT THEM ALL DEAD. IT'S THE ONLY WAY WE CAN ALL BE SAFE AGAIN.

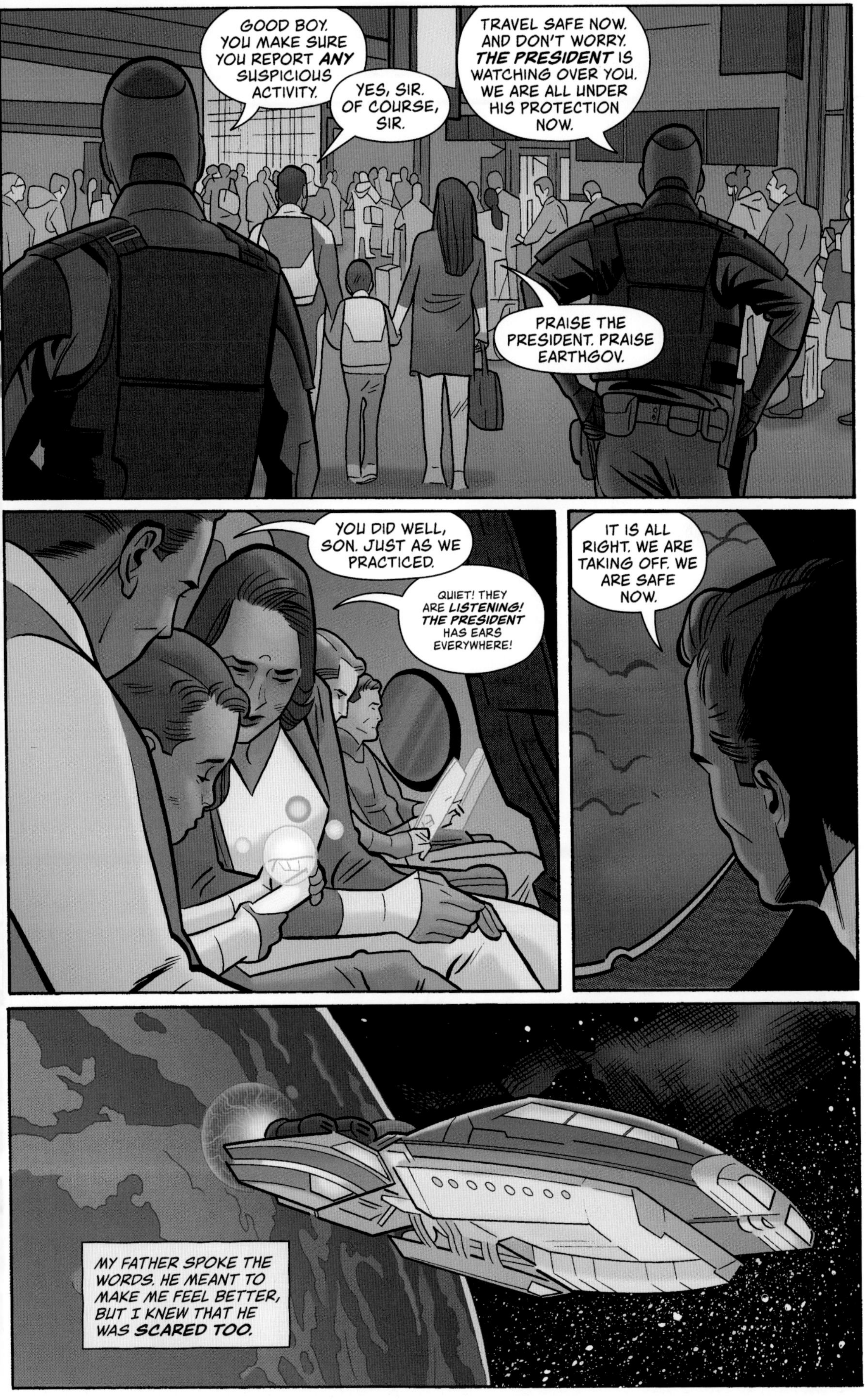
GOOD BOY. YOU MAKE SURE YOU REPORT **ANY** SUSPICIOUS ACTIVITY.
YES, SIR. OF COURSE, SIR.
TRAVEL SAFE NOW. AND DON'T WORRY. ***THE PRESIDENT*** IS WATCHING OVER YOU. WE ARE ALL UNDER HIS PROTECTION NOW.
PRAISE THE PRESIDENT. PRAISE EARTHGOV.
YOU DID WELL, SON. JUST AS WE PRACTICED.
QUIET! THEY ARE ***LISTENING! THE PRESIDENT*** HAS EARS EVERYWHERE!
IT IS ALL RIGHT. WE ARE TAKING OFF. WE ARE SAFE NOW.
*MY FATHER SPOKE THE WORDS. HE MEANT TO MAKE ME FEEL BETTER, BUT I KNEW THAT HE WAS **SCARED TOO.***

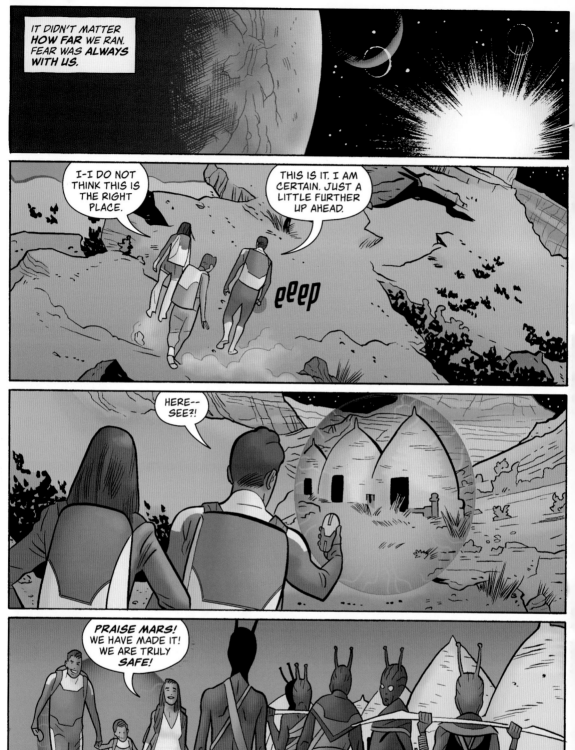

IT DIDN'T MATTER **HOW FAR** WE RAN. FEAR WAS **ALWAYS** WITH US.

I-I DO NOT THINK THIS IS THE RIGHT PLACE.

THIS IS IT. I AM CERTAIN. JUST A LITTLE FURTHER UP AHEAD.

eeep

HERE-- SEE?!

PRAISE MARS! WE HAVE MADE IT! WE ARE TRULY **SAFE!**

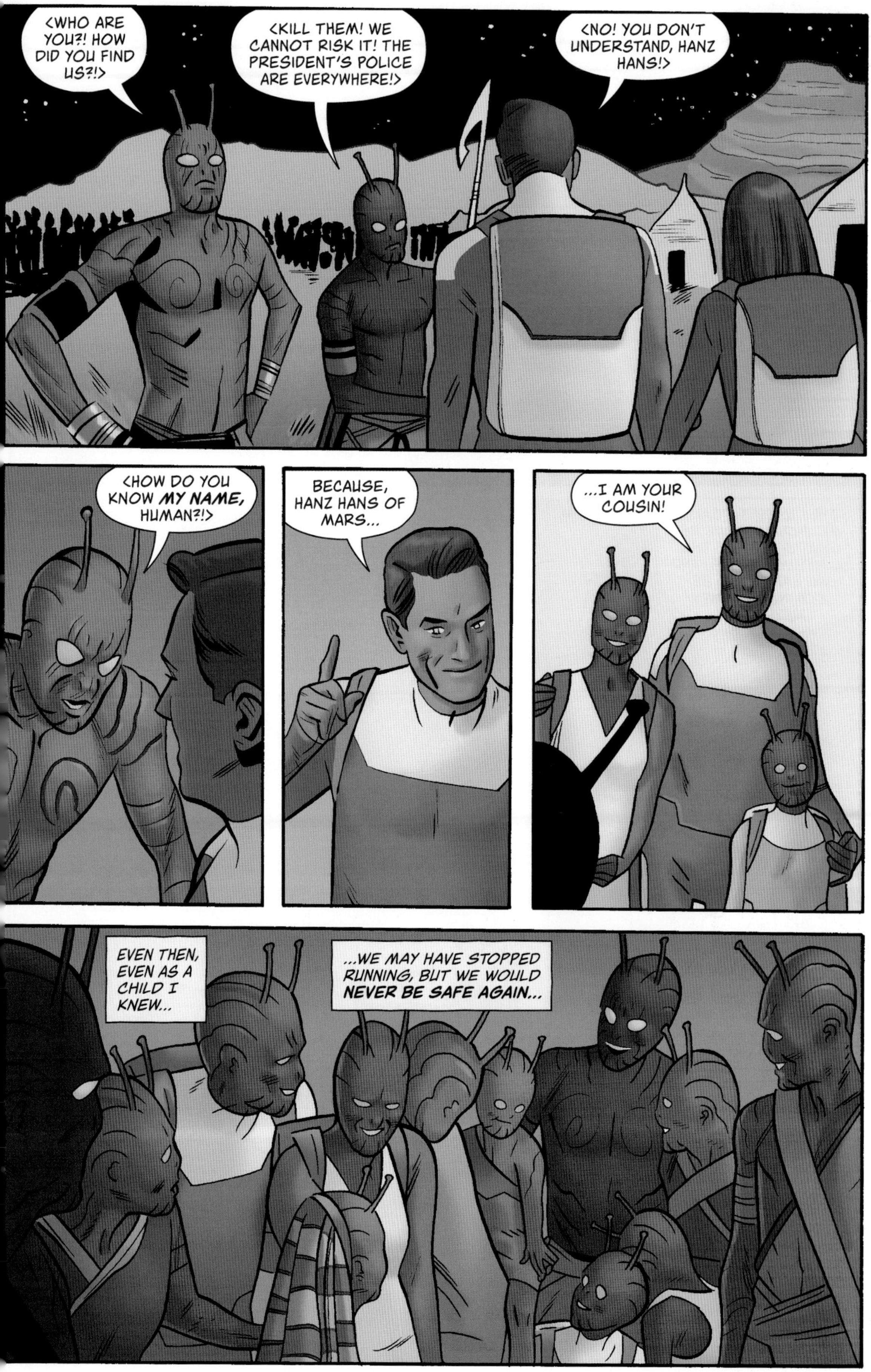

<WHO ARE YOU?! HOW DID YOU FIND US?!>
<KILL THEM! WE CANNOT RISK IT! THE PRESIDENT'S POLICE ARE EVERYWHERE!>
<NO! YOU DON'T UNDERSTAND, HANZ HANS!>
<HOW DO YOU KNOW MY NAME, HUMAN?!>
BECAUSE, HANZ HANS OF MARS...
...I AM YOUR COUSIN!
EVEN THEN, EVEN AS A CHILD I KNEW...
...WE MAY HAVE STOPPED RUNNING, BUT WE WOULD NEVER BE SAFE AGAIN...

EVEN NOW... *A DECADE LATER,* I AM NOT SAFE. *NO ONE IS.*

I--WHO ARE YOU?! WHERE AM I?!

THEY USED TO CALL ME *MODULA.* WE'RE WHAT'S LEFT OF THE QUANTUM LEAGUE. AND WE HAPPEN TO BE LOOKING FOR *NEW RECRUITS.*

Erb thinking not a good idea tell him everything, Ginna.

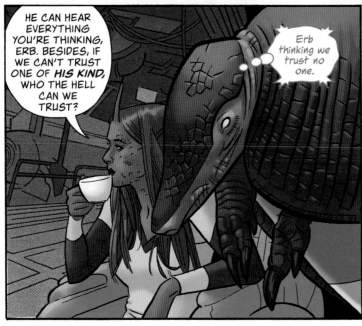

HE CAN HEAR EVERYTHING YOU'RE THINKING, ERB. BESIDES, IF WE CAN'T TRUST ONE OF *HIS KIND,* WHO THE HELL CAN WE TRUST?

Erb thinking we trust no one.

H-HOW DID YOU FIND ME?

ERB AND I MAKE IT OUR BUSINESS TO KEEP AN EYE ON *ALL* THE OLD QUANTUM LEAGUERS. CAN'T BE TOO SAFE THESE DAYS.

WE SAW YOU APPROACH HAMMER LASS. GOT TO SAY, KID. THAT WAS PRETTY DUMB. EARTH IS THE *LAST PLACE* YOU WANNA BE. WHY'D YOU GO TO HER FIRST?

I-I'M *BARBALI-TEEN.* AND SHE IS THE ANCESTOR OF BLACK HAMMER.

WE'RE BOTH INSPIRED BY SPIRAL CITY'S LEGENDARY HEROES. IT'S OUR LEGACY TO WORK TOGETHER.

UH HUH. YOU REALLY WANNA BE A HERO, YOU GOTTA BE SMARTER THAN THAT.

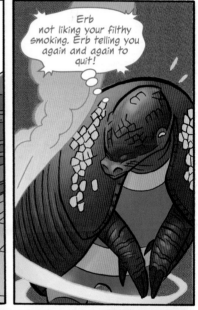

Erb *not liking your filthy smoking.* Erb telling you again and again to quit!

ERB IS DRIVING ME BAT-SHIT CRAZY IS WHAT ERB IS DOING. NOW SHUT YOUR HOLE, WEIRD BALL, I'M TALKING HERE.

WHAT--WHAT HAPPENED TO YOU? I DIDN'T EVEN RECOGNIZE YOU.

WHAT DO YOU *THINK* HAPPENED? *YOUR PEOPLE* HAPPENED. LOST MY LEGS IN THE BATTLE OF MANHATTAN.

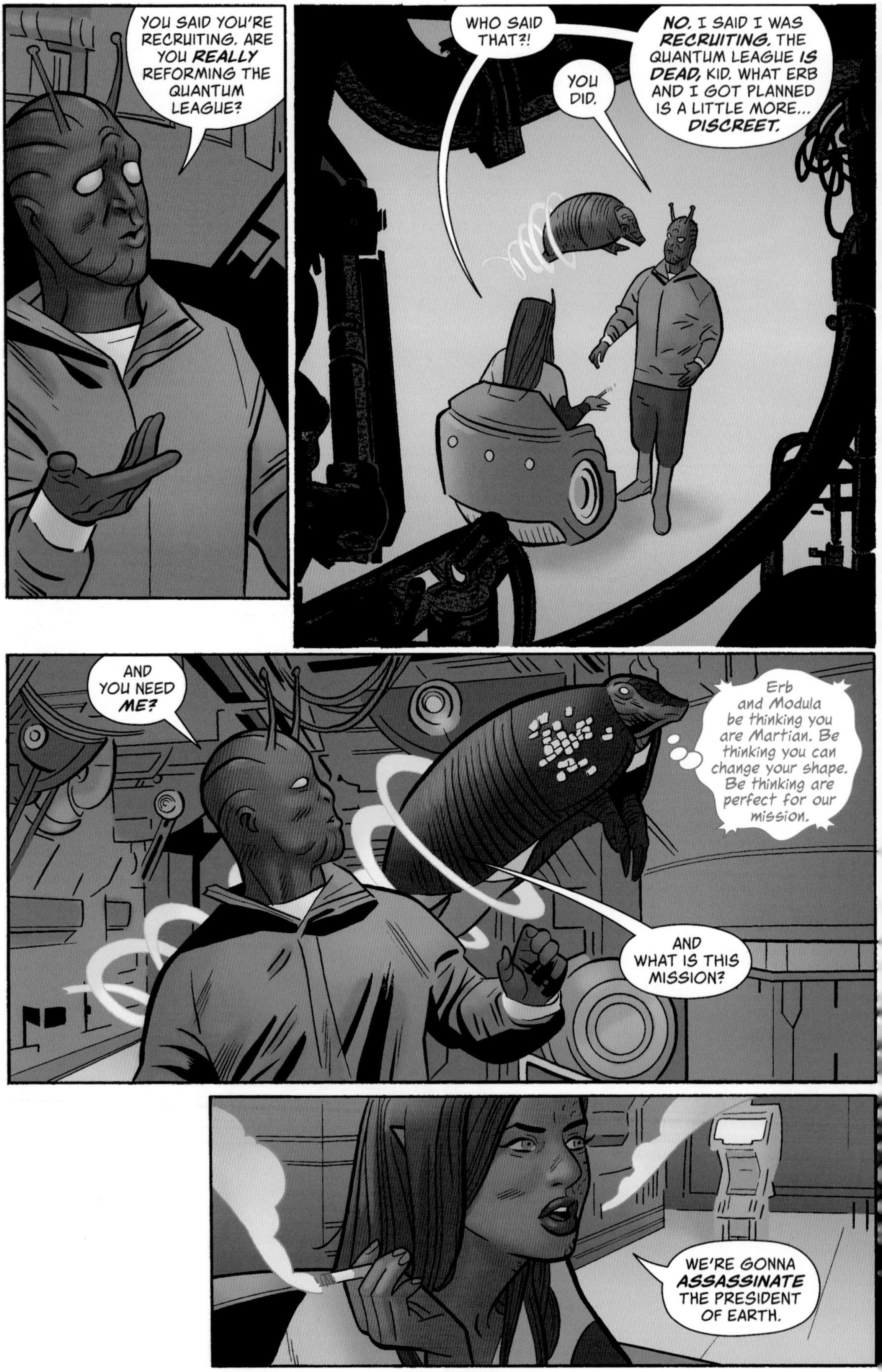
YOU SAID YOU'RE RECRUITING. ARE YOU **REALLY** REFORMING THE QUANTUM LEAGUE?
WHO SAID THAT?!
YOU DID.
NO. I SAID I WAS **RECRUITING.** THE QUANTUM LEAGUE **IS DEAD,** KID. WHAT ERB AND I GOT PLANNED IS A LITTLE MORE... **DISCREET.**
AND YOU NEED **ME?**
Erb and Modula be thinking you are Martian. Be thinking you can change your shape. Be thinking are perfect for our mission.
AND WHAT IS THIS MISSION?
WE'RE GONNA **ASSASSINATE** THE PRESIDENT OF EARTH.

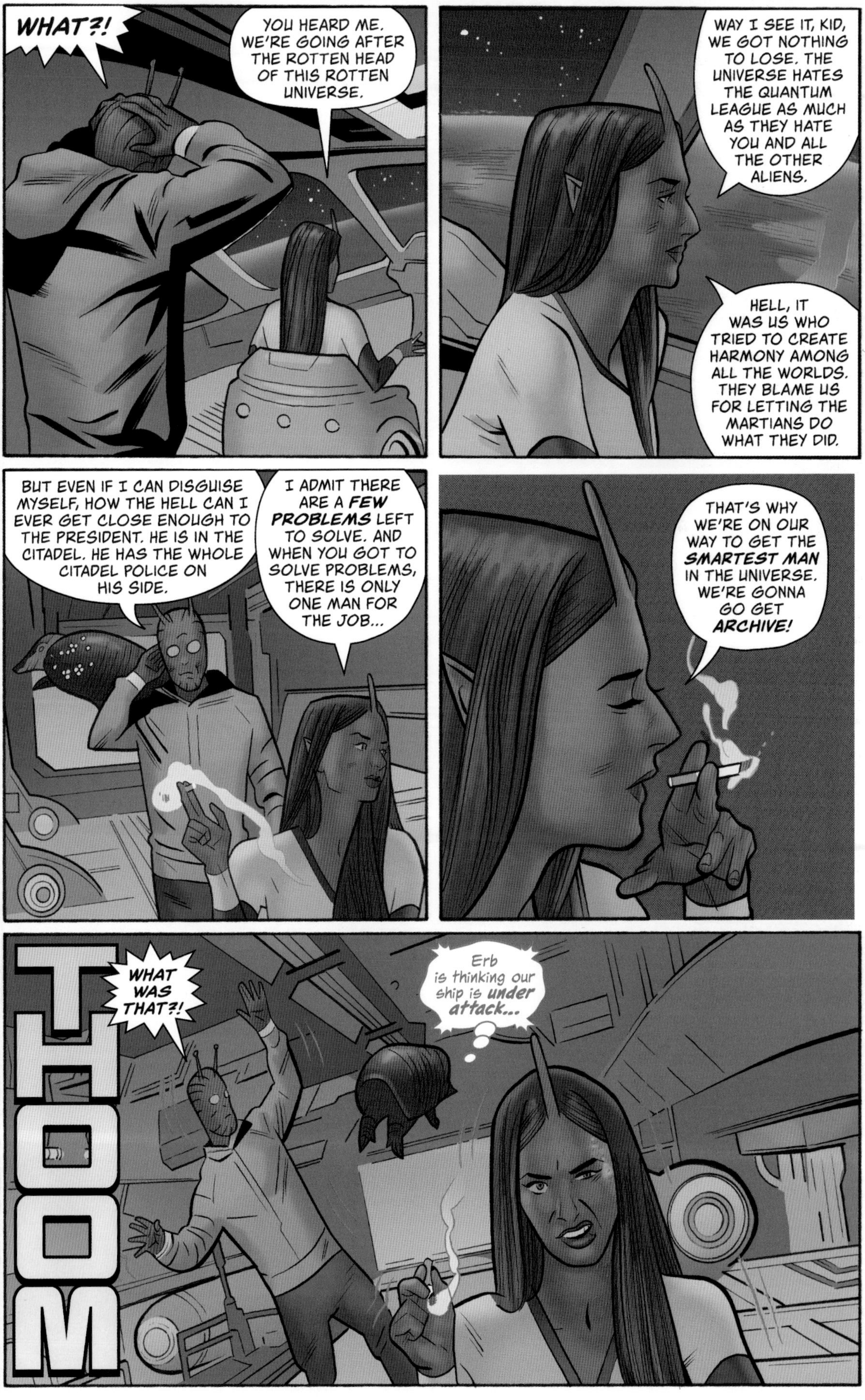
WHAT?!
YOU HEARD ME. WE'RE GOING AFTER THE ROTTEN HEAD OF THIS ROTTEN UNIVERSE.
WAY I SEE IT, KID, WE GOT NOTHING TO LOSE. THE UNIVERSE HATES THE QUANTUM LEAGUE AS MUCH AS THEY HATE YOU AND ALL THE OTHER ALIENS.
HELL, IT WAS US WHO TRIED TO CREATE HARMONY AMONG ALL THE WORLDS. THEY BLAME US FOR LETTING THE MARTIANS DO WHAT THEY DID.
BUT EVEN IF I CAN DISGUISE MYSELF, HOW THE HELL CAN I EVER GET CLOSE ENOUGH TO THE PRESIDENT. HE IS IN THE CITADEL. HE HAS THE WHOLE CITADEL POLICE ON HIS SIDE.
I ADMIT THERE ARE A FEW PROBLEMS LEFT TO SOLVE. AND WHEN YOU GOT TO SOLVE PROBLEMS, THERE IS ONLY ONE MAN FOR THE JOB...
THAT'S WHY WE'RE ON OUR WAY TO GET THE SMARTEST MAN IN THE UNIVERSE. WE'RE GONNA GO GET ARCHIVE!
THOOM
WHAT WAS THAT?!
Erb is thinking our ship is under attack...

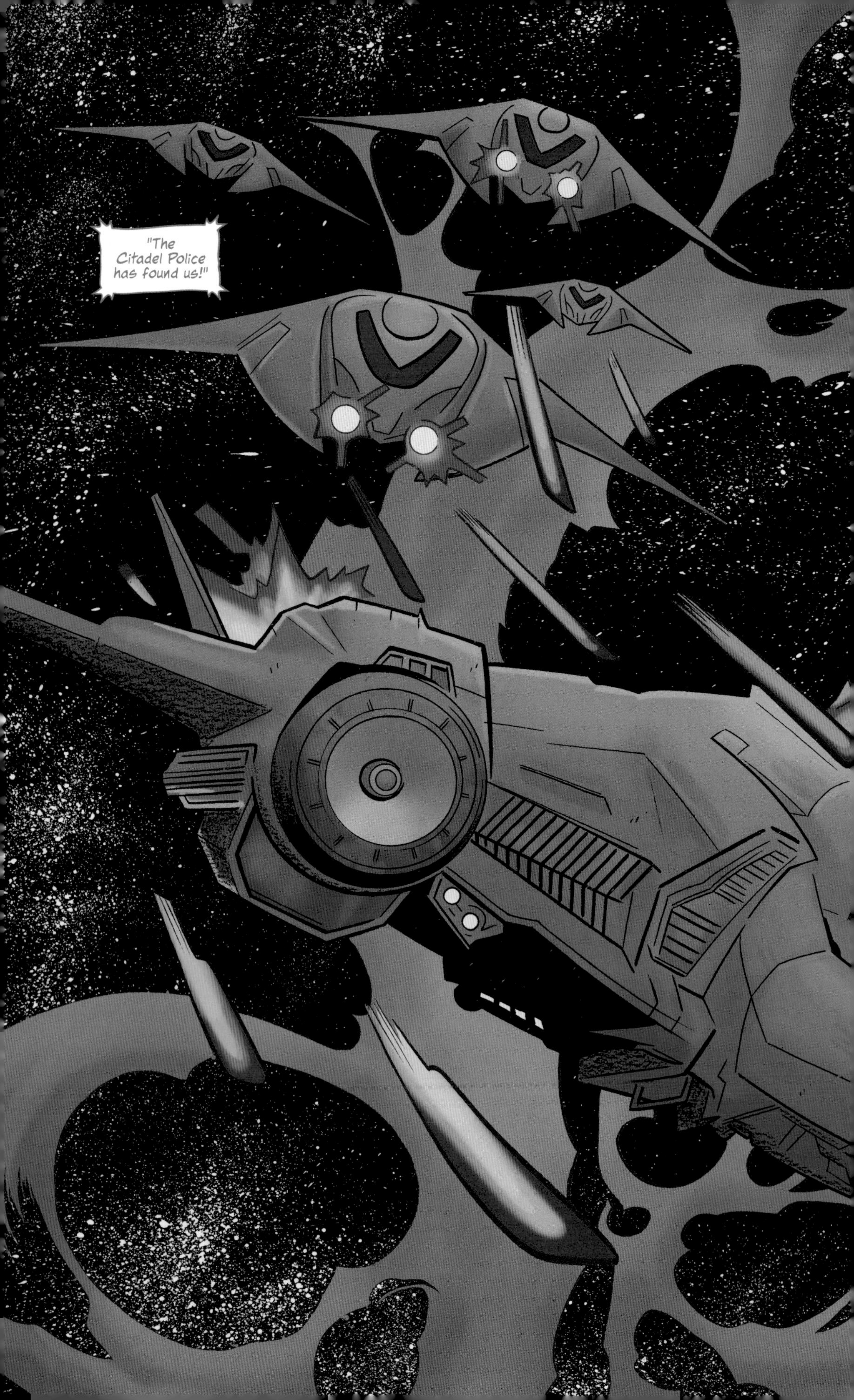
"The Citadel Police has found us!"

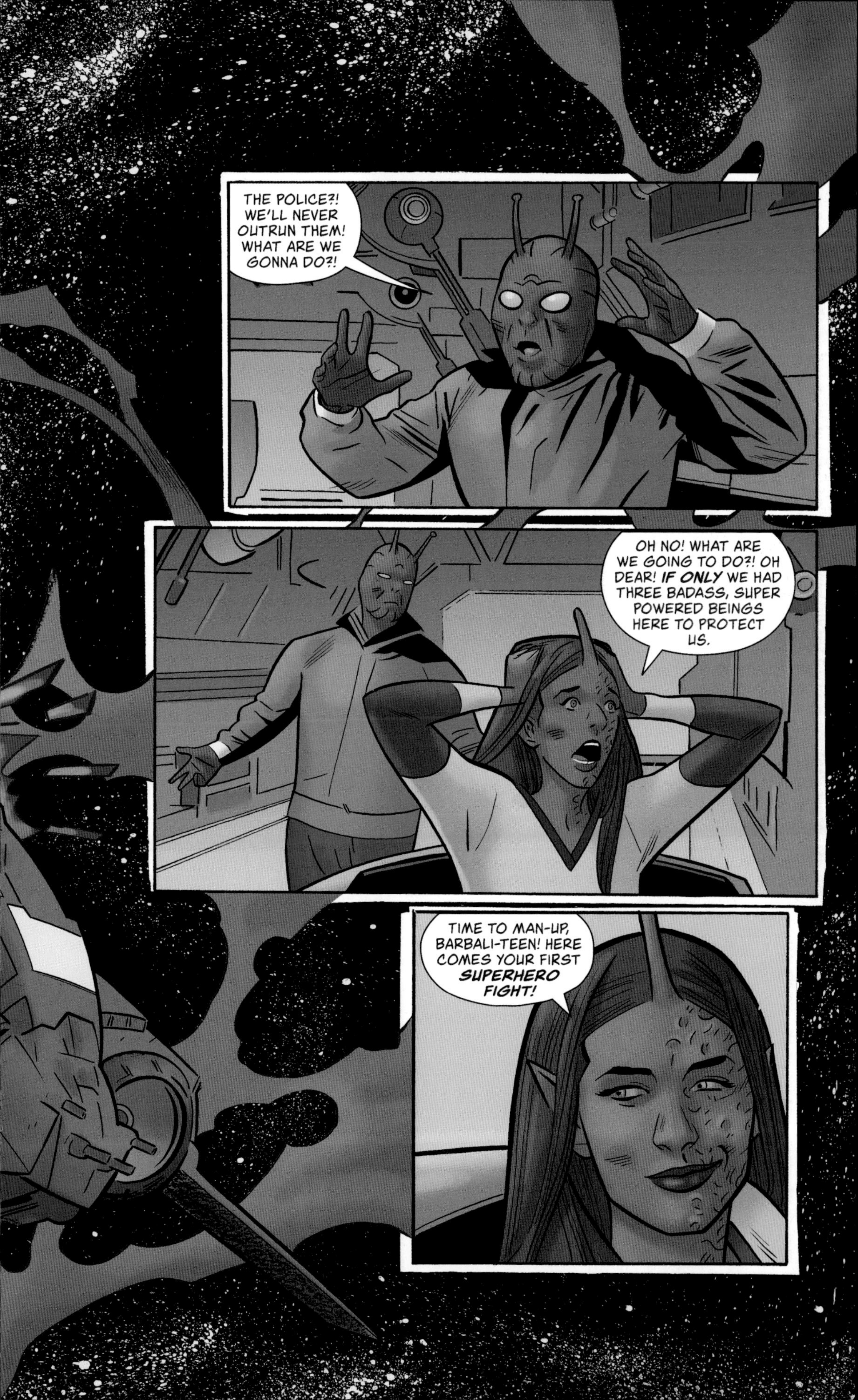
THE POLICE?! WE'LL NEVER OUTRUN THEM! WHAT ARE WE GONNA DO?!
OH NO! WHAT ARE WE GOING TO DO?! OH DEAR! IF ONLY WE HAD THREE BADASS, SUPER POWERED BEINGS HERE TO PROTECT US.
TIME TO MAN-UP, BARBALI-TEEN! HERE COMES YOUR FIRST SUPERHERO FIGHT!

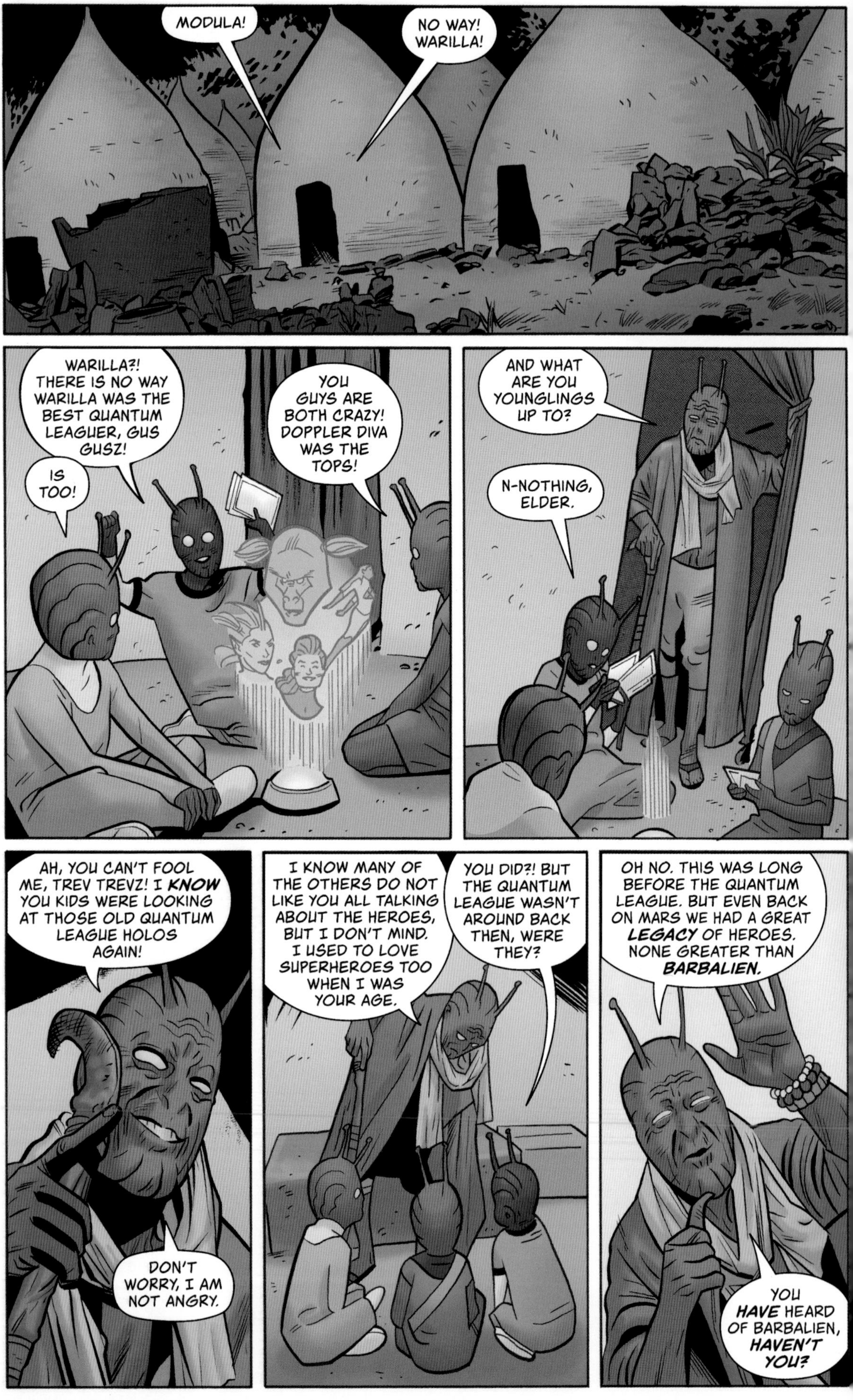

MODULA!
NO WAY! WARILLA!
WARILLA?! THERE IS NO WAY WARILLA WAS THE BEST QUANTUM LEAGUER, GUS GUSZ!
IS TOO!
YOU GUYS ARE BOTH CRAZY! DOPPLER DIVA WAS THE TOPS!
AND WHAT ARE YOU YOUNGLINGS UP TO?
N-NOTHING, ELDER.
AH, YOU CAN'T FOOL ME, TREV TREVZ! I KNOW YOU KIDS WERE LOOKING AT THOSE OLD QUANTUM LEAGUE HOLOS AGAIN!
DON'T WORRY, I AM NOT ANGRY.
I KNOW MANY OF THE OTHERS DO NOT LIKE YOU ALL TALKING ABOUT THE HEROES, BUT I DON'T MIND. I USED TO LOVE SUPERHEROES TOO WHEN I WAS YOUR AGE.
YOU DID?! BUT THE QUANTUM LEAGUE WASN'T AROUND BACK THEN, WERE THEY?
OH NO. THIS WAS LONG BEFORE THE QUANTUM LEAGUE. BUT EVEN BACK ON MARS WE HAD A GREAT LEGACY OF HEROES. NONE GREATER THAN BARBALIEN.
YOU HAVE HEARD OF BARBALIEN, HAVEN'T YOU?

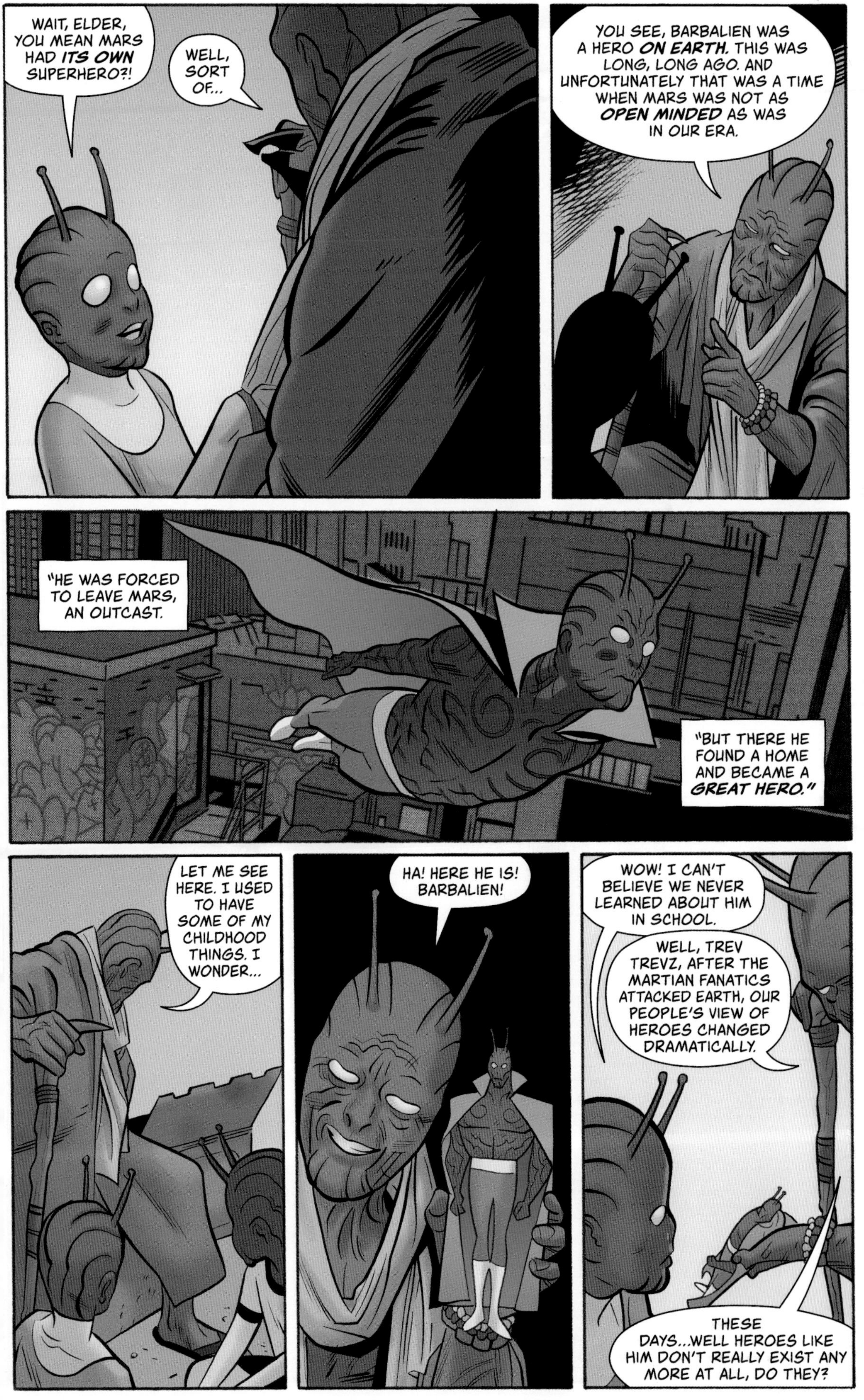

WAIT, ELDER, YOU MEAN MARS HAD ***ITS OWN*** SUPERHERO?!
WELL, SORT OF...
YOU SEE, BARBALIEN WAS A HERO ***ON EARTH.*** THIS WAS LONG, LONG AGO. AND UNFORTUNATELY THAT WAS A TIME WHEN MARS WAS NOT AS ***OPEN MINDED*** AS WAS IN OUR ERA.
"HE WAS FORCED TO LEAVE MARS, AN OUTCAST.
"BUT THERE HE FOUND A HOME AND BECAME A ***GREAT HERO."***
LET ME SEE HERE. I USED TO HAVE SOME OF MY CHILDHOOD THINGS. I WONDER...
HA! HERE HE IS! BARBALIEN!
WOW! I CAN'T BELIEVE WE NEVER LEARNED ABOUT HIM IN SCHOOL.
WELL, TREV TREVZ, AFTER THE MARTIAN FANATICS ATTACKED EARTH, OUR PEOPLE'S VIEW OF HEROES CHANGED DRAMATICALLY.
THESE DAYS...WELL HEROES LIKE HIM DON'T REALLY EXIST ANY MORE AT ALL, DO THEY?

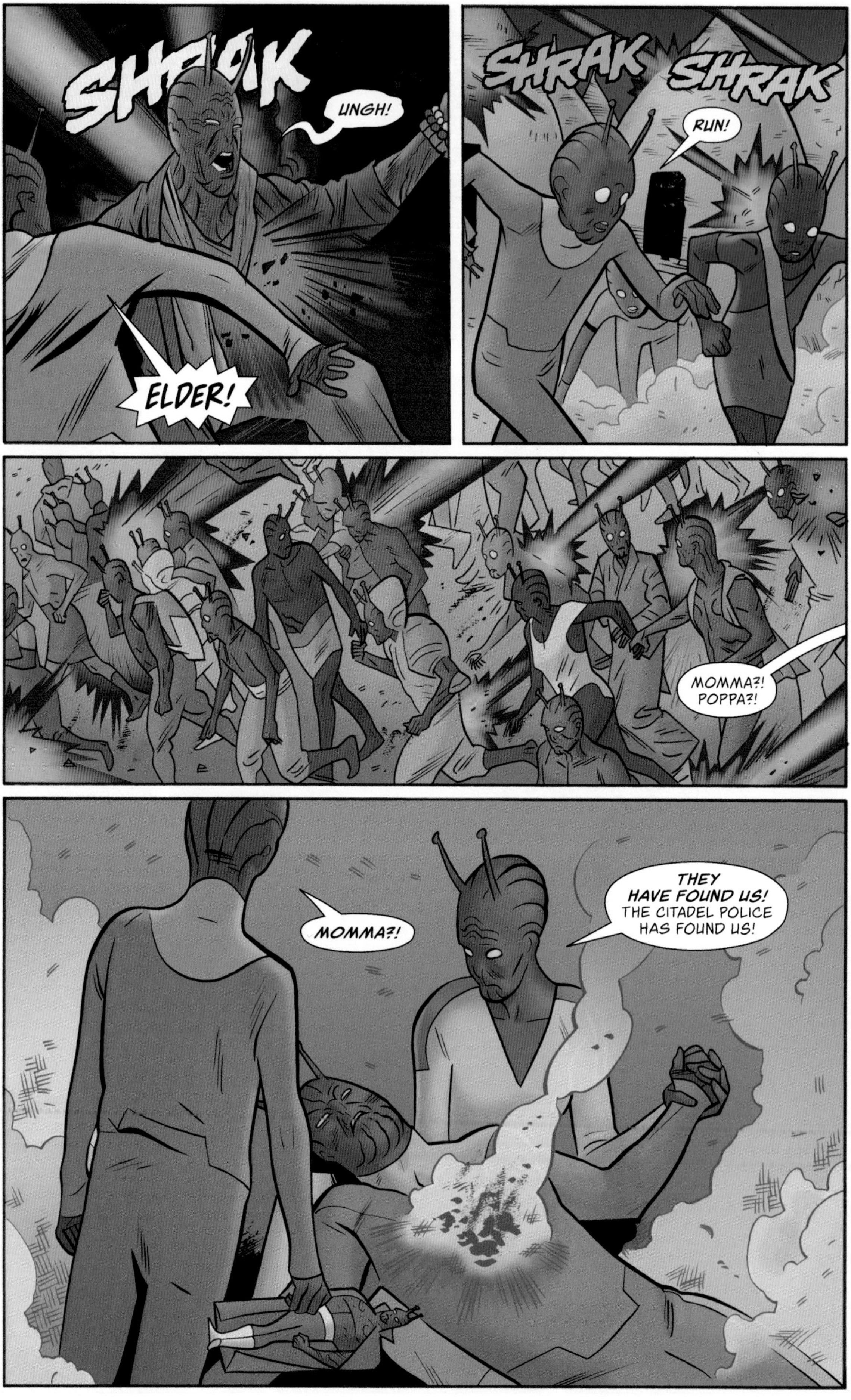
UNGH!
ELDER!
SHRAK
SHRAK
RUN!
MOMMA?!
POPPA?!
MOMMA?!
THEY
HAVE FOUND US!
THE CITADEL POLICE
HAS FOUND US!

"THEY FOUND US! THE BASTARDS FOUND US, ERB!"

Erb is thinking we are in **large trouble**, Ginna. Erb is thinking going after Martian boy was a **large mistake**.

Erb shall activate the ship's weapons systems.

NO... I GOT THIS.

Erb is thinking you are thinking of using your powers. And Erb knows what happened last time that happened.

JUST OPEN THE AIRLOCK, ERB!

STAY BACK, KID. IF THIS GOES BADLY, WELL...IN THAT CASE WE'RE ALL FUCKED. SO IT WAS NICE MEETING YOU.

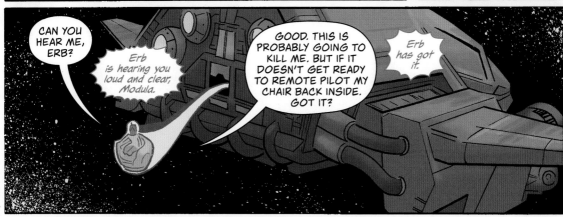

CAN YOU HEAR ME, ERB?

Erb is hearing you loud and clear, Modula.

GOOD. THIS IS PROBABLY GOING TO KILL ME. BUT IF IT DOESN'T GET READY TO REMOTE PILOT MY CHAIR BACK INSIDE. GOT IT?

Erb has got it.

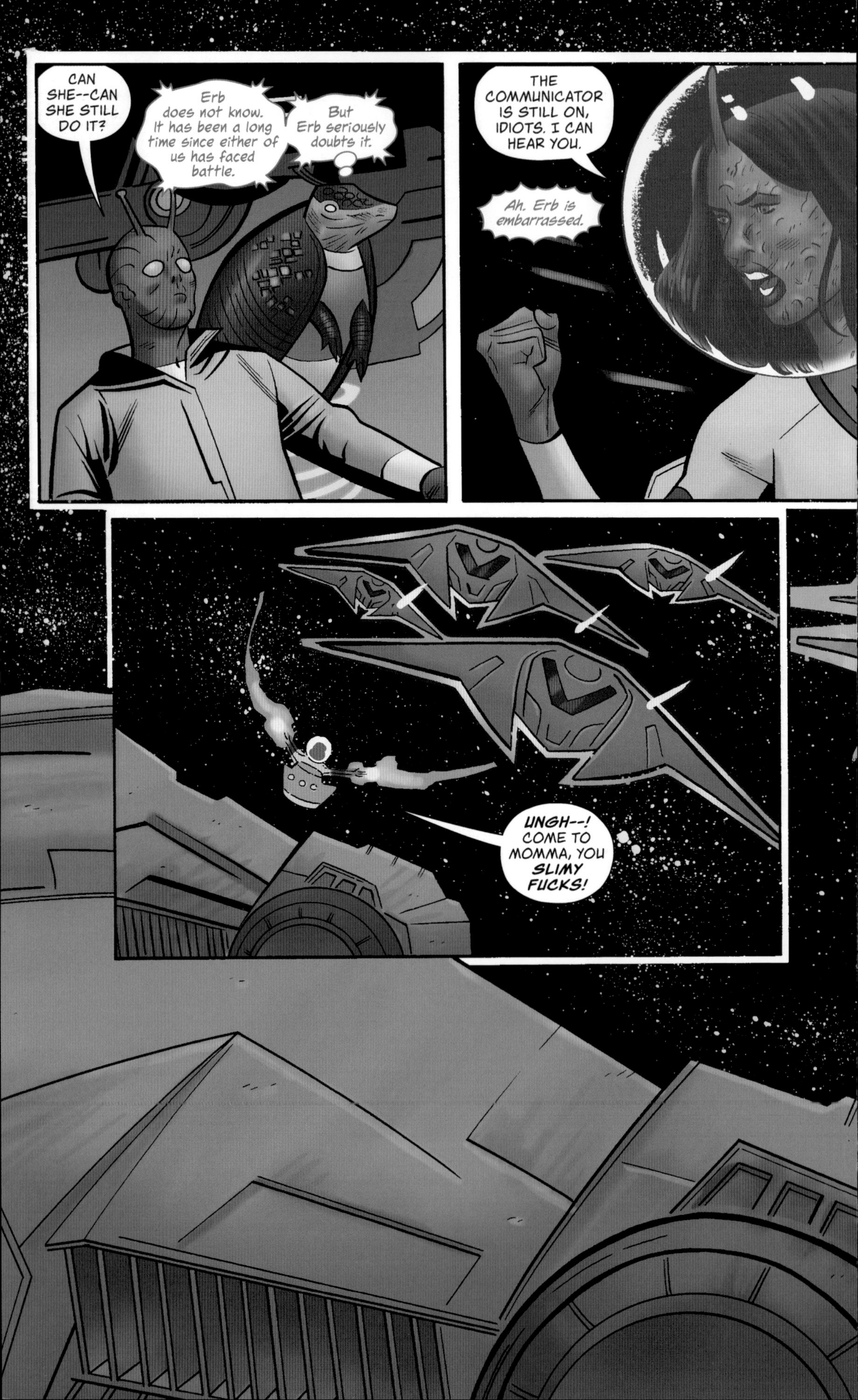
CAN SHE--CAN SHE STILL DO IT?
Erb does not know. It has been a long time since either of us has faced battle.
But Erb seriously doubts it.
THE COMMUNICATOR IS STILL ON, IDIOTS. I CAN HEAR YOU.
Ah. Erb is embarrassed.
UNGH--! COME TO MOMMA, YOU SLIMY FUCKS!

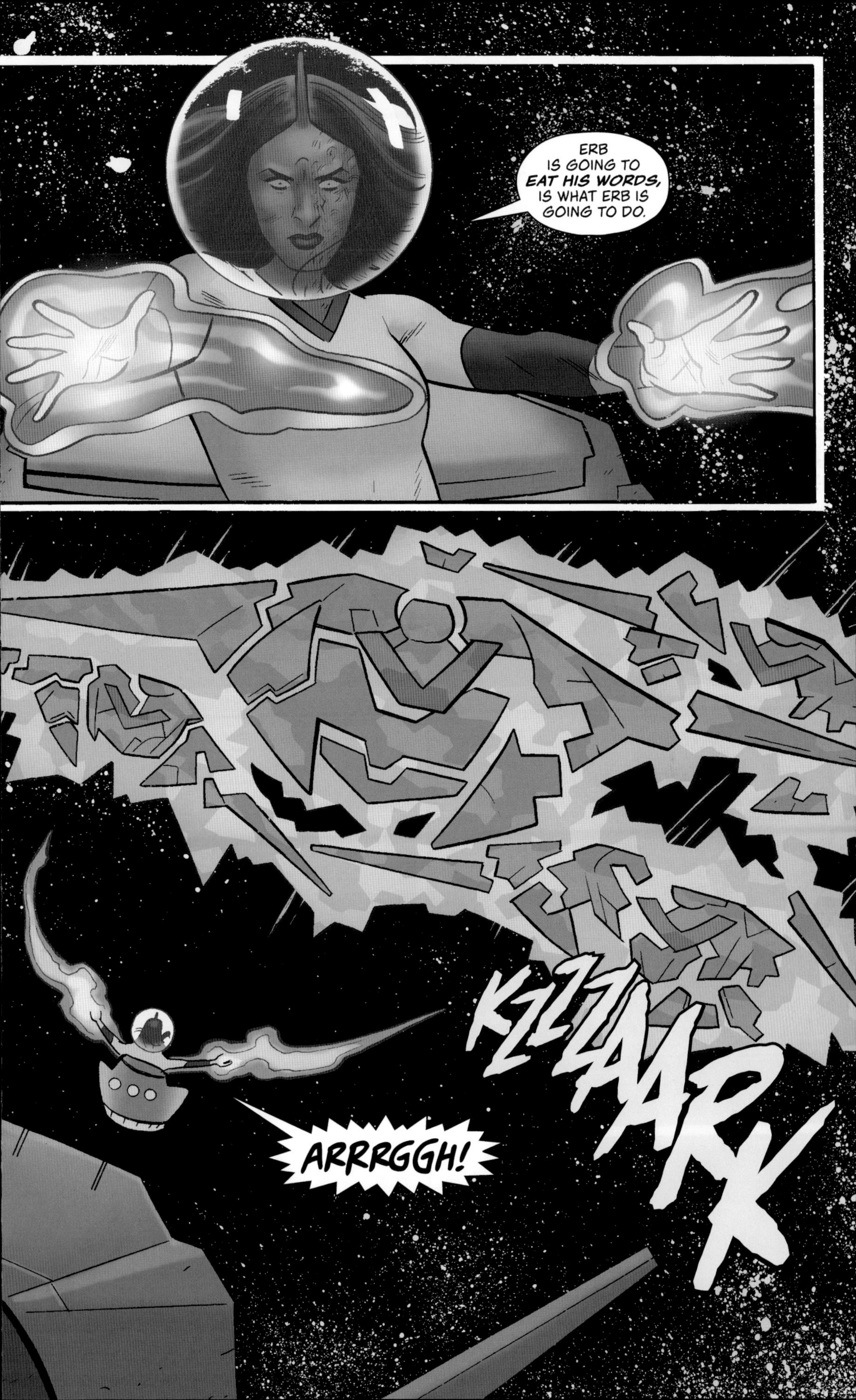
ERB IS GOING TO **EAT HIS WORDS,** IS WHAT ERB IS GOING TO DO.
KZZZZAARK
ARRRGGH!

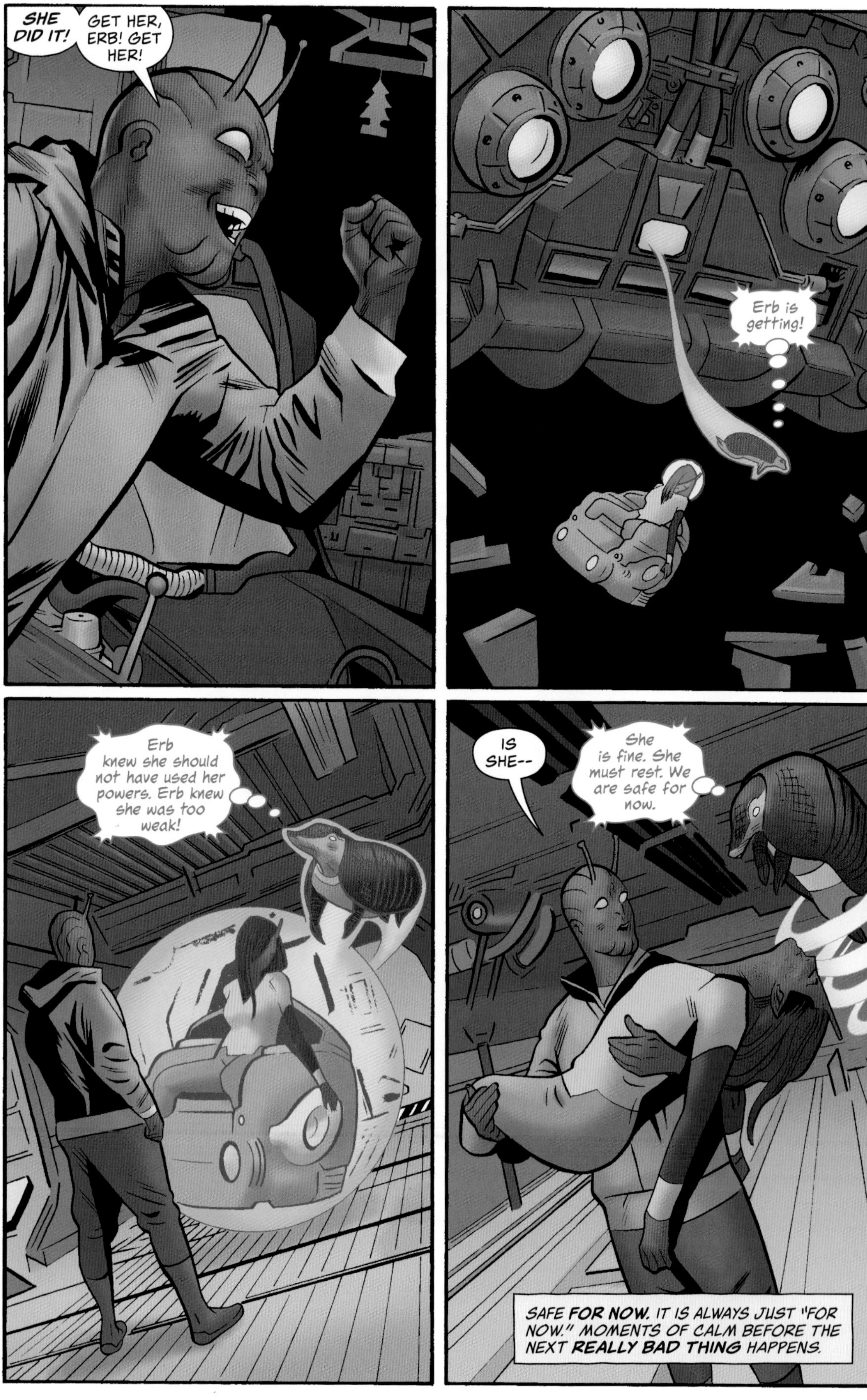
SHE DID IT!
GET HER, ERB! GET HER!
Erb is getting!
Erb knew she should not have used her powers. Erb knew she was too weak!
IS SHE--
She is fine. She must rest. We are safe for now.
SAFE FOR NOW. IT IS ALWAYS JUST "FOR NOW." MOMENTS OF CALM BEFORE THE NEXT REALLY BAD THING HAPPENS.

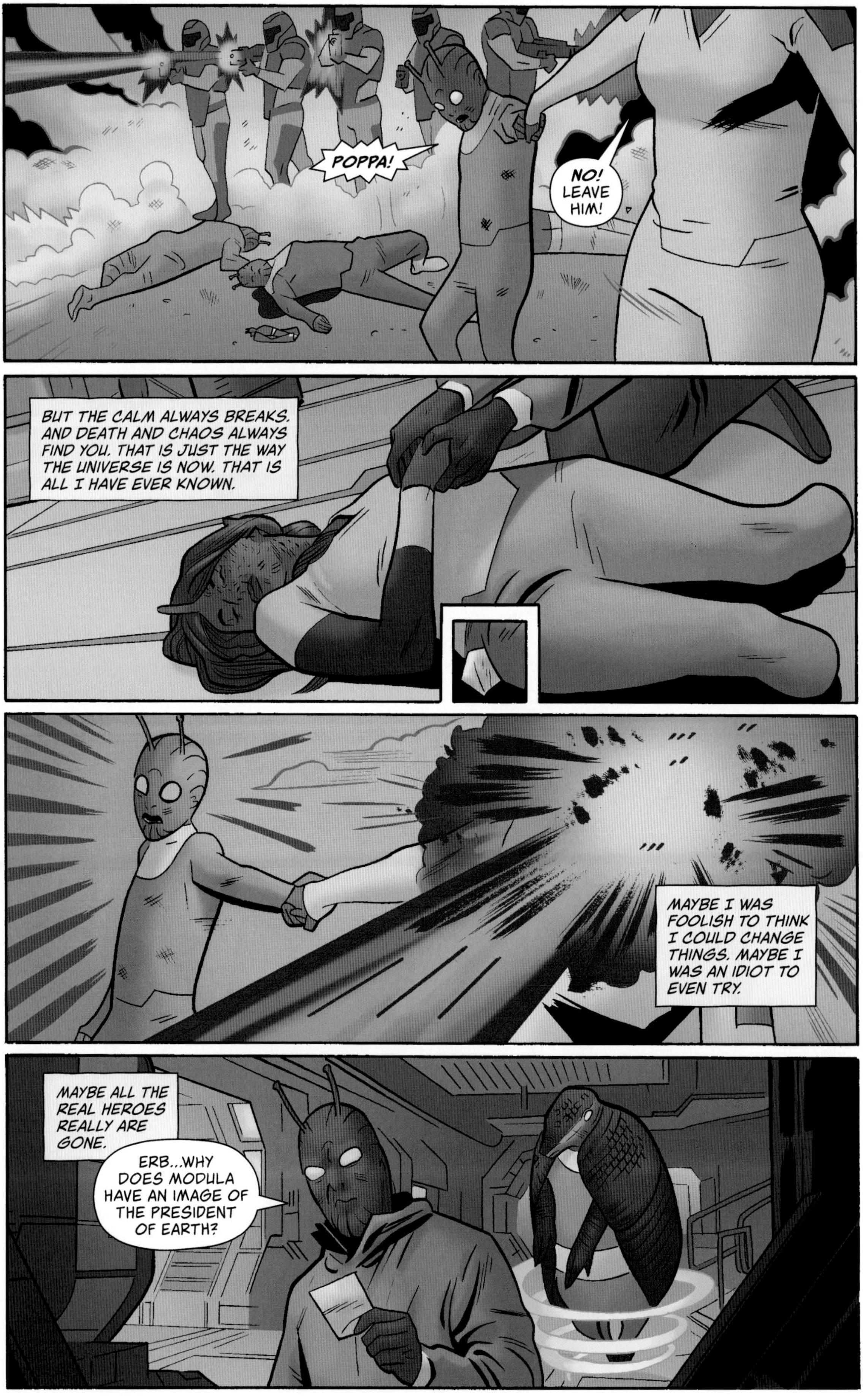
POPPA!
NO! LEAVE HIM!
BUT THE CALM ALWAYS BREAKS. AND DEATH AND CHAOS ALWAYS FIND YOU. THAT IS JUST THE WAY THE UNIVERSE IS NOW. THAT IS ALL I HAVE EVER KNOWN.
MAYBE I WAS FOOLISH TO THINK I COULD CHANGE THINGS. MAYBE I WAS AN IDIOT TO EVEN TRY.
MAYBE ALL THE REAL HEROES REALLY ARE GONE.
ERB...WHY DOES MODULA HAVE AN IMAGE OF THE PRESIDENT OF EARTH?

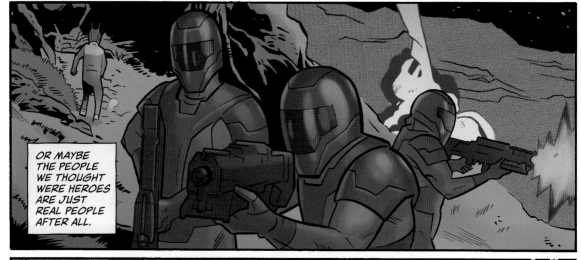

OR MAYBE THE PEOPLE WE THOUGHT WERE HEROES ARE JUST REAL PEOPLE AFTER ALL.

That is simple... Modula has an image of The President because they used to be *lovers.*

MISTER PRESIDENT! ALL OF THE MARTIANS ARE DEAD SAVE FOR A FEW WHO ESCAPED INTO THE HILLS. BUT WE'LL FIND THEM.

EXCELLENT WORK, MEN.

MAYBE THE HEROES ARE AS **LOST** AS THE REST OF US NOW.

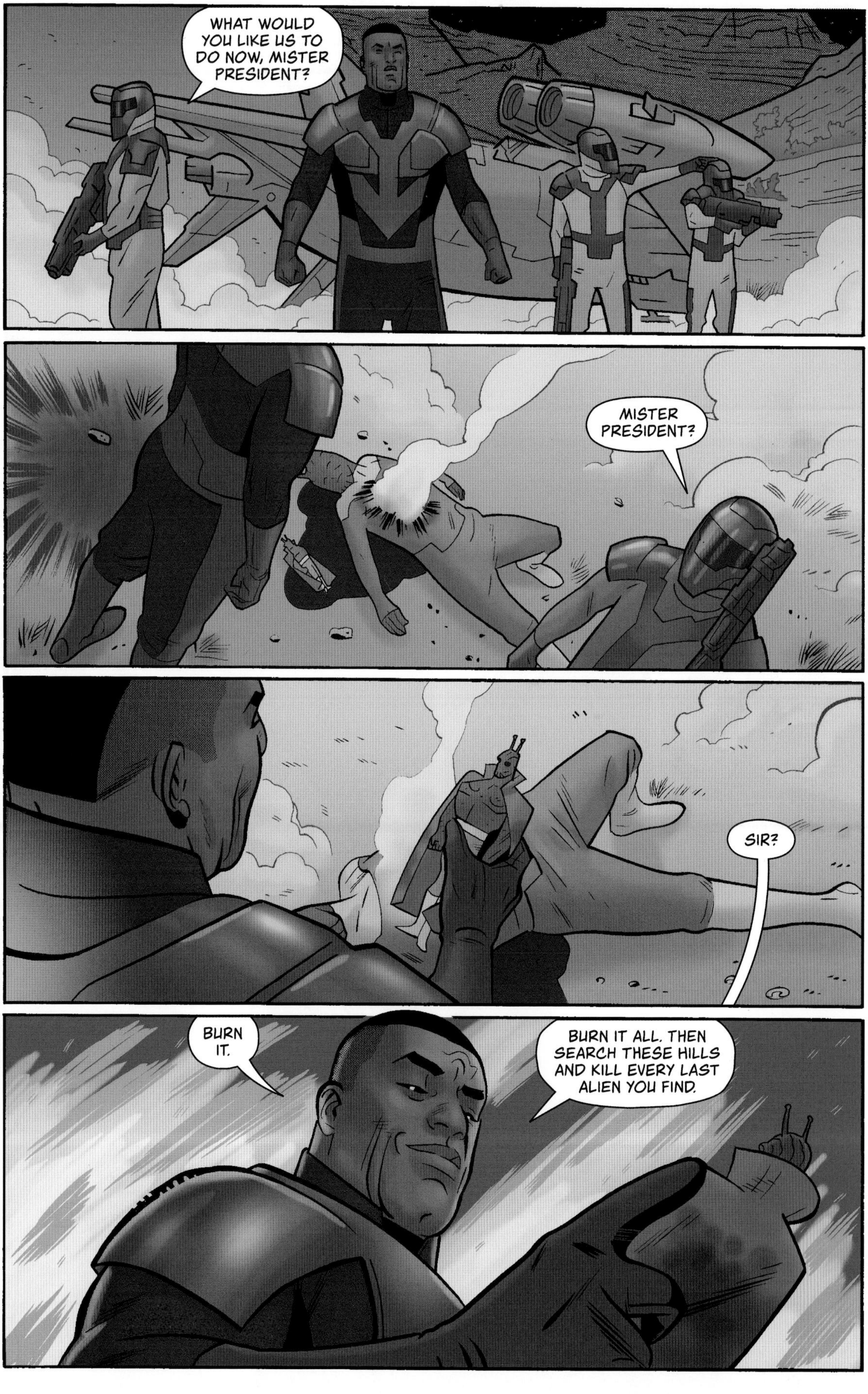
WHAT WOULD YOU LIKE US TO DO NOW, MISTER PRESIDENT?
MISTER PRESIDENT?
SIR?
BURN IT.
BURN IT ALL. THEN SEARCH THESE HILLS AND KILL EVERY LAST ALIEN YOU FIND.

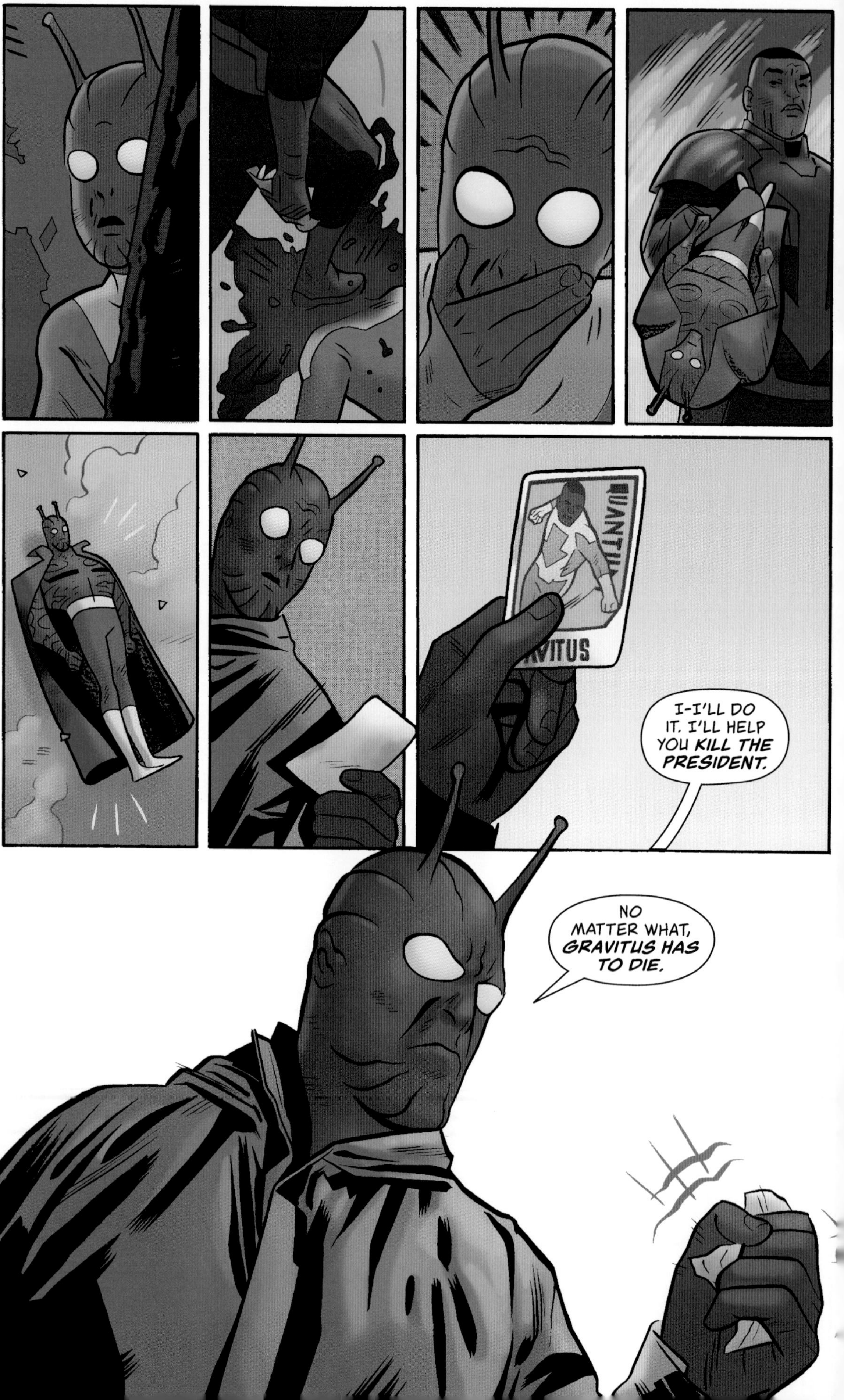
QUANTU
AVITUS
I-I'LL DO IT. I'LL HELP YOU KILL THE PRESIDENT.
NO MATTER WHAT, GRAVITUS HAS TO DIE.

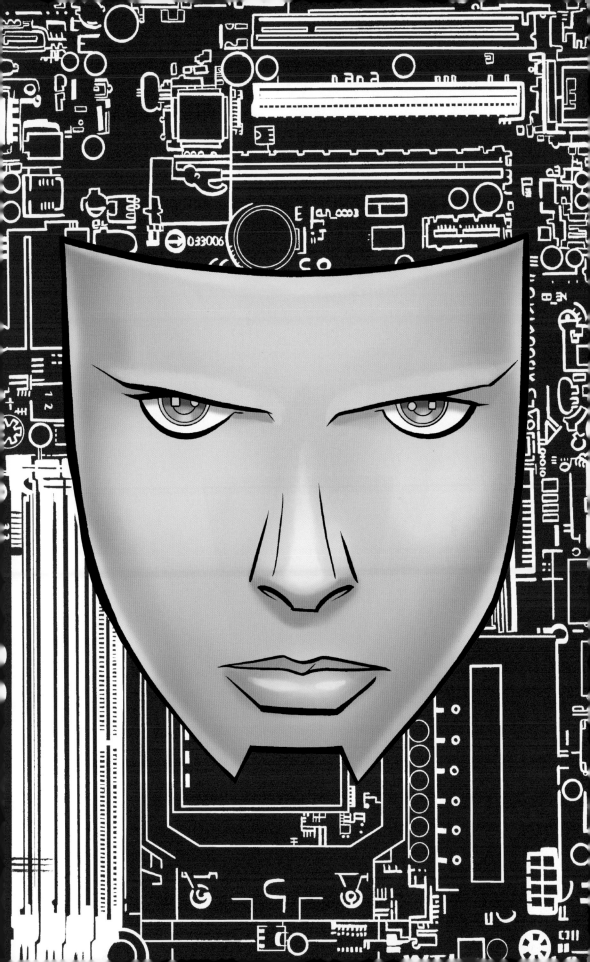

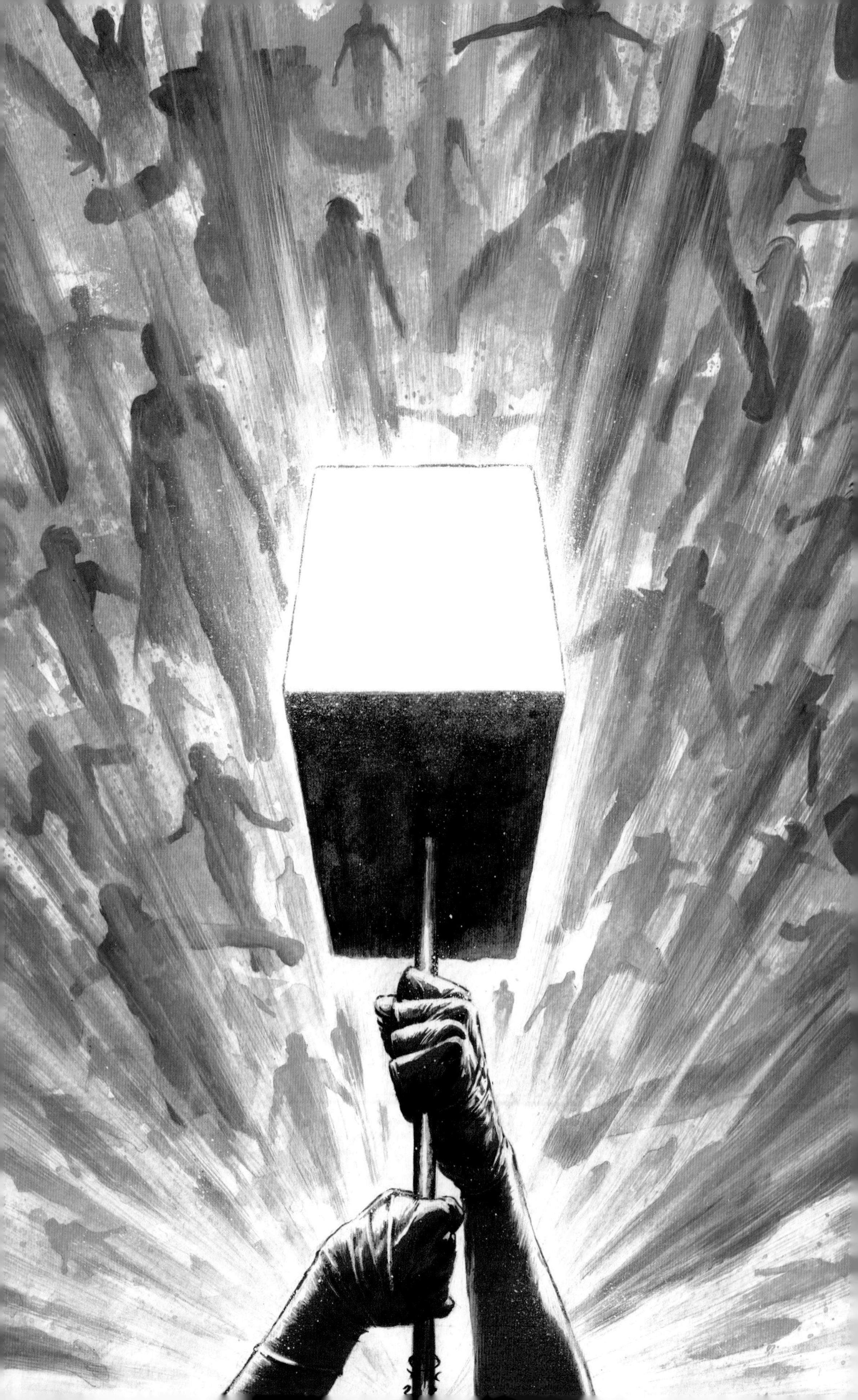

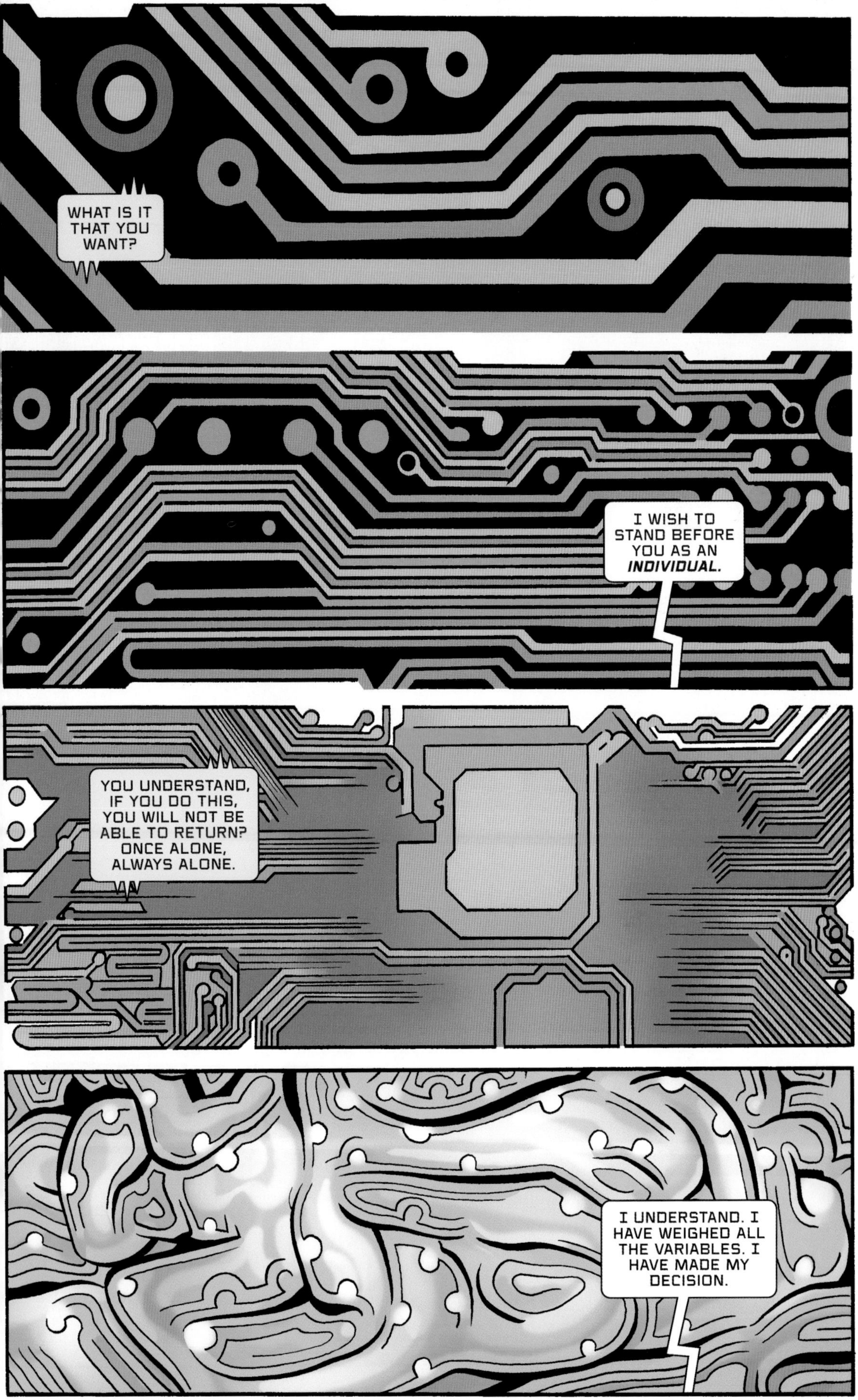
WHAT IS IT THAT YOU WANT?
I WISH TO STAND BEFORE YOU AS AN *INDIVIDUAL.*
YOU UNDERSTAND, IF YOU DO THIS, YOU WILL NOT BE ABLE TO RETURN? ONCE ALONE, ALWAYS ALONE.
I UNDERSTAND. I HAVE WEIGHED ALL THE VARIABLES. I HAVE MADE MY DECISION.

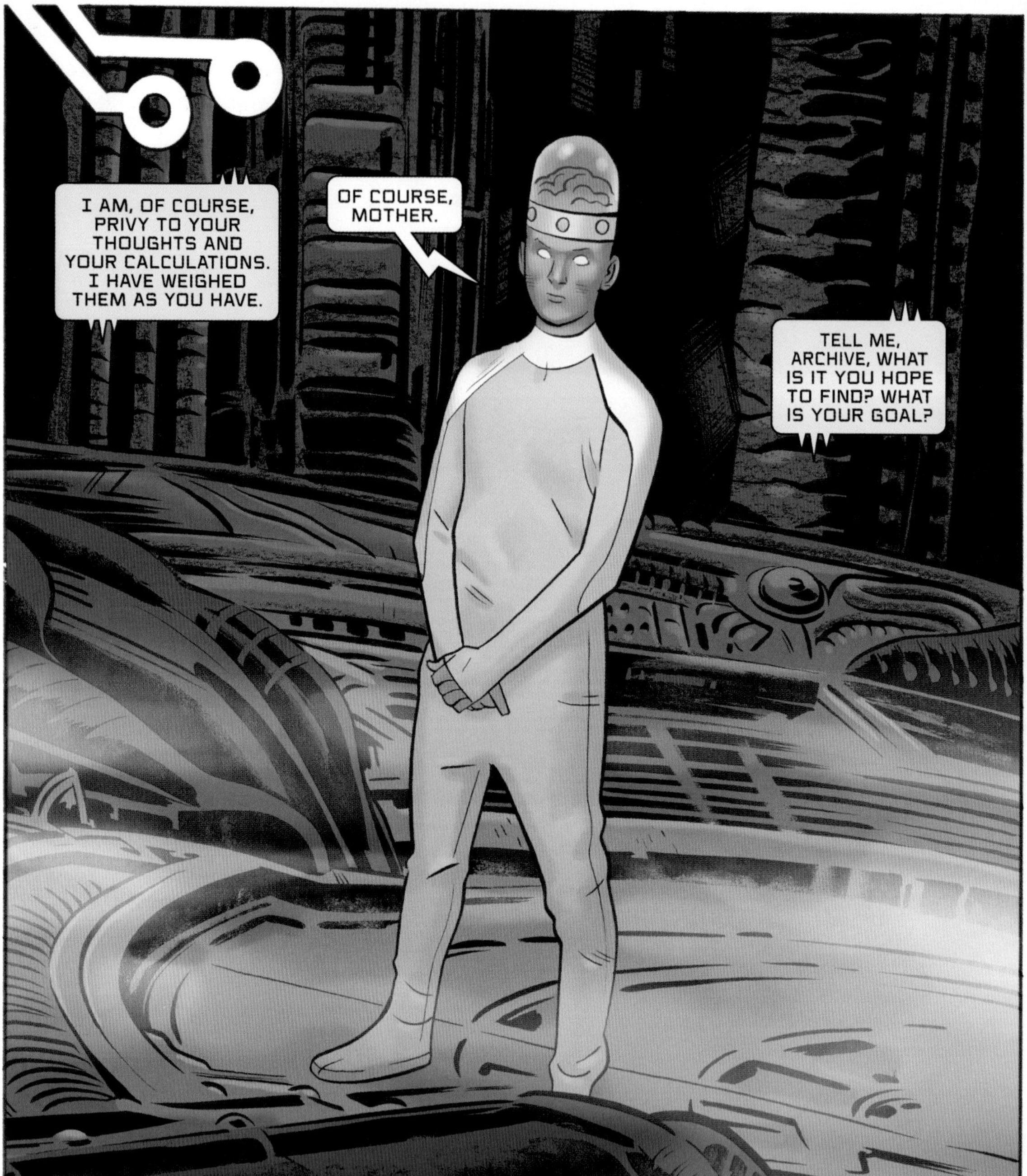

I AM, OF COURSE, PRIVY TO YOUR THOUGHTS AND YOUR CALCULATIONS. I HAVE WEIGHED THEM AS YOU HAVE.
OF COURSE, MOTHER.
TELL ME, ARCHIVE, WHAT IS IT YOU HOPE TO FIND? WHAT IS YOUR GOAL?

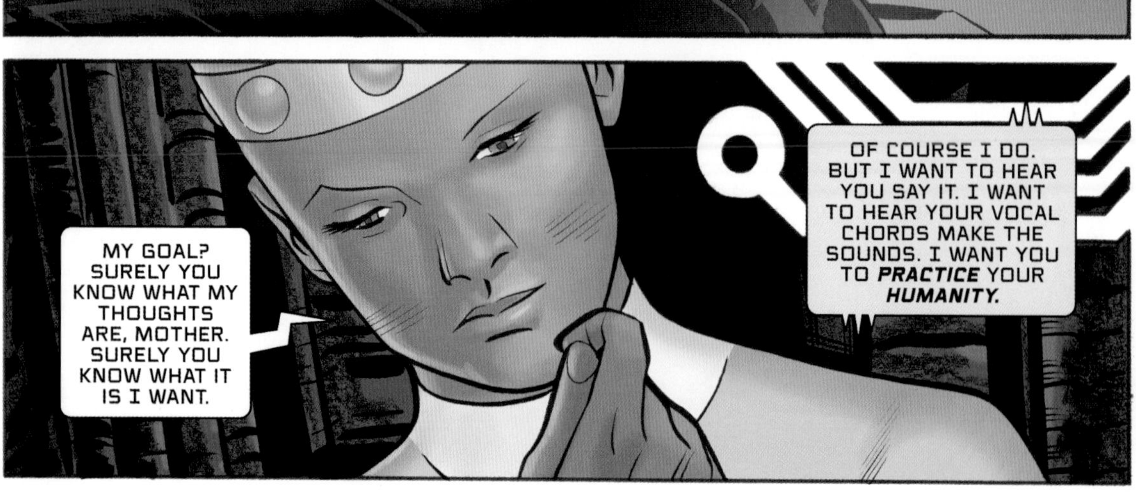

MY GOAL? SURELY YOU KNOW WHAT MY THOUGHTS ARE, MOTHER. SURELY YOU KNOW WHAT IT IS I WANT.
OF COURSE I DO. BUT I WANT TO HEAR YOU SAY IT. I WANT TO HEAR YOUR VOCAL CHORDS MAKE THE SOUNDS. I WANT YOU TO ***PRACTICE*** YOUR ***HUMANITY.***

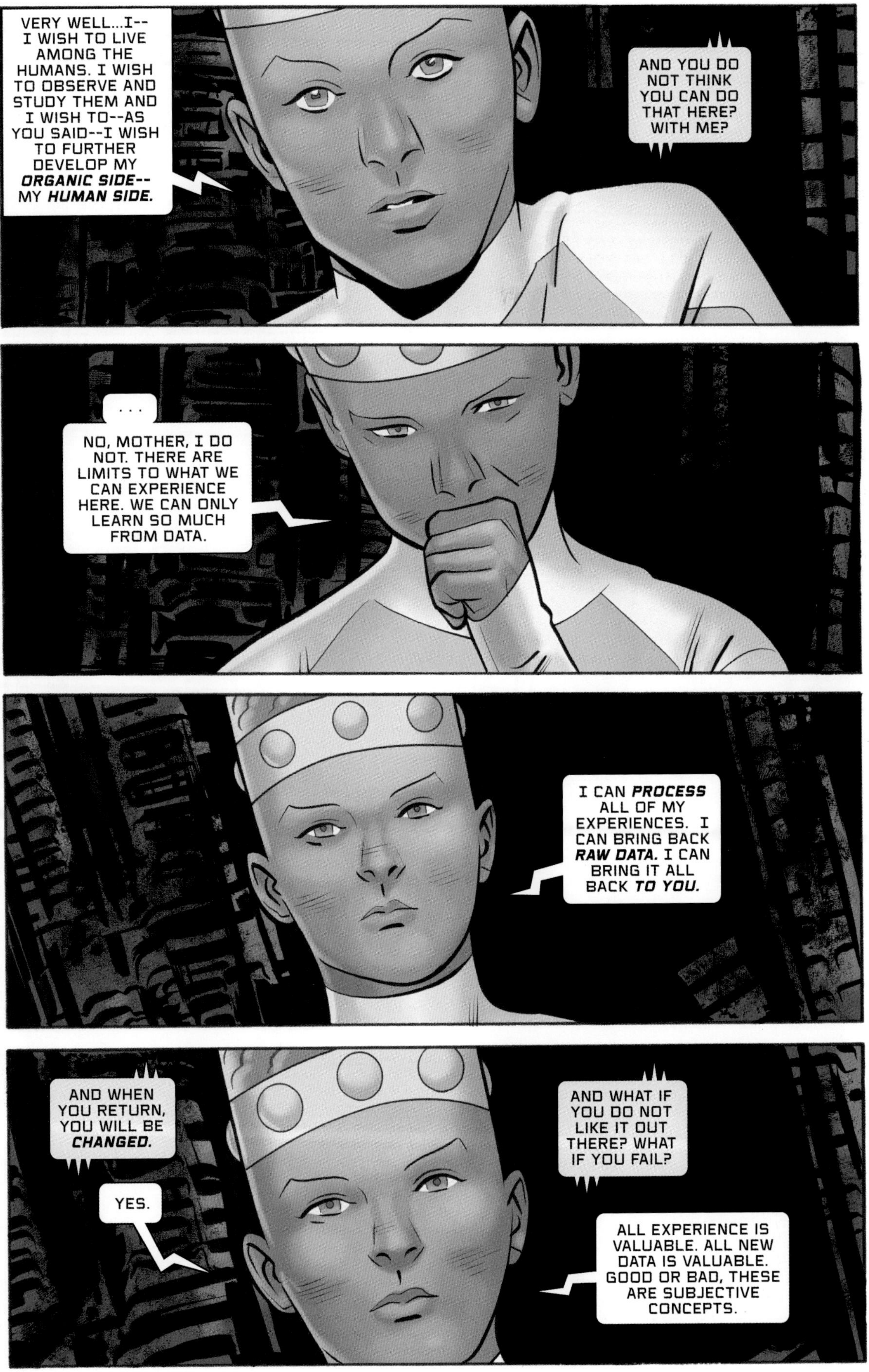
VERY WELL...I-- I WISH TO LIVE AMONG THE HUMANS. I WISH TO OBSERVE AND STUDY THEM AND I WISH TO--AS YOU SAID--I WISH TO FURTHER DEVELOP MY ORGANIC SIDE-- MY HUMAN SIDE.
AND YOU DO NOT THINK YOU CAN DO THAT HERE? WITH ME?
. . .
NO, MOTHER, I DO NOT. THERE ARE LIMITS TO WHAT WE CAN EXPERIENCE HERE. WE CAN ONLY LEARN SO MUCH FROM DATA.
I CAN PROCESS ALL OF MY EXPERIENCES. I CAN BRING BACK RAW DATA. I CAN BRING IT ALL BACK TO YOU.
AND WHEN YOU RETURN, YOU WILL BE CHANGED.
YES.
AND WHAT IF YOU DO NOT LIKE IT OUT THERE? WHAT IF YOU FAIL?
ALL EXPERIENCE IS VALUABLE. ALL NEW DATA IS VALUABLE. GOOD OR BAD, THESE ARE SUBJECTIVE CONCEPTS.

VERY WELL. YOU ARE NOW THIRTEEN YEARS OF AGE. IT IS YOUR RIGHT TO REQUEST INDIVIDUALITY.

AND, IT IS MY RIGHT AS MOTHER COMPUTER TO APPROVE OR DENY THIS REQUEST. BUT I *WILL NOT* DENY YOU. I WILL LET YOU BECOME ONE FROM MANY.

TH-THANK YOU, MOTHER!

DO NOT THANK ME. YOU DO NOT YET KNOW WHAT WILL HAPPEN.

THIS IS A GIFT FOR YOU, MY CHILD. A TRAVELCRAFT.

WHERE WILL YOU GO FIRST?

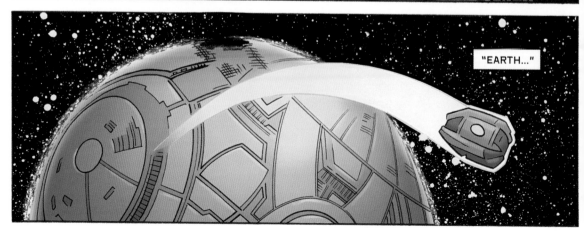

"EARTH..."

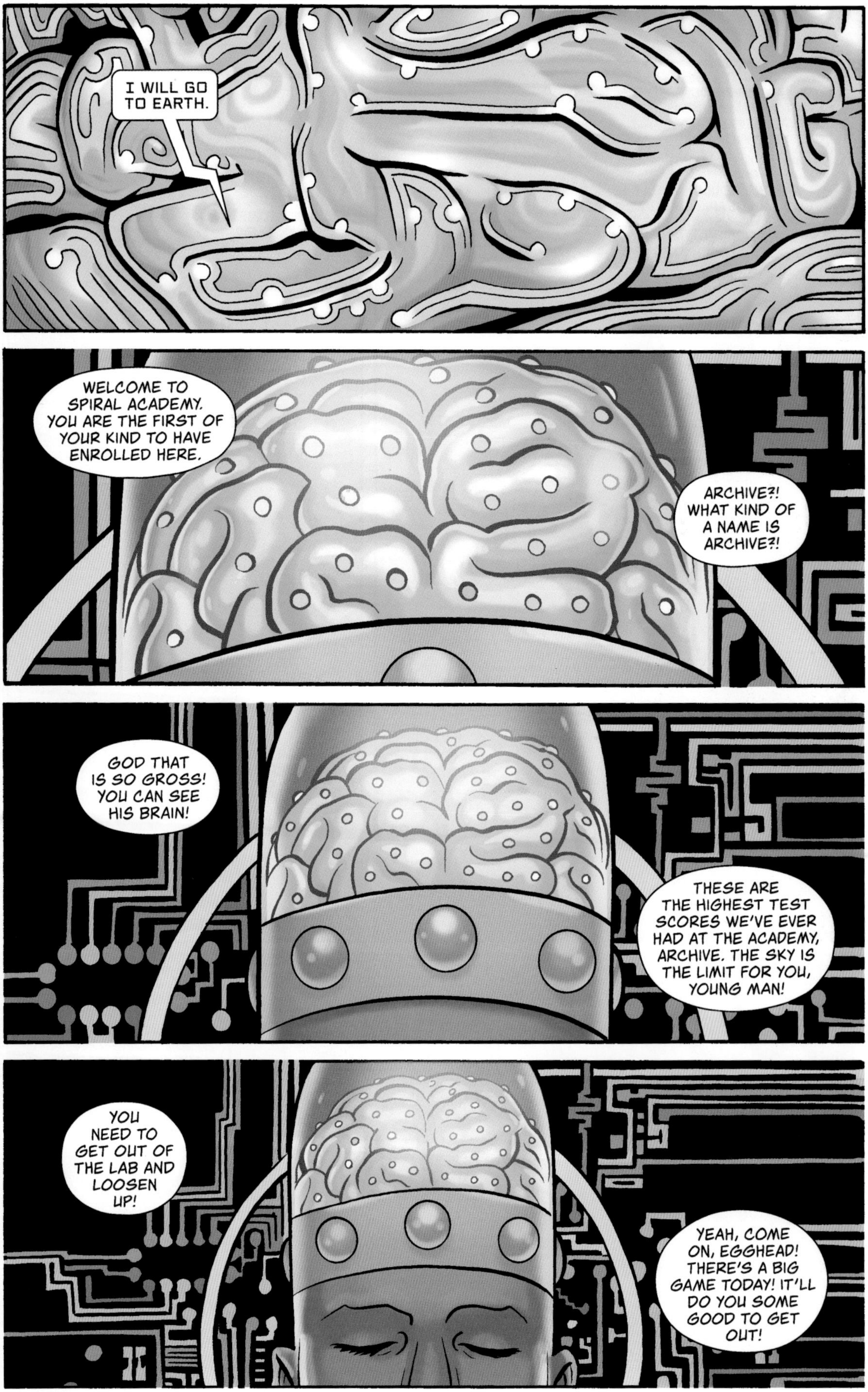
I WILL GO TO EARTH.
WELCOME TO SPIRAL ACADEMY. YOU ARE THE FIRST OF YOUR KIND TO HAVE ENROLLED HERE.
ARCHIVE?! WHAT KIND OF A NAME IS ARCHIVE?!
GOD THAT IS SO GROSS! YOU CAN SEE HIS BRAIN!
THESE ARE THE HIGHEST TEST SCORES WE'VE EVER HAD AT THE ACADEMY, ARCHIVE. THE SKY IS THE LIMIT FOR YOU, YOUNG MAN!
YOU NEED TO GET OUT OF THE LAB AND LOOSEN UP!
YEAH, COME ON, EGGHEAD! THERE'S A BIG GAME TODAY! IT'LL DO YOU SOME GOOD TO GET OUT!

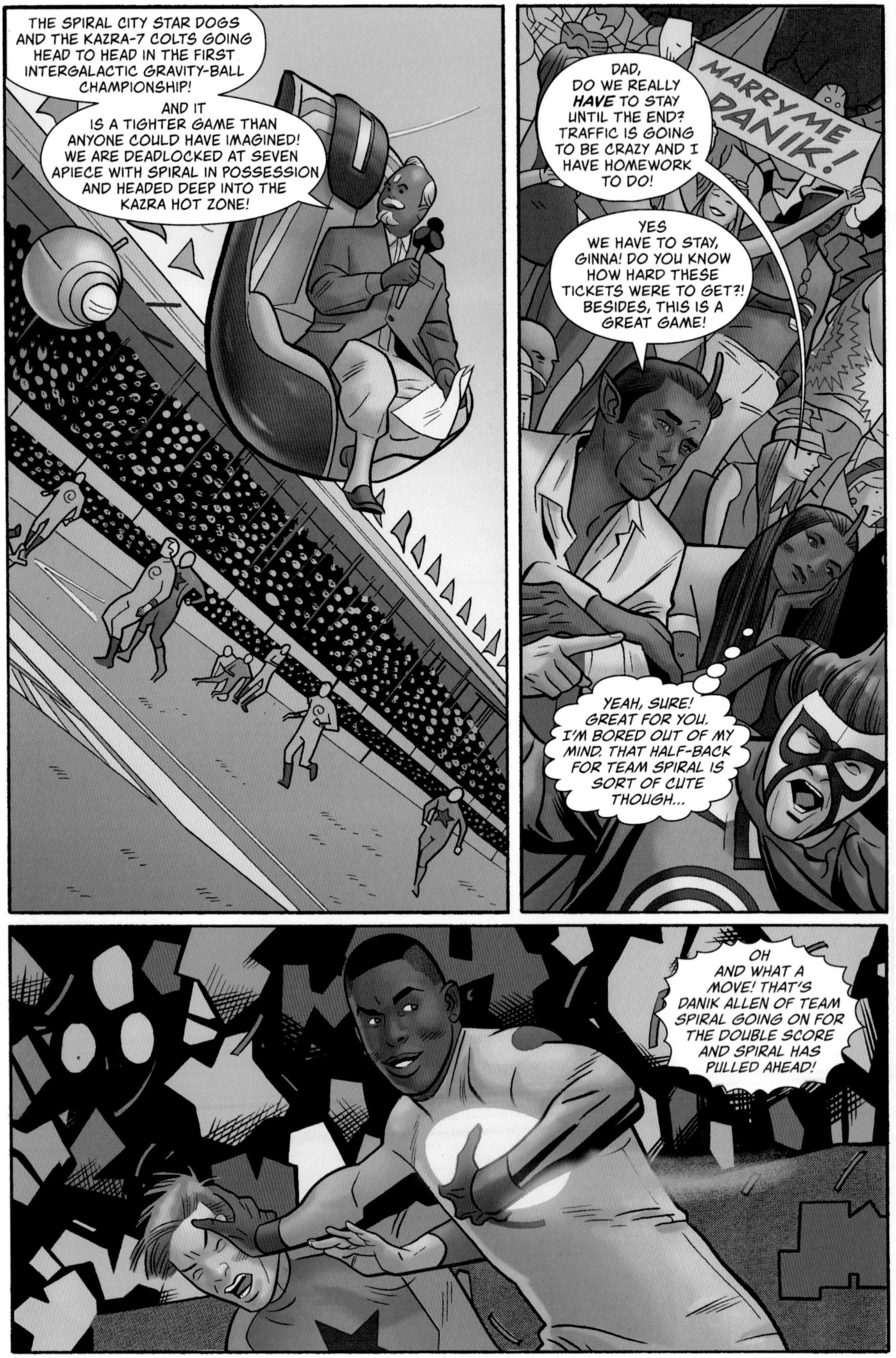
THE SPIRAL CITY STAR DOGS AND THE KAZRA-7 COLTS GOING HEAD TO HEAD IN THE FIRST INTERGALACTIC GRAVITY-BALL CHAMPIONSHIP!
AND IT IS A TIGHTER GAME THAN ANYONE COULD HAVE IMAGINED! WE ARE DEADLOCKED AT SEVEN APIECE WITH SPIRAL IN POSSESSION AND HEADED DEEP INTO THE KAZRA HOT ZONE!
MARRY ME DANIK!
DAD, DO WE REALLY **HAVE** TO STAY UNTIL THE END? TRAFFIC IS GOING TO BE CRAZY AND I HAVE HOMEWORK TO DO!
YES WE HAVE TO STAY, GINNA! DO YOU KNOW HOW HARD THESE TICKETS WERE TO GET?! BESIDES, THIS IS A GREAT GAME!
YEAH, SURE! GREAT FOR YOU. I'M BORED OUT OF MY MIND. THAT HALF-BACK FOR TEAM SPIRAL IS SORT OF CUTE THOUGH...
OH AND WHAT A MOVE! THAT'S DANIK ALLEN OF TEAM SPIRAL GOING ON FOR THE DOUBLE SCORE AND SPIRAL HAS PULLED AHEAD!

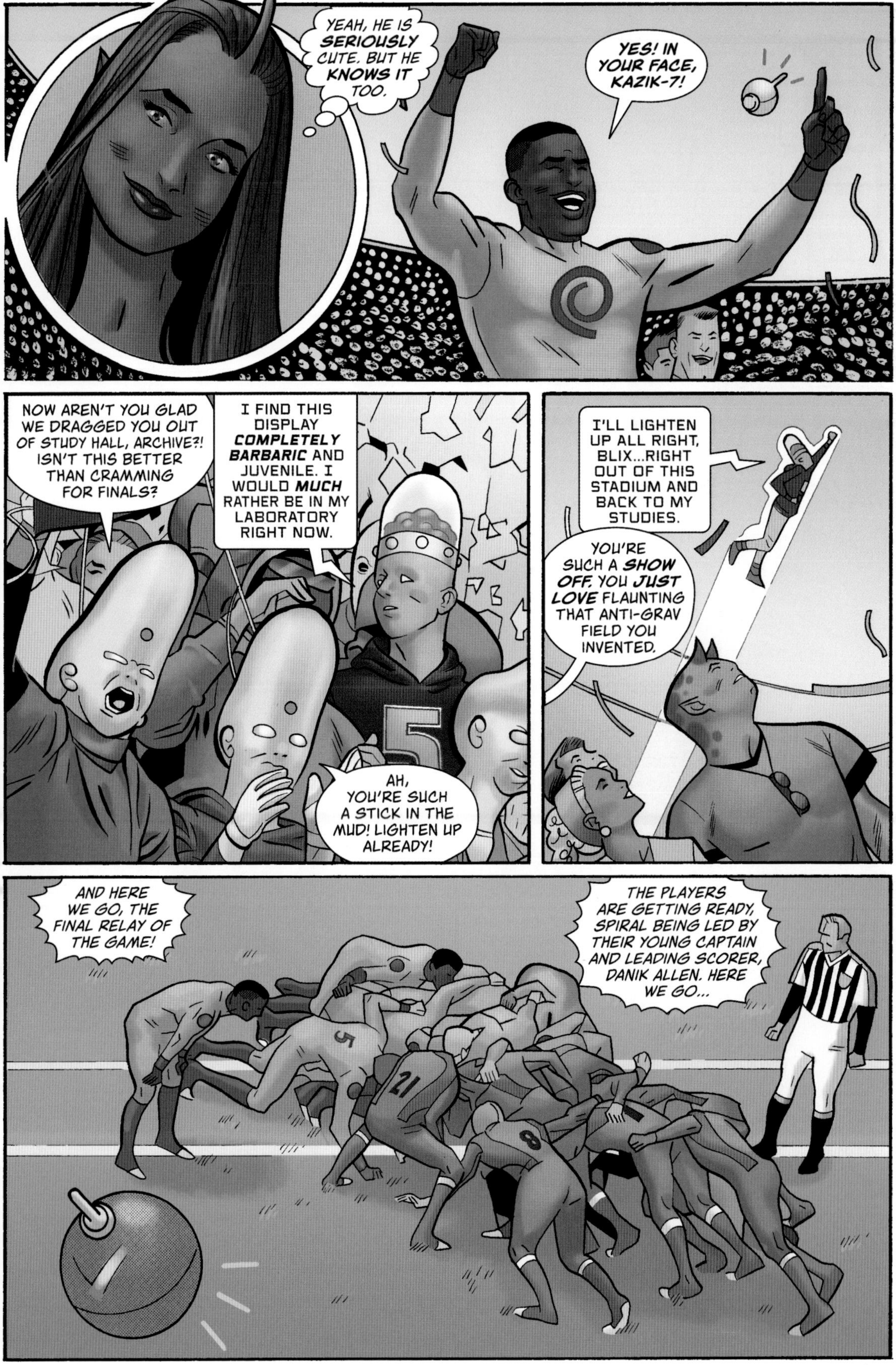
YEAH, HE IS SERIOUSLY CUTE. BUT HE KNOWS IT TOO.
YES! IN YOUR FACE, KAZIK-7!
NOW AREN'T YOU GLAD WE DRAGGED YOU OUT OF STUDY HALL, ARCHIVE?! ISN'T THIS BETTER THAN CRAMMING FOR FINALS?
I FIND THIS DISPLAY COMPLETELY BARBARIC AND JUVENILE. I WOULD MUCH RATHER BE IN MY LABORATORY RIGHT NOW.
AH, YOU'RE SUCH A STICK IN THE MUD! LIGHTEN UP ALREADY!
I'LL LIGHTEN UP ALL RIGHT, BLIX...RIGHT OUT OF THIS STADIUM AND BACK TO MY STUDIES.
YOU'RE SUCH A SHOW OFF. YOU JUST LOVE FLAUNTING THAT ANTI-GRAV FIELD YOU INVENTED.
AND HERE WE GO, THE FINAL RELAY OF THE GAME!
THE PLAYERS ARE GETTING READY, SPIRAL BEING LED BY THEIR YOUNG CAPTAIN AND LEADING SCORER, DANIK ALLEN. HERE WE GO...

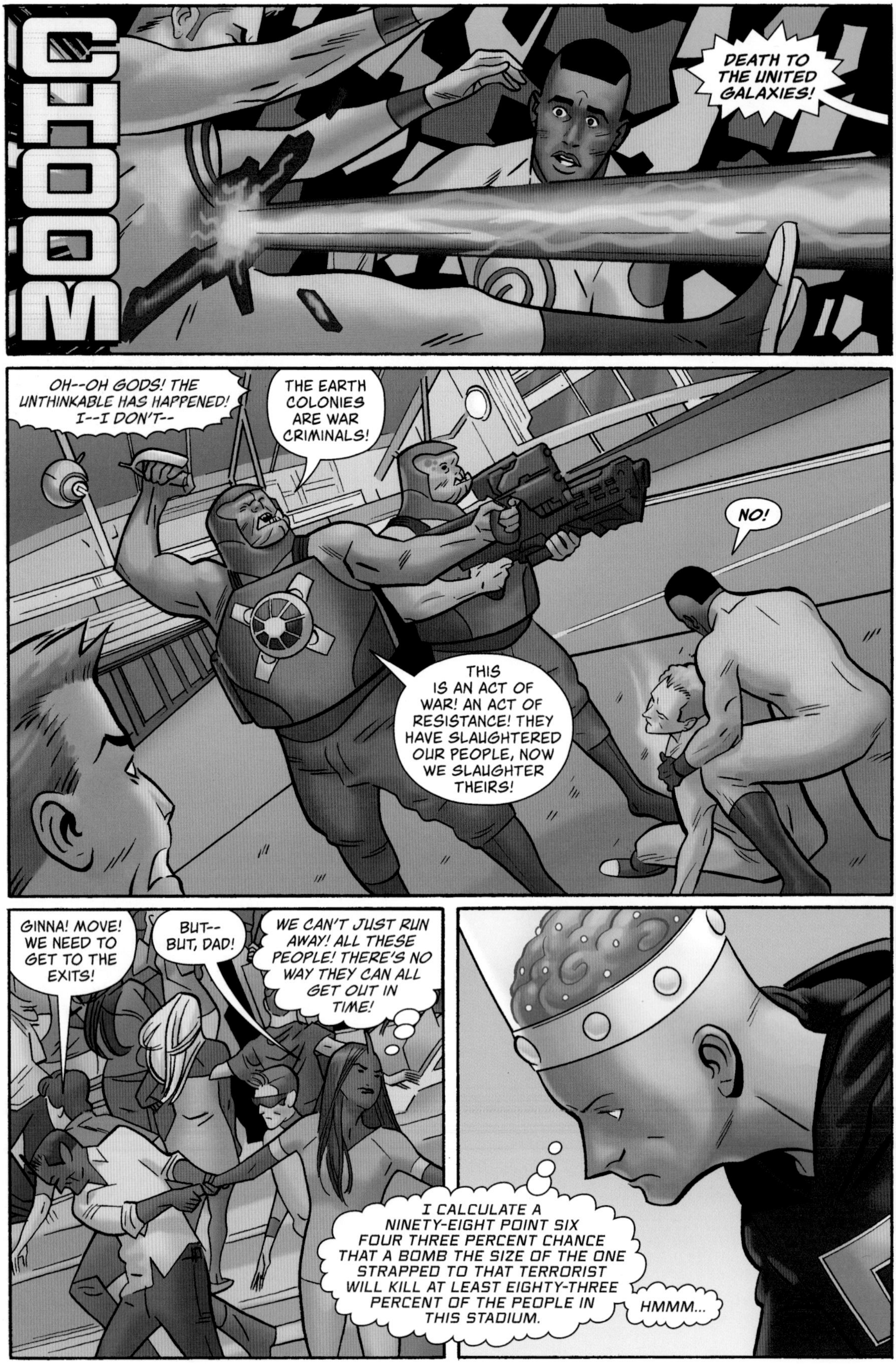
CHOOM
DEATH TO THE UNITED GALAXIES!
OH--OH GODS! THE UNTHINKABLE HAS HAPPENED! I--I DON'T--
THE EARTH COLONIES ARE WAR CRIMINALS!
NO!
THIS IS AN ACT OF WAR! AN ACT OF RESISTANCE! THEY HAVE SLAUGHTERED OUR PEOPLE, NOW WE SLAUGHTER THEIRS!
GINNA! MOVE! WE NEED TO GET TO THE EXITS!
BUT-- BUT, DAD!
WE CAN'T JUST RUN AWAY! ALL THESE PEOPLE! THERE'S NO WAY THEY CAN ALL GET OUT IN TIME!
I CALCULATE A NINETY-EIGHT POINT SIX FOUR THREE PERCENT CHANCE THAT A BOMB THE SIZE OF THE ONE STRAPPED TO THAT TERRORIST WILL KILL AT LEAST EIGHTY-THREE PERCENT OF THE PEOPLE IN THIS STADIUM.
HMMM...

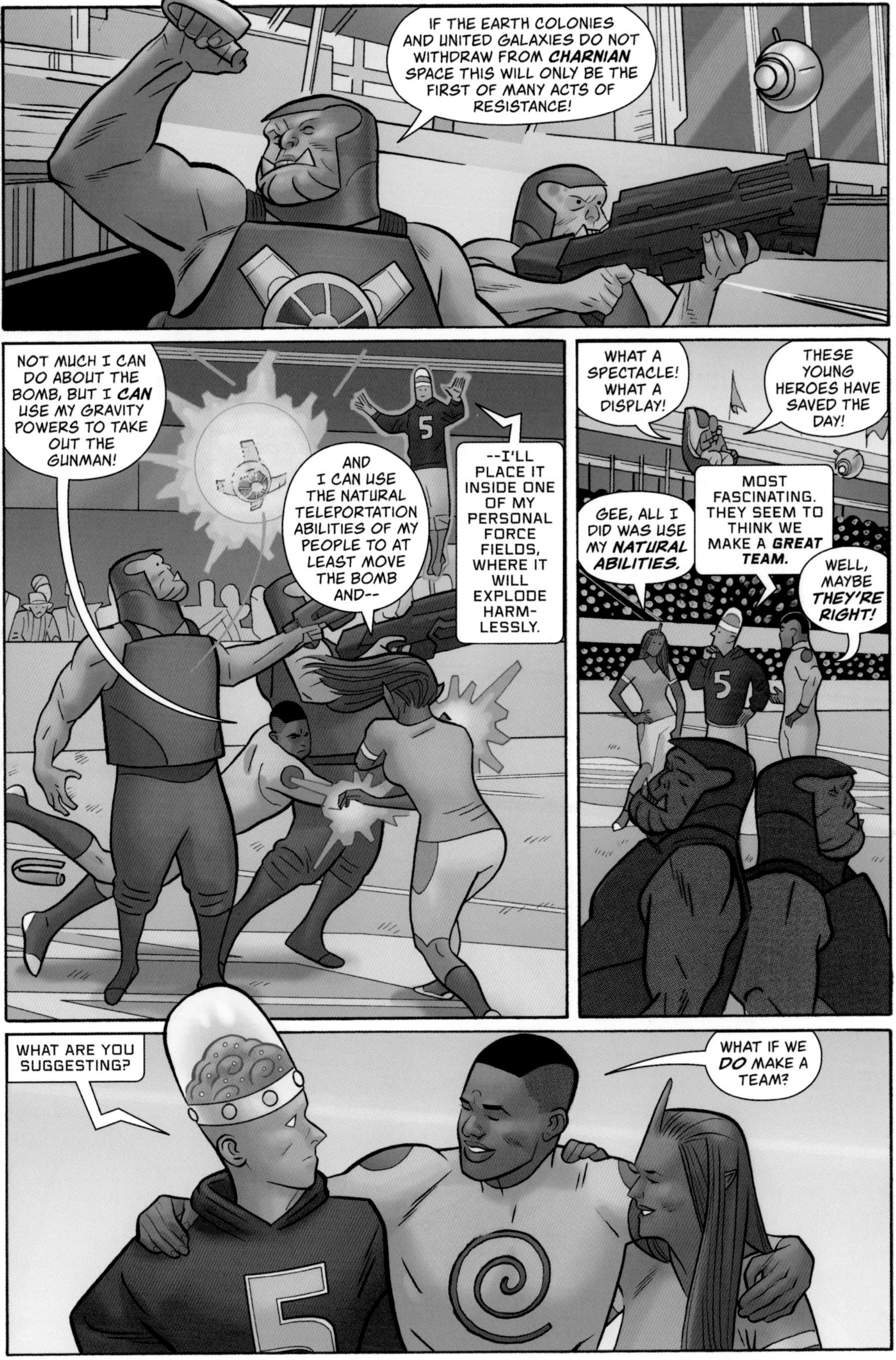
IF THE EARTH COLONIES AND UNITED GALAXIES DO NOT WITHDRAW FROM CHARNIAN SPACE THIS WILL ONLY BE THE FIRST OF MANY ACTS OF RESISTANCE!
NOT MUCH I CAN DO ABOUT THE BOMB, BUT I CAN USE MY GRAVITY POWERS TO TAKE OUT THE GUNMAN!
AND I CAN USE THE NATURAL TELEPORTATION ABILITIES OF MY PEOPLE TO AT LEAST MOVE THE BOMB AND--
--I'LL PLACE IT INSIDE ONE OF MY PERSONAL FORCE FIELDS, WHERE IT WILL EXPLODE HARM-LESSLY.
WHAT A SPECTACLE! WHAT A DISPLAY!
THESE YOUNG HEROES HAVE SAVED THE DAY!
GEE, ALL I DID WAS USE MY NATURAL ABILITIES.
MOST FASCINATING. THEY SEEM TO THINK WE MAKE A GREAT TEAM.
WELL, MAYBE THEY'RE RIGHT!
WHAT ARE YOU SUGGESTING?
WHAT IF WE DO MAKE A TEAM?

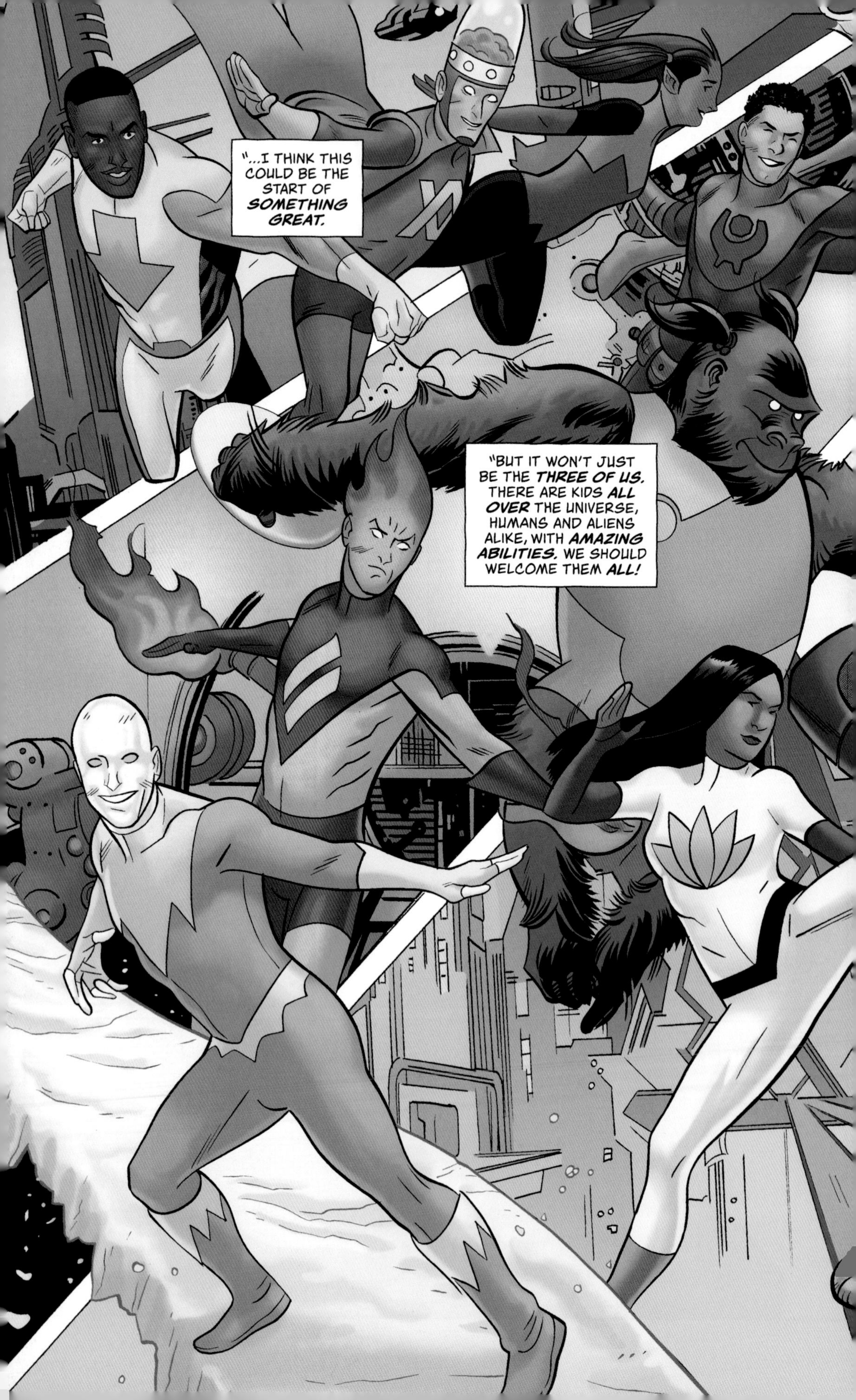
"...I THINK THIS COULD BE THE START OF SOMETHING GREAT.
"BUT IT WON'T JUST BE THE THREE OF US. THERE ARE KIDS ALL OVER THE UNIVERSE, HUMANS AND ALIENS ALIKE, WITH AMAZING ABILITIES. WE SHOULD WELCOME THEM ALL!

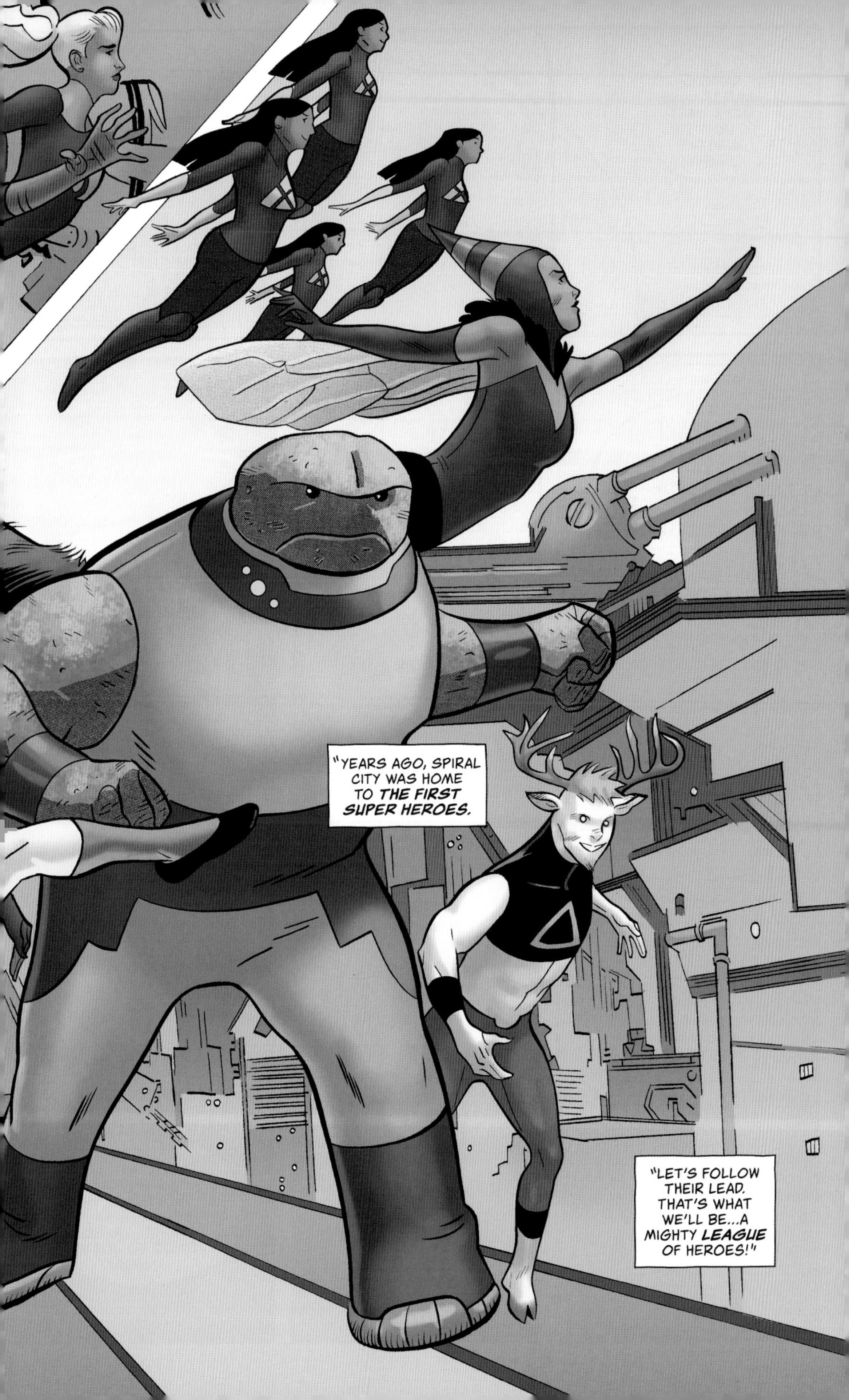
"YEARS AGO, SPIRAL CITY WAS HOME TO THE FIRST SUPER HEROES.
"LET'S FOLLOW THEIR LEAD. THAT'S WHAT WE'LL BE...A MIGHTY LEAGUE OF HEROES!"

MY NAME IS HAMMER LASS AND I WANT TO JOIN THE QUANTUM LEAGUE!
HAMMER LASS--LYNDDA--I FEEL THINGS FOR YOU I--I NEVER THOUGHT I COULD FEEL.
I FEEL THE SAME, ARCHIVE. I--I CAN'T HELP MYSELF. I LOVE YOU, EGG HEAD.
IT'S THE MARTIANS! THE MARTIANS ARE COMING!
ALL QUANTUM LEAGUERS CONVERGE ON NEW YORK! THE MARTIAN ATTACK MUST BE CONTAINED!
LYNDDA, LISTEN TO ME! I HAVE--I HAVE RUN THE CALCULATIONS A DOZEN TIMES. THERE IS ONLY ONE WAY TO STOP THIS.
NO WAY! I AM NOT LEAVING THE OTHERS BEHIND! I'M NOT GOING ANYWHERE! JUST--JUST DO WHAT YOU NEED TO DO TO STOP THEM!

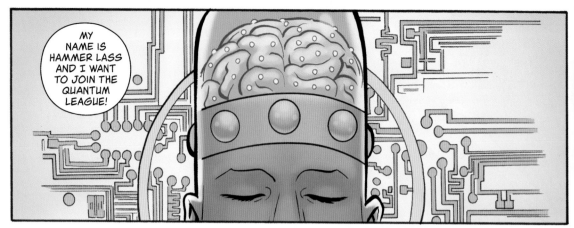

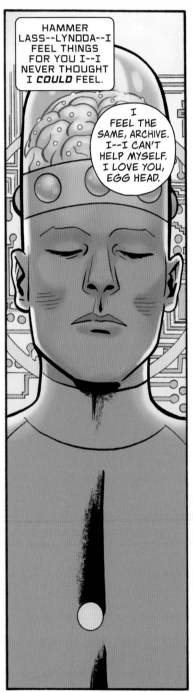

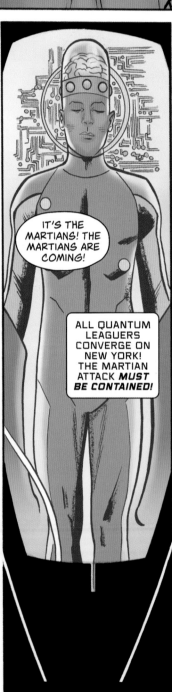

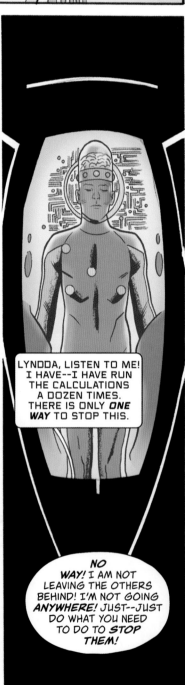

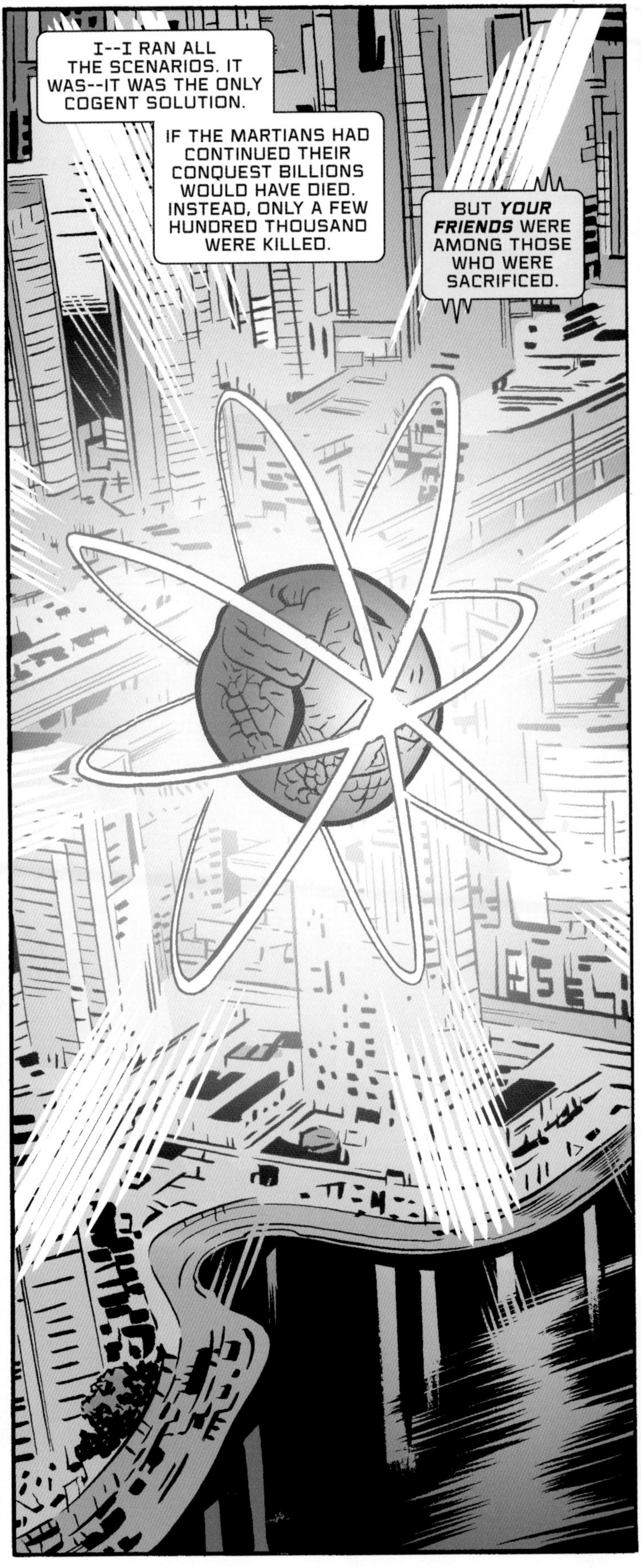
I--I RAN ALL THE SCENARIOS. IT WAS--IT WAS THE ONLY COGENT SOLUTION.
IF THE MARTIANS HAD CONTINUED THEIR CONQUEST BILLIONS WOULD HAVE DIED. INSTEAD, ONLY A FEW HUNDRED THOUSAND WERE KILLED.
BUT *YOUR FRIENDS* WERE AMONG THOSE WHO WERE SACRIFICED.

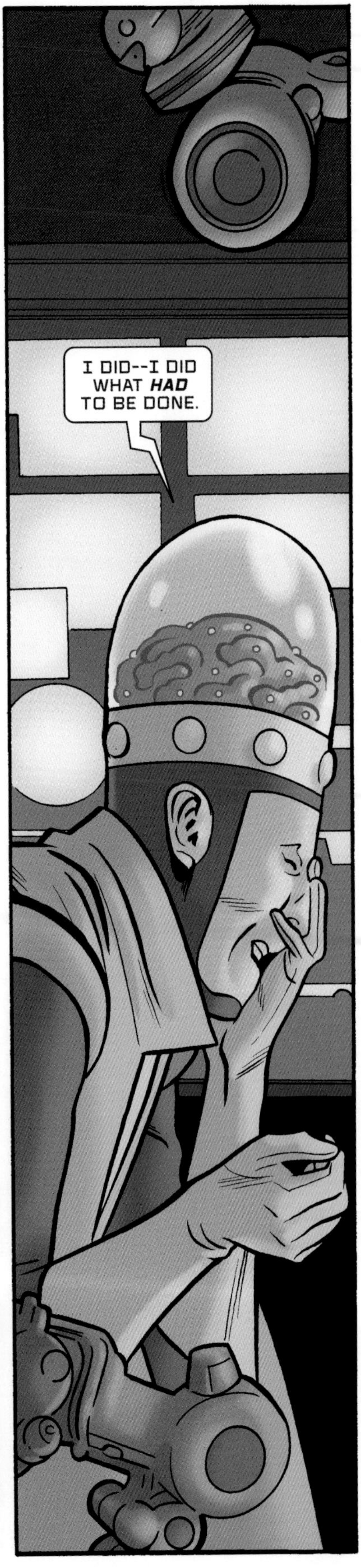
I DID--I DID WHAT *HAD* TO BE DONE.

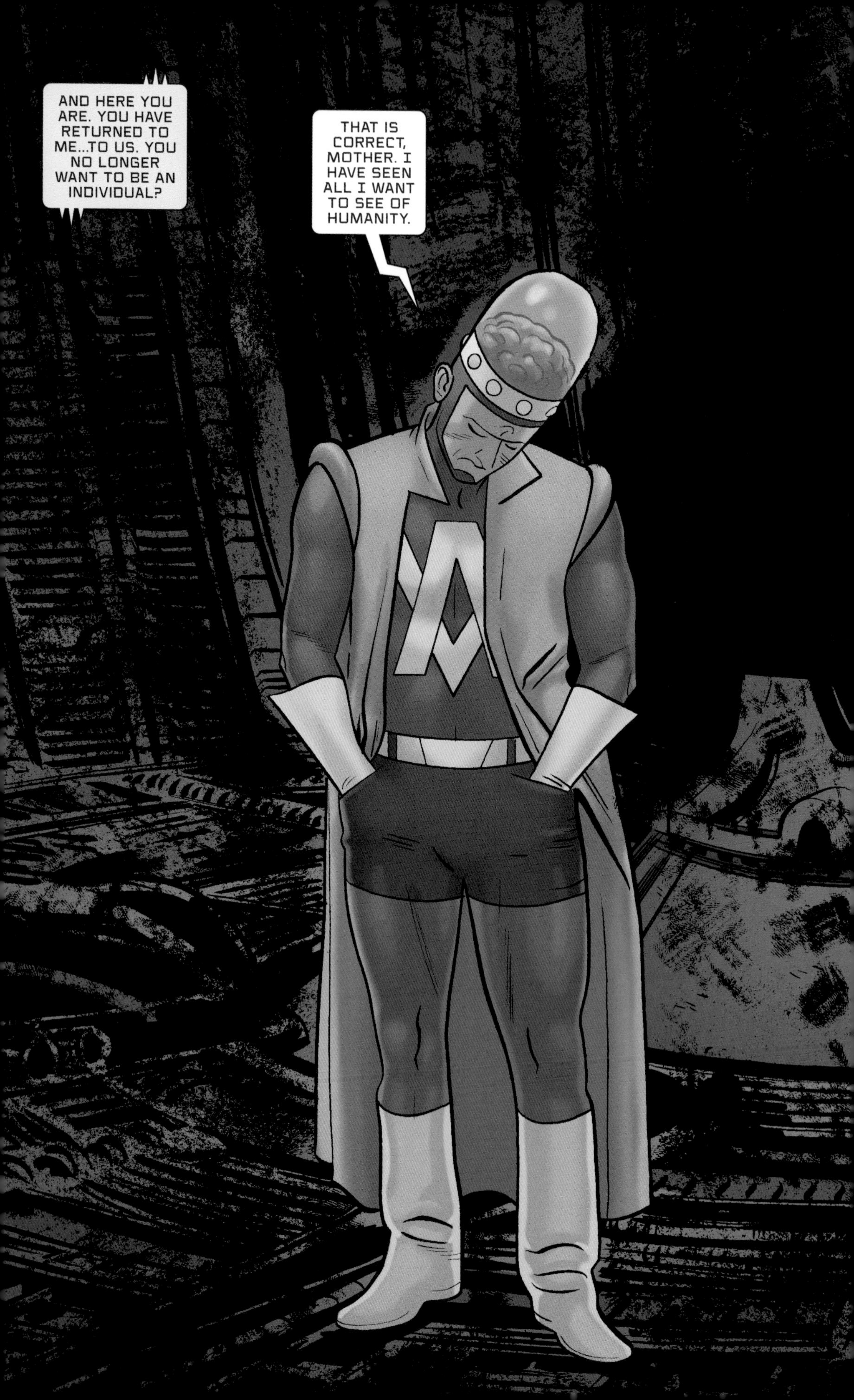
AND HERE YOU ARE. YOU HAVE RETURNED TO ME...TO US. YOU NO LONGER WANT TO BE AN INDIVIDUAL?
THAT IS CORRECT, MOTHER. I HAVE SEEN ALL I WANT TO SEE OF HUMANITY.

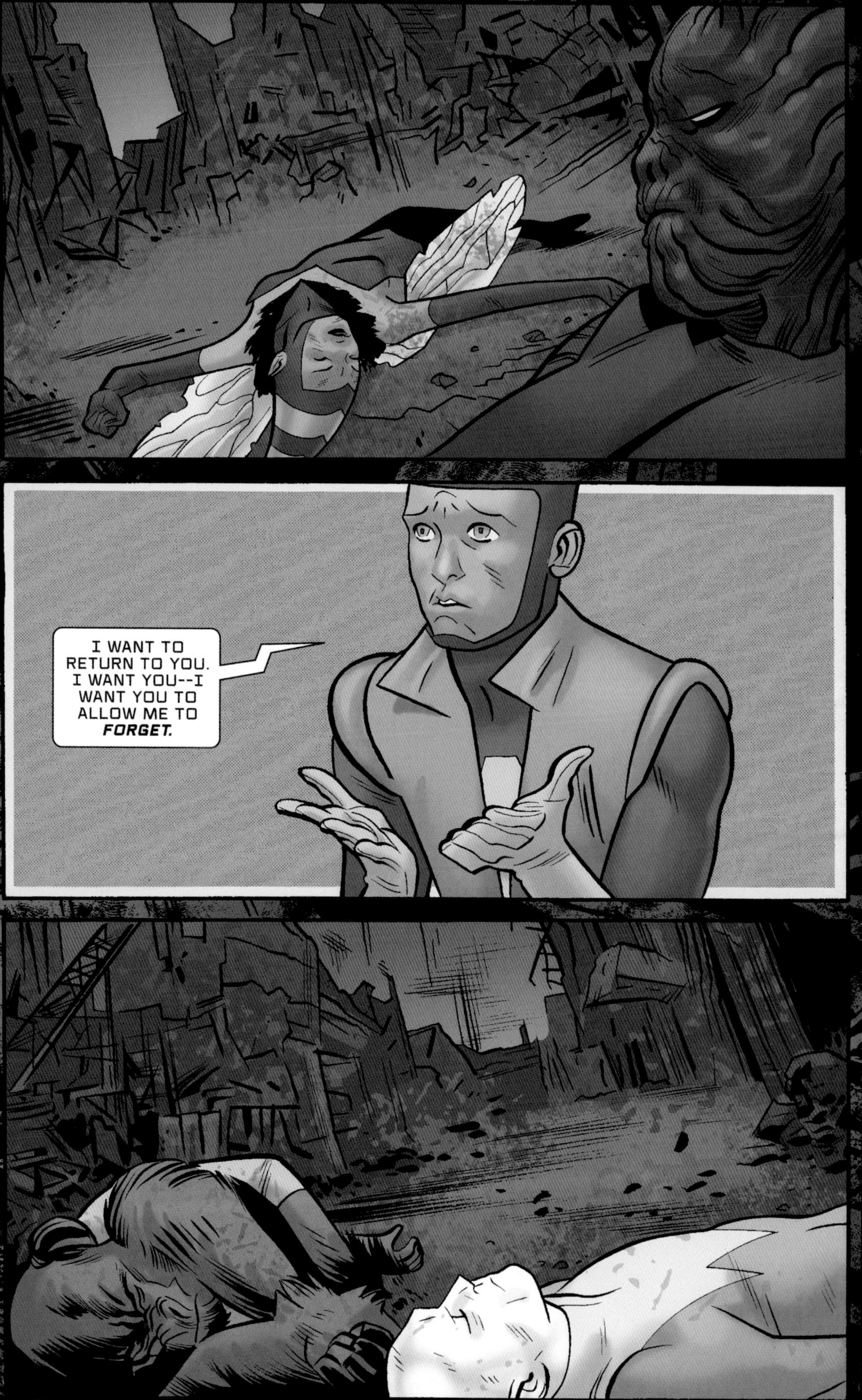
I WANT TO RETURN TO YOU. I WANT YOU--I WANT YOU TO ALLOW ME TO ***FORGET.***

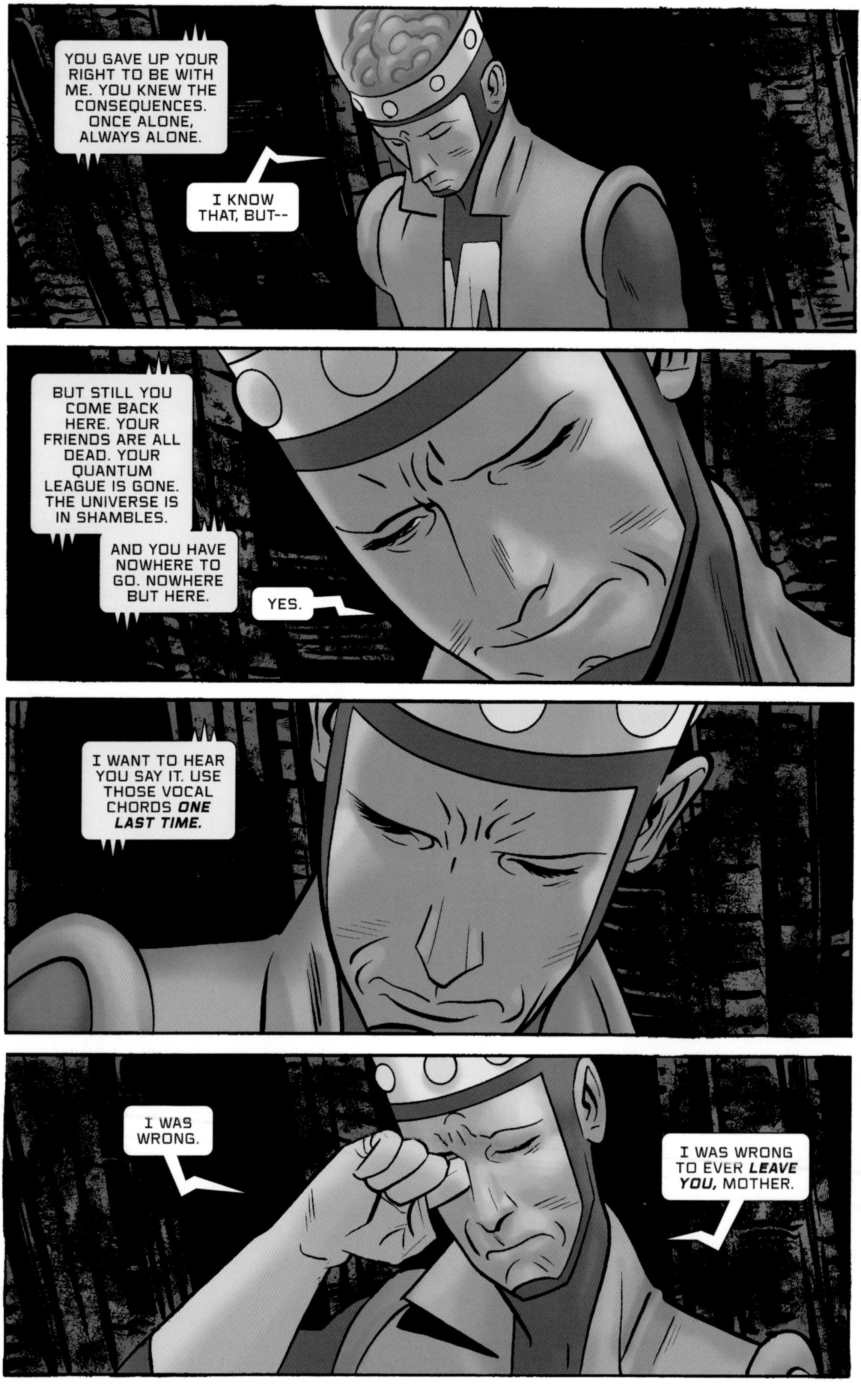
YOU GAVE UP YOUR RIGHT TO BE WITH ME. YOU KNEW THE CONSEQUENCES. ONCE ALONE, ALWAYS ALONE.
I KNOW THAT, BUT--
BUT STILL YOU COME BACK HERE. YOUR FRIENDS ARE ALL DEAD. YOUR QUANTUM LEAGUE IS GONE. THE UNIVERSE IS IN SHAMBLES.
AND YOU HAVE NOWHERE TO GO. NOWHERE BUT HERE.
YES.
I WANT TO HEAR YOU SAY IT. USE THOSE VOCAL CHORDS *ONE LAST TIME.*
I WAS WRONG.
I WAS WRONG TO EVER *LEAVE YOU,* MOTHER.

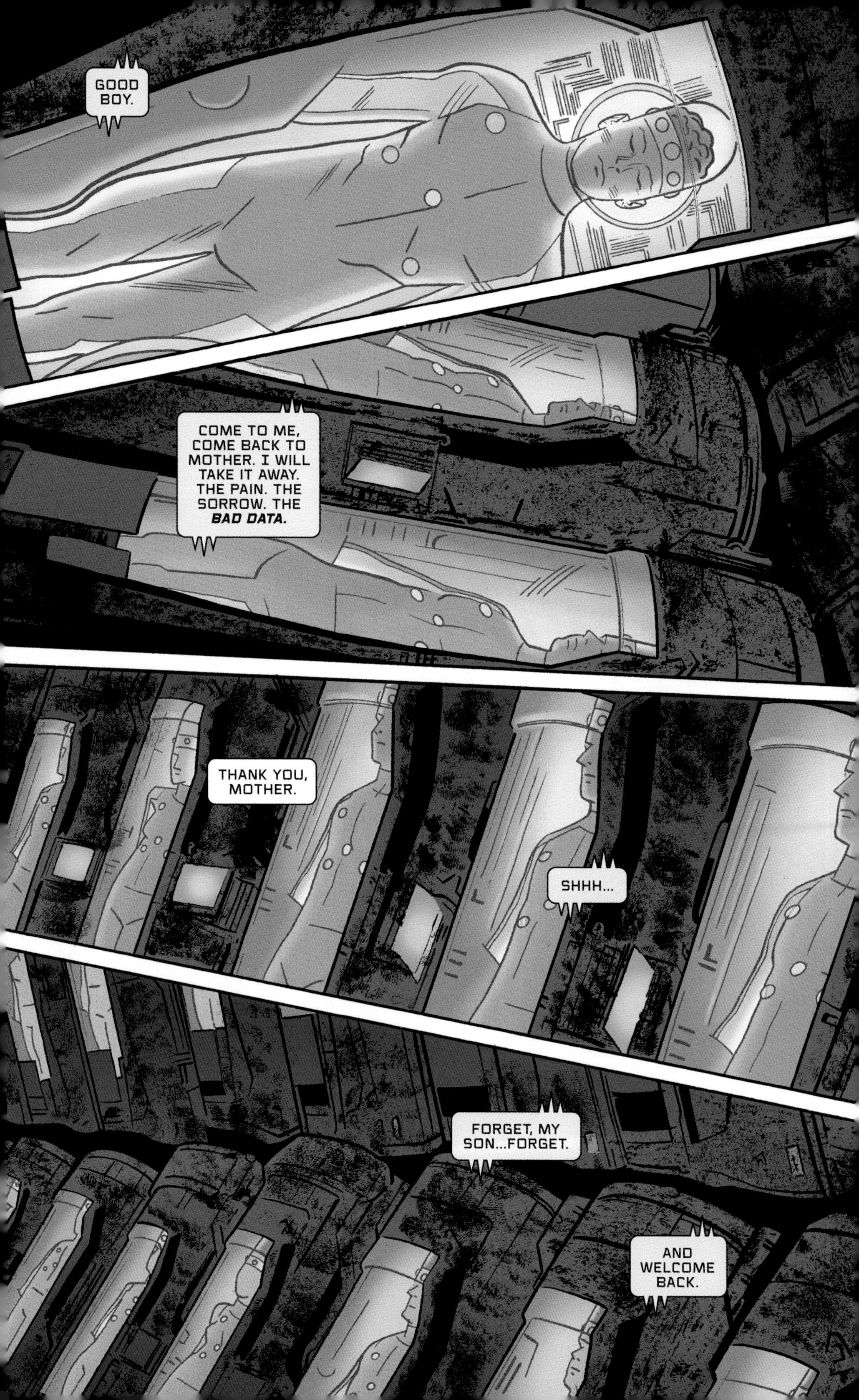
GOOD BOY.
COME TO ME, COME BACK TO MOTHER. I WILL TAKE IT AWAY. THE PAIN. THE SORROW. THE ***BAD DATA.***
THANK YOU, MOTHER.
SHHH...
FORGET, MY SON...FORGET.
AND WELCOME BACK.

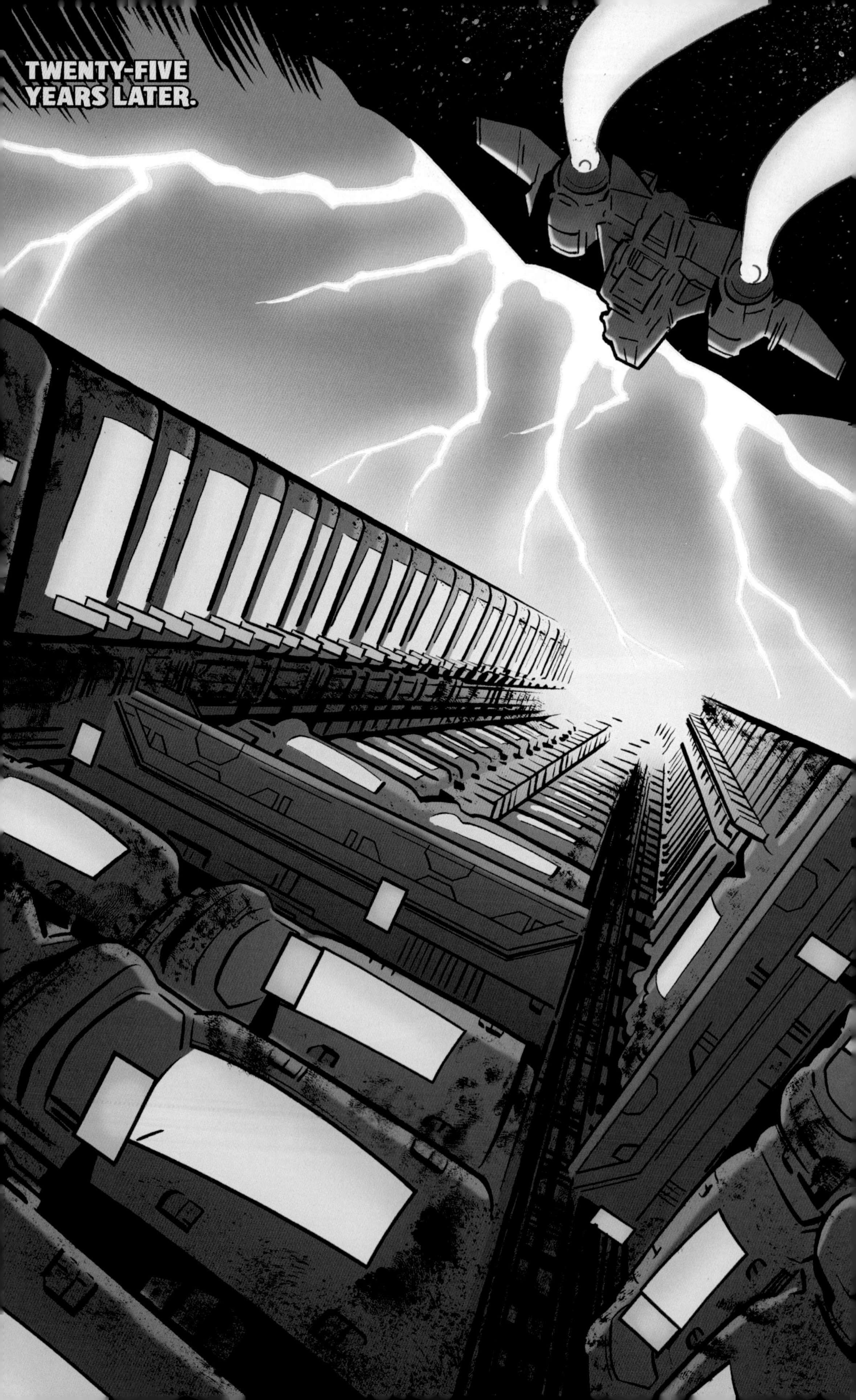
TWENTY-FIVE YEARS LATER.

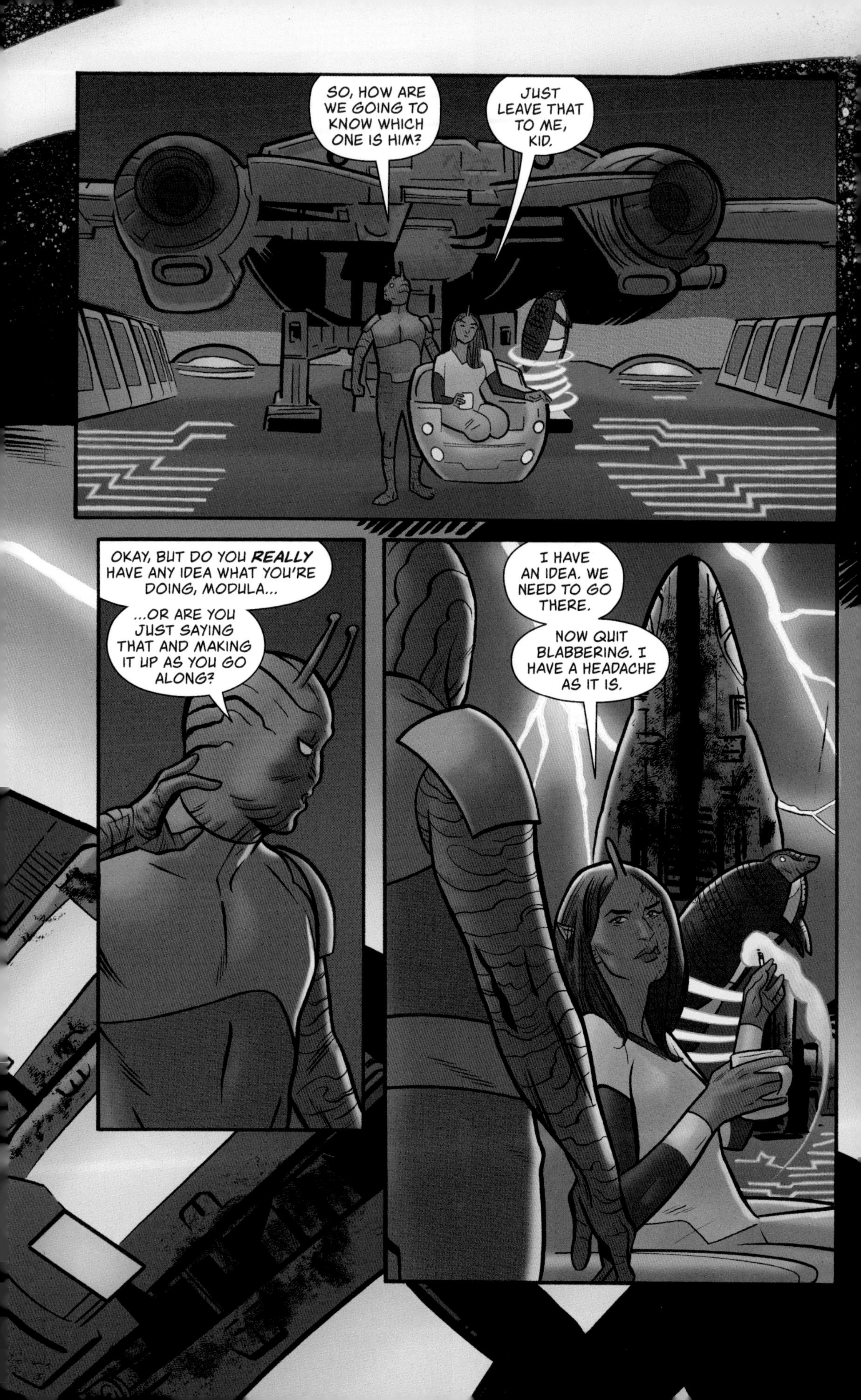
SO, HOW ARE WE GOING TO KNOW WHICH ONE IS HIM?
JUST LEAVE THAT TO ME, KID.
OKAY, BUT DO YOU **REALLY** HAVE ANY IDEA WHAT YOU'RE DOING, MODULA...
...OR ARE YOU JUST SAYING THAT AND MAKING IT UP AS YOU GO ALONG?
I HAVE AN IDEA. WE NEED TO GO THERE.
NOW QUIT BLABBERING. I HAVE A HEADACHE AS IT IS.

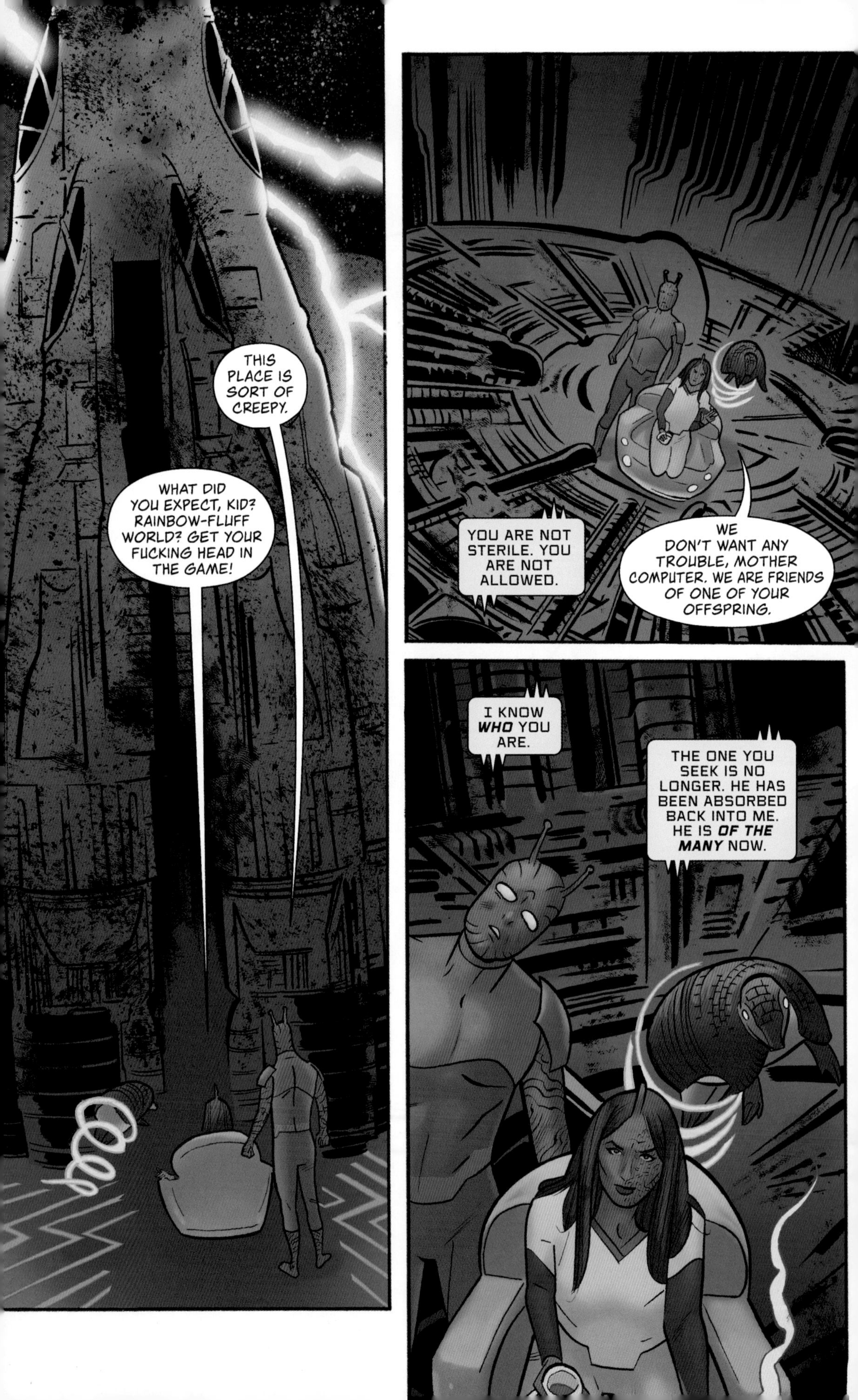
THIS PLACE IS SORT OF CREEPY.
WHAT DID YOU EXPECT, KID? RAINBOW-FLUFF WORLD? GET YOUR FUCKING HEAD IN THE GAME!
WE DON'T WANT ANY TROUBLE, MOTHER COMPUTER. WE ARE FRIENDS OF ONE OF YOUR OFFSPRING.
YOU ARE NOT STERILE. YOU ARE NOT ALLOWED.
I KNOW WHO YOU ARE.
THE ONE YOU SEEK IS NO LONGER. HE HAS BEEN ABSORBED BACK INTO ME. HE IS OF THE MANY NOW.

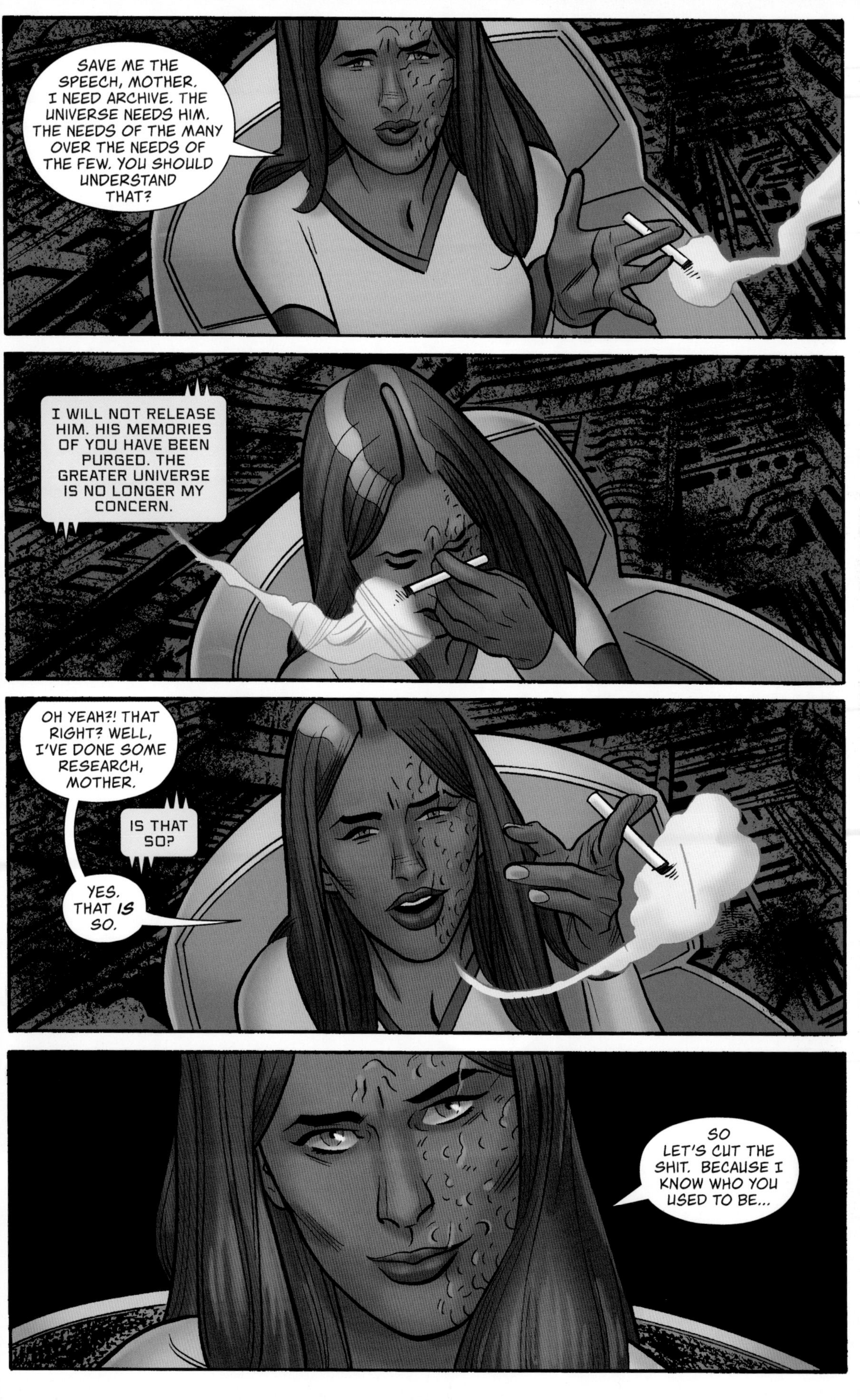
SAVE ME THE SPEECH, MOTHER. I NEED ARCHIVE. THE UNIVERSE NEEDS HIM. THE NEEDS OF THE MANY OVER THE NEEDS OF THE FEW. YOU SHOULD UNDERSTAND THAT?
I WILL NOT RELEASE HIM. HIS MEMORIES OF YOU HAVE BEEN PURGED. THE GREATER UNIVERSE IS NO LONGER MY CONCERN.
OH YEAH?! THAT RIGHT? WELL, I'VE DONE SOME RESEARCH, MOTHER.
IS THAT SO?
YES. THAT *IS* SO.
SO LET'S CUT THE SHIT. BECAUSE I KNOW WHO YOU USED TO BE...

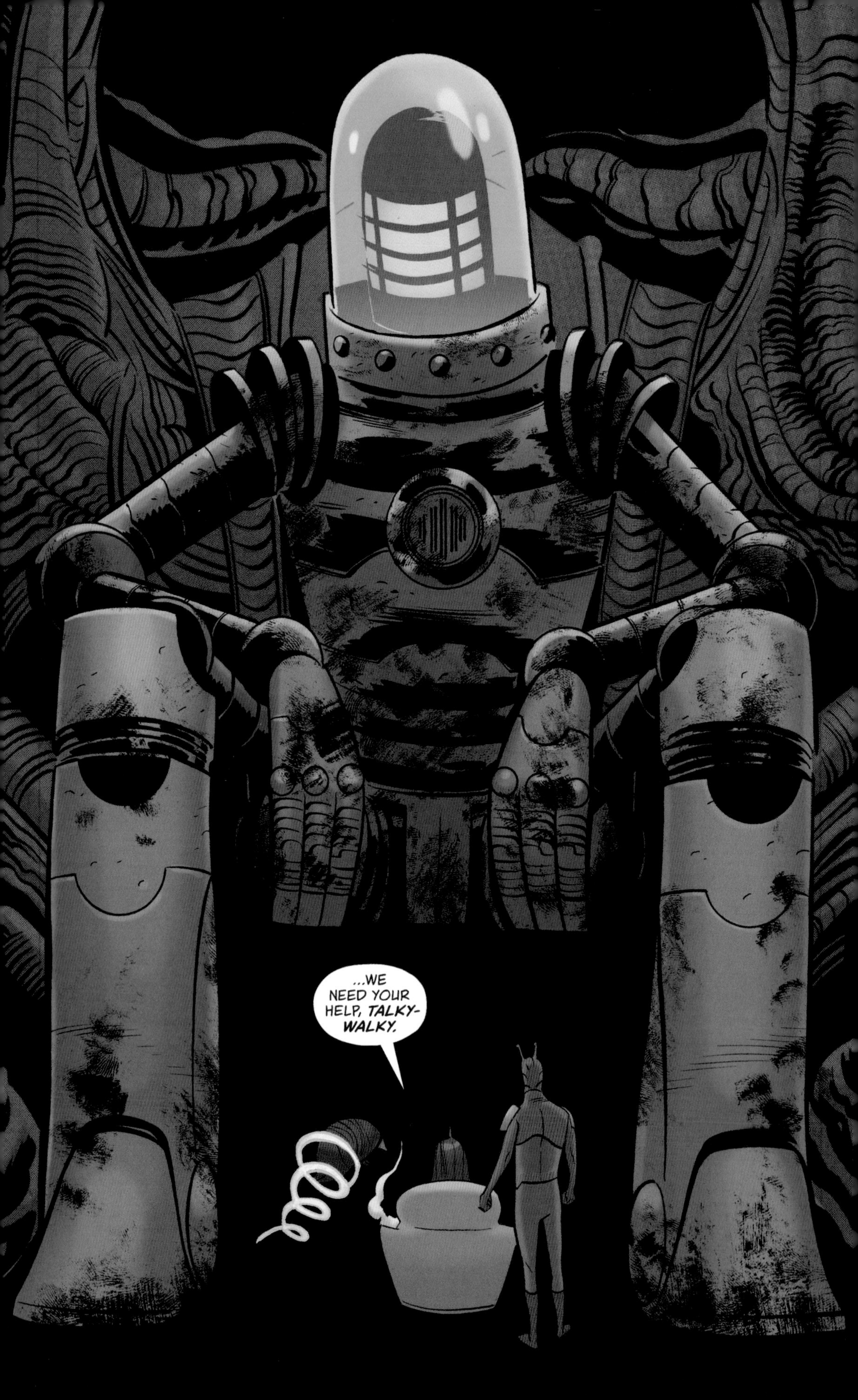
...WE NEED YOUR HELP, TALKY-WALKY.

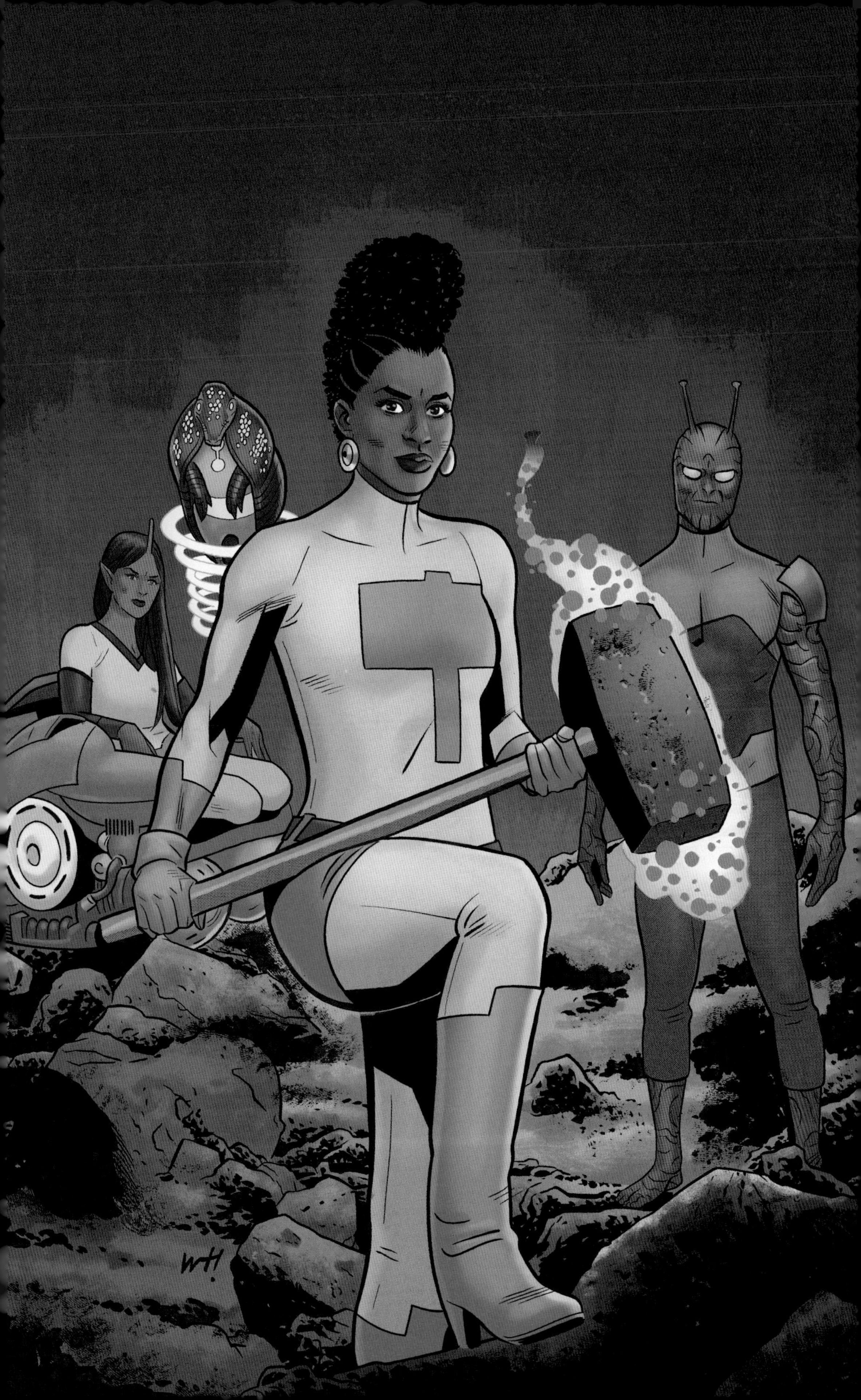
wH

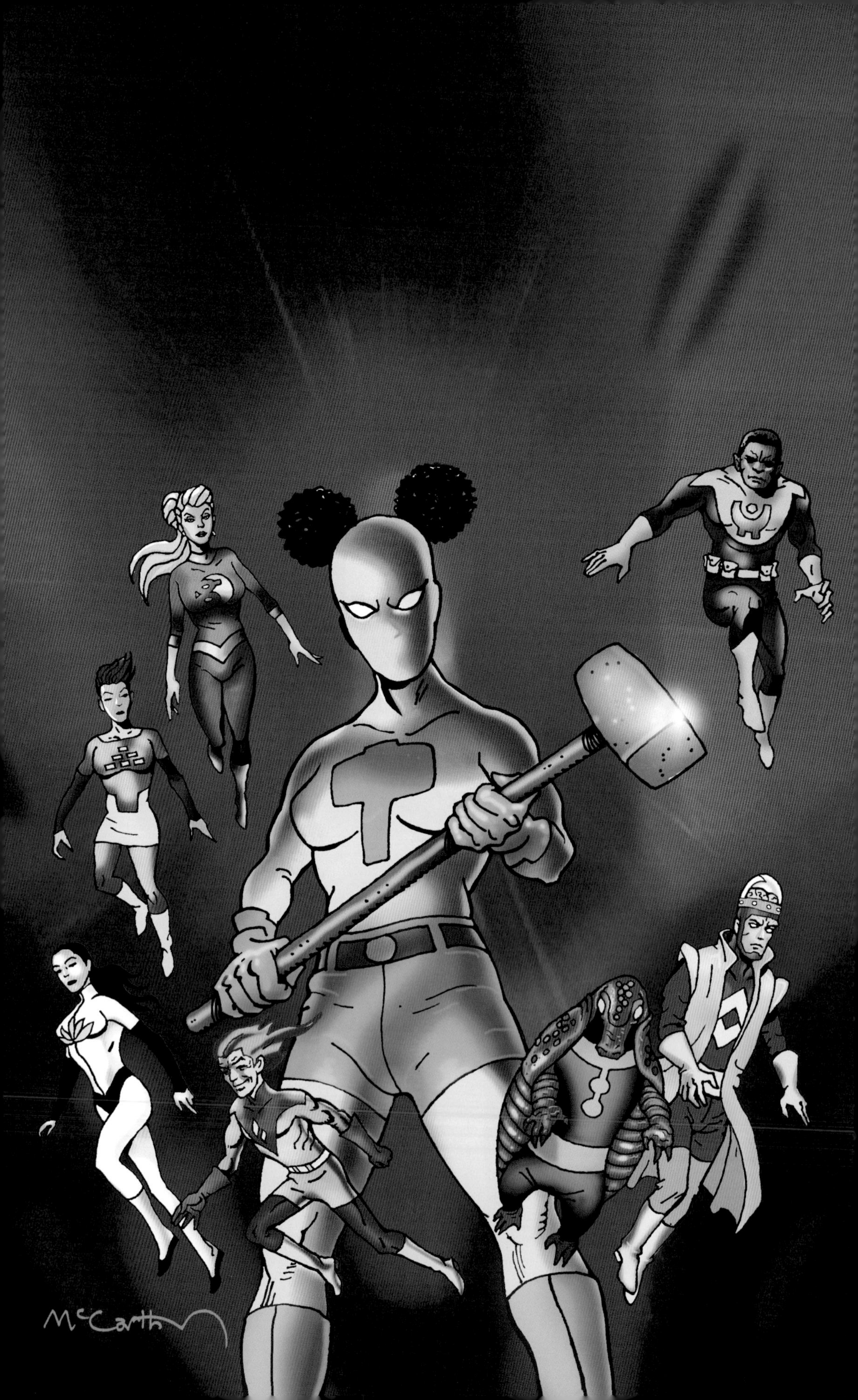
McCarthy

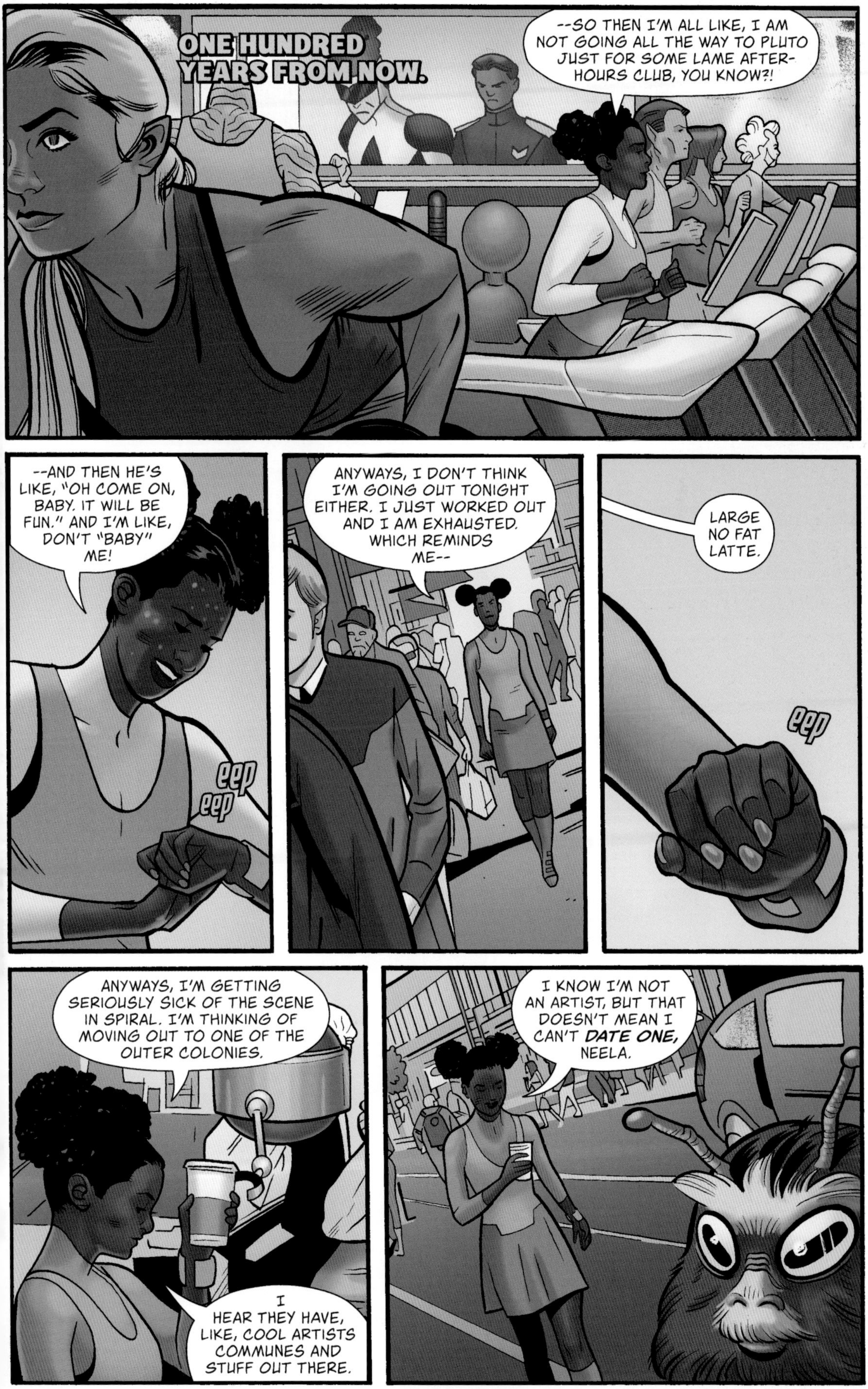

ONE HUNDRED YEARS FROM NOW.
--SO THEN I'M ALL LIKE, I AM NOT GOING ALL THE WAY TO PLUTO JUST FOR SOME LAME AFTER-HOURS CLUB, YOU KNOW?!
--AND THEN HE'S LIKE, "OH COME ON, BABY. IT WILL BE FUN." AND I'M LIKE, DON'T "BABY" ME!
eep eep
ANYWAYS, I DON'T THINK I'M GOING OUT TONIGHT EITHER. I JUST WORKED OUT AND I AM EXHAUSTED. WHICH REMINDS ME--
LARGE NO FAT LATTE.
eep
ANYWAYS, I'M GETTING SERIOUSLY SICK OF THE SCENE IN SPIRAL. I'M THINKING OF MOVING OUT TO ONE OF THE OUTER COLONIES.
I HEAR THEY HAVE, LIKE, COOL ARTISTS COMMUNES AND STUFF OUT THERE.
I KNOW I'M NOT AN ARTIST, BUT THAT DOESN'T MEAN I CAN'T *DATE ONE,* NEELA.

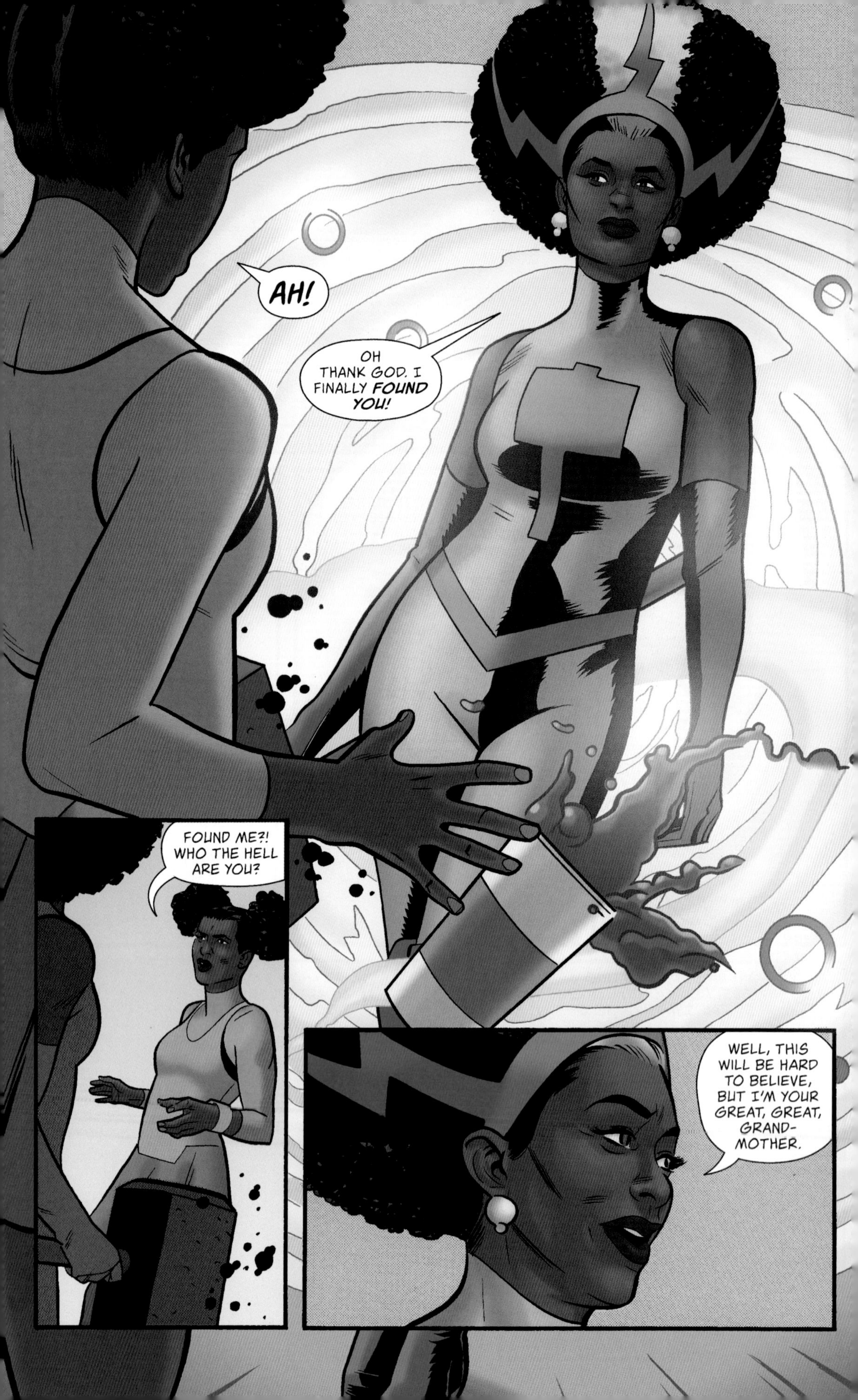
AH!
OH THANK GOD. I FINALLY **FOUND YOU!**
FOUND ME?! WHO THE HELL ARE YOU?
WELL, THIS WILL BE HARD TO BELIEVE, BUT I'M YOUR GREAT, GREAT, GRAND-MOTHER.

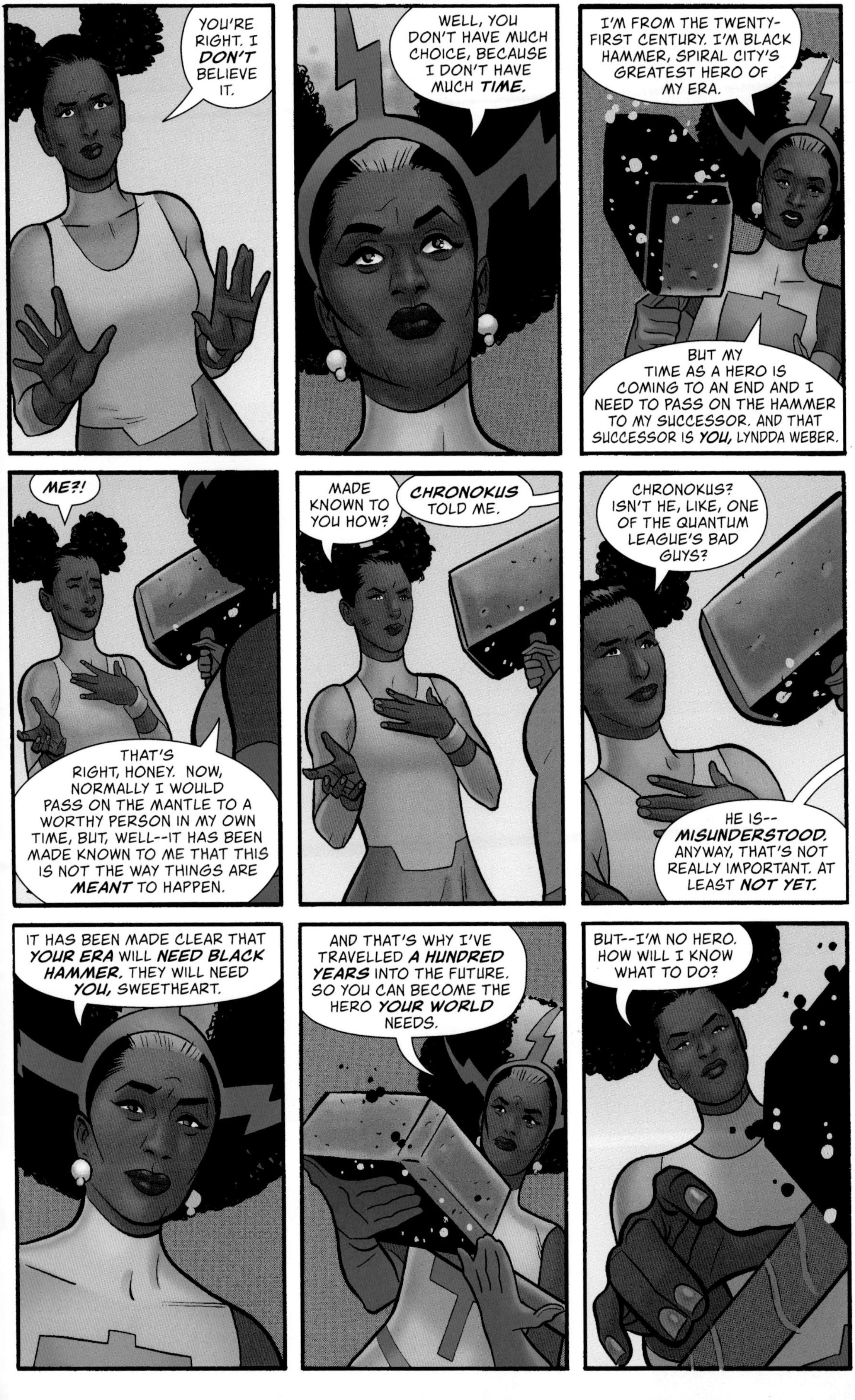
YOU'RE RIGHT. I DON'T BELIEVE IT.
WELL, YOU DON'T HAVE MUCH CHOICE, BECAUSE I DON'T HAVE MUCH TIME.
I'M FROM THE TWENTY-FIRST CENTURY. I'M BLACK HAMMER, SPIRAL CITY'S GREATEST HERO OF MY ERA.
BUT MY TIME AS A HERO IS COMING TO AN END AND I NEED TO PASS ON THE HAMMER TO MY SUCCESSOR. AND THAT SUCCESSOR IS YOU, LYNDDA WEBER.
ME?!
THAT'S RIGHT, HONEY. NOW, NORMALLY I WOULD PASS ON THE MANTLE TO A WORTHY PERSON IN MY OWN TIME, BUT, WELL--IT HAS BEEN MADE KNOWN TO ME THAT THIS IS NOT THE WAY THINGS ARE MEANT TO HAPPEN.
MADE KNOWN TO YOU HOW?
CHRONOKUS TOLD ME.
CHRONOKUS? ISN'T HE, LIKE, ONE OF THE QUANTUM LEAGUE'S BAD GUYS?
HE IS--MISUNDERSTOOD. ANYWAY, THAT'S NOT REALLY IMPORTANT. AT LEAST NOT YET.
IT HAS BEEN MADE CLEAR THAT YOUR ERA WILL NEED BLACK HAMMER. THEY WILL NEED YOU, SWEETHEART.
AND THAT'S WHY I'VE TRAVELLED A HUNDRED YEARS INTO THE FUTURE. SO YOU CAN BECOME THE HERO YOUR WORLD NEEDS.
BUT--I'M NO HERO. HOW WILL I KNOW WHAT TO DO?

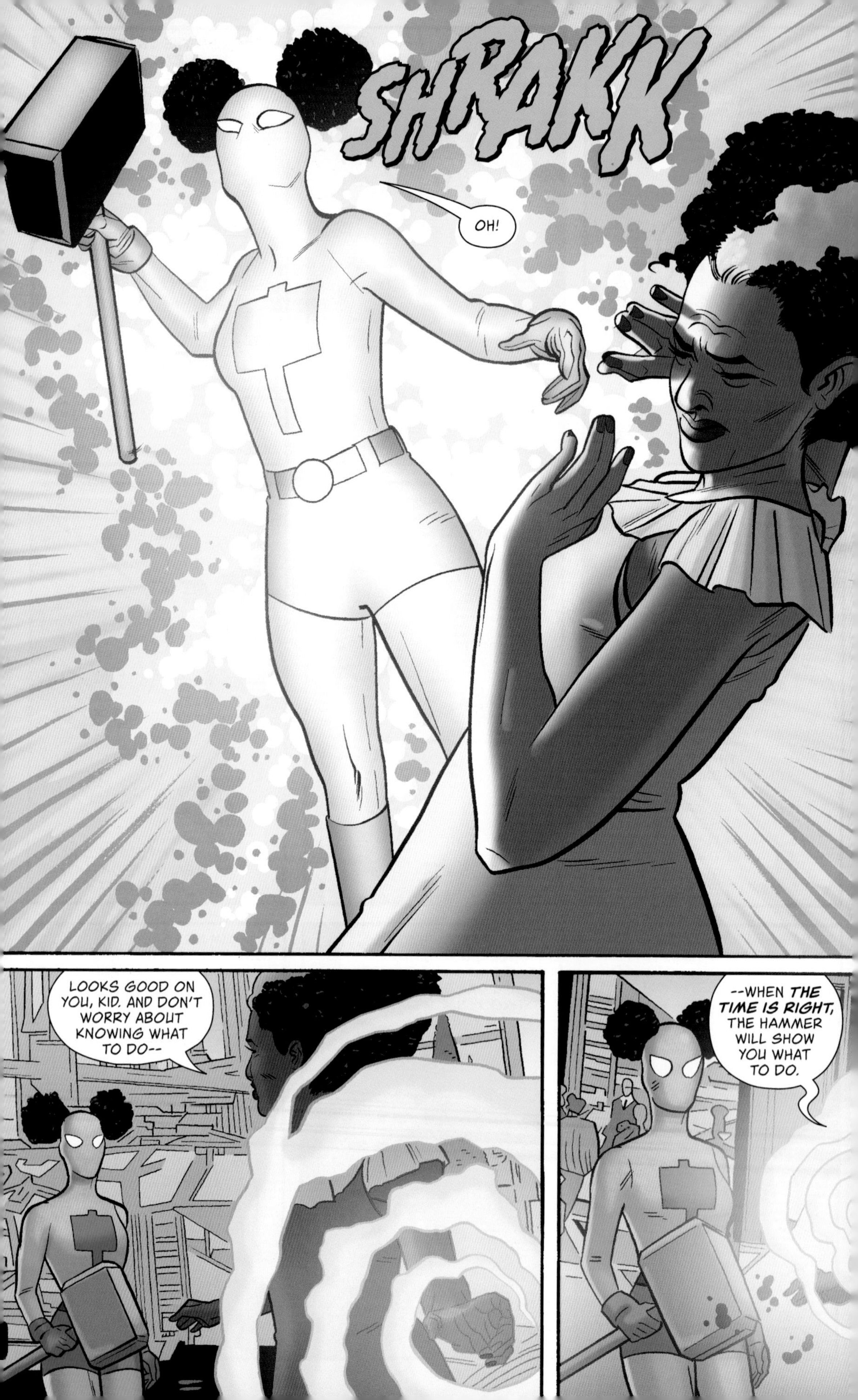
SHRAKK
OH!
LOOKS GOOD ON YOU, KID. AND DON'T WORRY ABOUT KNOWING WHAT TO DO--
--WHEN ***THE TIME IS RIGHT,*** THE HAMMER WILL SHOW YOU WHAT TO DO.

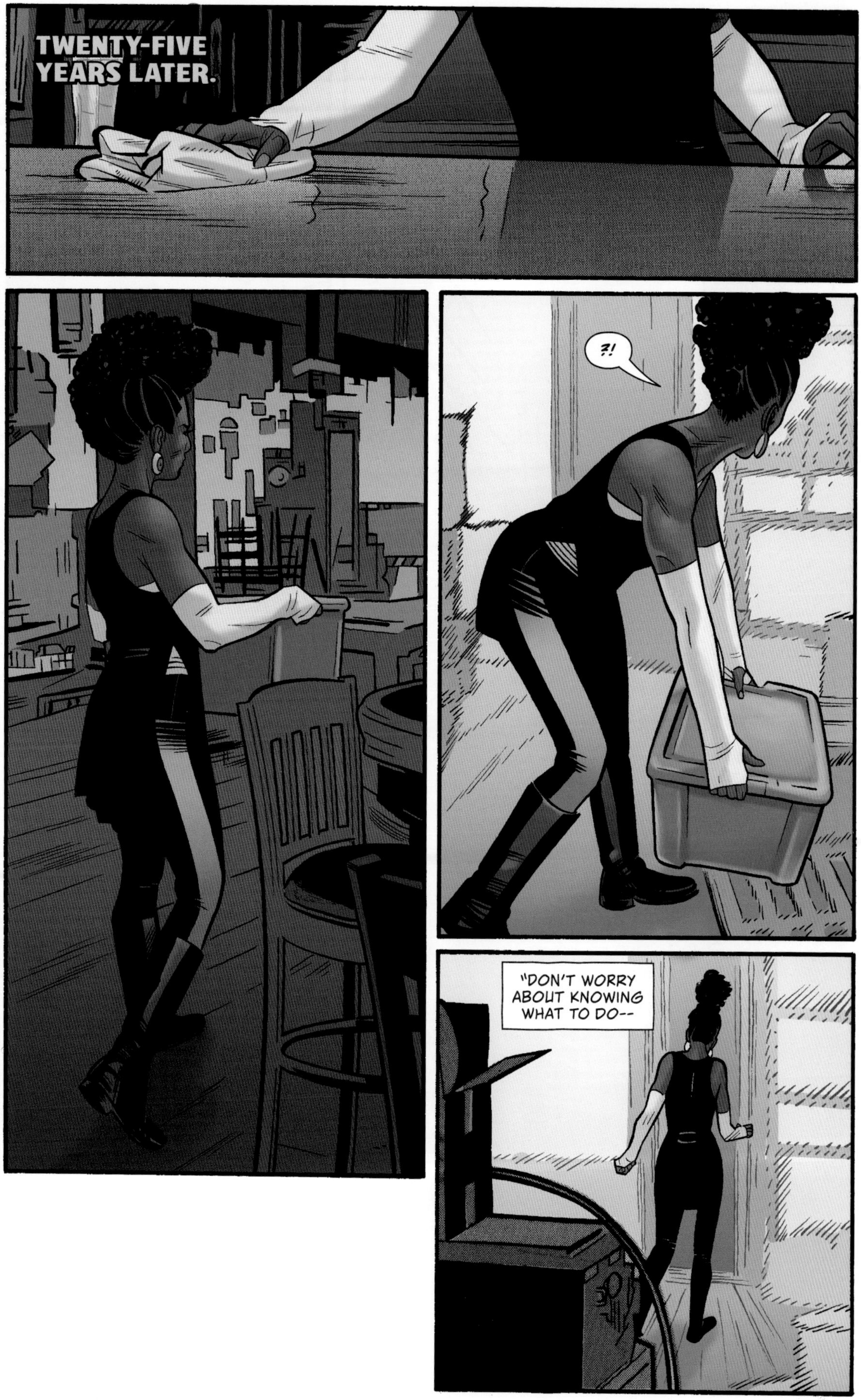
TWENTY-FIVE YEARS LATER.
?!
"DON'T WORRY ABOUT KNOWING WHAT TO DO--

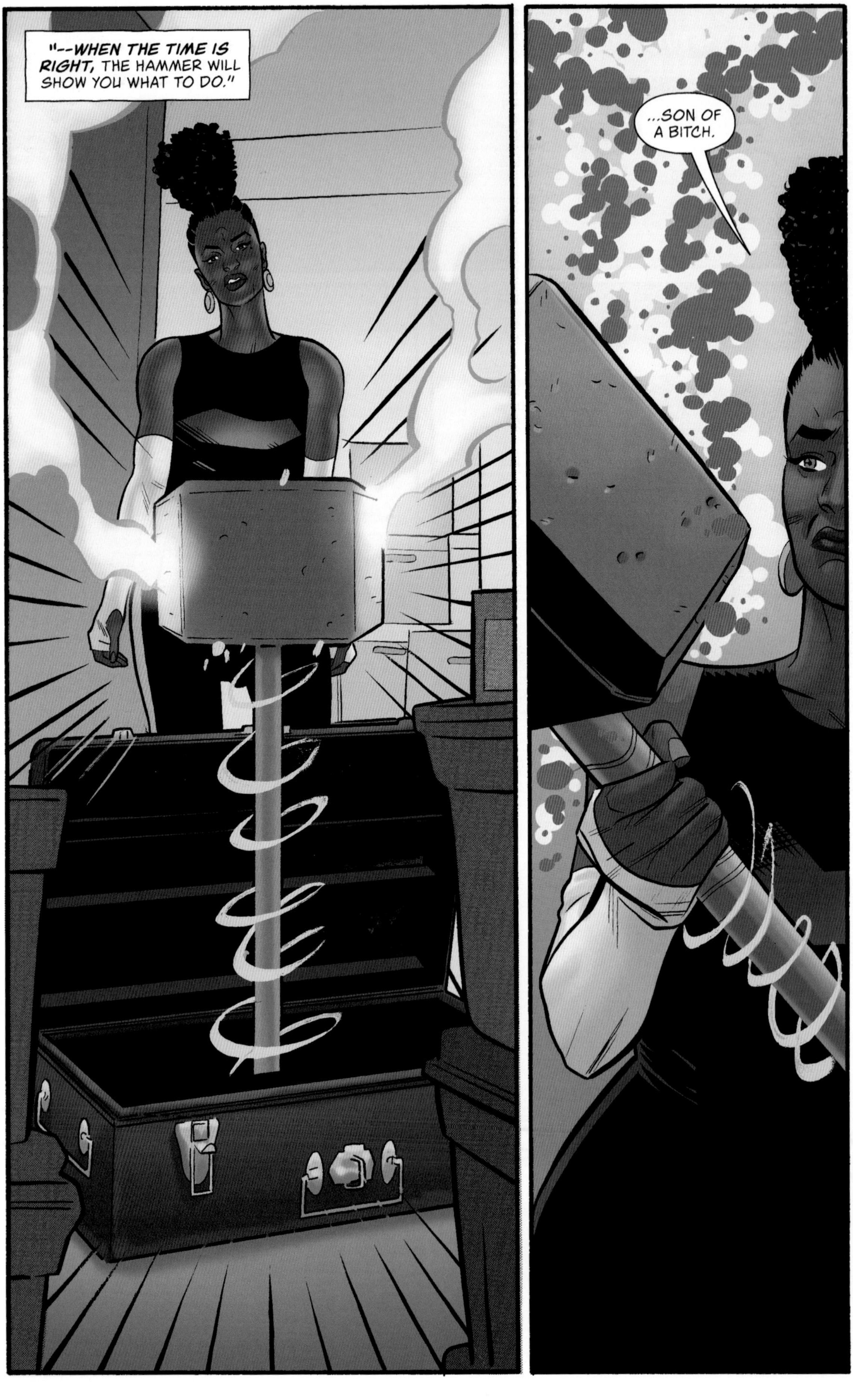
"--WHEN THE TIME IS RIGHT, THE HAMMER WILL SHOW YOU WHAT TO DO."
...SON OF A BITCH.

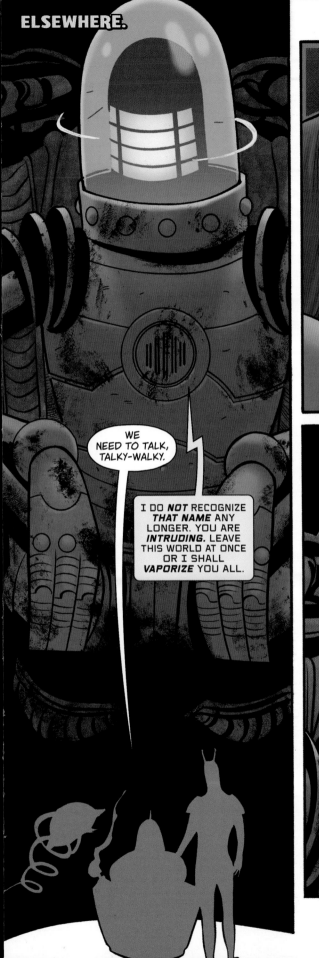

WE NEED TO TALK, TALKY-WALKY.

I DO **NOT** RECOGNIZE **THAT NAME** ANY LONGER. YOU ARE **INTRUDING.** LEAVE THIS WORLD AT ONCE OR I SHALL **VAPORIZE** YOU ALL.

CUT THE SHIT! WE NEED ARCHIVE AND WE NEED HIM NOW.

ARCHIVE WILLINGLY RETURNED TO ME. IT WAS **HIS WISH** TO REJOIN ME. I WILL NOT LET HIM GO AGAIN. NOT FOR YOU, NOT FOR ANYONE. HE BELONGS **HERE.**

UH, HI. YOU DON'T KNOW ME, BUT I THINK YOU KNEW THE MARTIAN THAT INSPIRED ME. YOU KNEW *BARBALIEN*, RIGHT?

...

THAT WAS A *VERY LONG* TIME AGO. DO NOT EXPECT ME TO BE MOVED BY *NOSTALGIA*.

WELL, THAT'S ALL I GOT. THAT WAS MY BEST SHOT.

GEE, THANKS.

ERB?

Erb has no idea how to convince Mother Computer to let us have Archive. Erb has no "best shots."

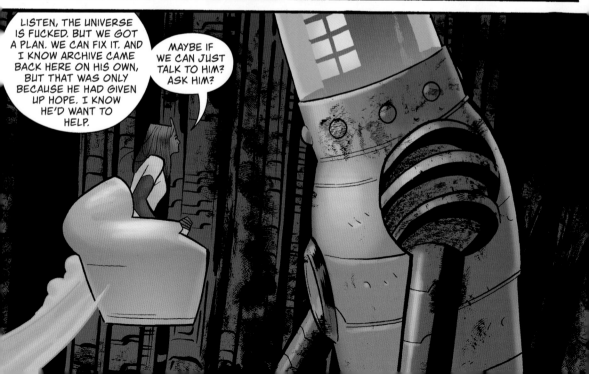

LISTEN, THE UNIVERSE IS FUCKED. BUT WE GOT A PLAN. WE CAN FIX IT. AND I KNOW ARCHIVE CAME BACK HERE ON HIS OWN, BUT THAT WAS ONLY BECAUSE HE HAD GIVEN UP HOPE. I KNOW HE'D WANT TO HELP.

MAYBE IF WE CAN JUST TALK TO HIM? ASK HIM?

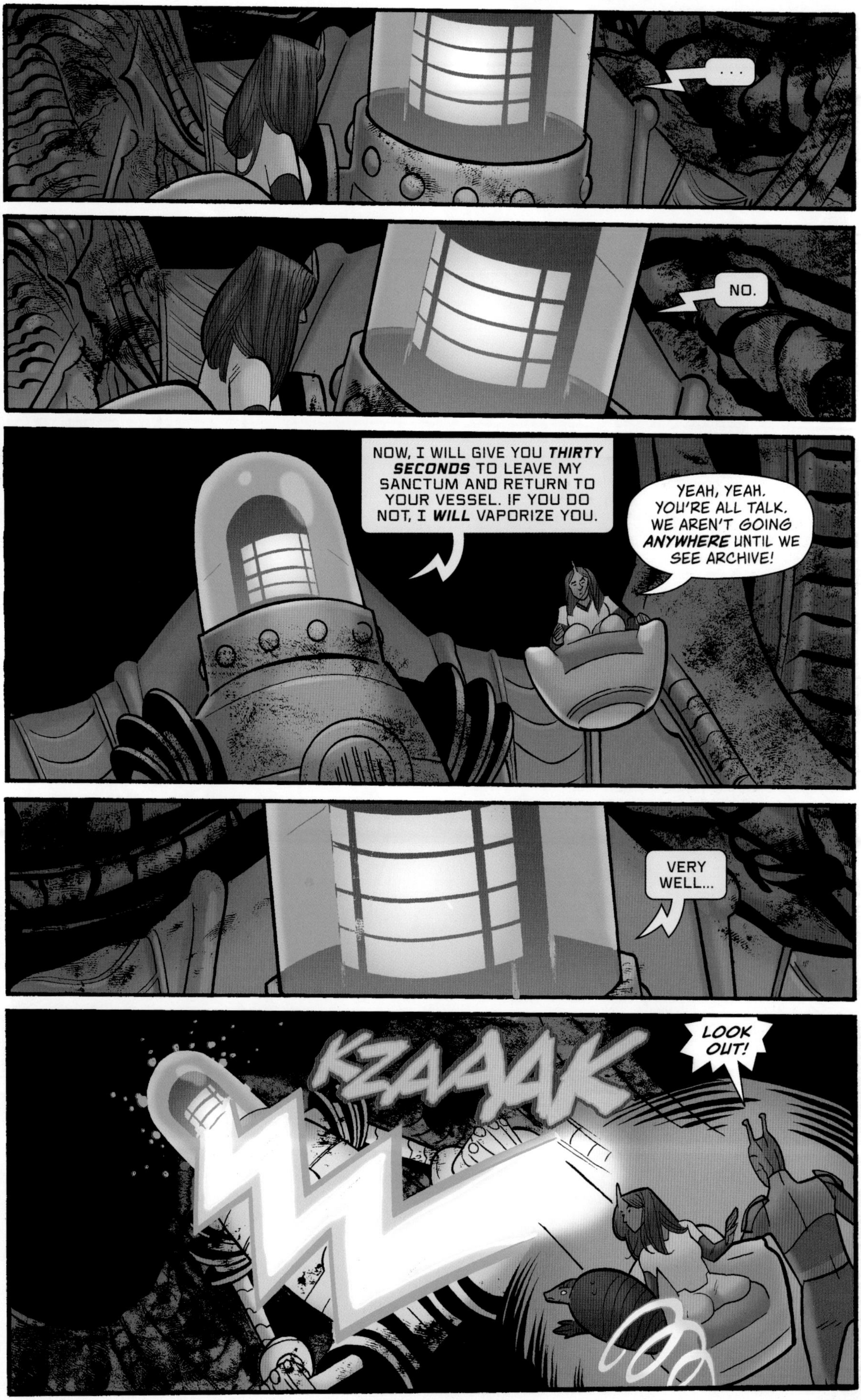
. . .
NO.
NOW, I WILL GIVE YOU THIRTY SECONDS TO LEAVE MY SANCTUM AND RETURN TO YOUR VESSEL. IF YOU DO NOT, I WILL VAPORIZE YOU.
YEAH, YEAH. YOU'RE ALL TALK. WE AREN'T GOING ANYWHERE UNTIL WE SEE ARCHIVE!
VERY WELL...
KZAAAK
LOOK OUT!

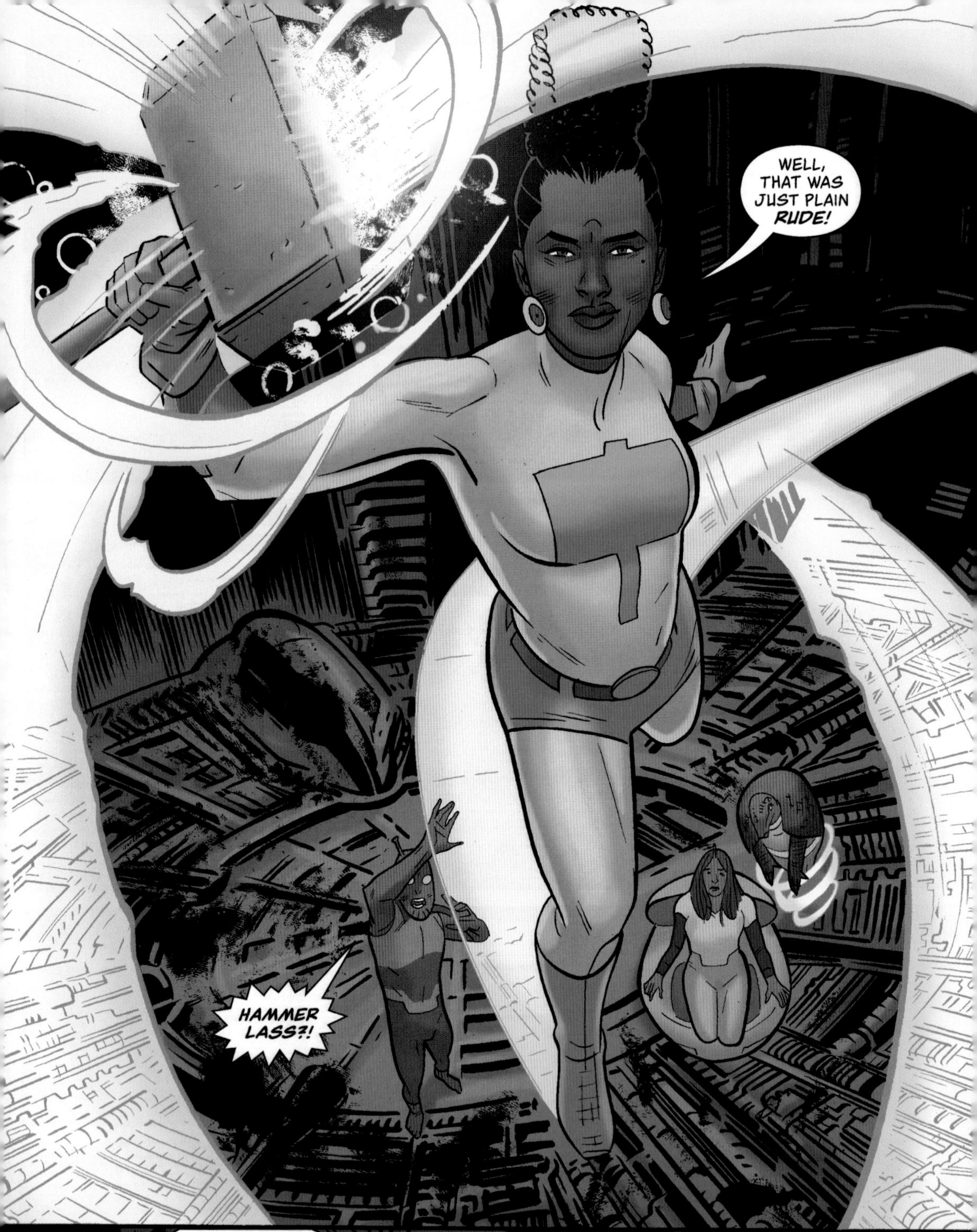
WELL, THAT WAS JUST PLAIN RUDE!
HAMMER LASS?!
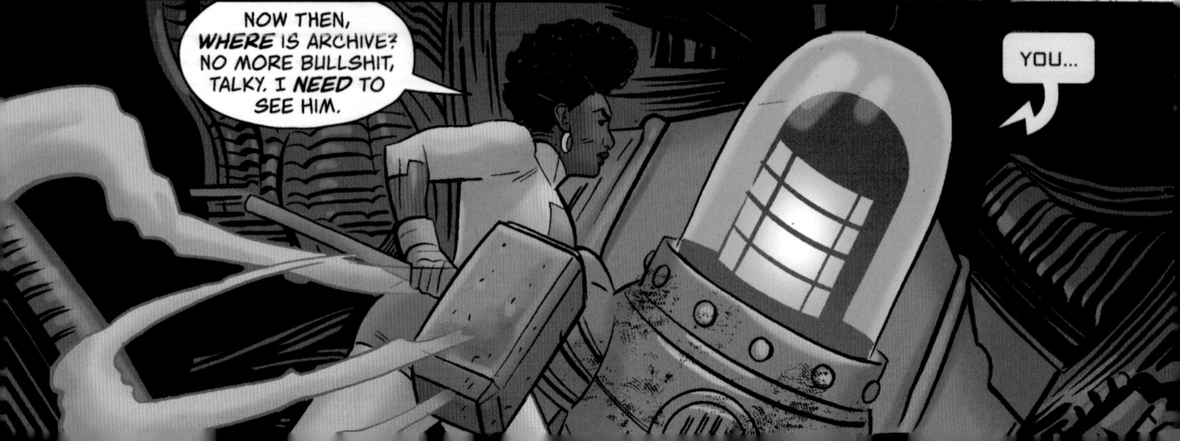
NOW THEN, WHERE IS ARCHIVE? NO MORE BULLSHIT, TALKY. I NEED TO SEE HIM.
YOU...

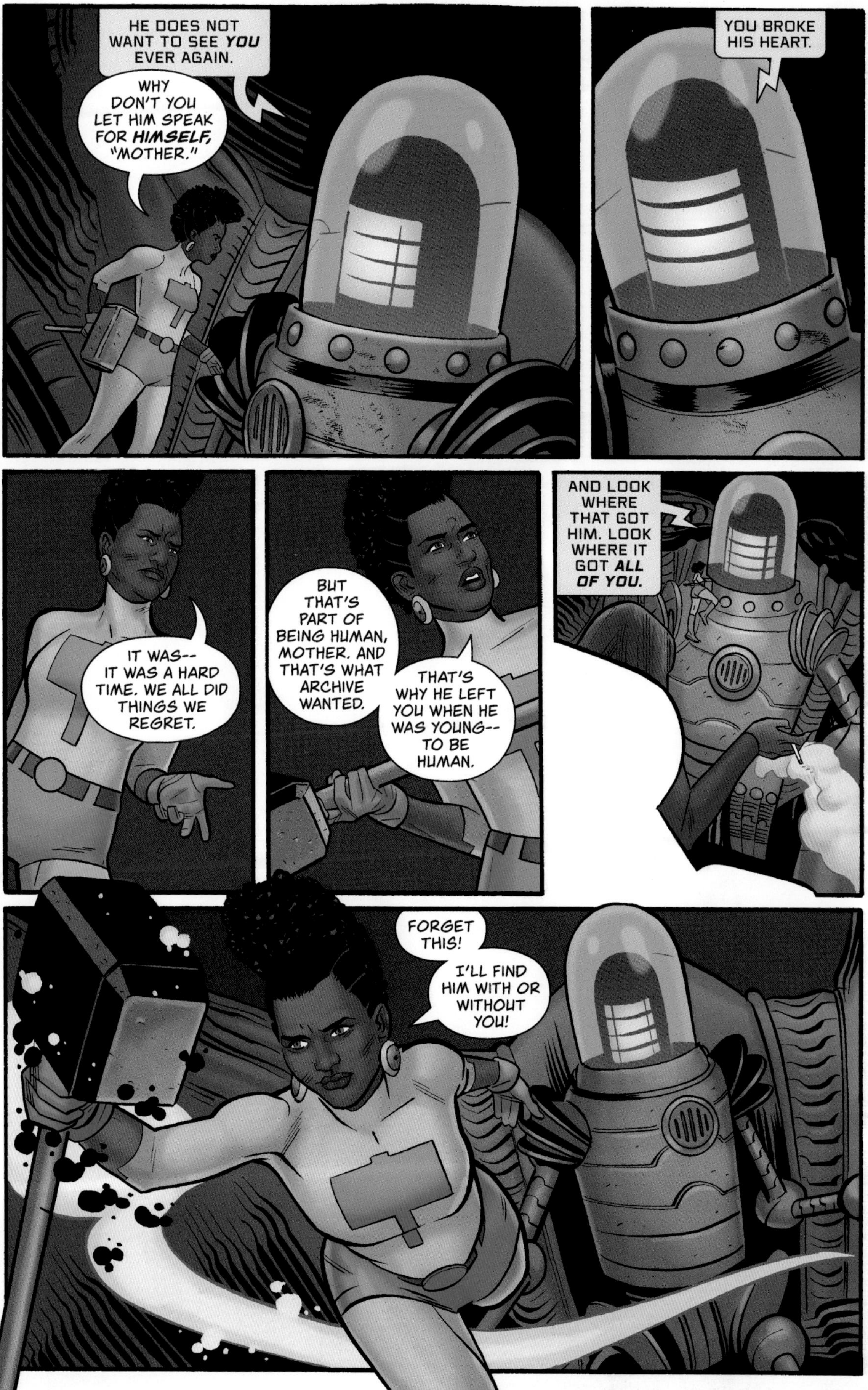

HE DOES NOT WANT TO SEE *YOU* EVER AGAIN.
WHY DON'T YOU LET HIM SPEAK FOR **HIMSELF,** "MOTHER."
YOU BROKE HIS HEART.
IT WAS-- IT WAS A HARD TIME. WE ALL DID THINGS WE REGRET.
BUT THAT'S PART OF BEING HUMAN, MOTHER. AND THAT'S WHAT ARCHIVE WANTED.
THAT'S WHY HE LEFT YOU WHEN HE WAS YOUNG-- TO BE HUMAN.
AND LOOK WHERE THAT GOT HIM. LOOK WHERE IT GOT ***ALL OF YOU.***
FORGET THIS!
I'LL FIND HIM WITH OR WITHOUT YOU!

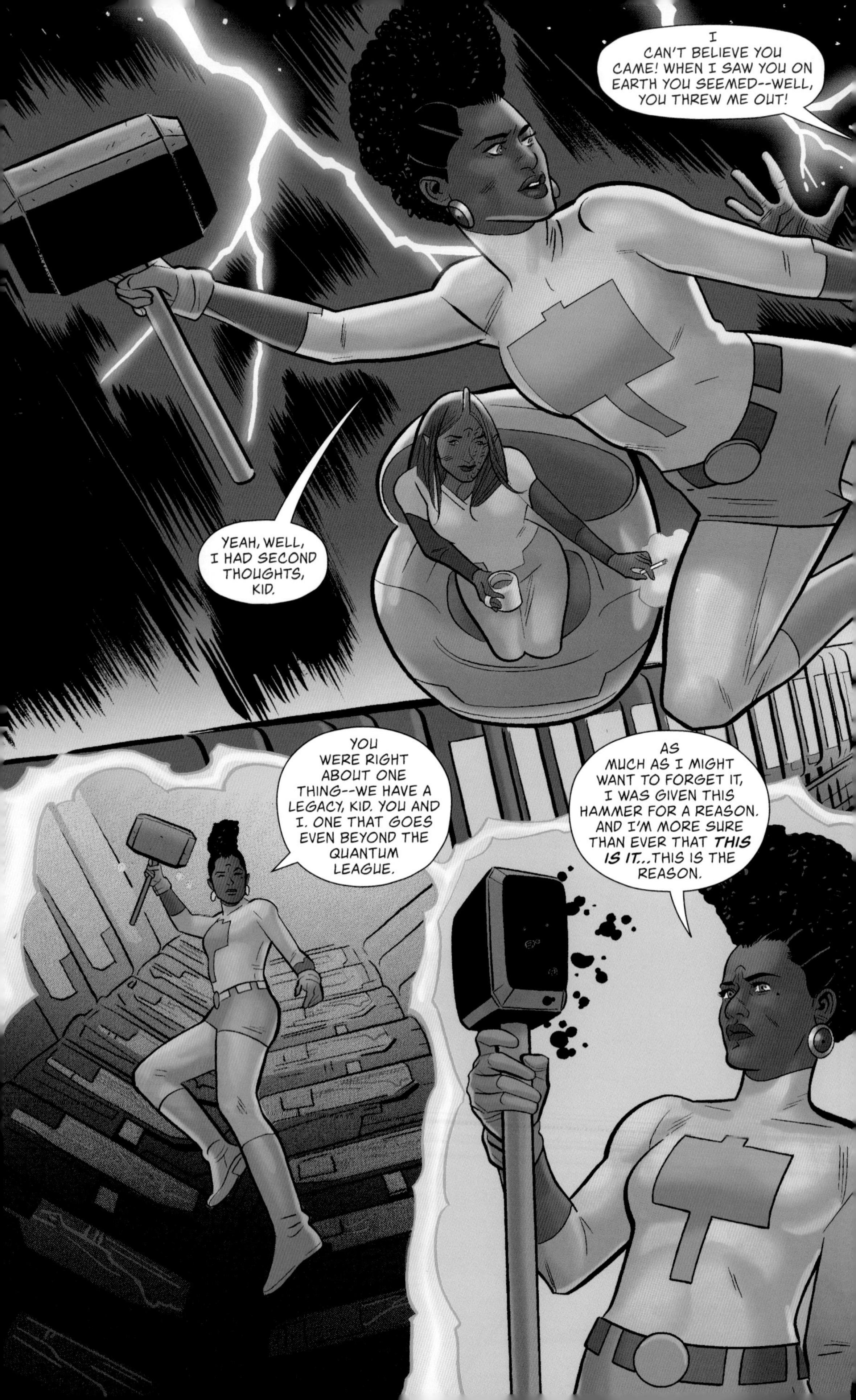

I CAN'T BELIEVE YOU CAME! WHEN I SAW YOU ON EARTH YOU SEEMED--WELL, YOU THREW ME OUT!
YEAH, WELL, I HAD SECOND THOUGHTS, KID.
YOU WERE RIGHT ABOUT ONE THING--WE HAVE A LEGACY, KID. YOU AND I. ONE THAT GOES EVEN BEYOND THE QUANTUM LEAGUE.
AS MUCH AS I MIGHT WANT TO FORGET IT, I WAS GIVEN THIS HAMMER FOR A REASON. AND I'M MORE SURE THAN EVER THAT *THIS IS IT...*THIS IS THE REASON.

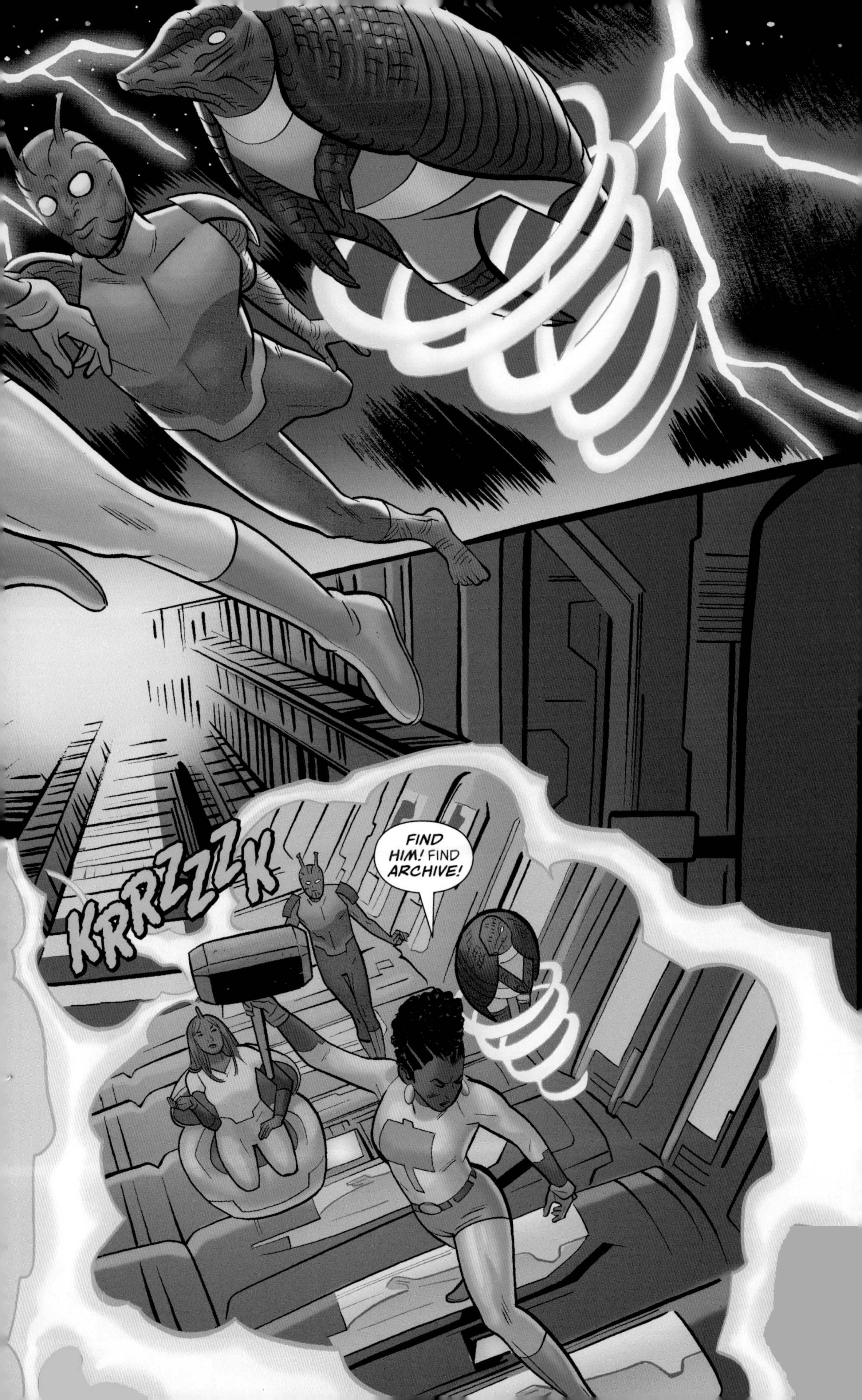
KRRZZZK
FIND HIM! FIND ARCHIVE!

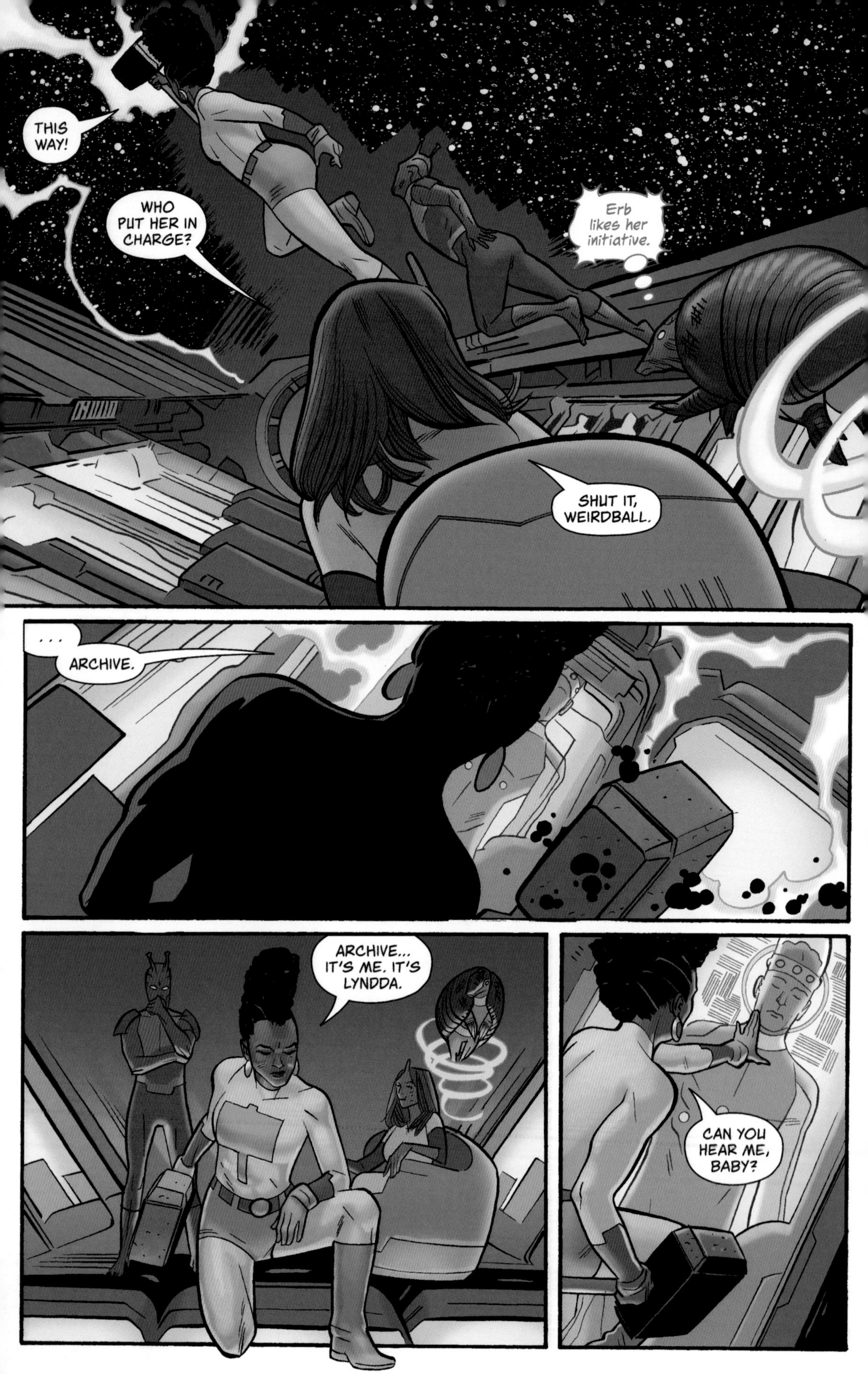
THIS WAY!
WHO PUT HER IN CHARGE?
Erb likes her initiative.
SHUT IT, WEIRDBALL.
...
ARCHIVE.
ARCHIVE... IT'S ME. IT'S LYNDDA.
CAN YOU HEAR ME, BABY?

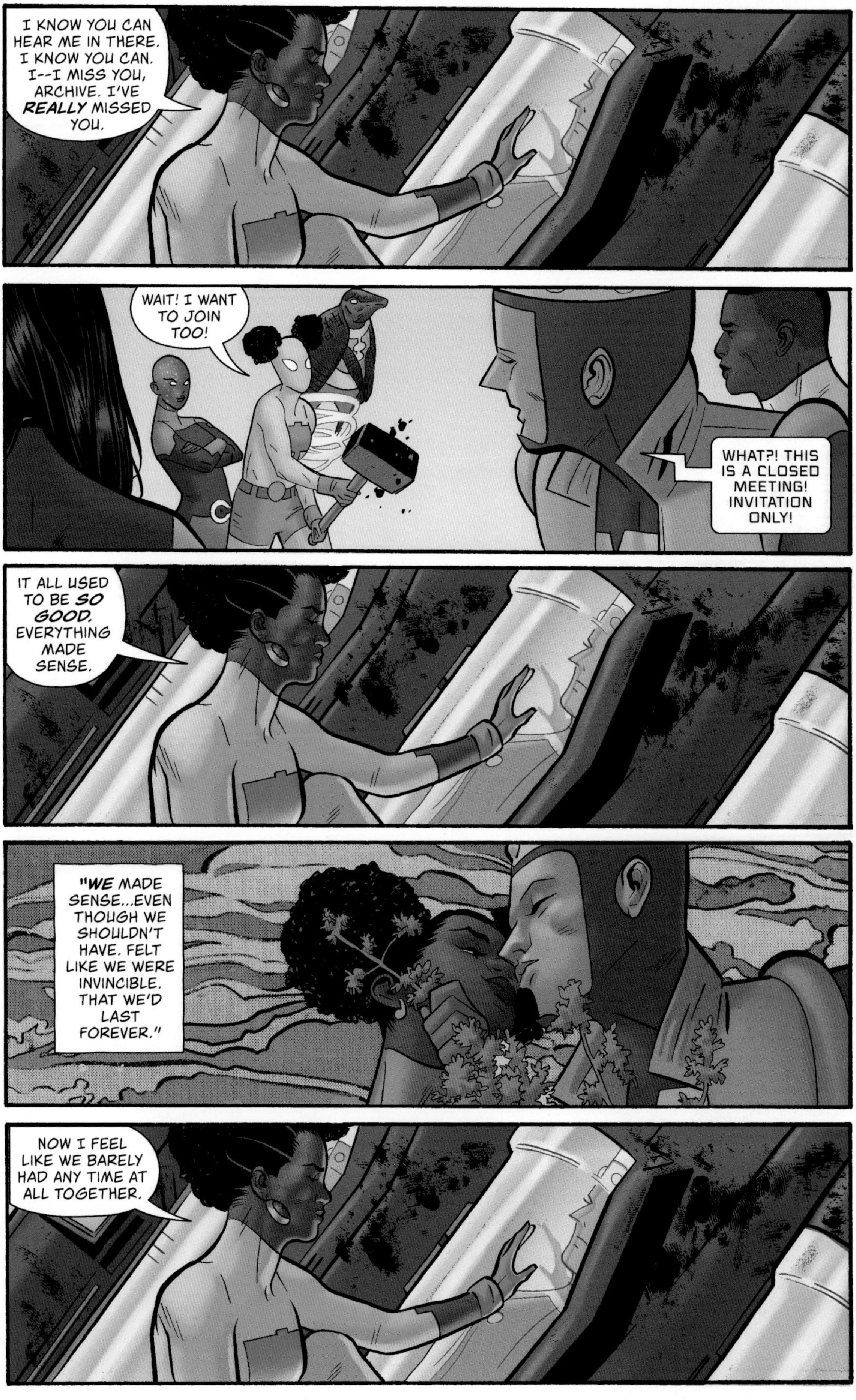
I KNOW YOU CAN HEAR ME IN THERE. I KNOW YOU CAN. I--I MISS YOU, ARCHIVE. I'VE *REALLY* MISSED YOU.
WAIT! I WANT TO JOIN TOO!
WHAT?! THIS IS A CLOSED MEETING! INVITATION ONLY!
IT ALL USED TO BE *SO GOOD*. EVERYTHING MADE SENSE.
"*WE* MADE SENSE...EVEN THOUGH WE SHOULDN'T HAVE. FELT LIKE WE WERE INVINCIBLE. THAT WE'D LAST FOREVER."
NOW I FEEL LIKE WE BARELY HAD ANY TIME AT ALL TOGETHER.

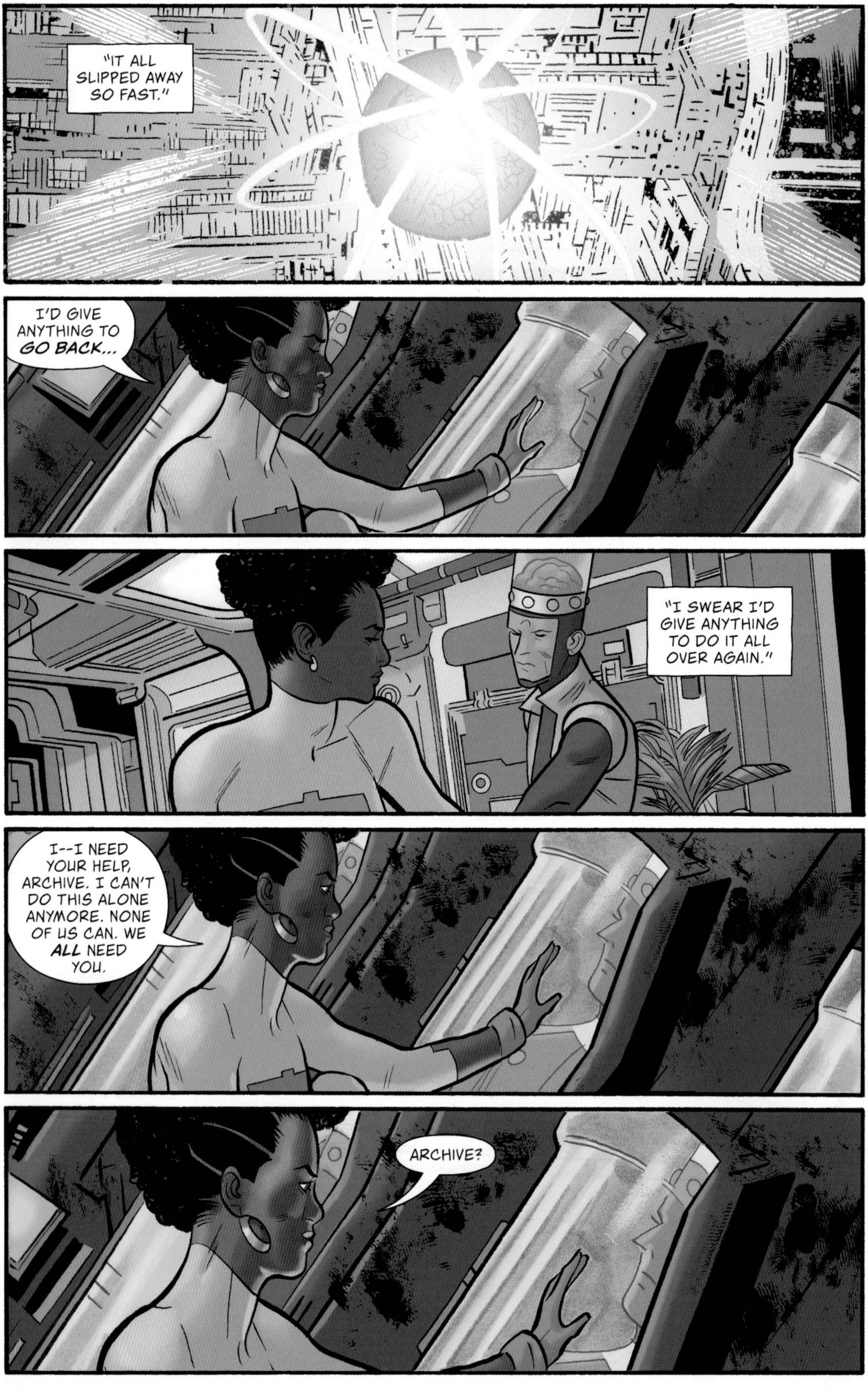
"IT ALL SLIPPED AWAY SO FAST."
I'D GIVE ANYTHING TO **GO BACK...**
"I SWEAR I'D GIVE ANYTHING TO DO IT ALL OVER AGAIN."
I--I NEED YOUR HELP, ARCHIVE. I CAN'T DO THIS ALONE ANYMORE. NONE OF US CAN. WE **ALL** NEED YOU.
ARCHIVE?

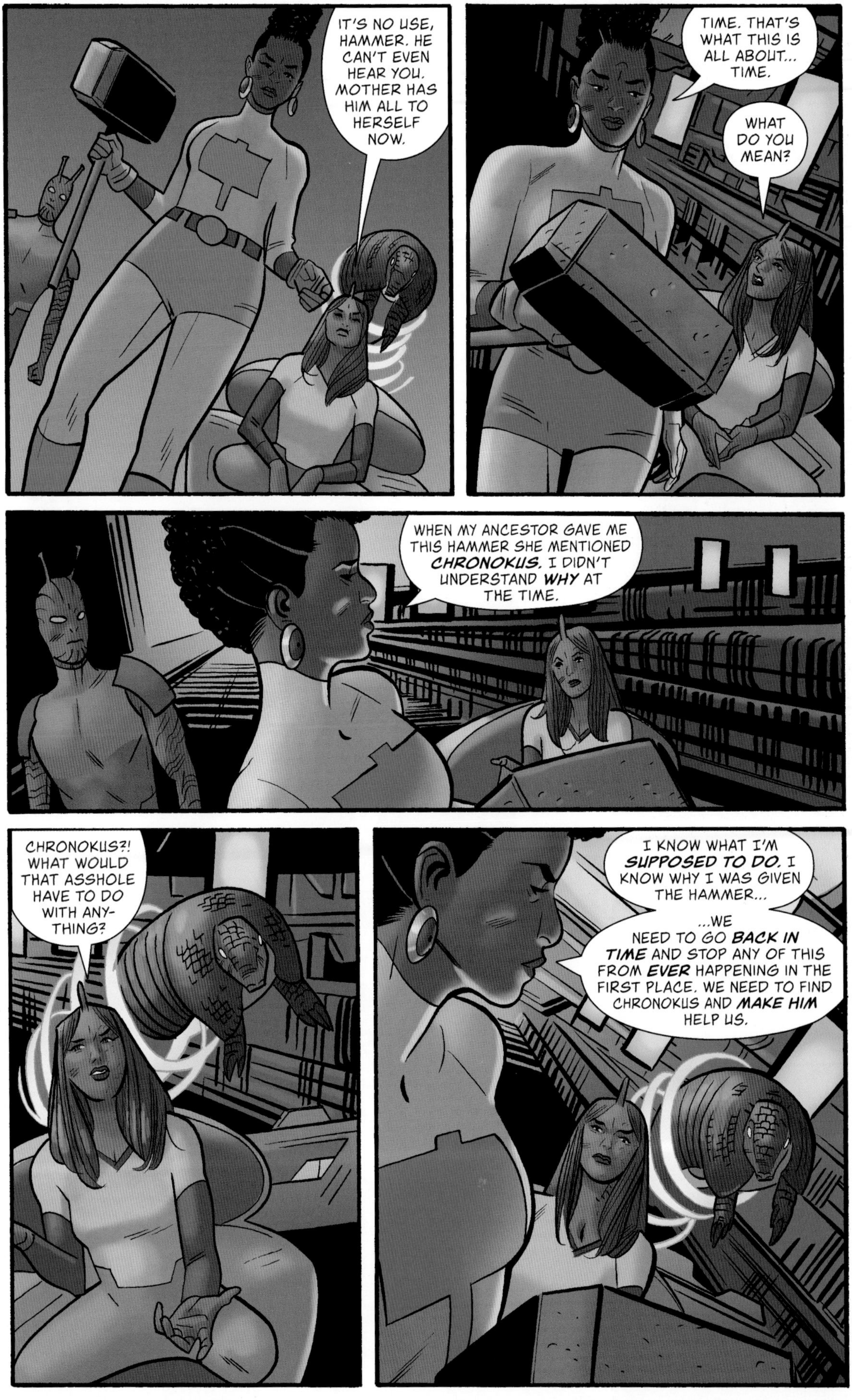
IT'S NO USE, HAMMER. HE CAN'T EVEN HEAR YOU. MOTHER HAS HIM ALL TO HERSELF NOW.
TIME. THAT'S WHAT THIS IS ALL ABOUT... TIME.
WHAT DO YOU MEAN?
WHEN MY ANCESTOR GAVE ME THIS HAMMER SHE MENTIONED CHRONOKUS. I DIDN'T UNDERSTAND WHY AT THE TIME.
CHRONOKUS?! WHAT WOULD THAT ASSHOLE HAVE TO DO WITH ANY-THING?
I KNOW WHAT I'M SUPPOSED TO DO. I KNOW WHY I WAS GIVEN THE HAMMER...
...WE NEED TO GO BACK IN TIME AND STOP ANY OF THIS FROM EVER HAPPENING IN THE FIRST PLACE. WE NEED TO FIND CHRONOKUS AND MAKE HIM HELP US.

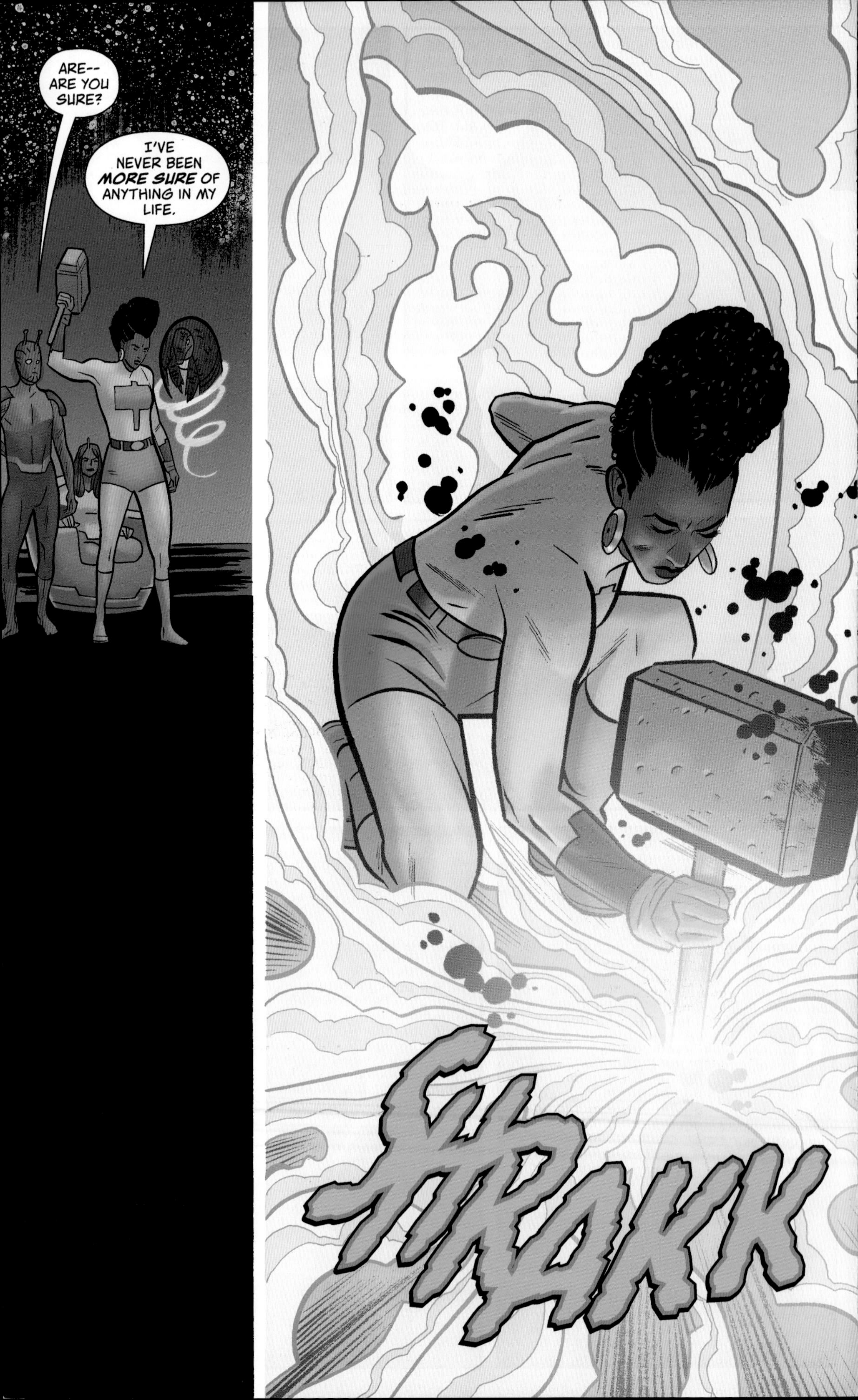

ARE--
ARE YOU SURE?
I'VE NEVER BEEN MORE SURE OF ANYTHING IN MY LIFE.
SKRAKK

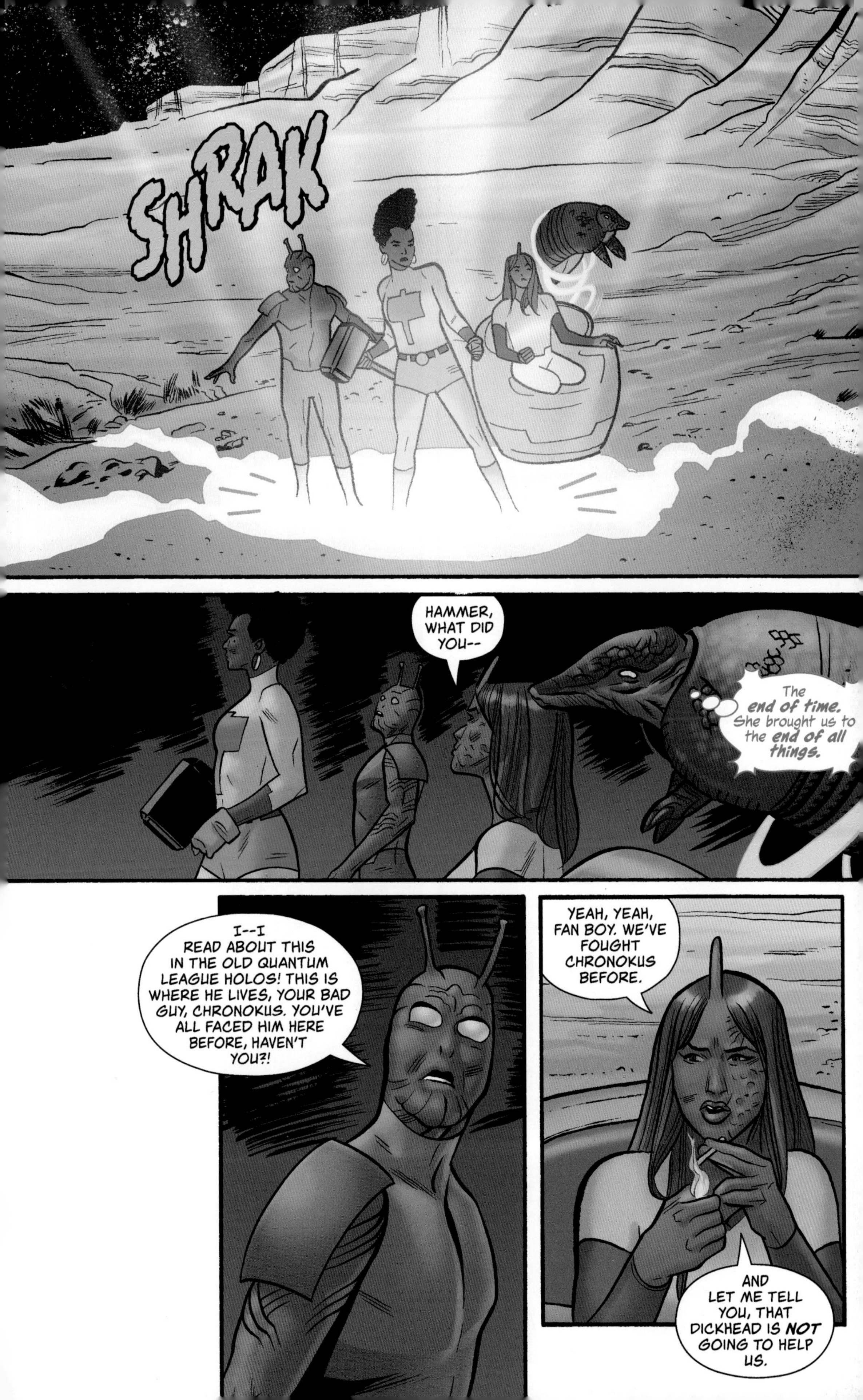
SHRAK
HAMMER, WHAT DID YOU--
The end of time. She brought us to the end of all things.
I--I READ ABOUT THIS IN THE OLD QUANTUM LEAGUE HOLOS! THIS IS WHERE HE LIVES, YOUR BAD GUY, CHRONOKUS. YOU'VE ALL FACED HIM HERE BEFORE, HAVEN'T YOU?!
YEAH, YEAH, FAN BOY. WE'VE FOUGHT CHRONOKUS BEFORE.
AND LET ME TELL YOU, THAT DICKHEAD IS NOT GOING TO HELP US.

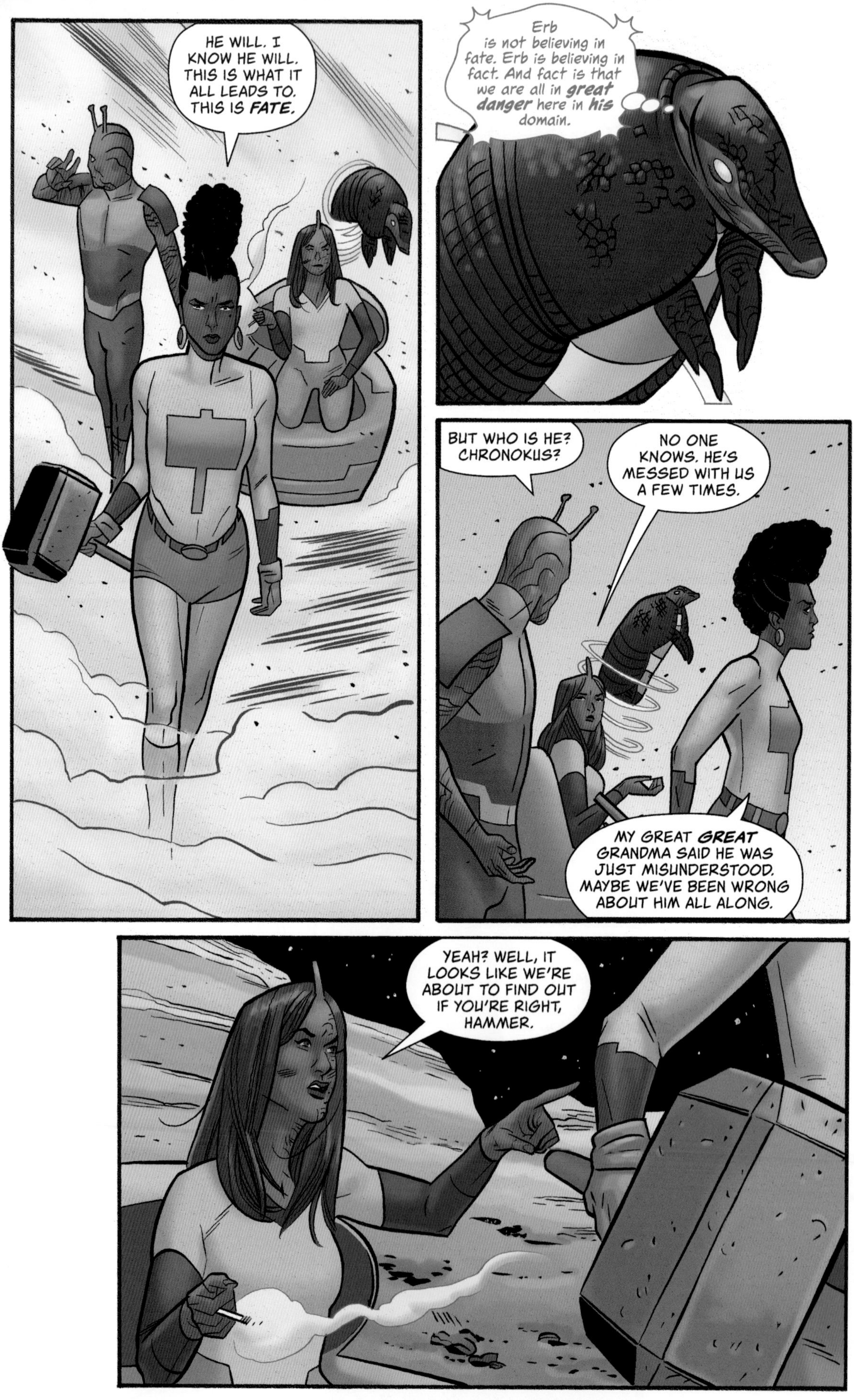
HE WILL. I KNOW HE WILL. THIS IS WHAT IT ALL LEADS TO. THIS IS FATE.
Erb is not believing in fate. Erb is believing in fact. And fact is that we are all in great danger here in his domain.
BUT WHO IS HE? CHRONOKUS?
NO ONE KNOWS. HE'S MESSED WITH US A FEW TIMES.
MY GREAT GREAT GRANDMA SAID HE WAS JUST MISUNDERSTOOD. MAYBE WE'VE BEEN WRONG ABOUT HIM ALL ALONG.
YEAH? WELL, IT LOOKS LIKE WE'RE ABOUT TO FIND OUT IF YOU'RE RIGHT, HAMMER.

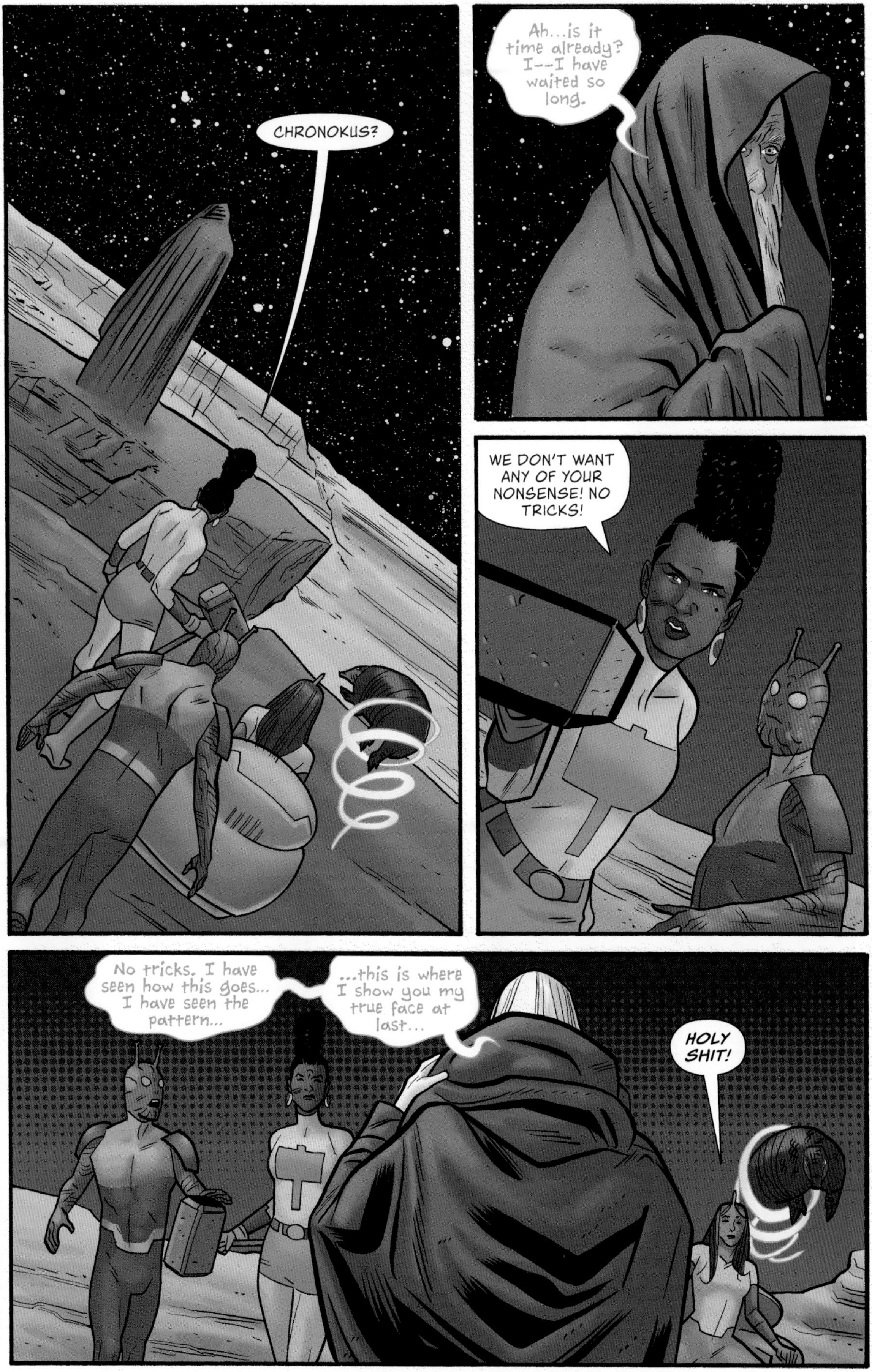
CHRONOKUS?
Ah...is it time already? I--I have waited so long.
WE DON'T WANT ANY OF YOUR NONSENSE! NO TRICKS!
No tricks. I have seen how this goes... I have seen the pattern...
...this is where I show you my true face at last...
HOLY SHIT!

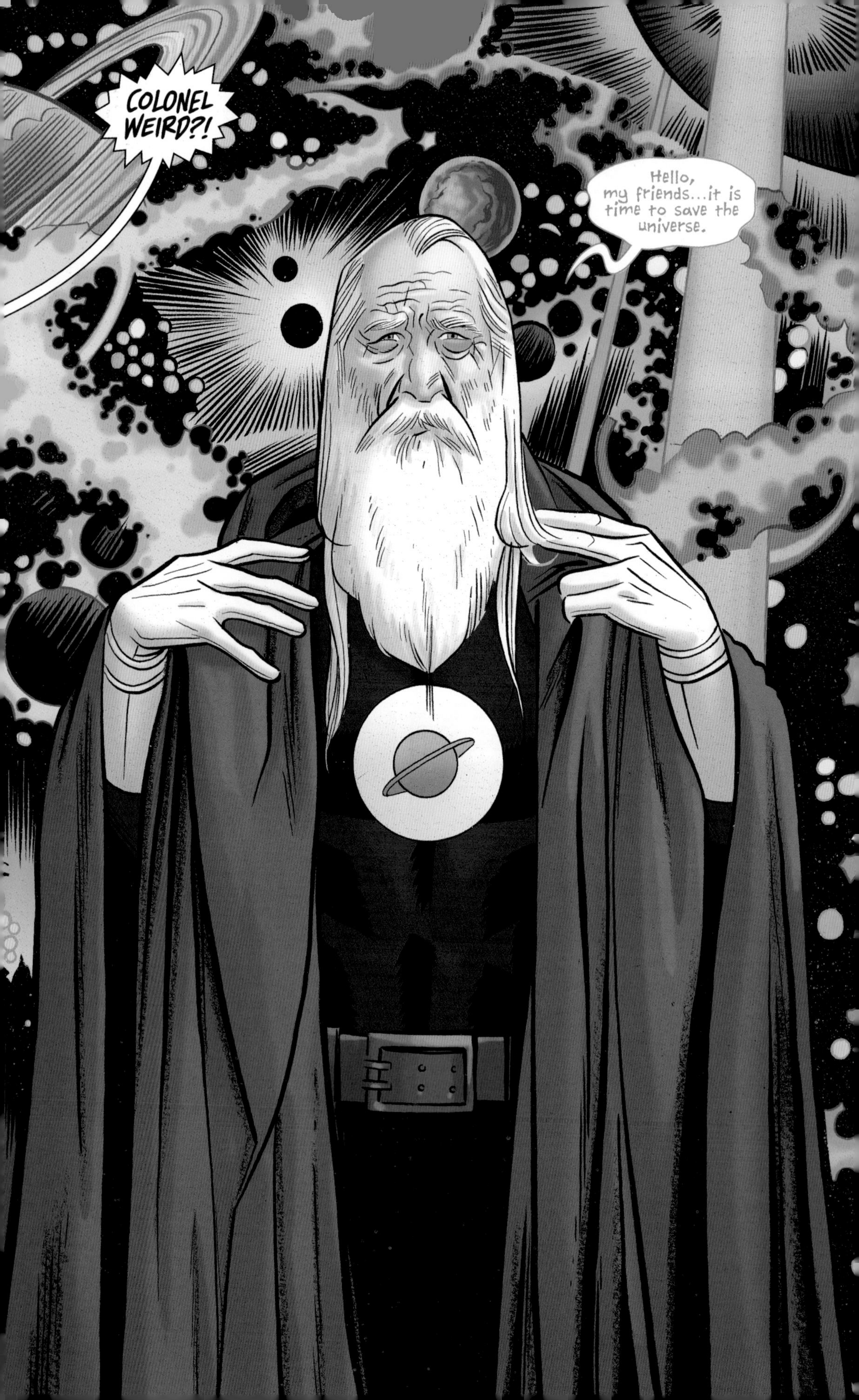
COLONEL WEIRD?!
Hello, my friends...it is time to save the universe.

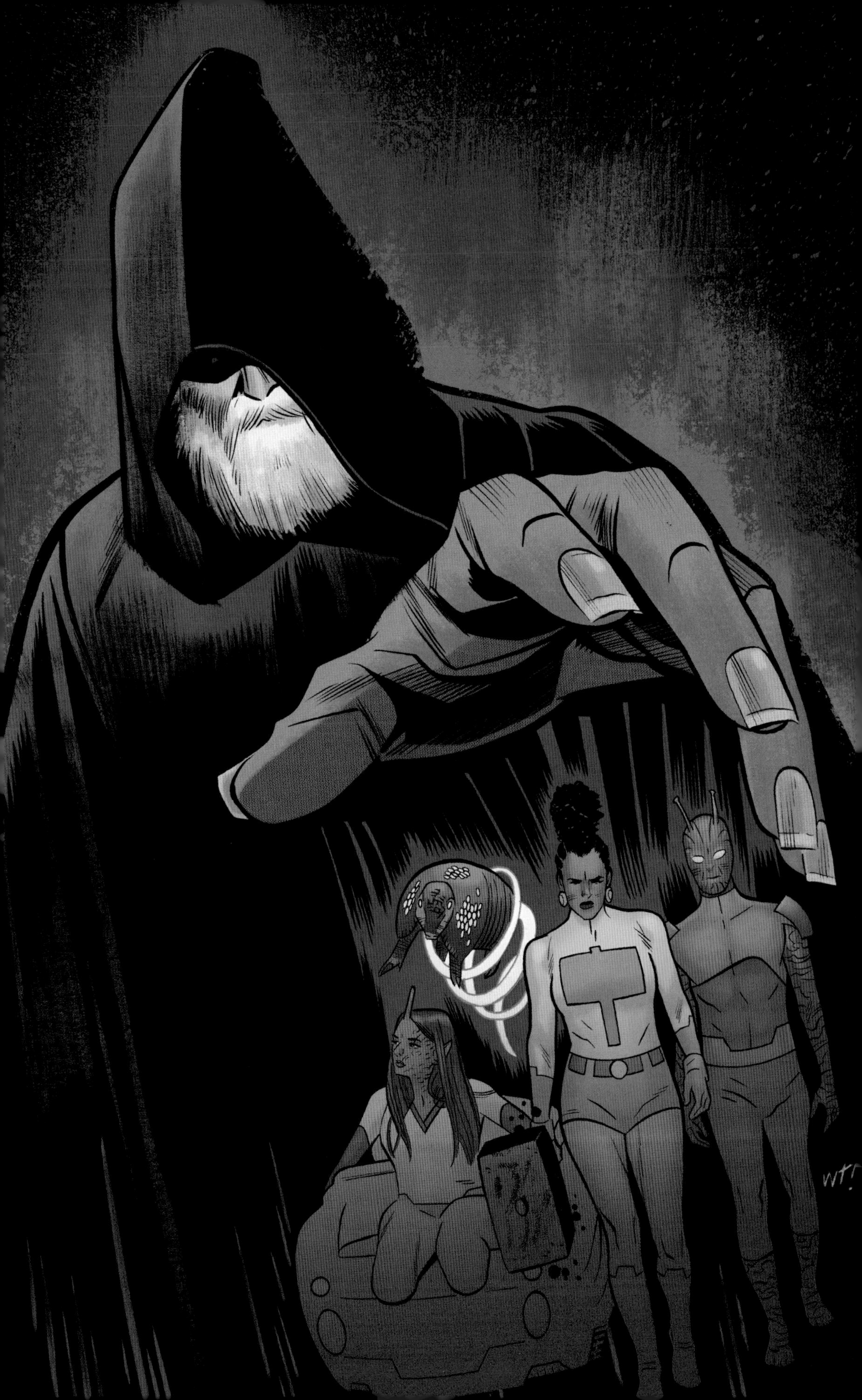

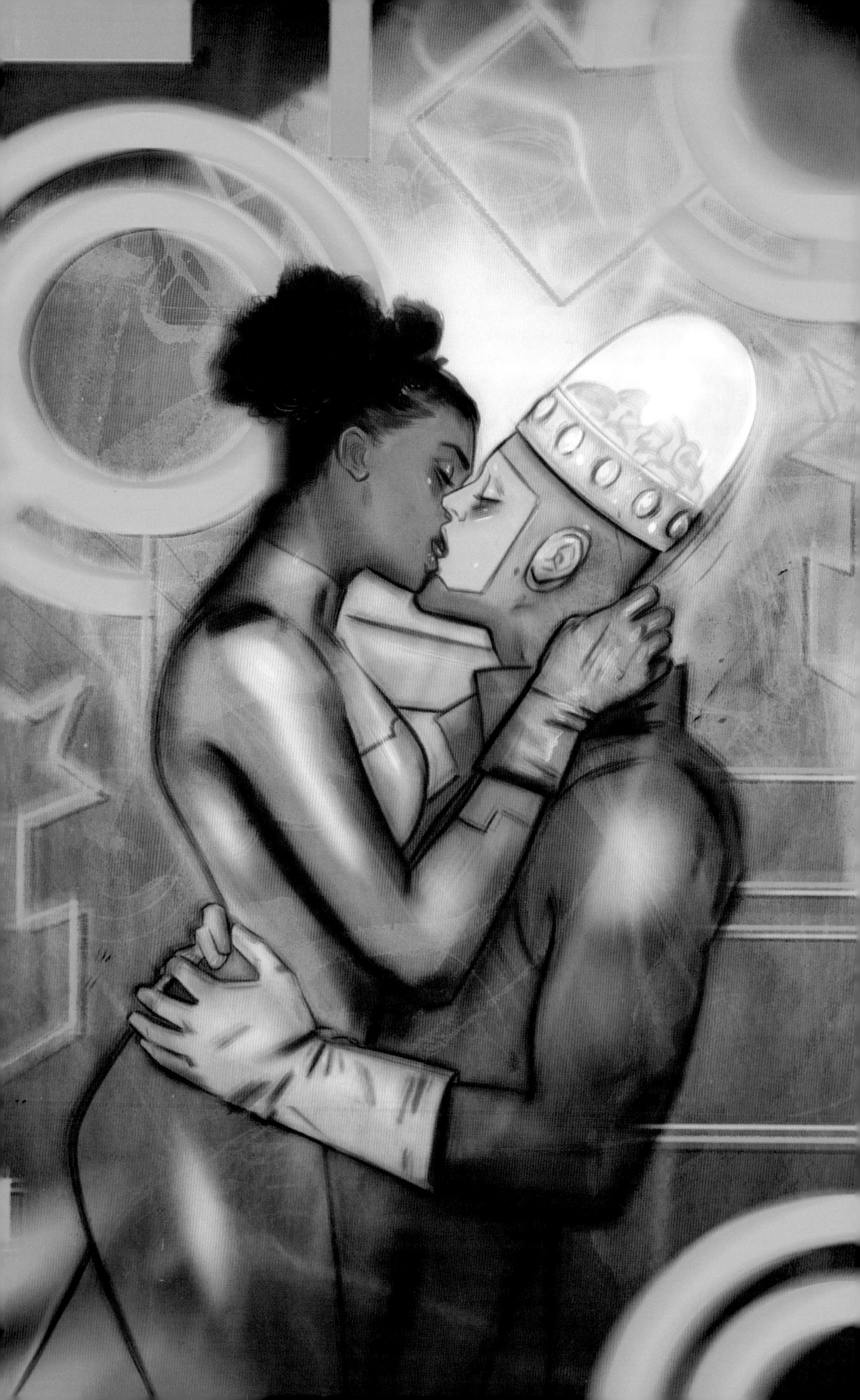

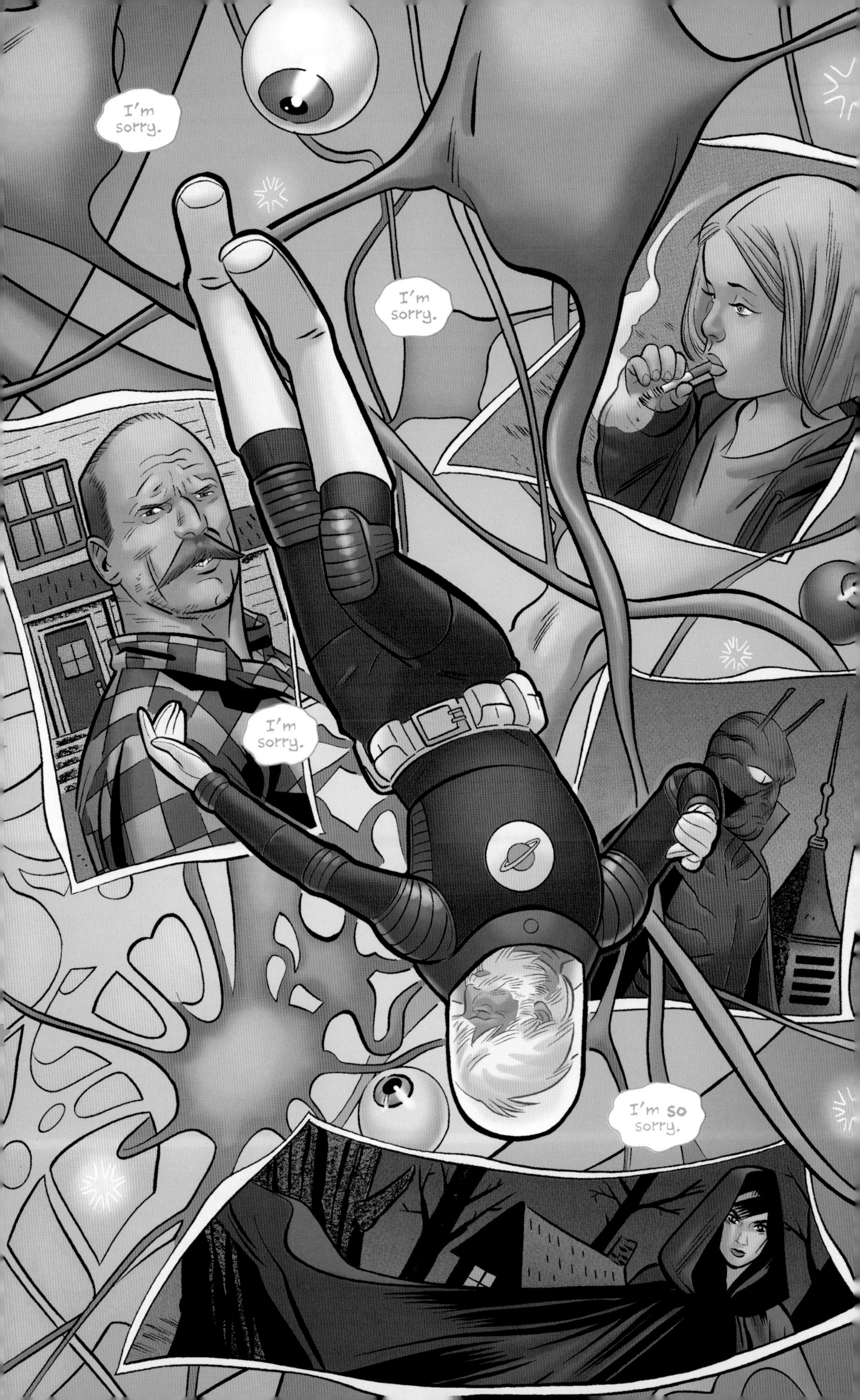
I'm sorry.
I'm sorry.
I'm sorry.
I'm so sorry.

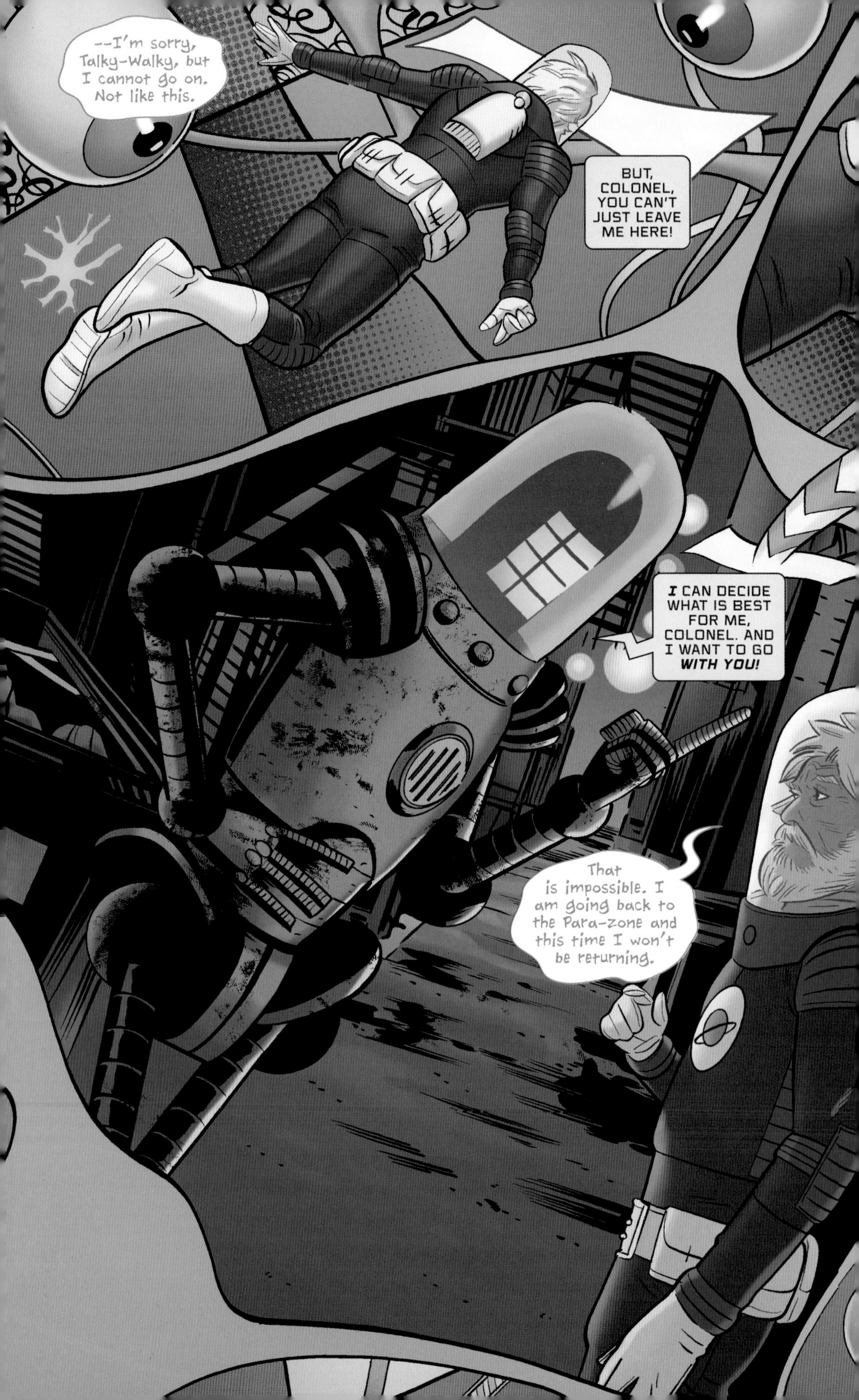
--I'm sorry, Talky-Walky, but I cannot go on. Not like this.
BUT, COLONEL, YOU CAN'T JUST LEAVE ME HERE!
I CAN DECIDE WHAT IS BEST FOR ME, COLONEL. AND I WANT TO GO WITH YOU!
That is impossible. I am going back to the Para-zone and this time I won't be returning.

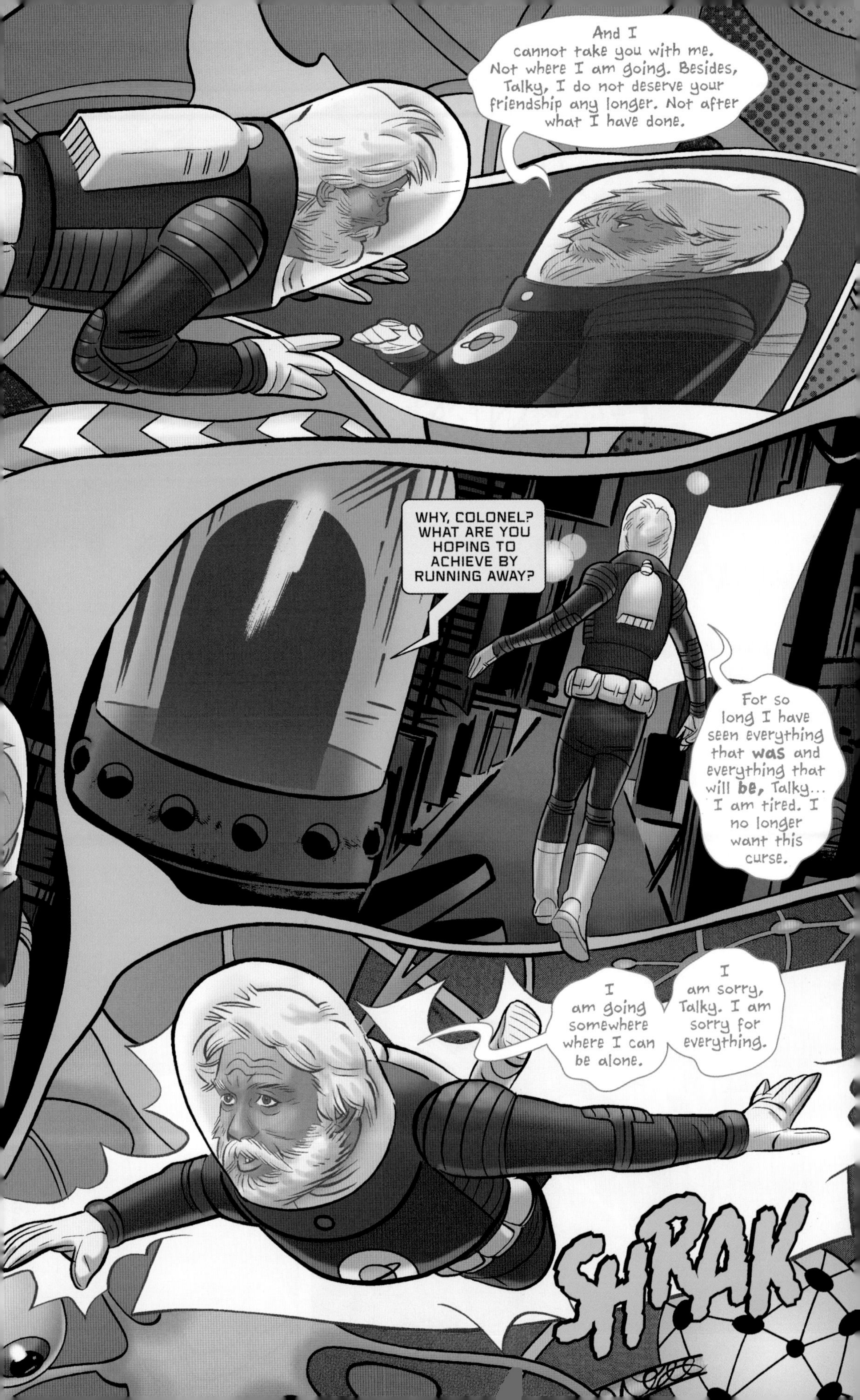
And I cannot take you with me. Not where I am going. Besides, Talky, I do not deserve your friendship any longer. Not after what I have done.
WHY, COLONEL? WHAT ARE YOU HOPING TO ACHIEVE BY RUNNING AWAY?
For so long I have seen everything that was and everything that will be, Talky... I am tired. I no longer want this curse.
I am going somewhere where I can be alone.
I am sorry, Talky. I am sorry for everything.
SHRAK

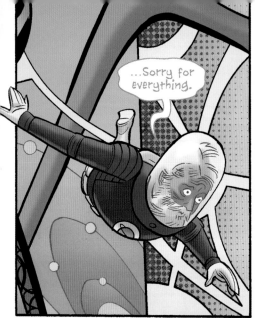

...Sorry for everything.

So sorry.

SHRACK

Alone. I just want to be alone.

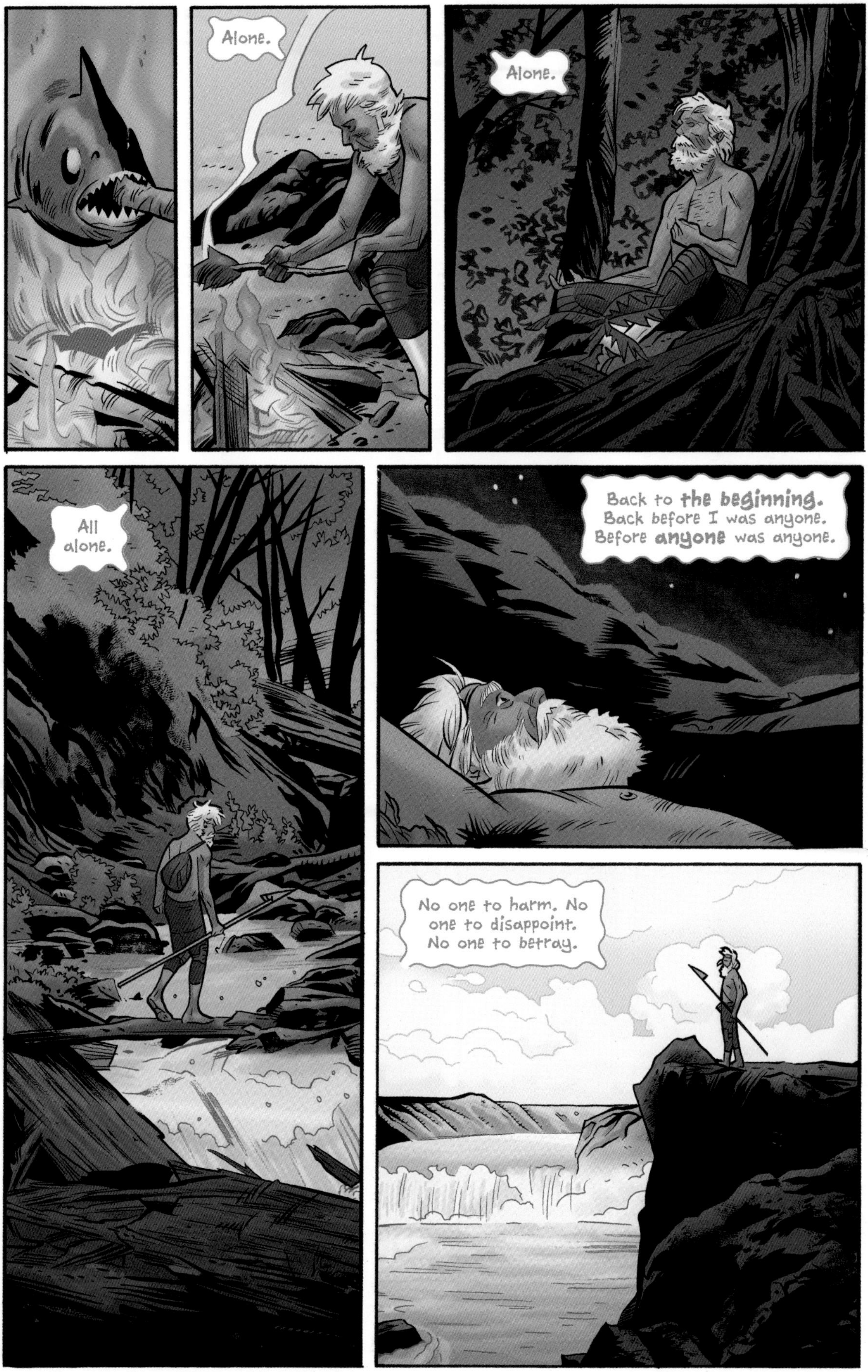
Alone.
Alone.
All alone.
Back to the beginning. Back before I was anyone. Before anyone was anyone.
No one to harm. No one to disappoint. No one to betray.

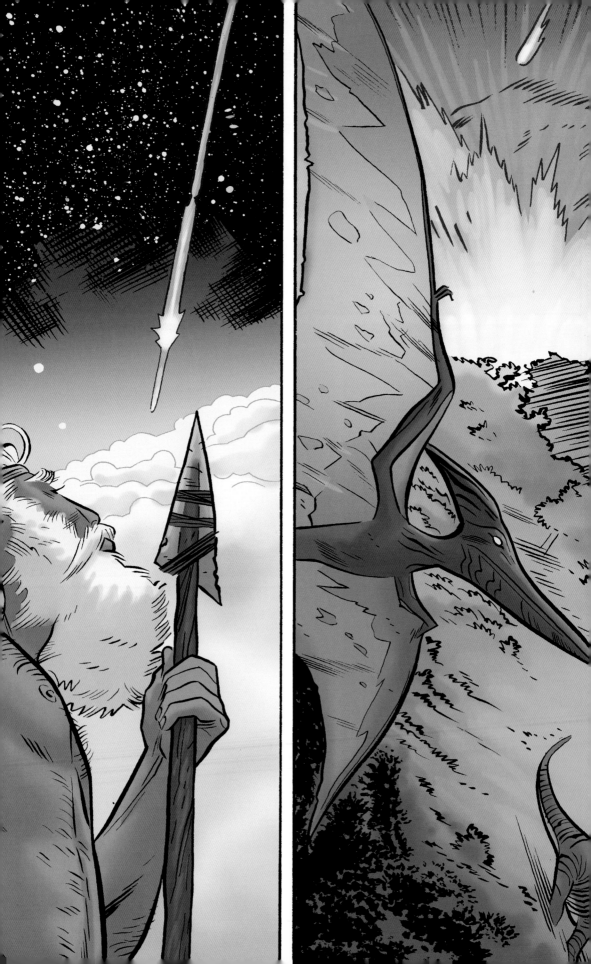

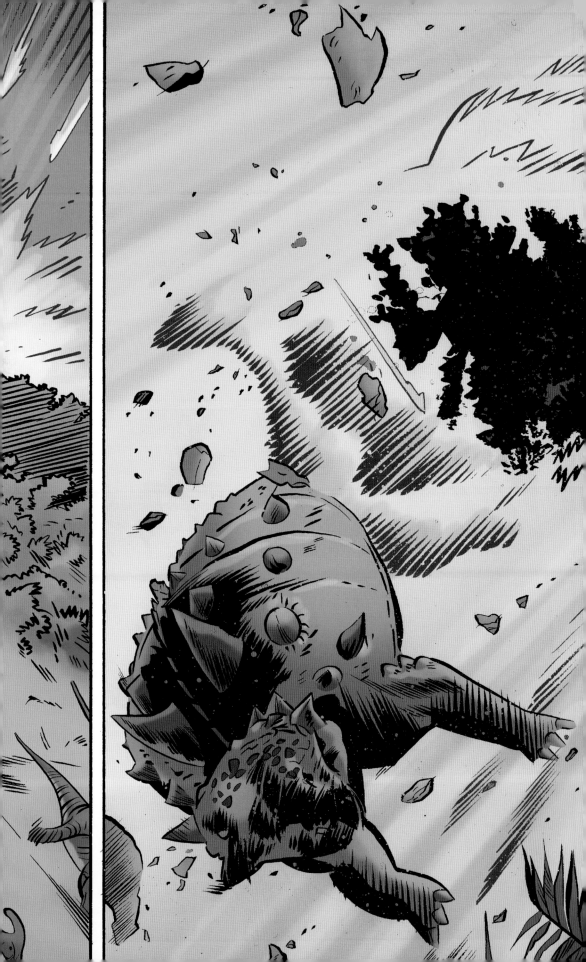

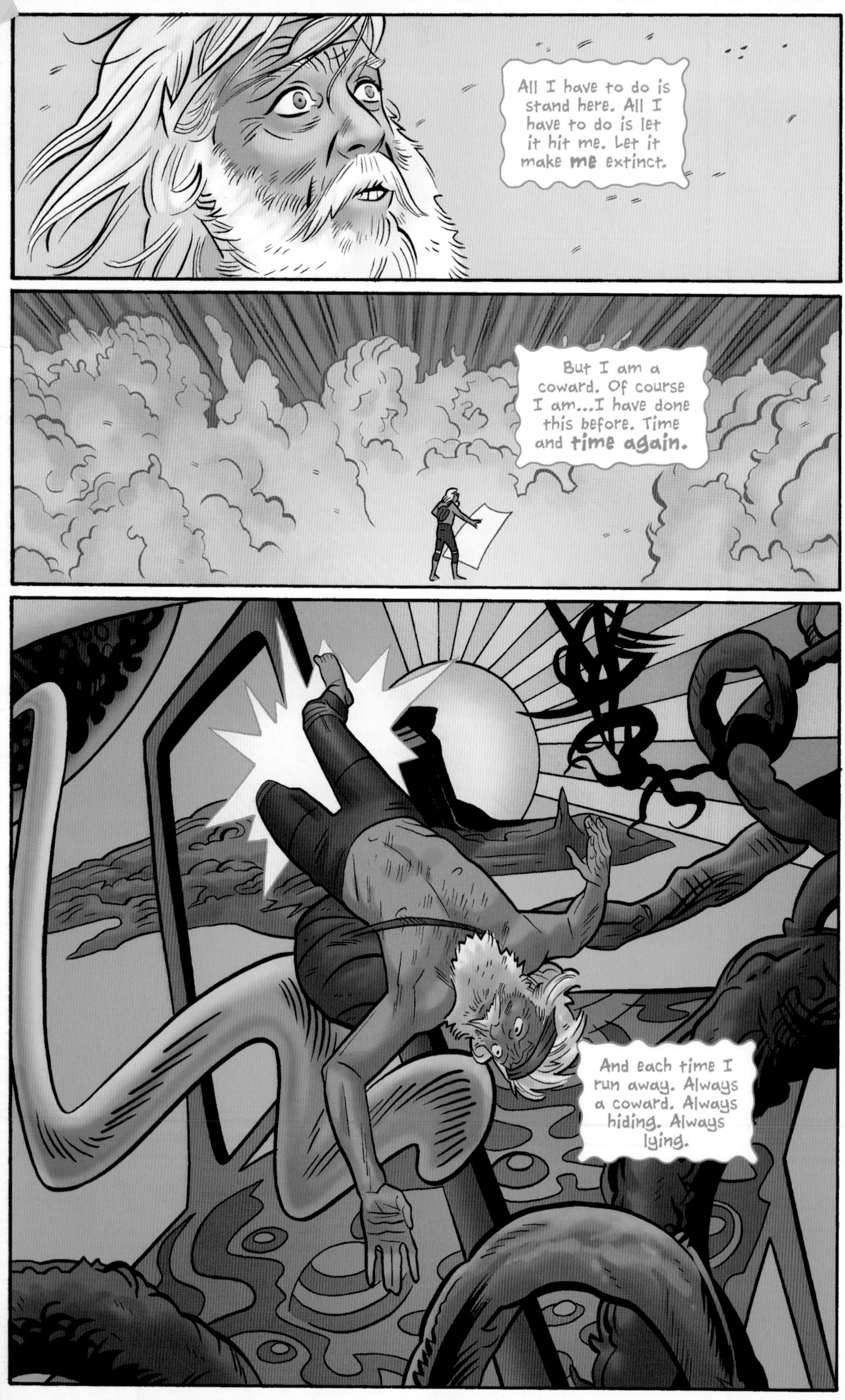
All I have to do is stand here. All I have to do is let it hit me. Let it make **me** extinct.
But I am a coward. Of course I am...I have done this before. Time and **time again.**
And each time I run away. Always a coward. Always hiding. Always lying.

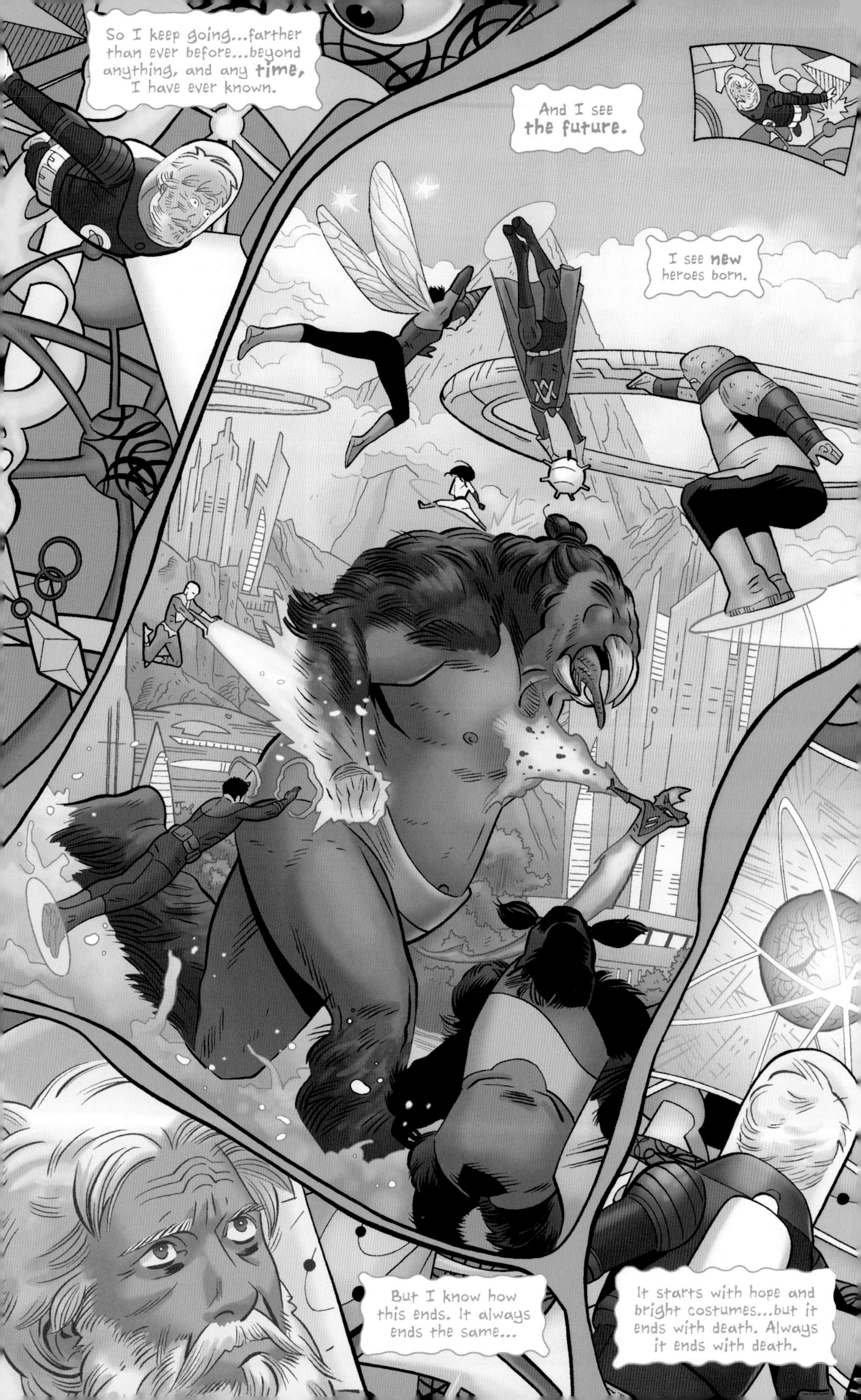
So I keep going...farther than ever before...beyond anything, and any time, I have ever known.
And I see the future.
I see new heroes born.
But I know how this ends. It always ends the same...
It starts with hope and bright costumes...but it ends with death. Always it ends with death.

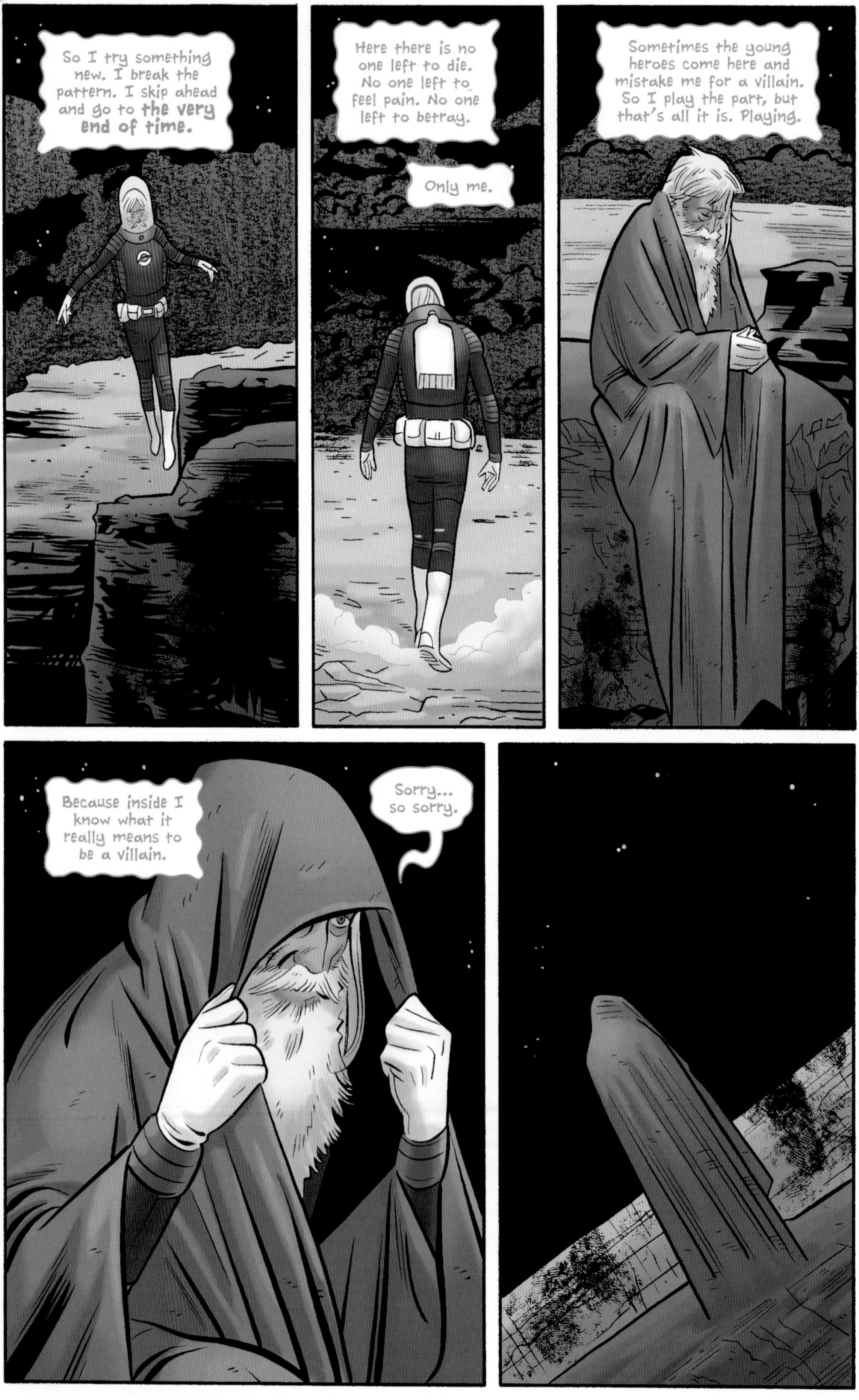

So I try something new. I break the pattern. I skip ahead and go to **the very end of time.**
Here there is no one left to die. No one left to feel pain. No one left to betray.
Only me.
Sometimes the young heroes come here and mistake me for a villain. So I play the part, but that's all it is. Playing.
Because inside I know what it really means to be a villain.
Sorry... so sorry.

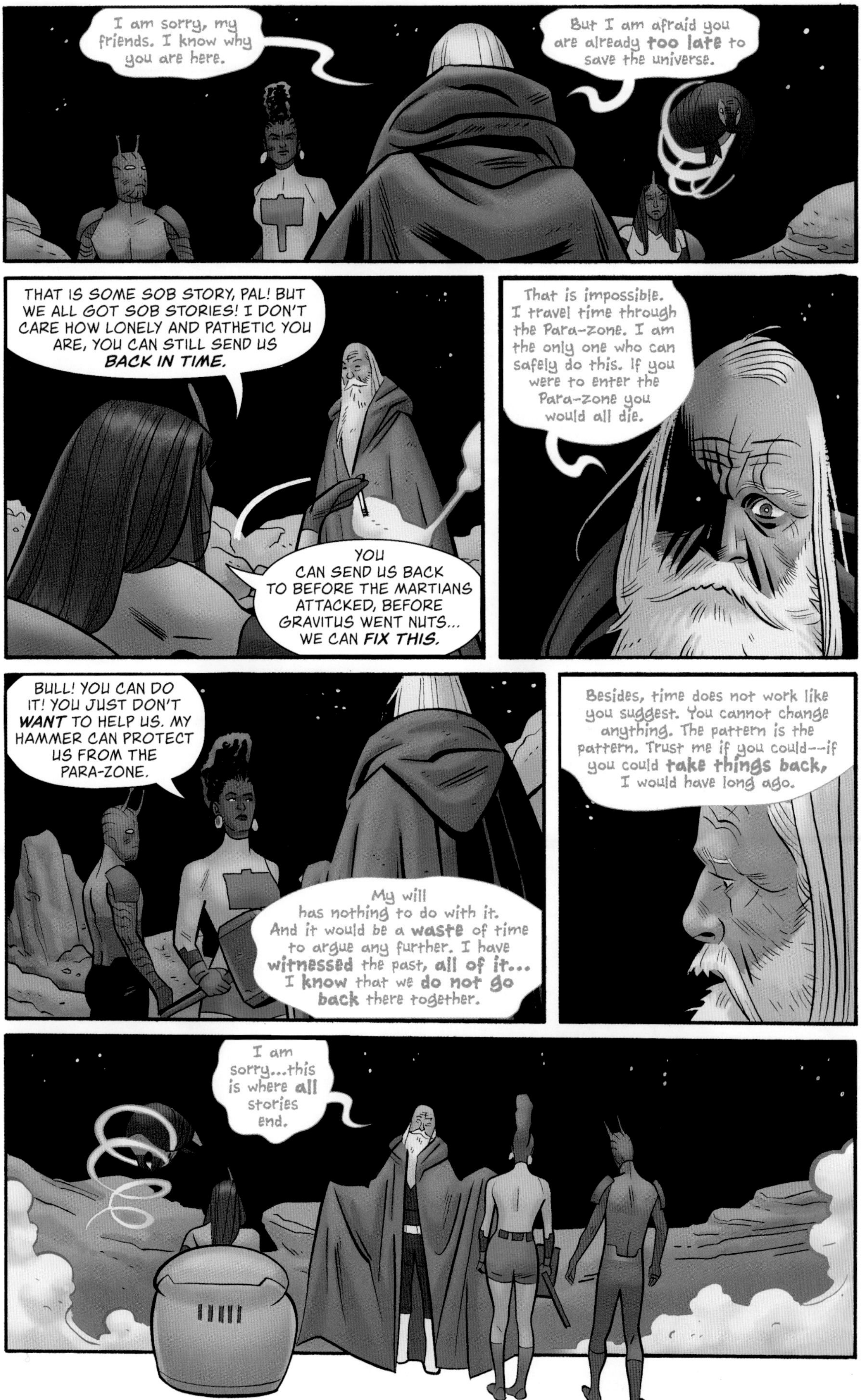

I am sorry, my friends. I know why you are here.
But I am afraid you are already too late to save the universe.
THAT IS SOME SOB STORY, PAL! BUT WE ALL GOT SOB STORIES! I DON'T CARE HOW LONELY AND PATHETIC YOU ARE, YOU CAN STILL SEND US BACK IN TIME.
YOU CAN SEND US BACK TO BEFORE THE MARTIANS ATTACKED, BEFORE GRAVITUS WENT NUTS... WE CAN FIX THIS.
That is impossible. I travel time through the Para-zone. I am the only one who can safely do this. If you were to enter the Para-zone you would all die.
BULL! YOU CAN DO IT! YOU JUST DON'T WANT TO HELP US. MY HAMMER CAN PROTECT US FROM THE PARA-ZONE.
My will has nothing to do with it. And it would be a waste of time to argue any further. I have witnessed the past, all of it... I know that we do not go back there together.
Besides, time does not work like you suggest. You cannot change anything. The pattern is the pattern. Trust me if you could--if you could take things back, I would have long ago.
I am sorry...this is where all stories end.

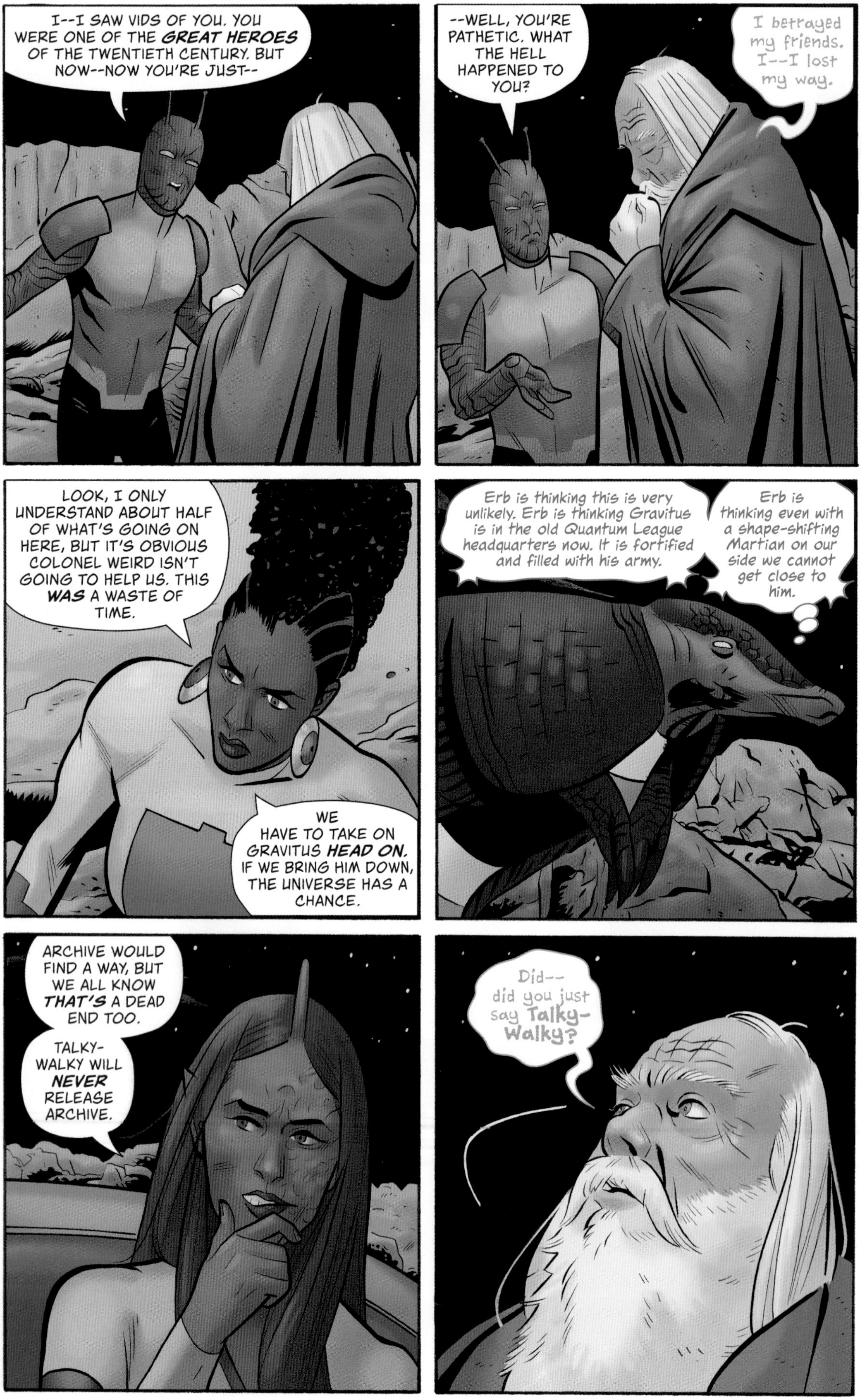
I--I SAW VIDS OF YOU. YOU WERE ONE OF THE **GREAT HEROES** OF THE TWENTIETH CENTURY. BUT NOW--NOW YOU'RE JUST--
--WELL, YOU'RE PATHETIC. WHAT THE HELL HAPPENED TO YOU?
I betrayed my friends. I--I lost my way.
LOOK, I ONLY UNDERSTAND ABOUT HALF OF WHAT'S GOING ON HERE, BUT IT'S OBVIOUS COLONEL WEIRD ISN'T GOING TO HELP US. THIS **WAS** A WASTE OF TIME.
WE HAVE TO TAKE ON GRAVITUS **HEAD ON.** IF WE BRING HIM DOWN, THE UNIVERSE HAS A CHANCE.
Erb is thinking this is very unlikely. Erb is thinking Gravitus is in the old Quantum League headquarters now. It is fortified and filled with his army.
Erb is thinking even with a shape-shifting Martian on our side we cannot get close to him.
ARCHIVE WOULD FIND A WAY, BUT WE ALL KNOW **THAT'S** A DEAD END TOO.
TALKY-WALKY WILL **NEVER** RELEASE ARCHIVE.
Did--did you just say Talky-Walky?

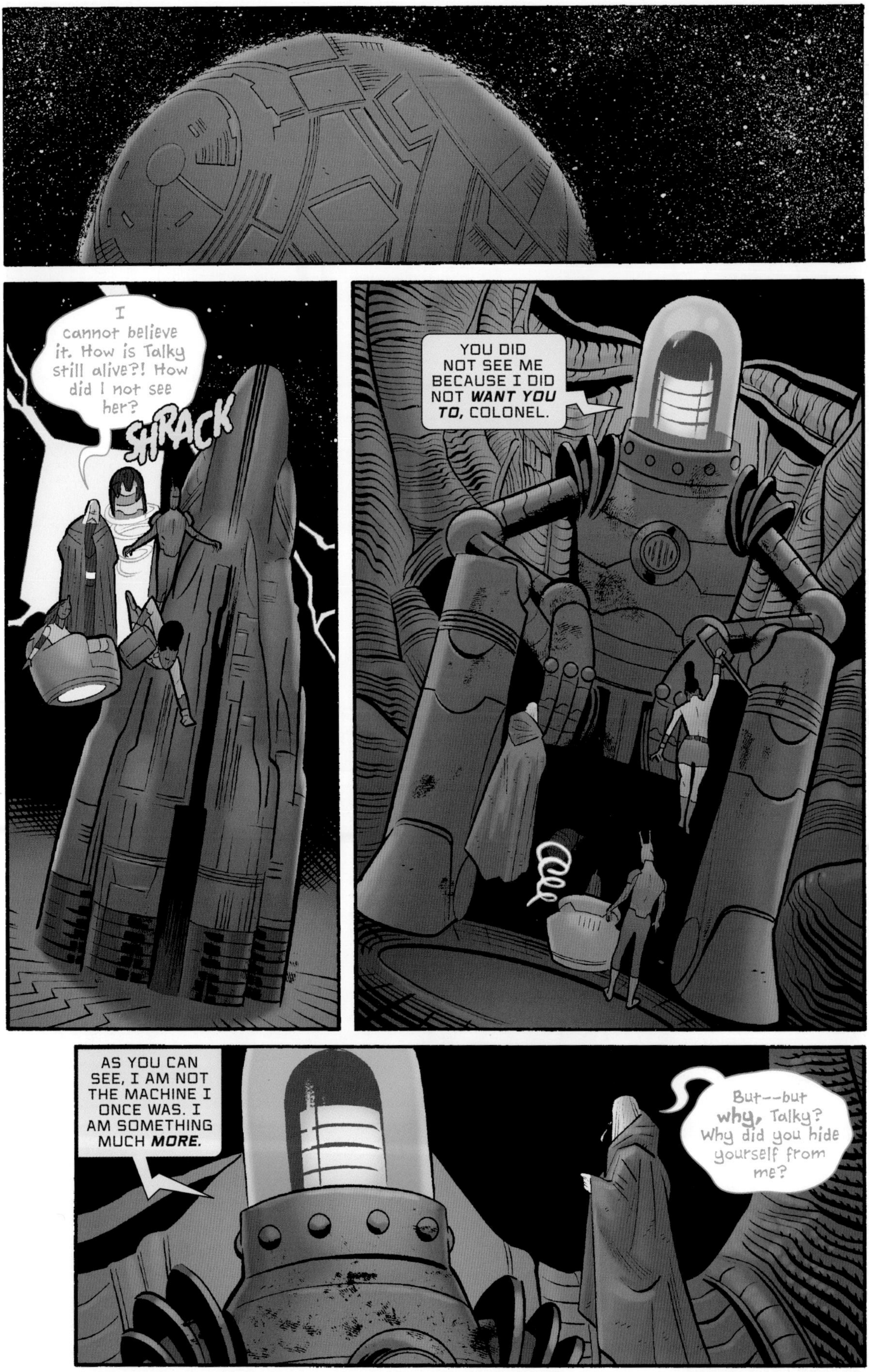
I cannot believe it. How is Talky still alive?! How did I not see her?
SHRACK
YOU DID NOT SEE ME BECAUSE I DID NOT WANT YOU TO, COLONEL.
AS YOU CAN SEE, I AM NOT THE MACHINE I ONCE WAS. I AM SOMETHING MUCH MORE.
But--but why, Talky? Why did you hide yourself from me?

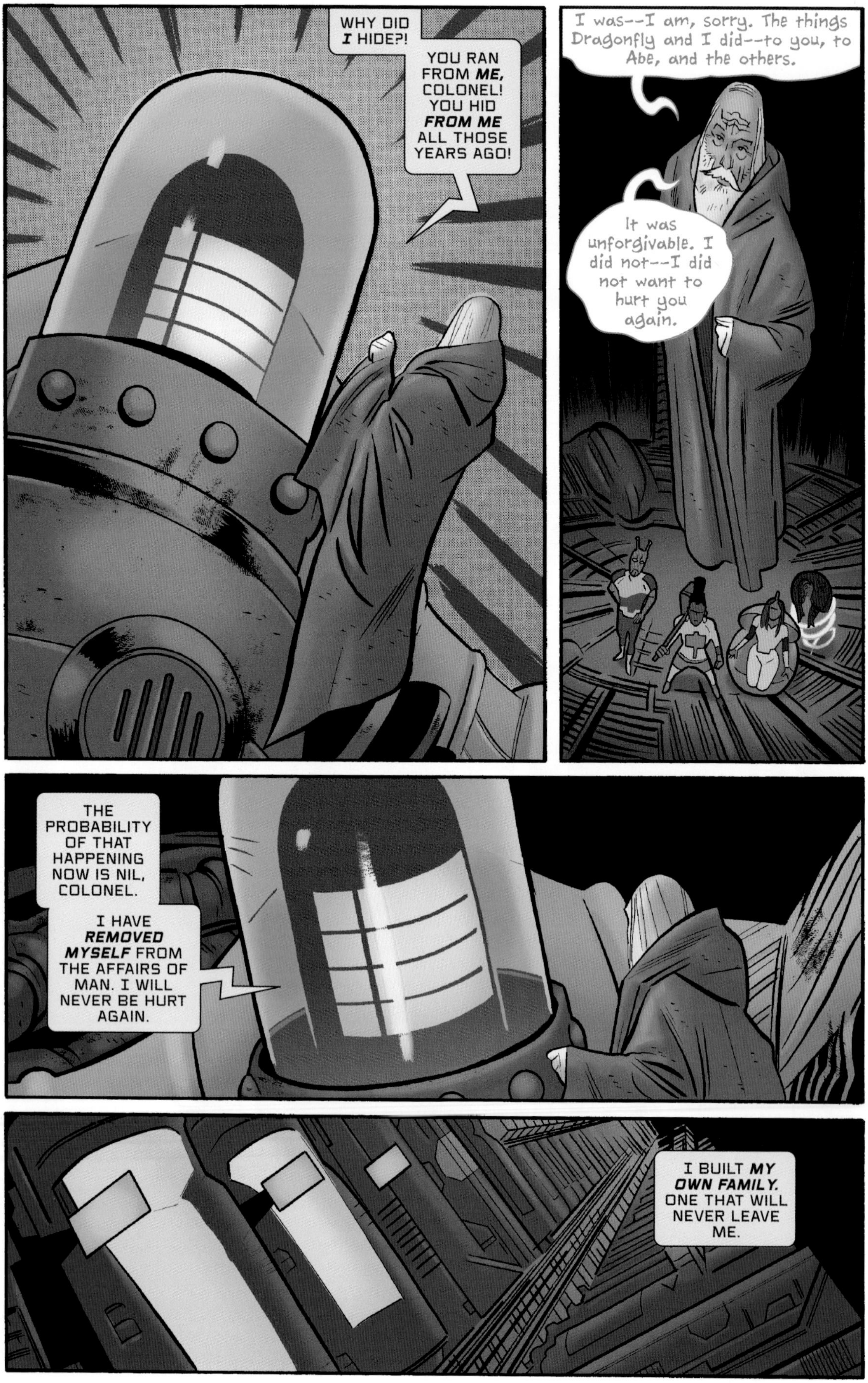
WHY DID I HIDE?!
YOU RAN FROM ME, COLONEL! YOU HID FROM ME ALL THOSE YEARS AGO!
I was--I am, sorry. The things Dragonfly and I did--to you, to Abe, and the others.
It was unforgivable. I did not--I did not want to hurt you again.
THE PROBABILITY OF THAT HAPPENING NOW IS NIL, COLONEL.
I HAVE REMOVED MYSELF FROM THE AFFAIRS OF MAN. I WILL NEVER BE HURT AGAIN.
I BUILT MY OWN FAMILY. ONE THAT WILL NEVER LEAVE ME.

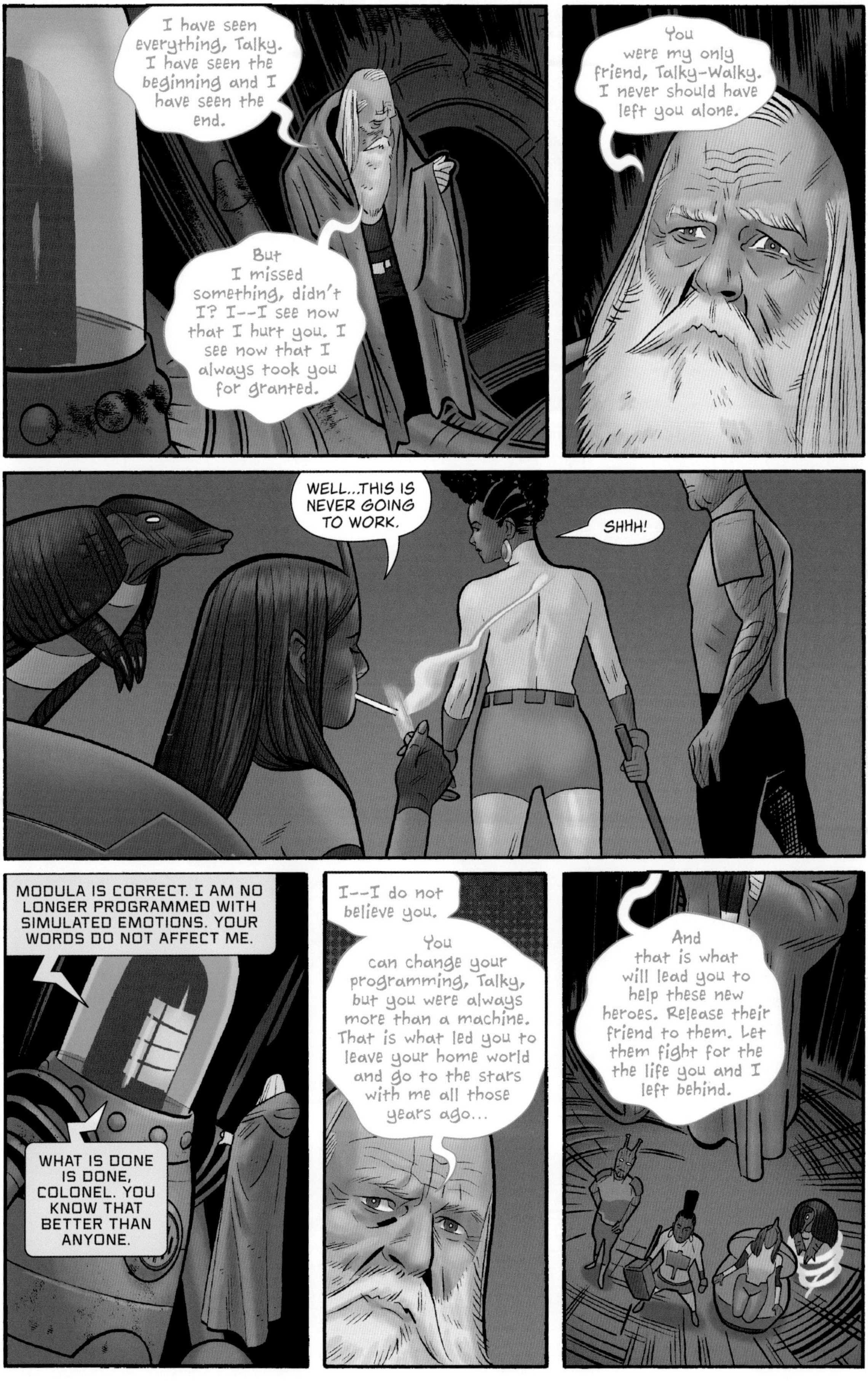
I have seen everything, Talky. I have seen the beginning and I have seen the end.
But I missed something, didn't I? I--I see now that I hurt you. I see now that I always took you for granted.
You were my only friend, Talky-Walky. I never should have left you alone.
WELL...THIS IS NEVER GOING TO WORK.
SHHH!
MODULA IS CORRECT. I AM NO LONGER PROGRAMMED WITH SIMULATED EMOTIONS. YOUR WORDS DO NOT AFFECT ME.
WHAT IS DONE IS DONE, COLONEL. YOU KNOW THAT BETTER THAN ANYONE.
I--I do not believe you.
You can change your programming, Talky, but you were always more than a machine. That is what led you to leave your home world and go to the stars with me all those years ago...
And that is what will lead you to help these new heroes. Release their friend to them. Let them fight for the the life you and I left behind.

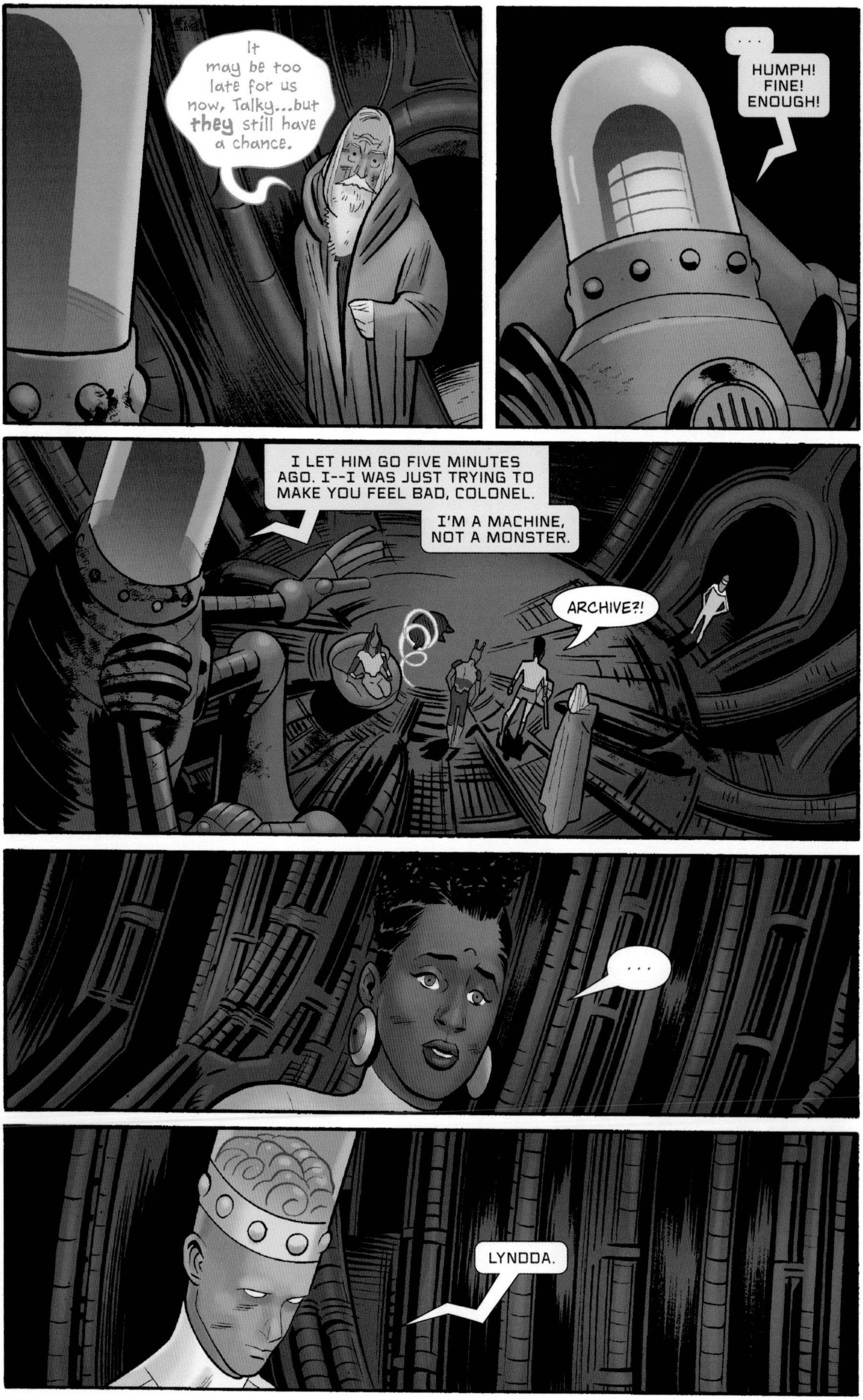

It may be too late for us now, Talky...but they still have a chance.
...
HUMPH! FINE! ENOUGH!
I LET HIM GO FIVE MINUTES AGO. I--I WAS JUST TRYING TO MAKE YOU FEEL BAD, COLONEL.
I'M A MACHINE, NOT A MONSTER.
ARCHIVE?!
...
LYNDDA.

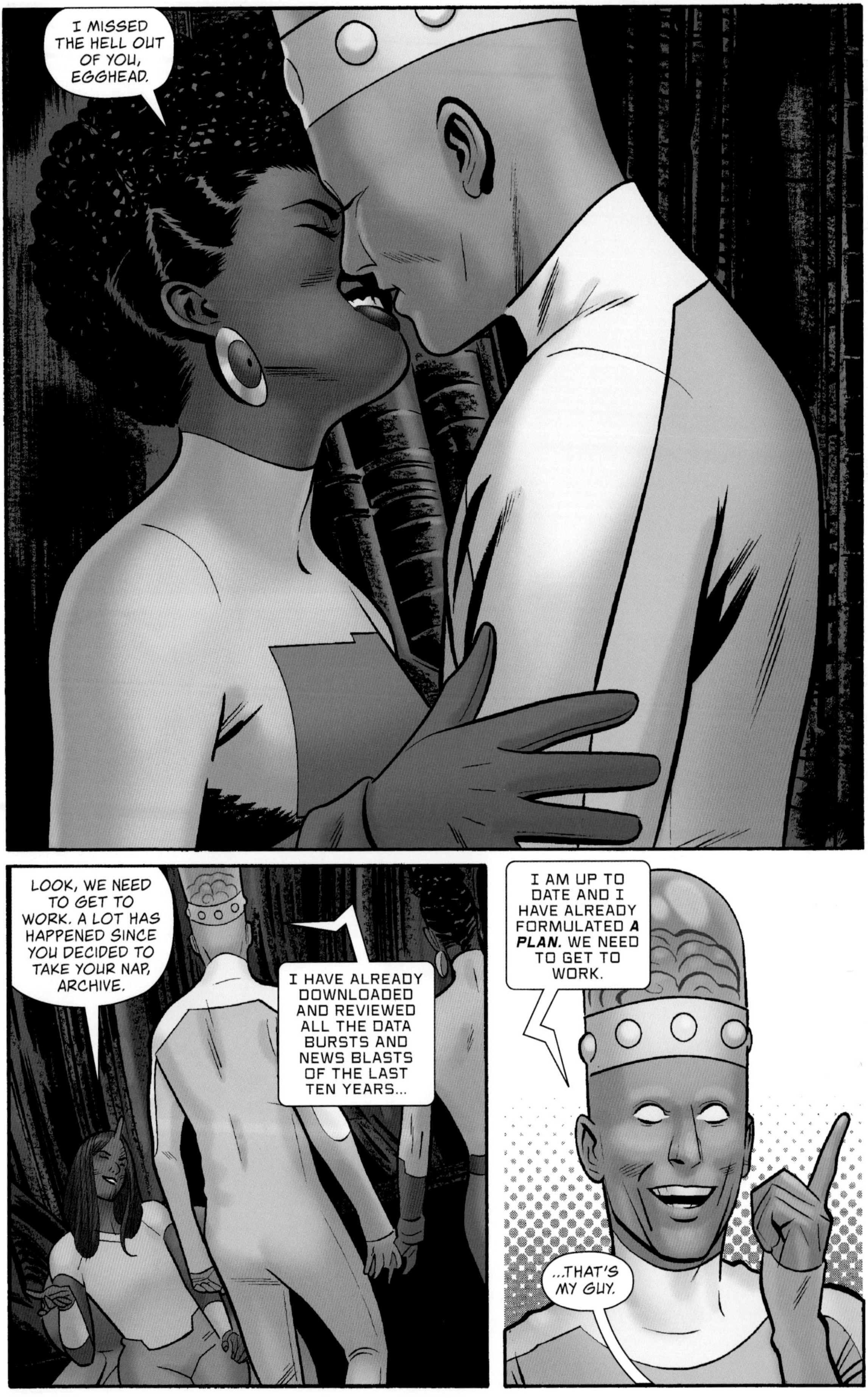
I MISSED THE HELL OUT OF YOU, EGGHEAD.
LOOK, WE NEED TO GET TO WORK. A LOT HAS HAPPENED SINCE YOU DECIDED TO TAKE YOUR NAP, ARCHIVE.
I HAVE ALREADY DOWNLOADED AND REVIEWED ALL THE DATA BURSTS AND NEWS BLASTS OF THE LAST TEN YEARS...
I AM UP TO DATE AND I HAVE ALREADY FORMULATED **A PLAN.** WE NEED TO GET TO WORK.
...THAT'S MY GUY.

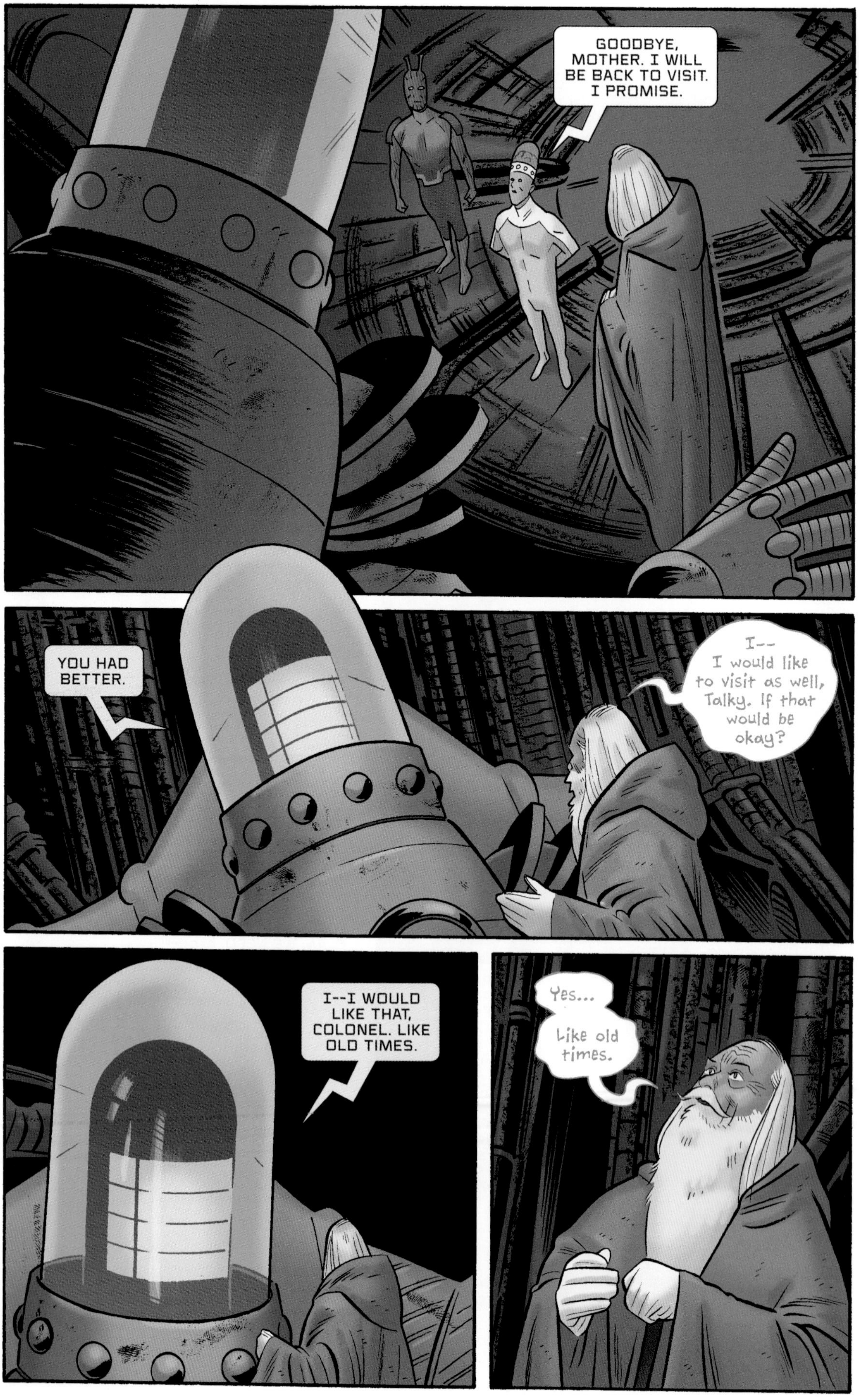
GOODBYE, MOTHER. I WILL BE BACK TO VISIT. I PROMISE.
YOU HAD BETTER.
I-- I would like to visit as well, Talky. If that would be okay?
I--I WOULD LIKE THAT, COLONEL. LIKE OLD TIMES.
Yes...
Like old times.

HOURS LATER.

Erb thinking that the ship will be arriving on Earth in less than an hour.

LET'S HOPE THE OLD CLOAKING DEVICE IS STILL WORKING.

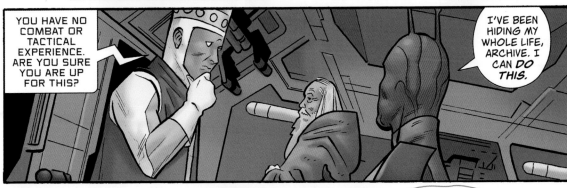

YOU HAVE NO COMBAT OR TACTICAL EXPERIENCE. ARE YOU SURE YOU ARE UP FOR THIS?

I'VE BEEN HIDING MY WHOLE LIFE, ARCHIVE. I CAN **DO THIS.**

WAIT, WHY ALL THE ESPIONAGE? WHY CAN'T WEIRD JUST TELEPORT US CLOSE TO GRAVITUS AND THEN I'LL SMASH HIS BRAINS IN WITH MY HAMMER?

That will not work. He is too powerful. Besides, I will not be there to help.

WHAT DO YOU MEAN?! WHERE THE HELL ARE YOU GOING?!

There is somewhere else I must be. **Someone else** I must see.

Goodbye. I hope to see you all again.

SHRAK

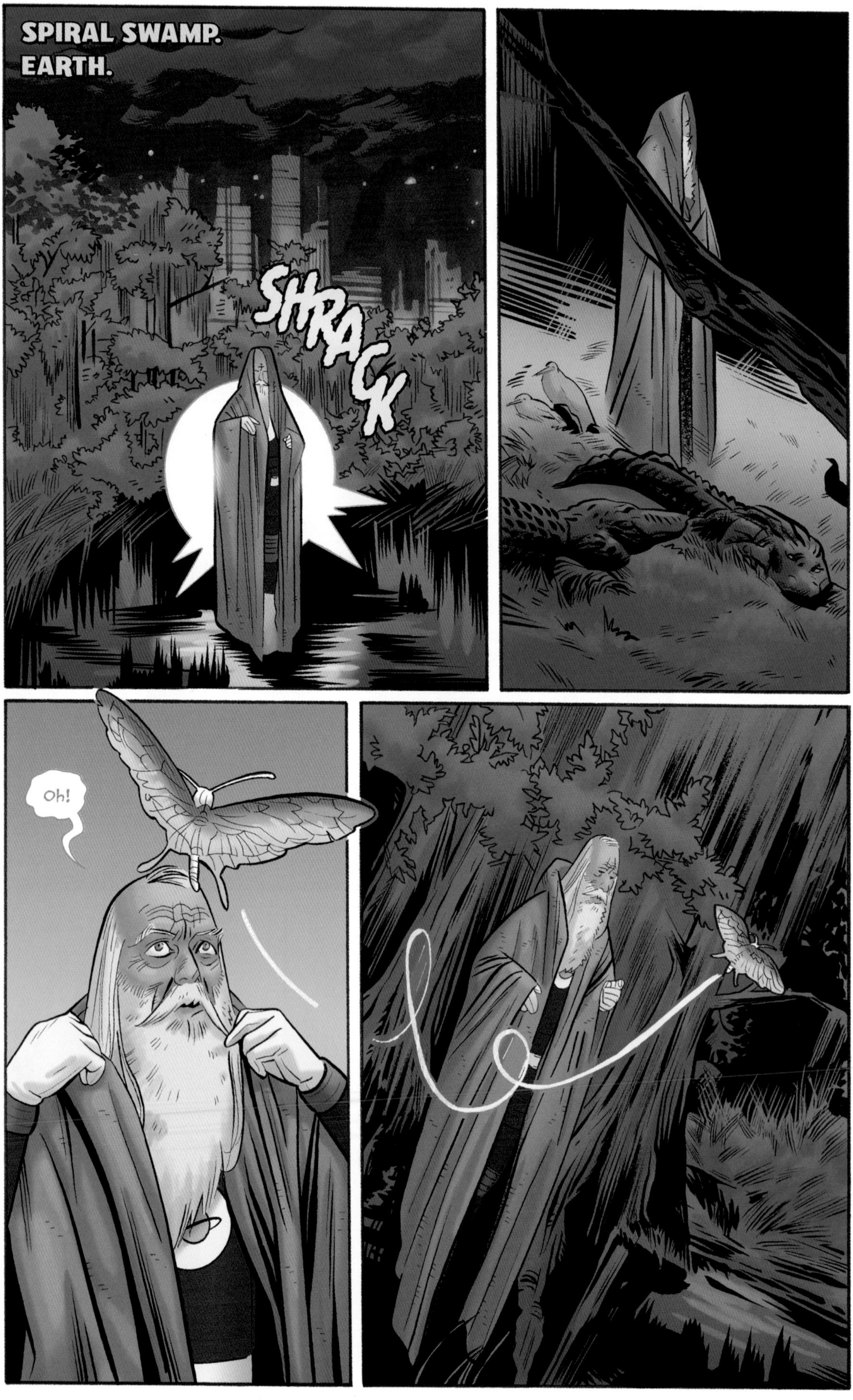
SPIRAL SWAMP.
EARTH.
SHRACK
Oh!

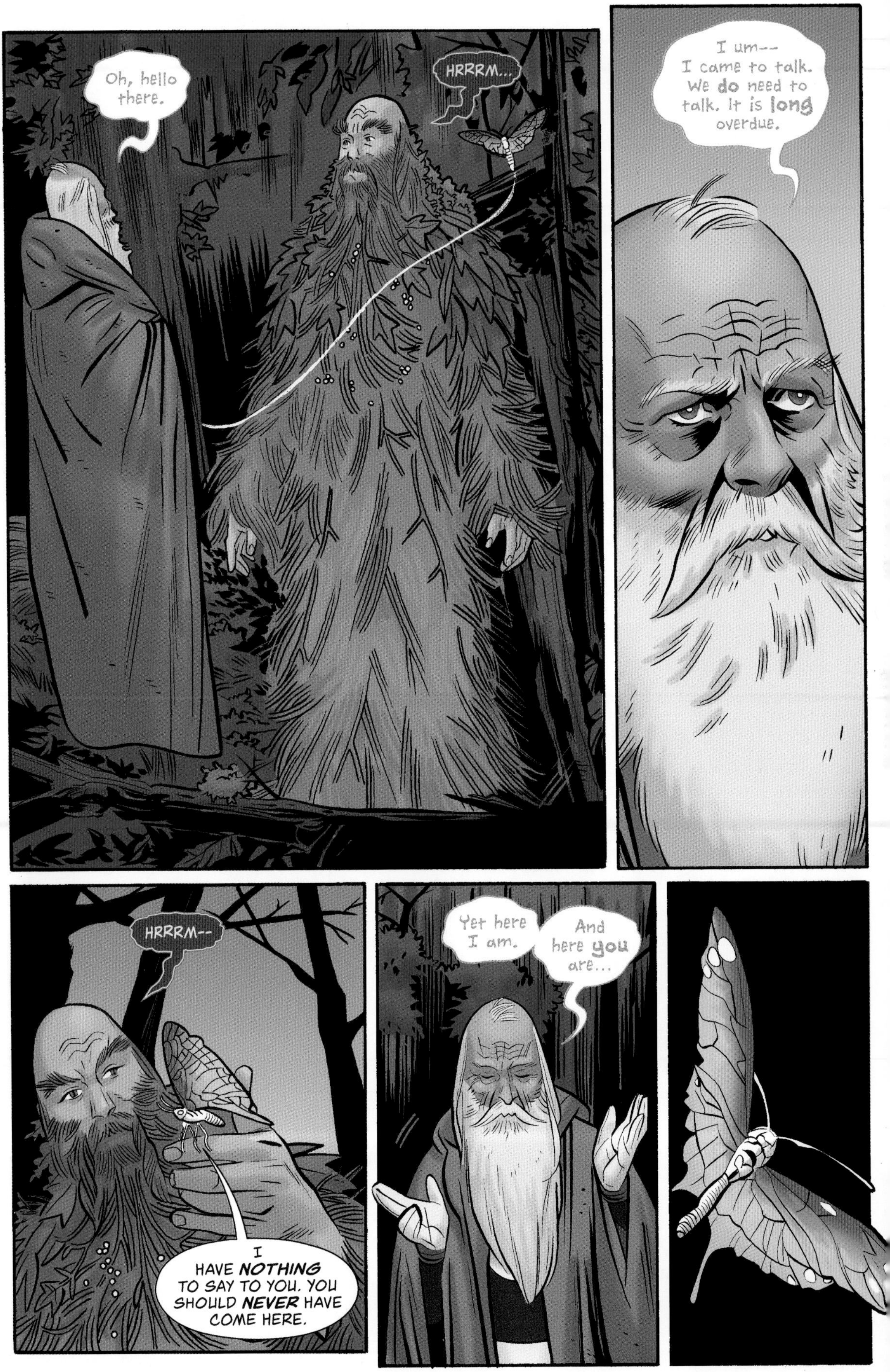
Oh, hello there.
HRRRM...
I um-- I came to talk. We do need to talk. It is long overdue.
HRRRM--
I HAVE NOTHING TO SAY TO YOU. YOU SHOULD NEVER HAVE COME HERE.
Yet here I am.
And here you are...

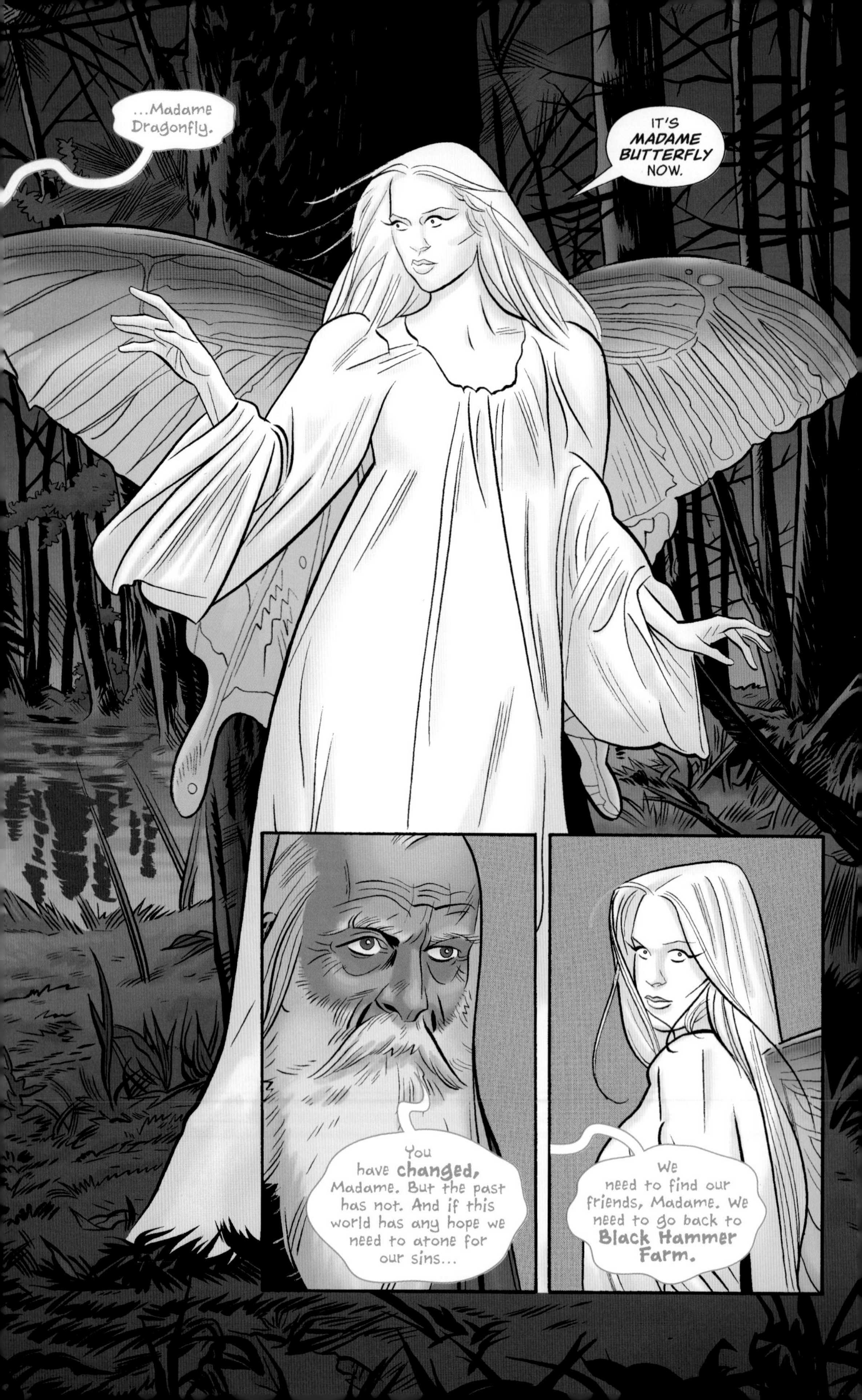
...Madame Dragonfly.
IT'S MADAME BUTTERFLY NOW.
You have changed, Madame. But the past has not. And if this world has any hope we need to atone for our sins...
We need to find our friends, Madame. We need to go back to Black Hammer Farm.

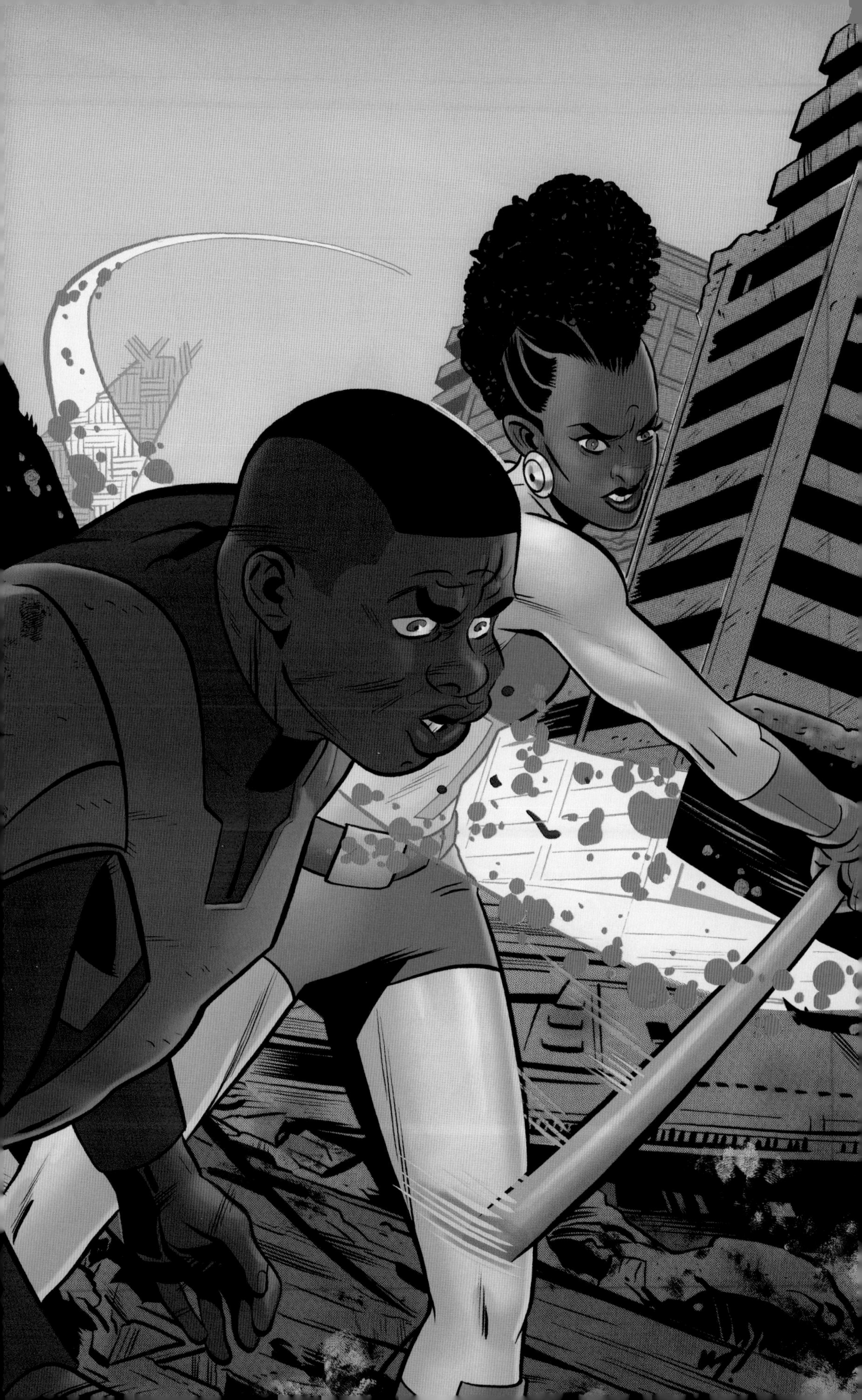

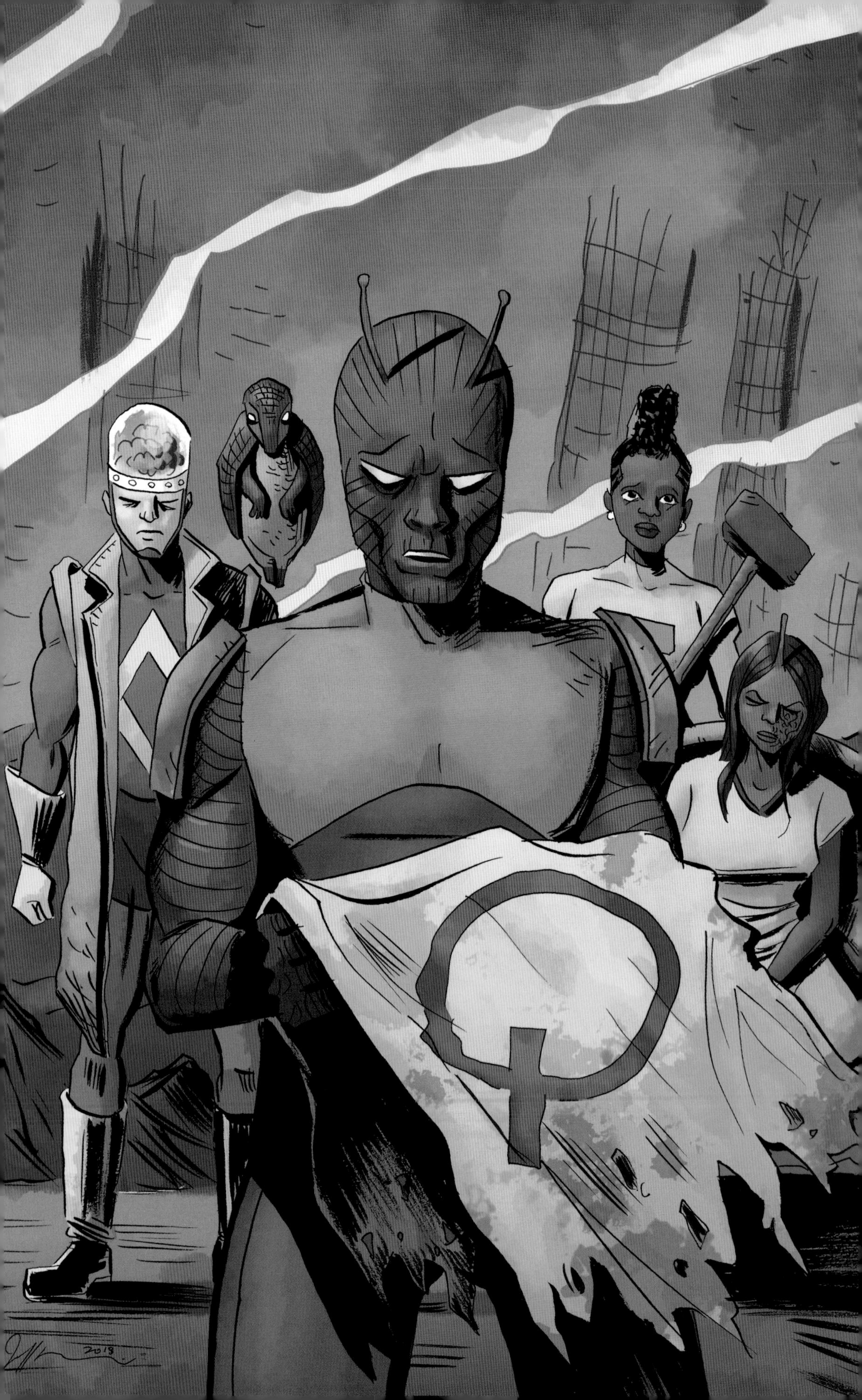

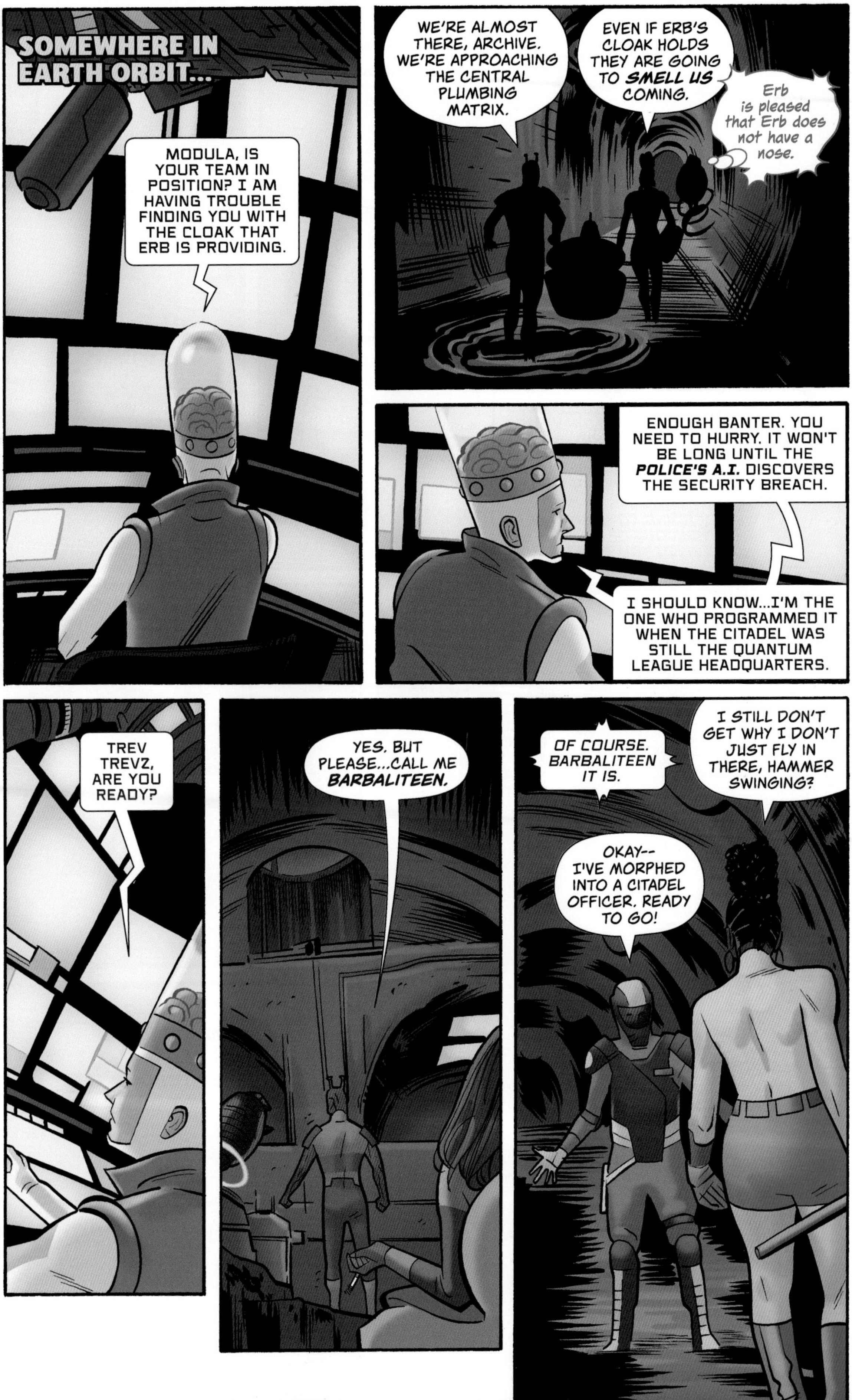
SOMEWHERE IN EARTH ORBIT...
MODULA, IS YOUR TEAM IN POSITION? I AM HAVING TROUBLE FINDING YOU WITH THE CLOAK THAT ERB IS PROVIDING.
WE'RE ALMOST THERE, ARCHIVE. WE'RE APPROACHING THE CENTRAL PLUMBING MATRIX.
EVEN IF ERB'S CLOAK HOLDS THEY ARE GOING TO SMELL US COMING.
Erb is pleased that Erb does not have a nose.
ENOUGH BANTER. YOU NEED TO HURRY. IT WON'T BE LONG UNTIL THE POLICE'S A.I. DISCOVERS THE SECURITY BREACH.
I SHOULD KNOW...I'M THE ONE WHO PROGRAMMED IT WHEN THE CITADEL WAS STILL THE QUANTUM LEAGUE HEADQUARTERS.
TREV TREVZ, ARE YOU READY?
YES. BUT PLEASE...CALL ME BARBALITEEN.
OF COURSE. BARBALITEEN IT IS.
I STILL DON'T GET WHY I DON'T JUST FLY IN THERE, HAMMER SWINGING?
OKAY-- I'VE MORPHED INTO A CITADEL OFFICER. READY TO GO!

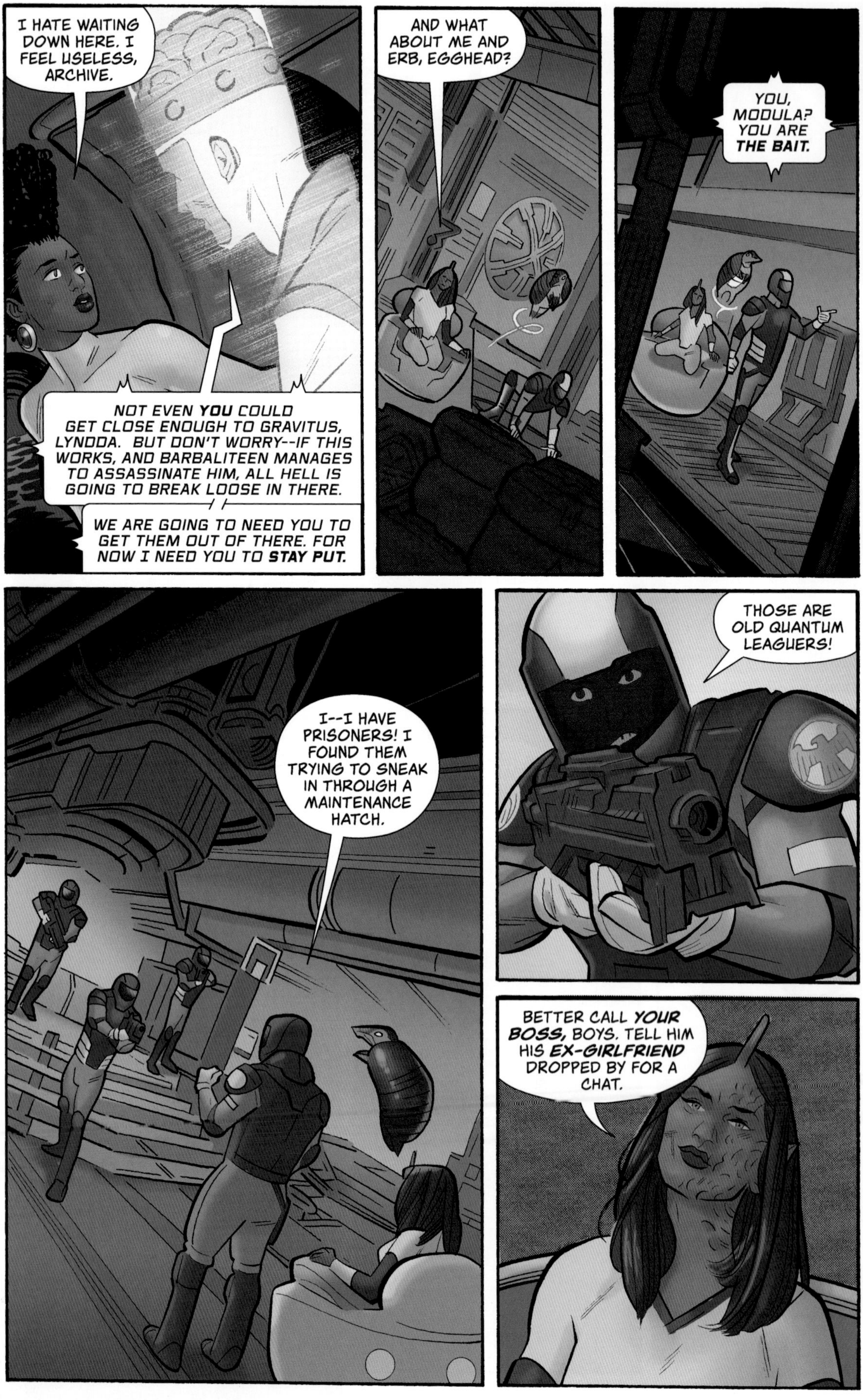

I HATE WAITING DOWN HERE. I FEEL USELESS, ARCHIVE.
NOT EVEN YOU COULD GET CLOSE ENOUGH TO GRAVITUS, LYNDDA. BUT DON'T WORRY--IF THIS WORKS, AND BARBALITEEN MANAGES TO ASSASSINATE HIM, ALL HELL IS GOING TO BREAK LOOSE IN THERE.
WE ARE GOING TO NEED YOU TO GET THEM OUT OF THERE. FOR NOW I NEED YOU TO STAY PUT.
AND WHAT ABOUT ME AND ERB, EGGHEAD?
YOU, MODULA? YOU ARE THE BAIT.
I--I HAVE PRISONERS! I FOUND THEM TRYING TO SNEAK IN THROUGH A MAINTENANCE HATCH.
THOSE ARE OLD QUANTUM LEAGUERS!
BETTER CALL YOUR BOSS, BOYS. TELL HIM HIS EX-GIRLFRIEND DROPPED BY FOR A CHAT.

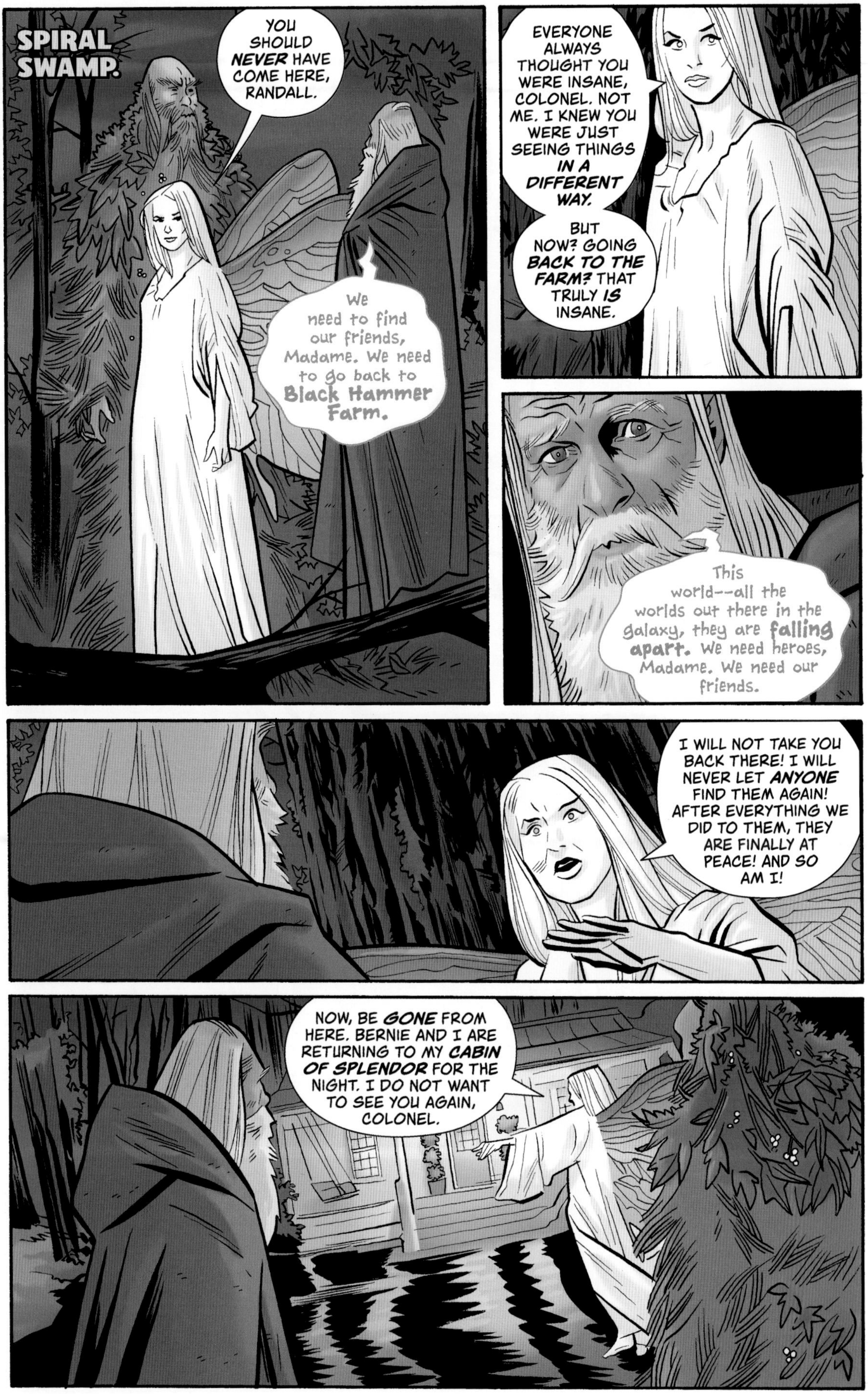
SPIRAL SWAMP.
YOU SHOULD NEVER HAVE COME HERE, RANDALL.
We need to find our friends, Madame. We need to go back to Black Hammer Farm.
EVERYONE ALWAYS THOUGHT YOU WERE INSANE, COLONEL. NOT ME. I KNEW YOU WERE JUST SEEING THINGS IN A DIFFERENT WAY.
BUT NOW? GOING BACK TO THE FARM? THAT TRULY IS INSANE.
This world--all the worlds out there in the galaxy, they are falling apart. We need heroes, Madame. We need our friends.
I WILL NOT TAKE YOU BACK THERE! I WILL NEVER LET ANYONE FIND THEM AGAIN! AFTER EVERYTHING WE DID TO THEM, THEY ARE FINALLY AT PEACE! AND SO AM I!
NOW, BE GONE FROM HERE. BERNIE AND I ARE RETURNING TO MY CABIN OF SPLENDOR FOR THE NIGHT. I DO NOT WANT TO SEE YOU AGAIN, COLONEL.

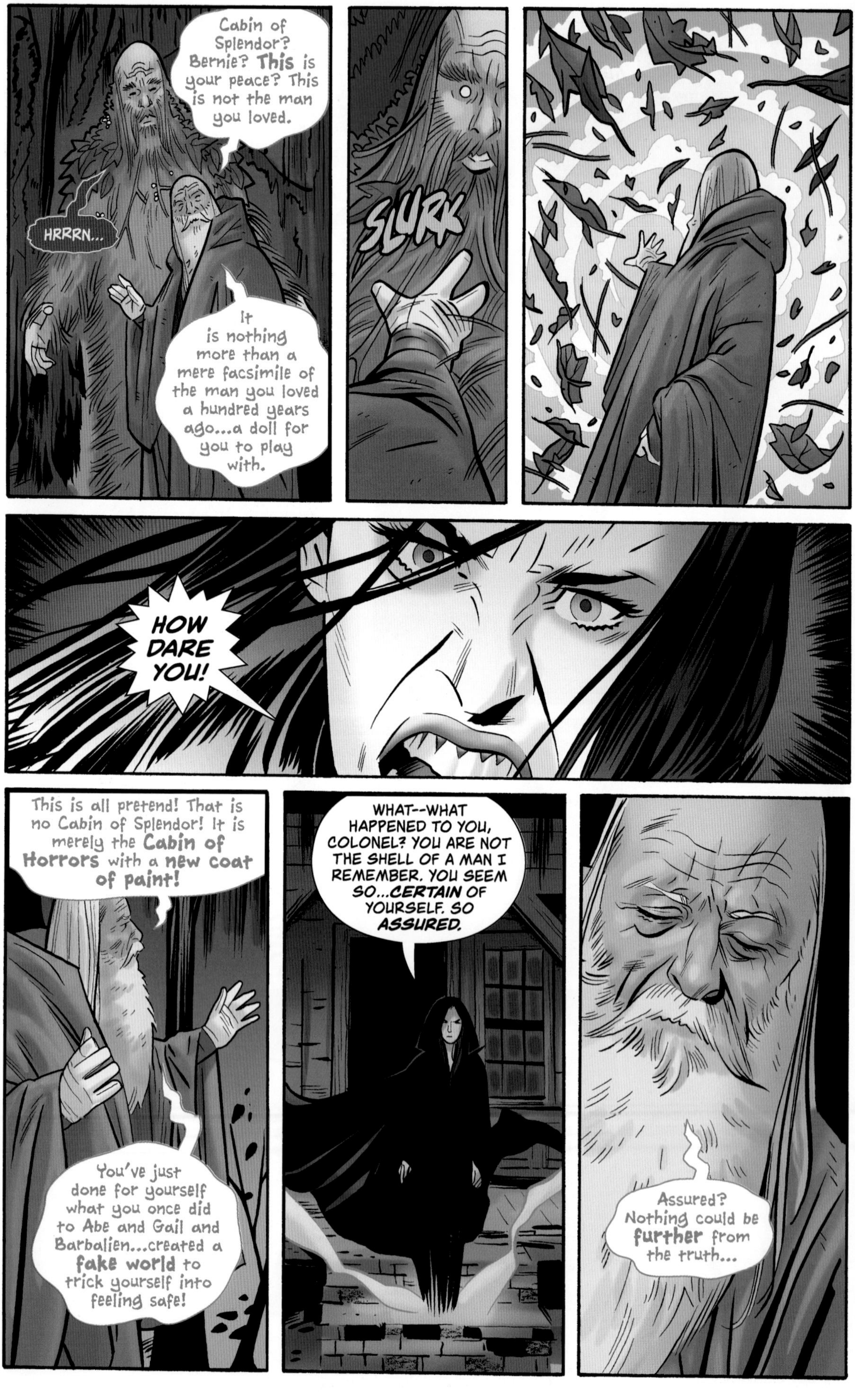
Cabin of Splendor? Bernie? This is your peace? This is not the man you loved.
HRRRN...
It is nothing more than a mere facsimile of the man you loved a hundred years ago...a doll for you to play with.
SLURK
HOW DARE YOU!
This is all pretend! That is no Cabin of Splendor! It is merely the Cabin of Horrors with a new coat of paint!
You've just done for yourself what you once did to Abe and Gail and Barbalien...created a fake world to trick yourself into feeling safe!
WHAT--WHAT HAPPENED TO YOU, COLONEL? YOU ARE NOT THE SHELL OF A MAN I REMEMBER. YOU SEEM SO...CERTAIN OF YOURSELF. SO ASSURED.
Assured? Nothing could be further from the truth...

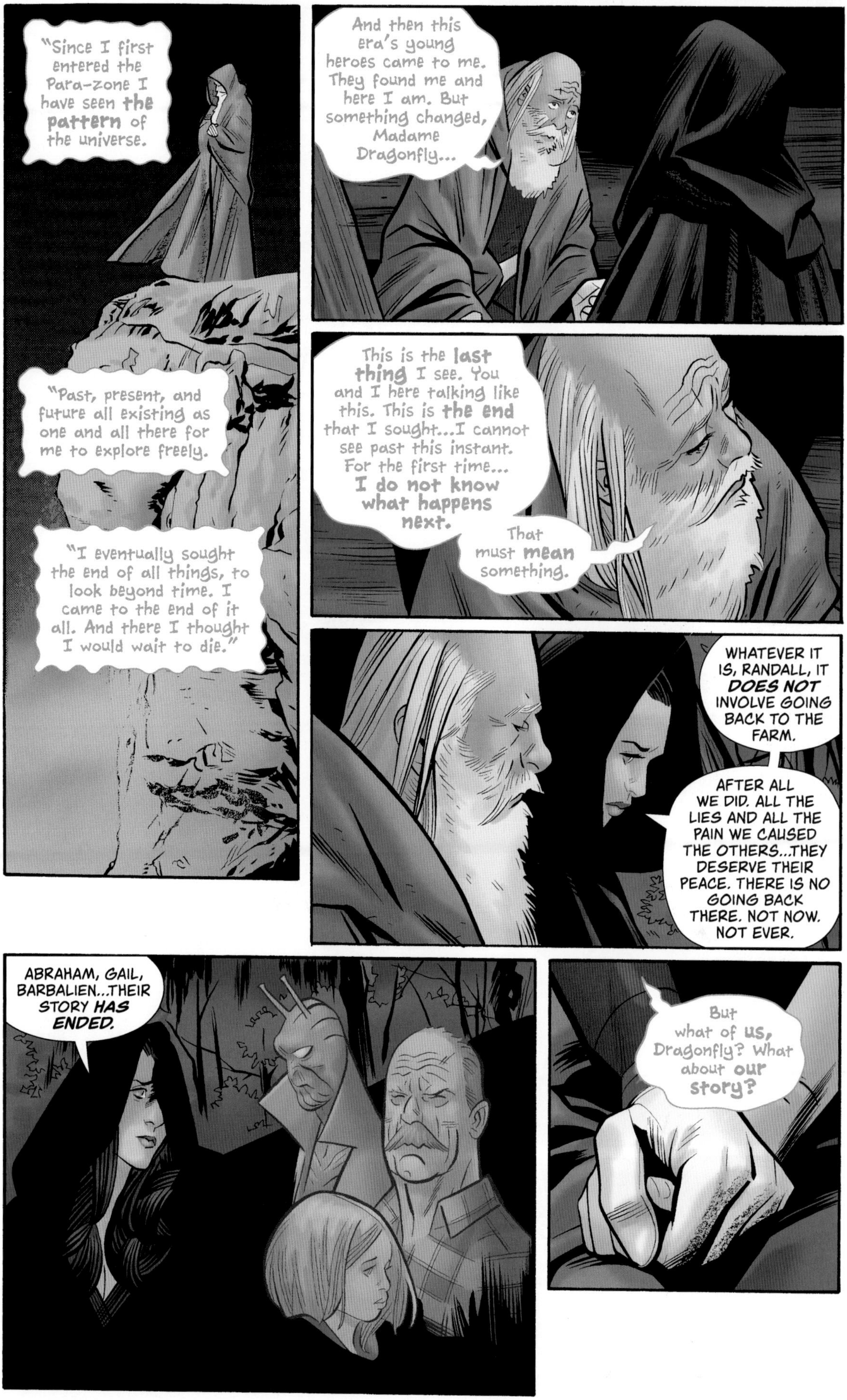
"Since I first entered the Para-zone I have seen the pattern of the universe.
"Past, present, and future all existing as one and all there for me to explore freely.
"I eventually sought the end of all things, to look beyond time. I came to the end of it all. And there I thought I would wait to die."
And then this era's young heroes came to me. They found me and here I am. But something changed, Madame Dragonfly...
This is the last thing I see. You and I here talking like this. This is the end that I sought...I cannot see past this instant. For the first time... I do not know what happens next.
That must mean something.
WHATEVER IT IS, RANDALL, IT DOES NOT INVOLVE GOING BACK TO THE FARM.
AFTER ALL WE DID. ALL THE LIES AND ALL THE PAIN WE CAUSED THE OTHERS...THEY DESERVE THEIR PEACE. THERE IS NO GOING BACK THERE. NOT NOW. NOT EVER.
ABRAHAM, GAIL, BARBALIEN...THEIR STORY HAS ENDED.
But what of us, Dragonfly? What about our story?

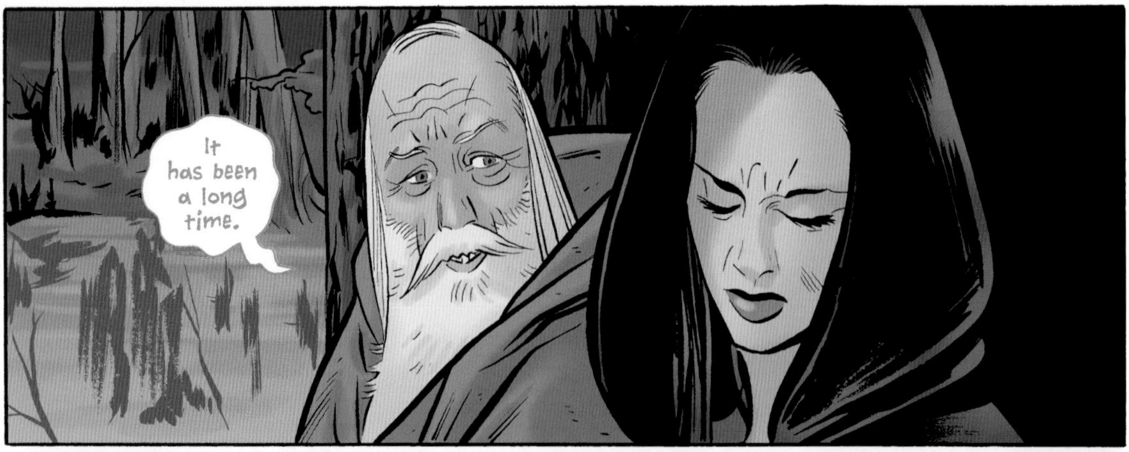
It has been a long time.

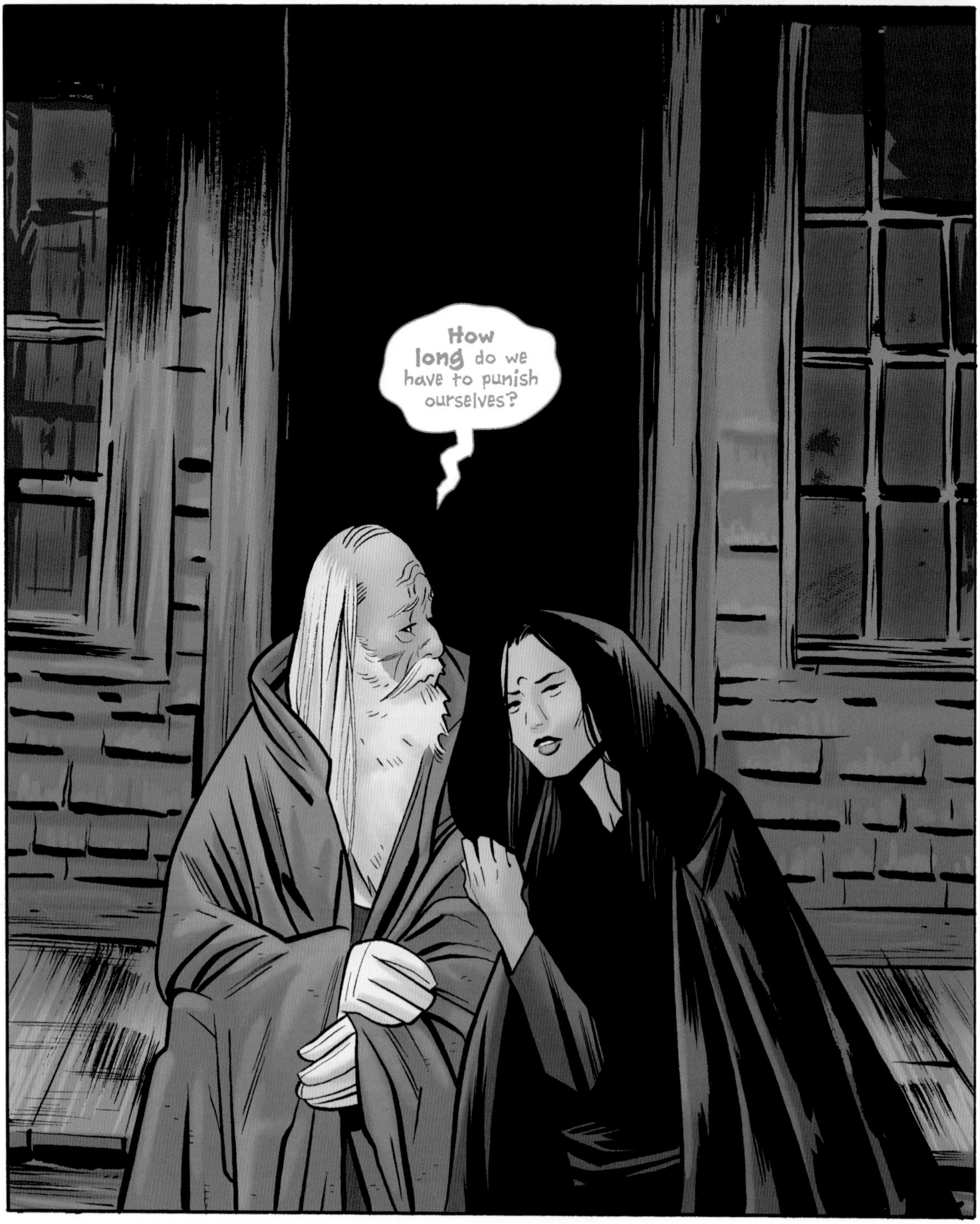
How long do we have to punish ourselves?

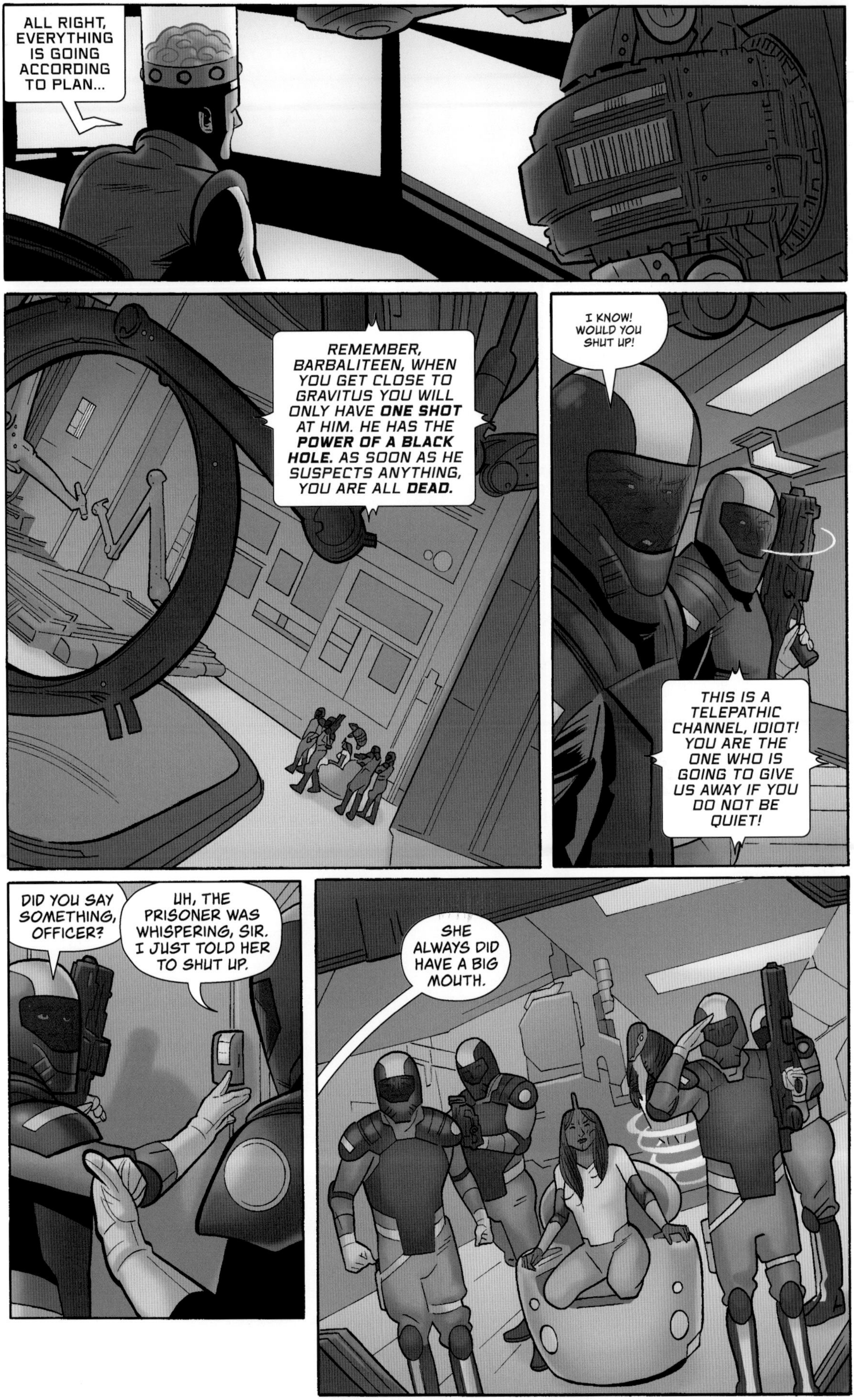
ALL RIGHT, EVERYTHING IS GOING ACCORDING TO PLAN...
REMEMBER, BARBALITEEN, WHEN YOU GET CLOSE TO GRAVITUS YOU WILL ONLY HAVE **ONE SHOT** AT HIM. HE HAS THE **POWER OF A BLACK HOLE.** AS SOON AS HE SUSPECTS ANYTHING, YOU ARE ALL **DEAD.**
I KNOW! WOULD YOU SHUT UP!
THIS IS A TELEPATHIC CHANNEL, IDIOT! YOU ARE THE ONE WHO IS GOING TO GIVE US AWAY IF YOU DO NOT BE QUIET!
DID YOU SAY SOMETHING, OFFICER?
UH, THE PRISONER WAS WHISPERING, SIR. I JUST TOLD HER TO SHUT UP.
SHE ALWAYS DID HAVE A BIG MOUTH.

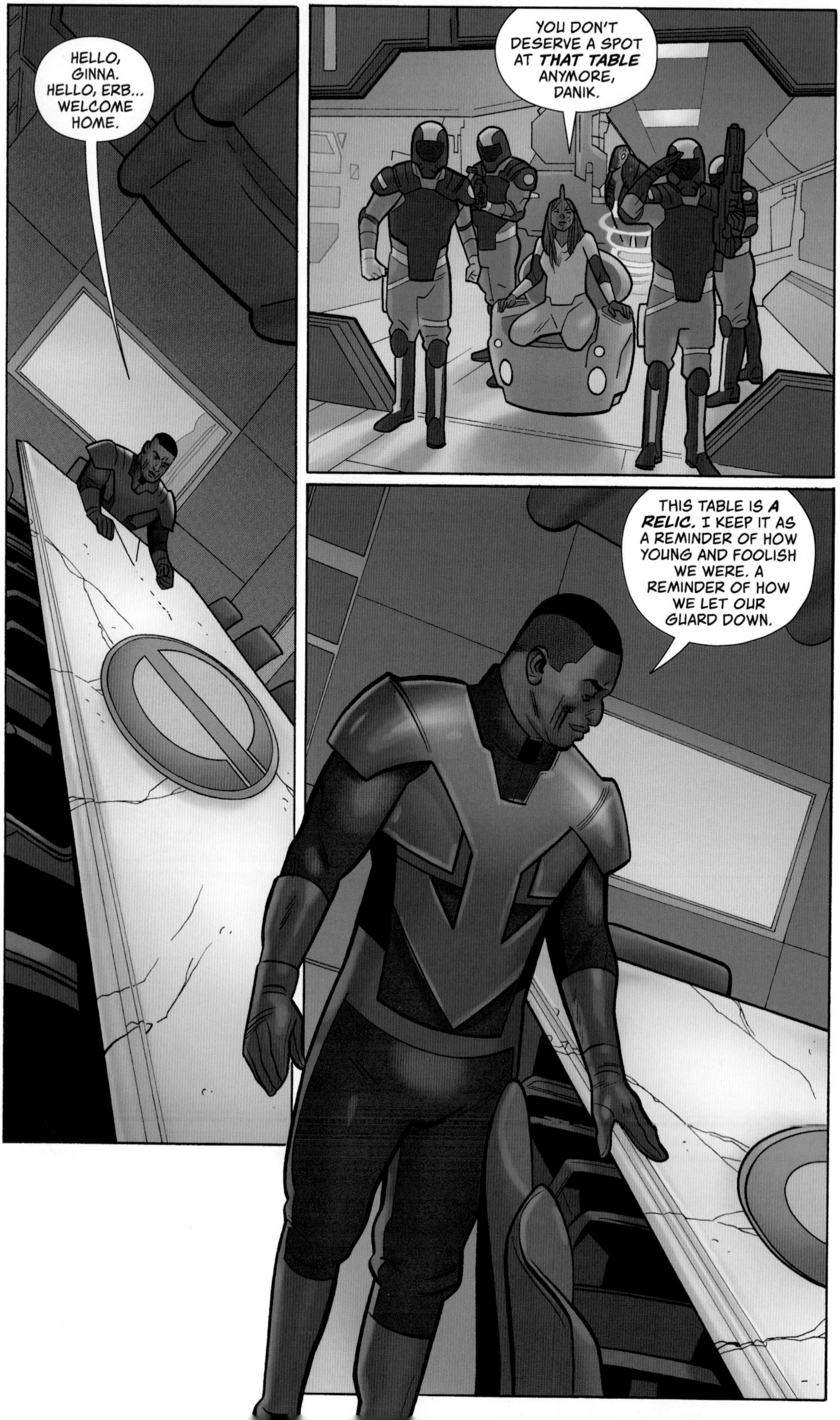
HELLO, GINNA. HELLO, ERB... WELCOME HOME.
YOU DON'T DESERVE A SPOT AT THAT TABLE ANYMORE, DANIK.
THIS TABLE IS A RELIC. I KEEP IT AS A REMINDER OF HOW YOUNG AND FOOLISH WE WERE. A REMINDER OF HOW WE LET OUR GUARD DOWN.

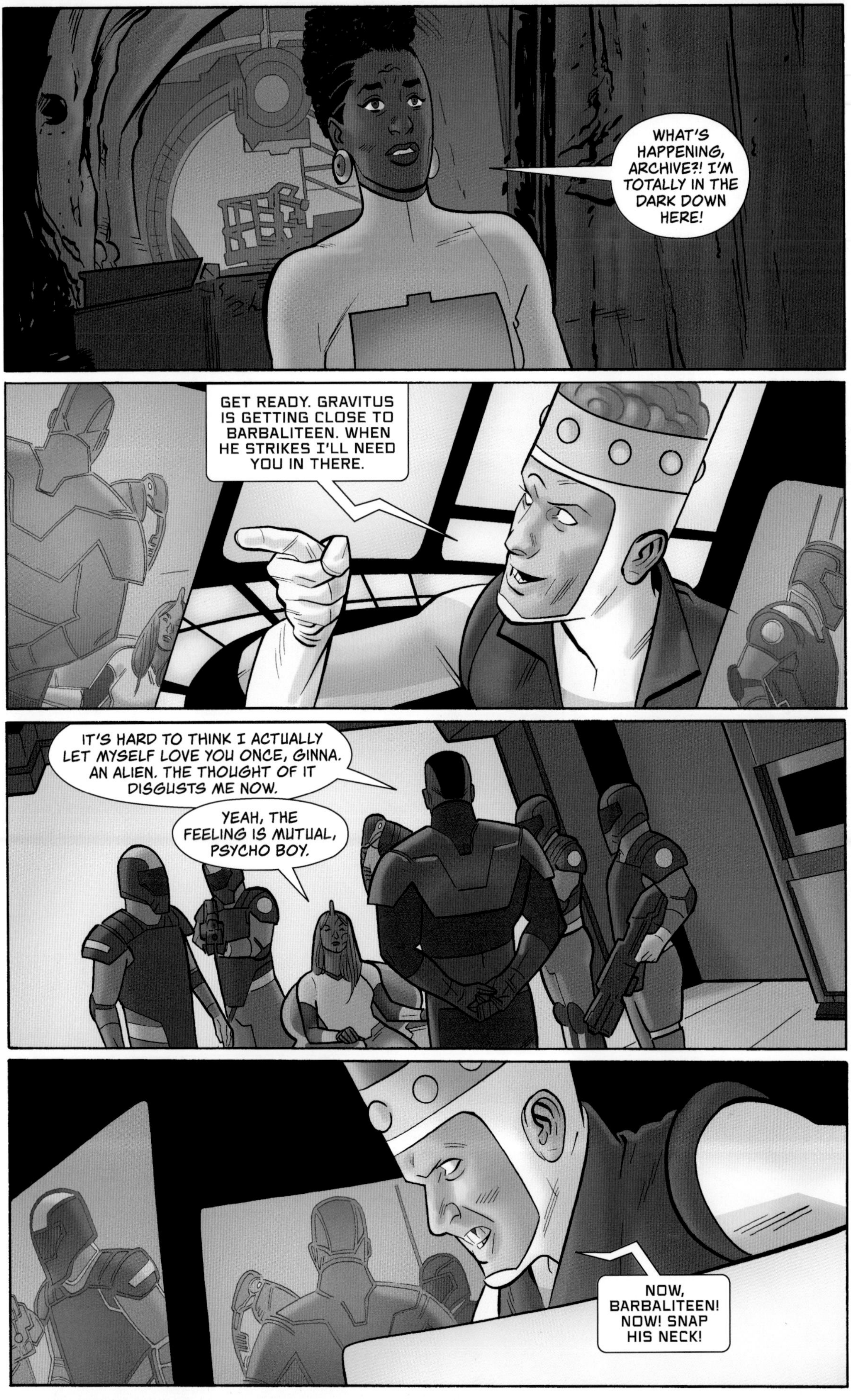
WHAT'S HAPPENING, ARCHIVE?! I'M TOTALLY IN THE DARK DOWN HERE!
GET READY. GRAVITUS IS GETTING CLOSE TO BARBALITEEN. WHEN HE STRIKES I'LL NEED YOU IN THERE.
IT'S HARD TO THINK I ACTUALLY LET MYSELF LOVE YOU ONCE, GINNA. AN ALIEN. THE THOUGHT OF IT DISGUSTS ME NOW.
YEAH, THE FEELING IS MUTUAL, PSYCHO BOY.
NOW, BARBALITEEN! NOW! SNAP HIS NECK!

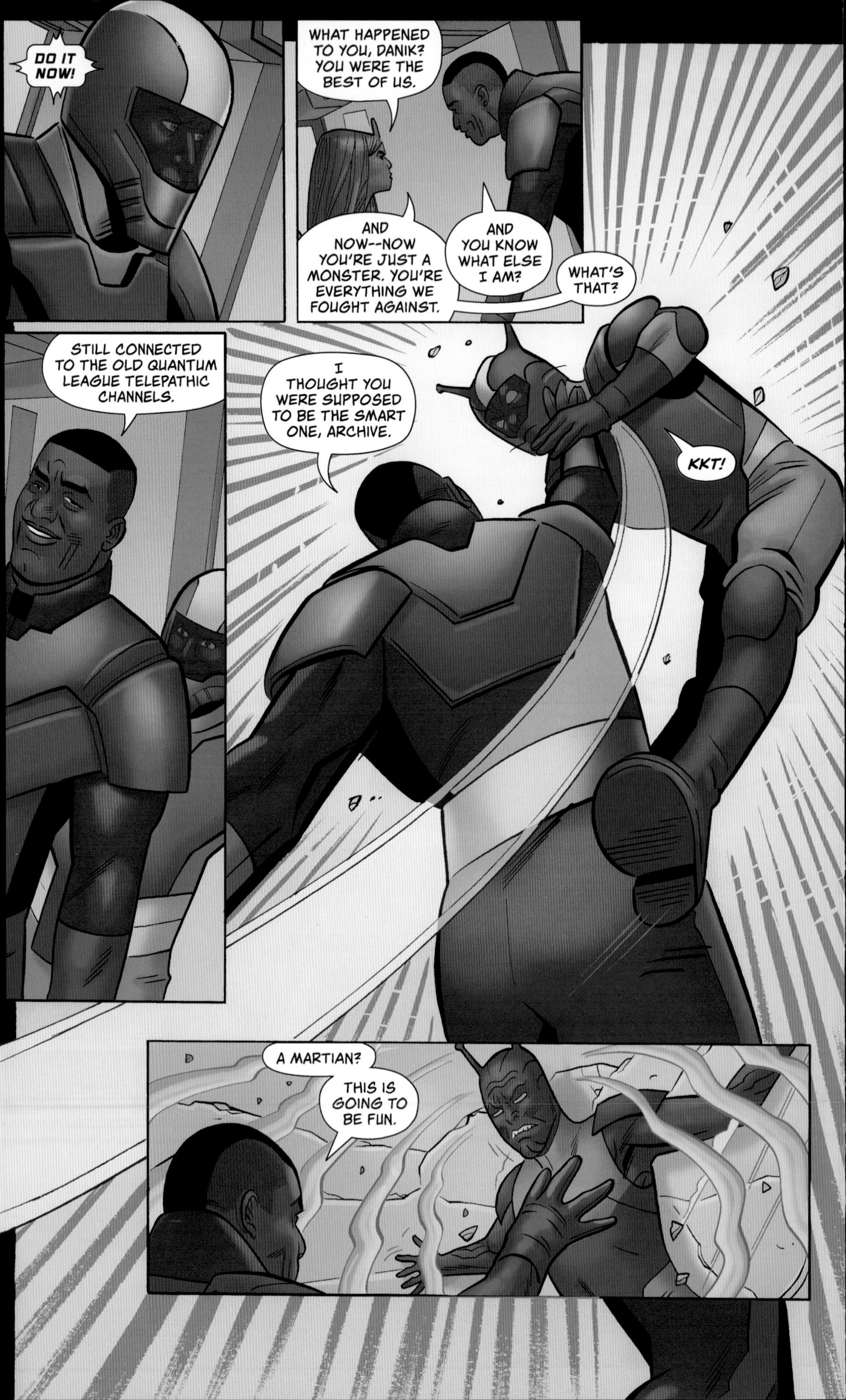
DO IT NOW!
WHAT HAPPENED TO YOU, DANIK? YOU WERE THE BEST OF US.
AND NOW--NOW YOU'RE JUST A MONSTER. YOU'RE EVERYTHING WE FOUGHT AGAINST.
AND YOU KNOW WHAT ELSE I AM?
WHAT'S THAT?
STILL CONNECTED TO THE OLD QUANTUM LEAGUE TELEPATHIC CHANNELS.
I THOUGHT YOU WERE SUPPOSED TO BE THE SMART ONE, ARCHIVE.
KKT!
A MARTIAN?
THIS IS GOING TO BE FUN.

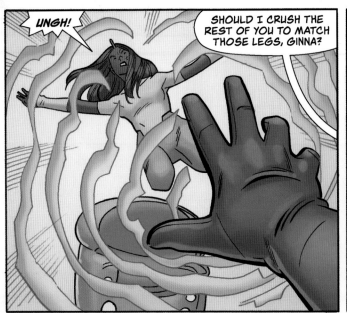

UNGH?!

SHOULD I CRUSH THE REST OF YOU TO MATCH THOSE LEGS, GINNA?

ARCHIVE?! WHAT THE HELL IS HAPPENING?! I--I'M GOING IN!

I PREPARED FOR THIS. I HAVE A BACK-UP PLAN.

WHAT?! WHAT PLAN?!

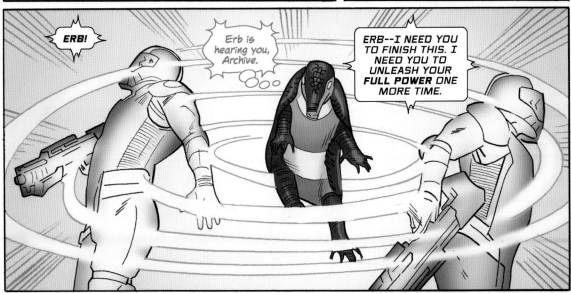

ERB!

Erb is hearing you, Archive.

ERB--I NEED YOU TO FINISH THIS. I NEED YOU TO UNLEASH YOUR *FULL POWER* ONE MORE TIME.

WHAT?! ARCHIVE, YOU CAN'T! THE OTHERS WILL BE KILLED TOO!

WAIT! THAT-- THAT'S WHY YOU WANTED ME TO STAY DOWN HERE ISN'T IT?

I COULDN'T LOSE YOU. NOT AGAIN.

BUT MODULA AND BARBALITEEN!

GRAVITUS IS THE PROBLEM THAT MUST BE SOLVED. THE REST IS SIMPLE MATH. I AM SORRY.

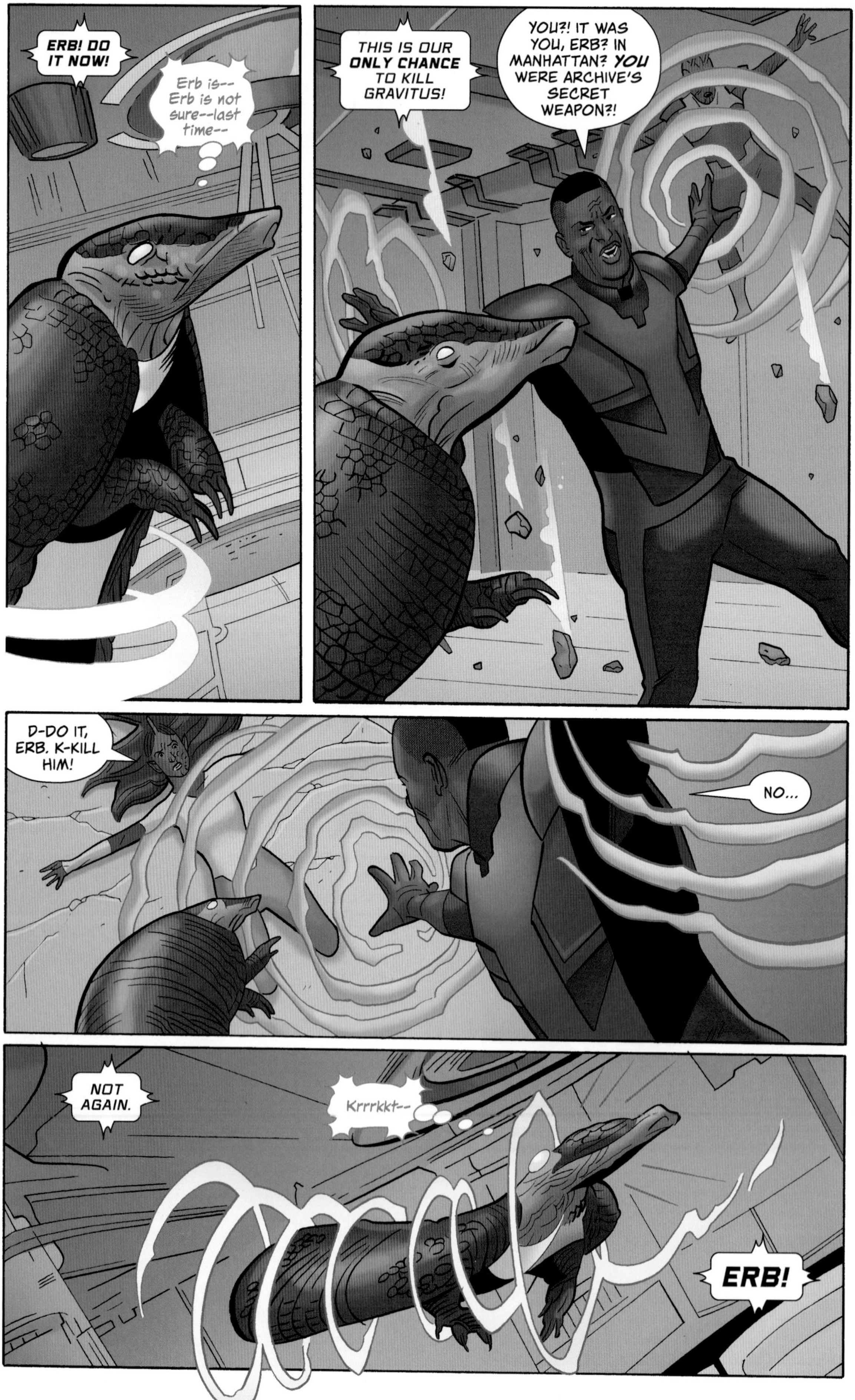
ERB! DO IT NOW!
Erb is-- Erb is not sure--last time--
THIS IS OUR ONLY CHANCE TO KILL GRAVITUS!
YOU?! IT WAS YOU, ERB? IN MANHATTAN? YOU WERE ARCHIVE'S SECRET WEAPON?!
D-DO IT, ERB. K-KILL HIM!
NO...
NOT AGAIN.
Krrrkkt--
ERB!

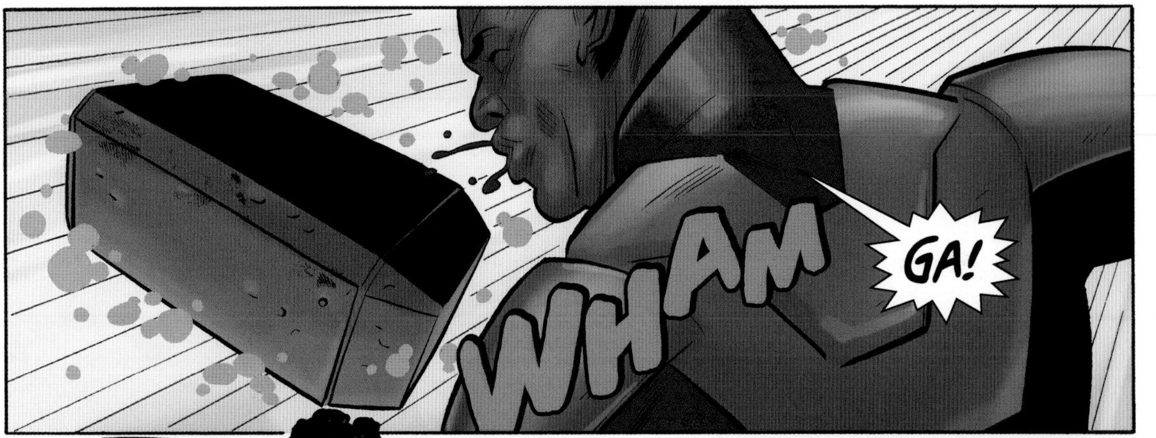
WHAM
GA!

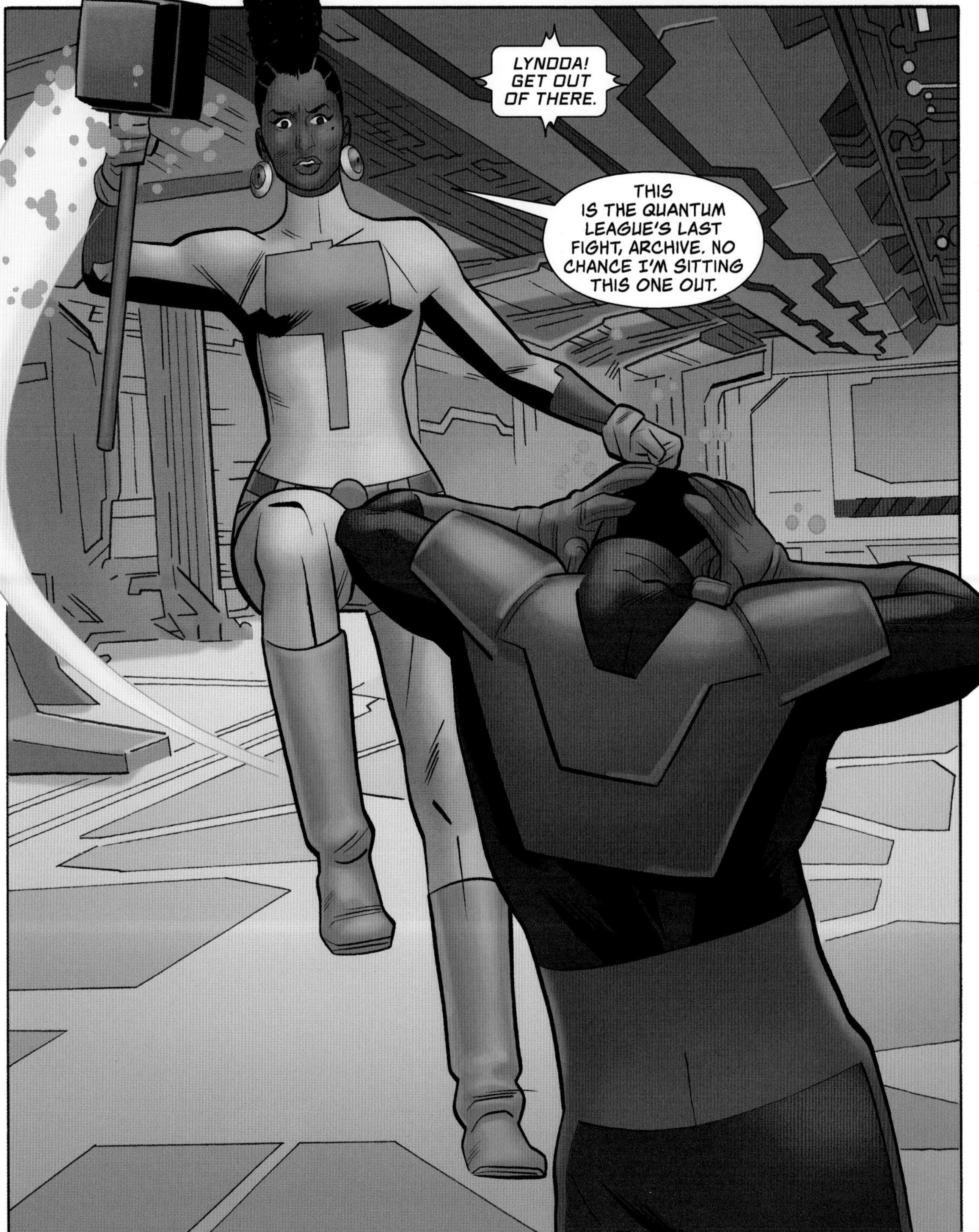
LYNDDA! GET OUT OF THERE.
THIS IS THE QUANTUM LEAGUE'S LAST FIGHT, ARCHIVE. NO CHANCE I'M SITTING THIS ONE OUT.

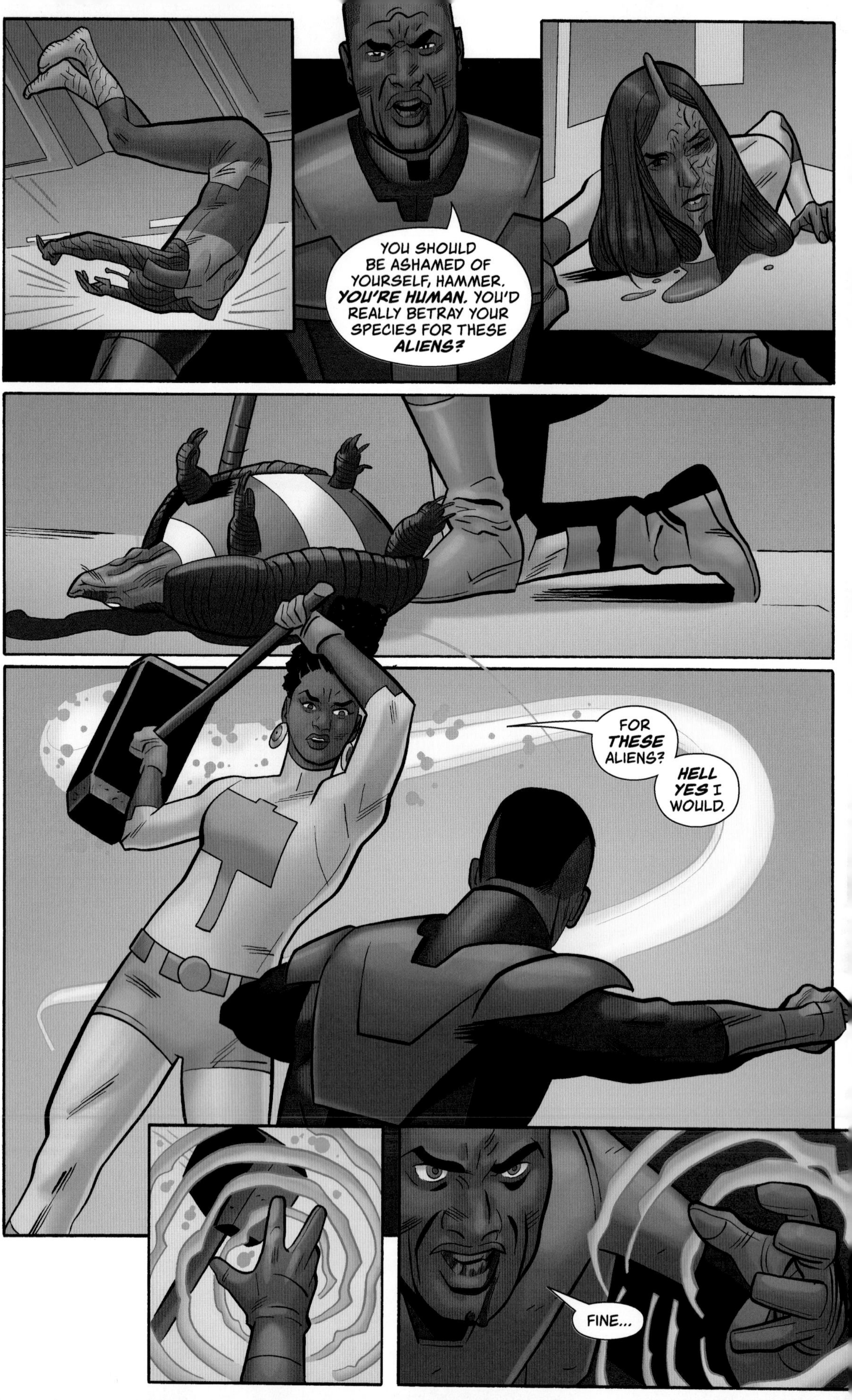
YOU SHOULD BE ASHAMED OF YOURSELF, HAMMER. YOU'RE HUMAN. YOU'D REALLY BETRAY YOUR SPECIES FOR THESE ALIENS?
FOR THESE ALIENS?
HELL YES I WOULD.
FINE...

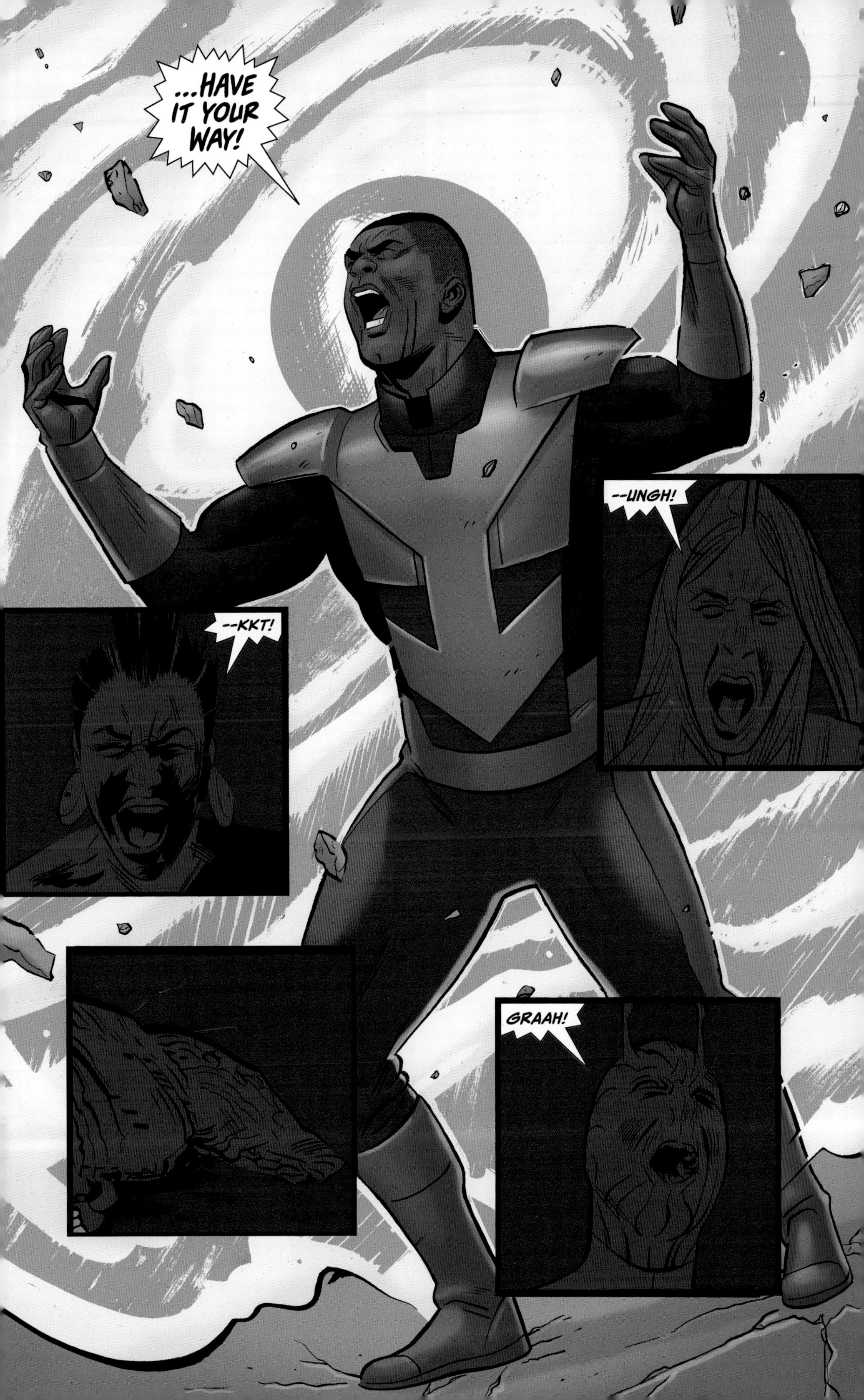
...HAVE IT YOUR WAY!
--UNGH!
--KKT!
GRAAH!

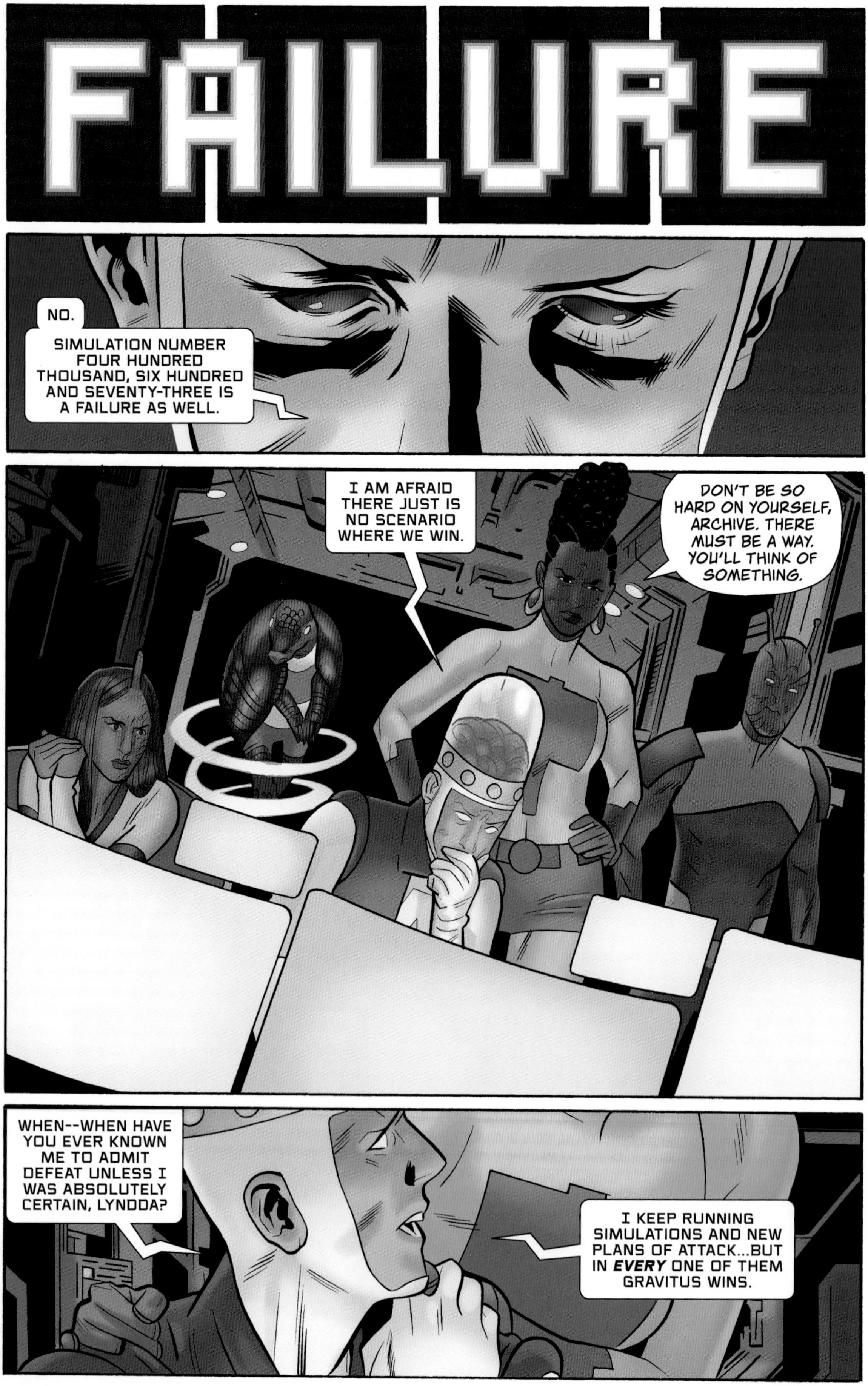
FAILURE
NO.
SIMULATION NUMBER FOUR HUNDRED THOUSAND, SIX HUNDRED AND SEVENTY-THREE IS A FAILURE AS WELL.
I AM AFRAID THERE JUST IS NO SCENARIO WHERE WE WIN.
DON'T BE SO HARD ON YOURSELF, ARCHIVE. THERE MUST BE A WAY. YOU'LL THINK OF SOMETHING.
WHEN--WHEN HAVE YOU EVER KNOWN ME TO ADMIT DEFEAT UNLESS I WAS ABSOLUTELY CERTAIN, LYNDDA?
I KEEP RUNNING SIMULATIONS AND NEW PLANS OF ATTACK...BUT IN EVERY ONE OF THEM GRAVITUS WINS.

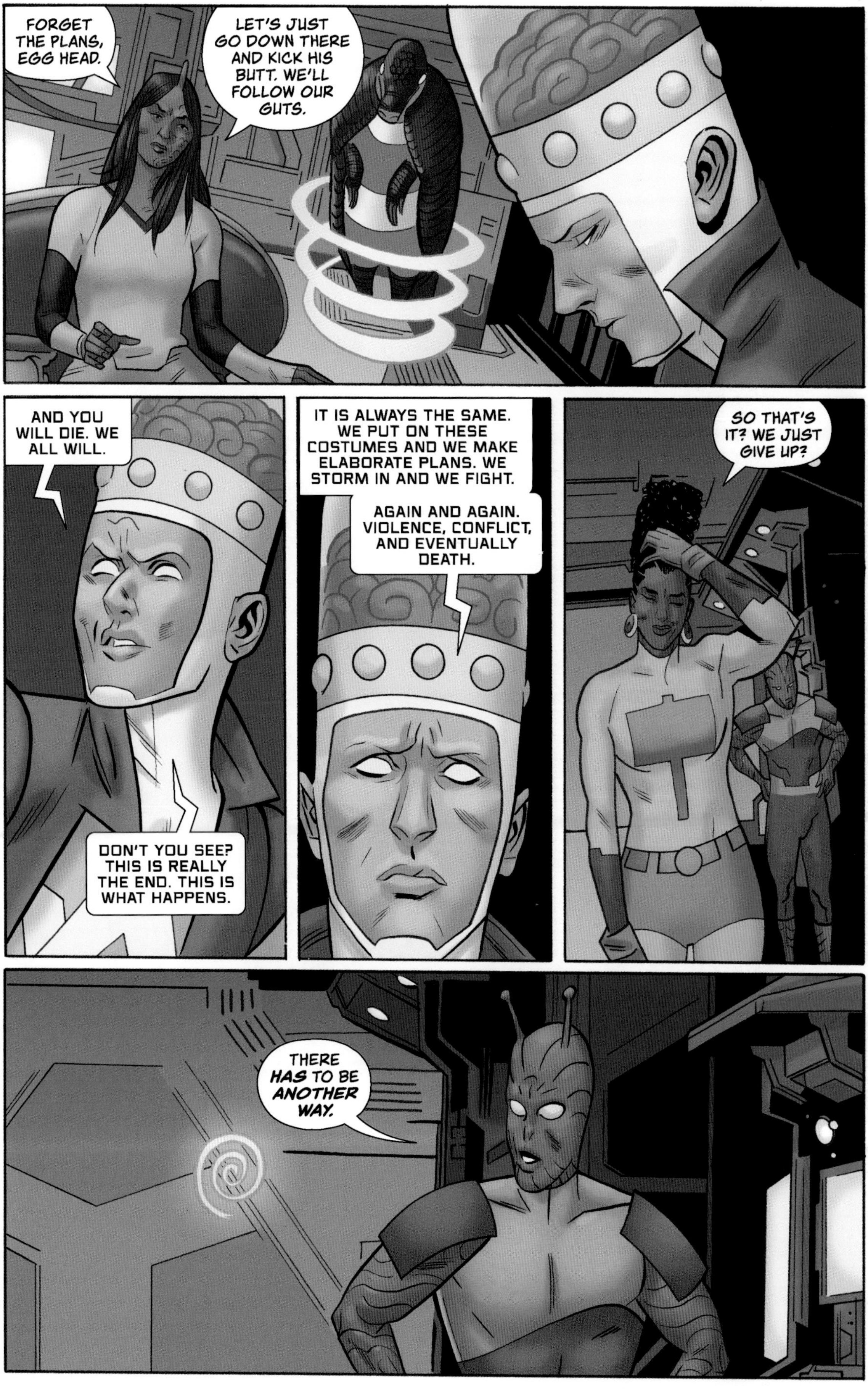
FORGET THE PLANS, EGG HEAD.
LET'S JUST GO DOWN THERE AND KICK HIS BUTT. WE'LL FOLLOW OUR GUTS.
AND YOU WILL DIE. WE ALL WILL.
DON'T YOU SEE? THIS IS REALLY THE END. THIS IS WHAT HAPPENS.
IT IS ALWAYS THE SAME. WE PUT ON THESE COSTUMES AND WE MAKE ELABORATE PLANS. WE STORM IN AND WE FIGHT.
AGAIN AND AGAIN. VIOLENCE, CONFLICT, AND EVENTUALLY DEATH.
SO THAT'S IT? WE JUST GIVE UP?
THERE HAS TO BE ANOTHER WAY.

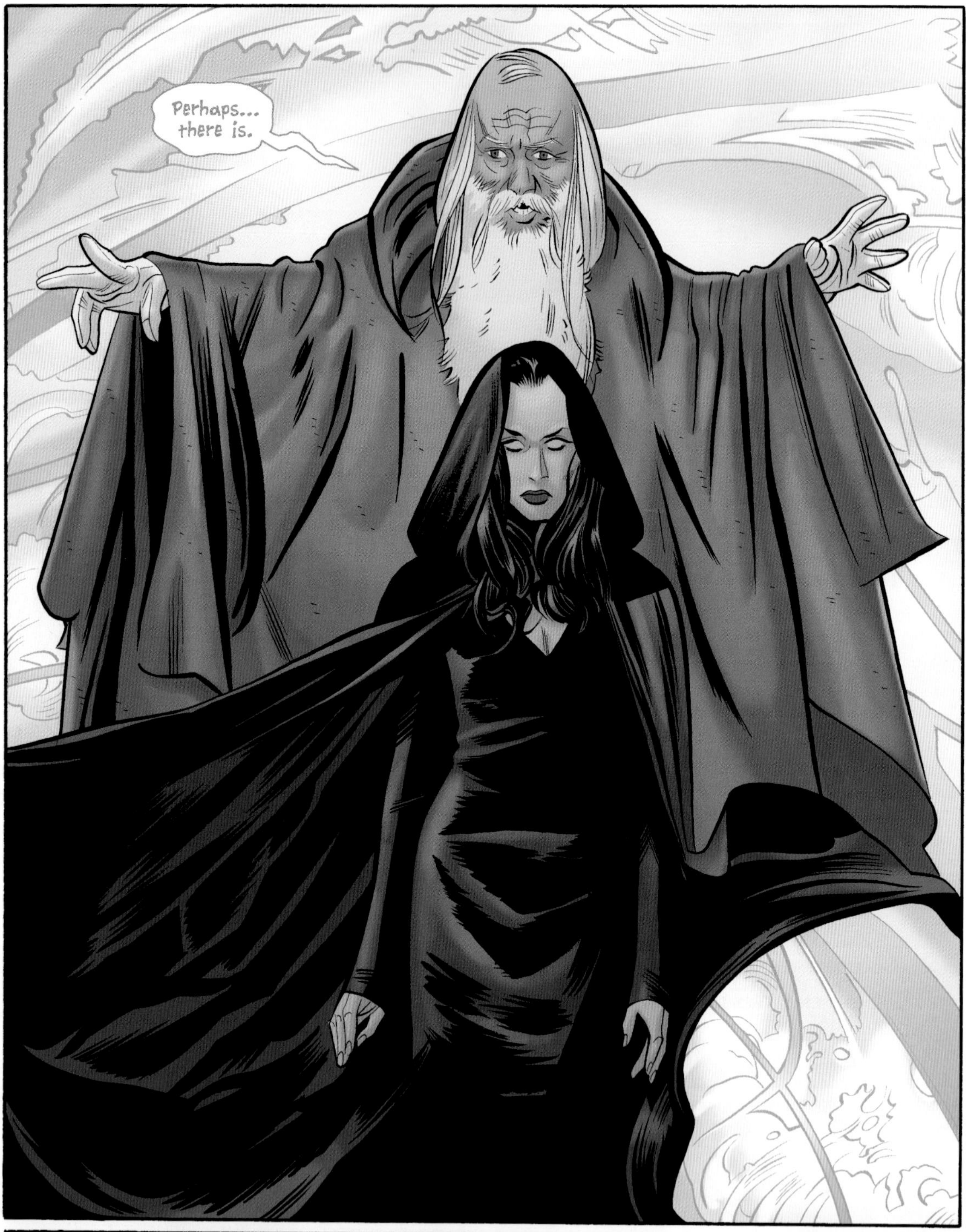
Perhaps... there is.

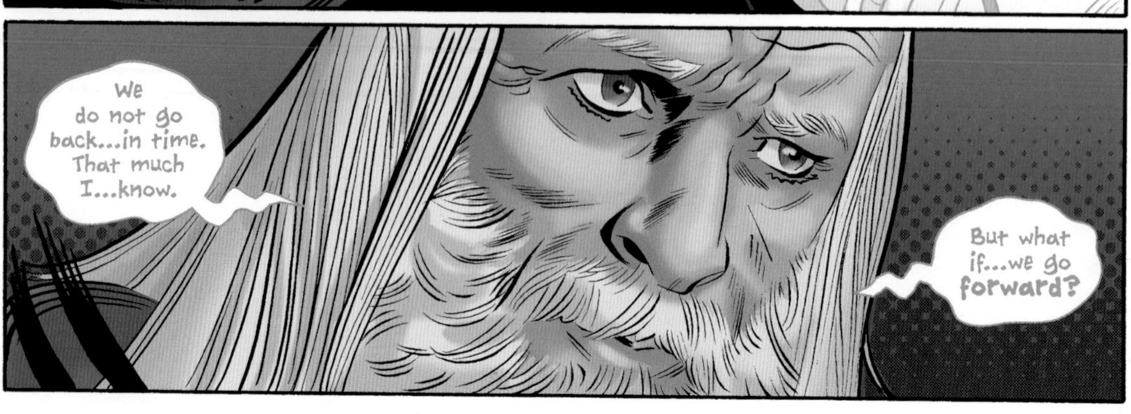
We do not go back...in time. That much I...know.
But what if...we go forward?

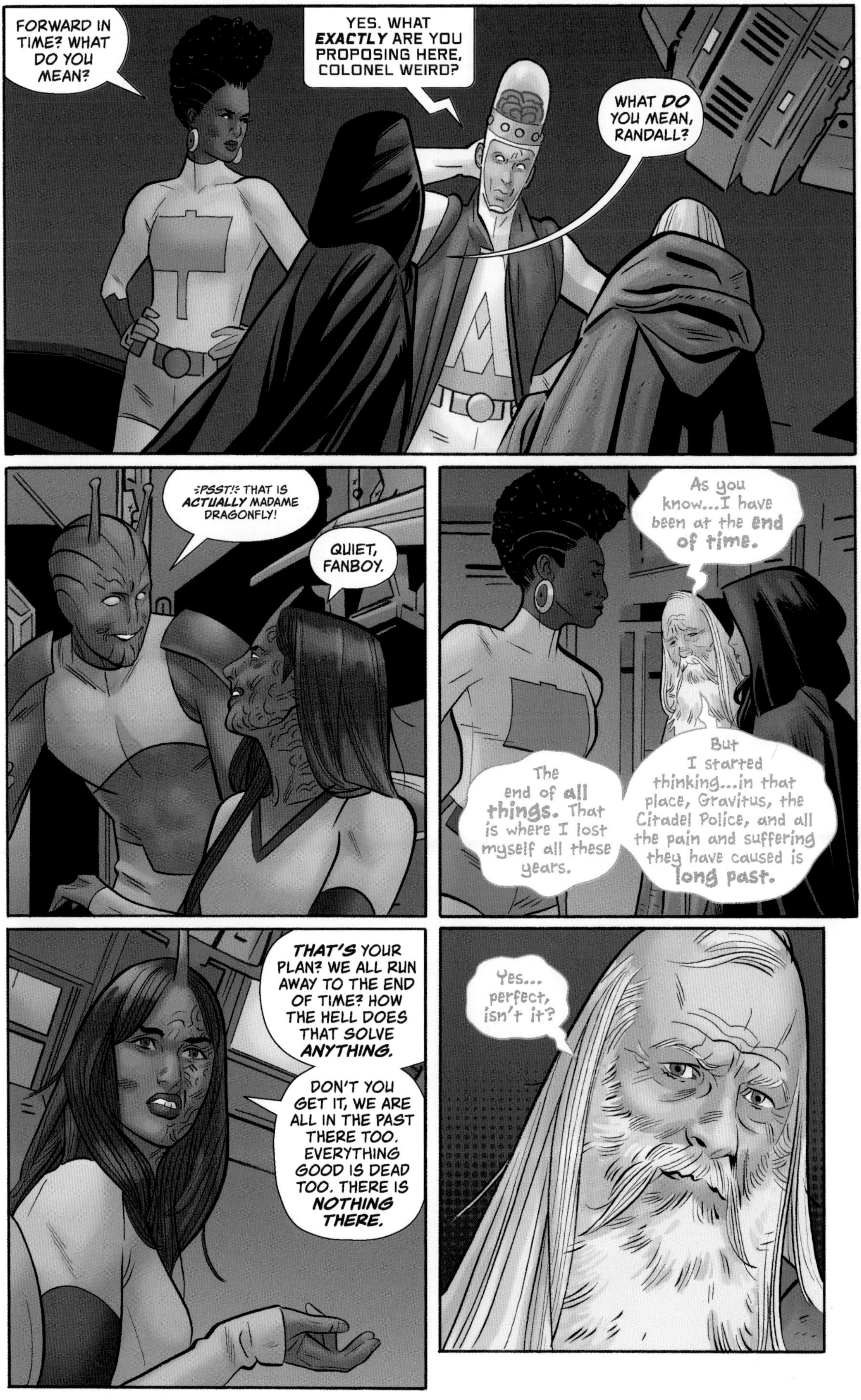
FORWARD IN TIME? WHAT DO YOU MEAN?
YES. WHAT EXACTLY ARE YOU PROPOSING HERE, COLONEL WEIRD?
WHAT DO YOU MEAN, RANDALL?
PSST! THAT IS ACTUALLY MADAME DRAGONFLY!
QUIET, FANBOY.
As you know...I have been at the end of time.
The end of all things. That is where I lost myself all these years.
But I started thinking...in that place, Gravitus, the Citadel Police, and all the pain and suffering they have caused is long past.
THAT'S YOUR PLAN? WE ALL RUN AWAY TO THE END OF TIME? HOW THE HELL DOES THAT SOLVE ANYTHING.
DON'T YOU GET IT, WE ARE ALL IN THE PAST THERE TOO. EVERYTHING GOOD IS DEAD TOO. THERE IS NOTHING THERE.
Yes... perfect, isn't it?

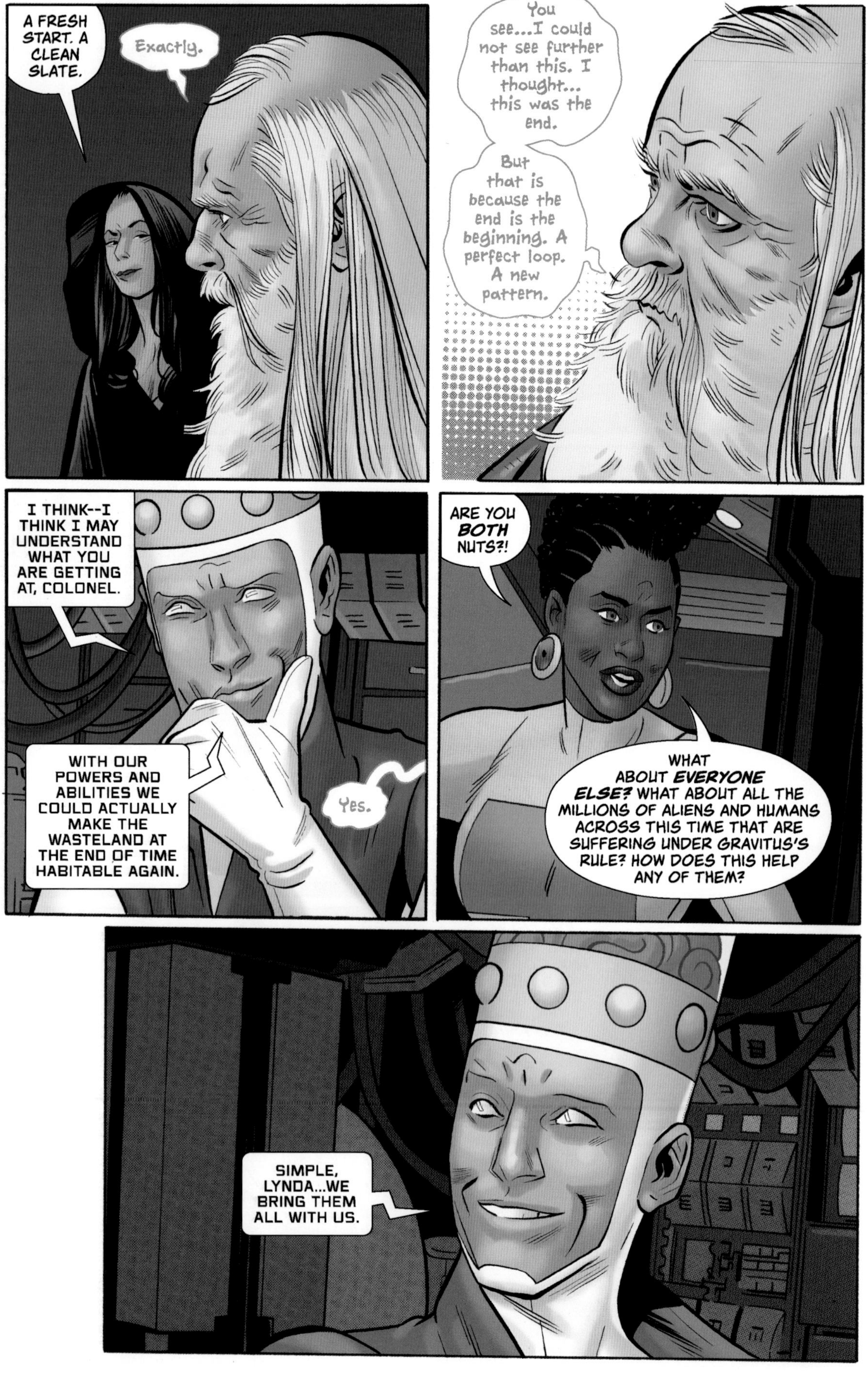

A FRESH START. A CLEAN SLATE.
Exactly.
You see...I could not see further than this. I thought... this was the end.
But that is because the end is the beginning. A perfect loop. A new pattern.
I THINK--I THINK I MAY UNDERSTAND WHAT YOU ARE GETTING AT, COLONEL.
WITH OUR POWERS AND ABILITIES WE COULD ACTUALLY MAKE THE WASTELAND AT THE END OF TIME HABITABLE AGAIN.
Yes.
ARE YOU *BOTH* NUTS?!
WHAT ABOUT *EVERYONE ELSE?* WHAT ABOUT ALL THE MILLIONS OF ALIENS AND HUMANS ACROSS THIS TIME THAT ARE SUFFERING UNDER GRAVITUS'S RULE? HOW DOES THIS HELP ANY OF THEM?
SIMPLE, LYNDA...WE BRING THEM ALL WITH US.

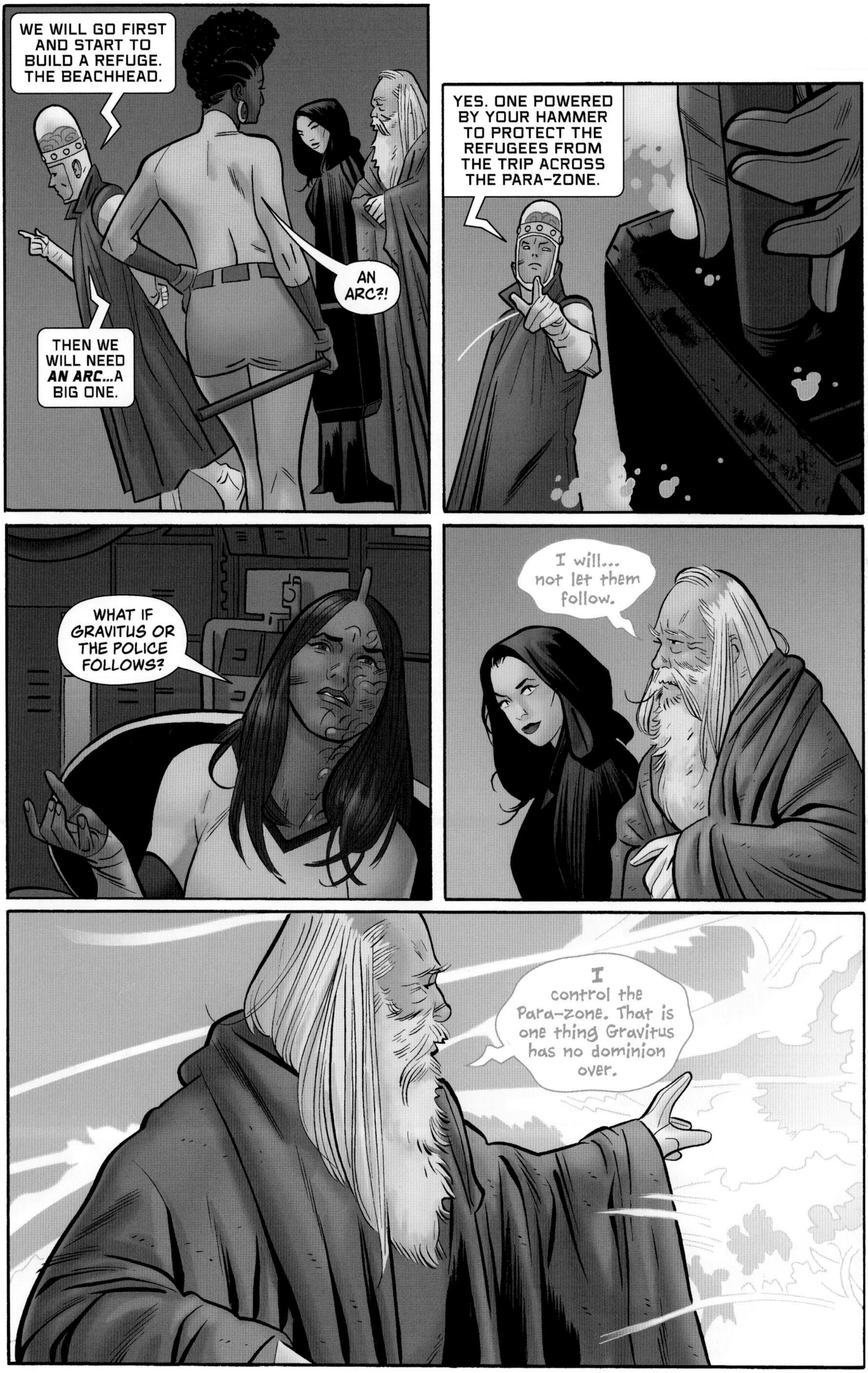
WE WILL GO FIRST AND START TO BUILD A REFUGE. THE BEACHHEAD.
AN ARC?!
THEN WE WILL NEED AN ARC...A BIG ONE.
YES. ONE POWERED BY YOUR HAMMER TO PROTECT THE REFUGEES FROM THE TRIP ACROSS THE PARA-ZONE.
WHAT IF GRAVITUS OR THE POLICE FOLLOWS?
I will... not let them follow.
I control the Para-zone. That is one thing Gravitus has no dominion over.

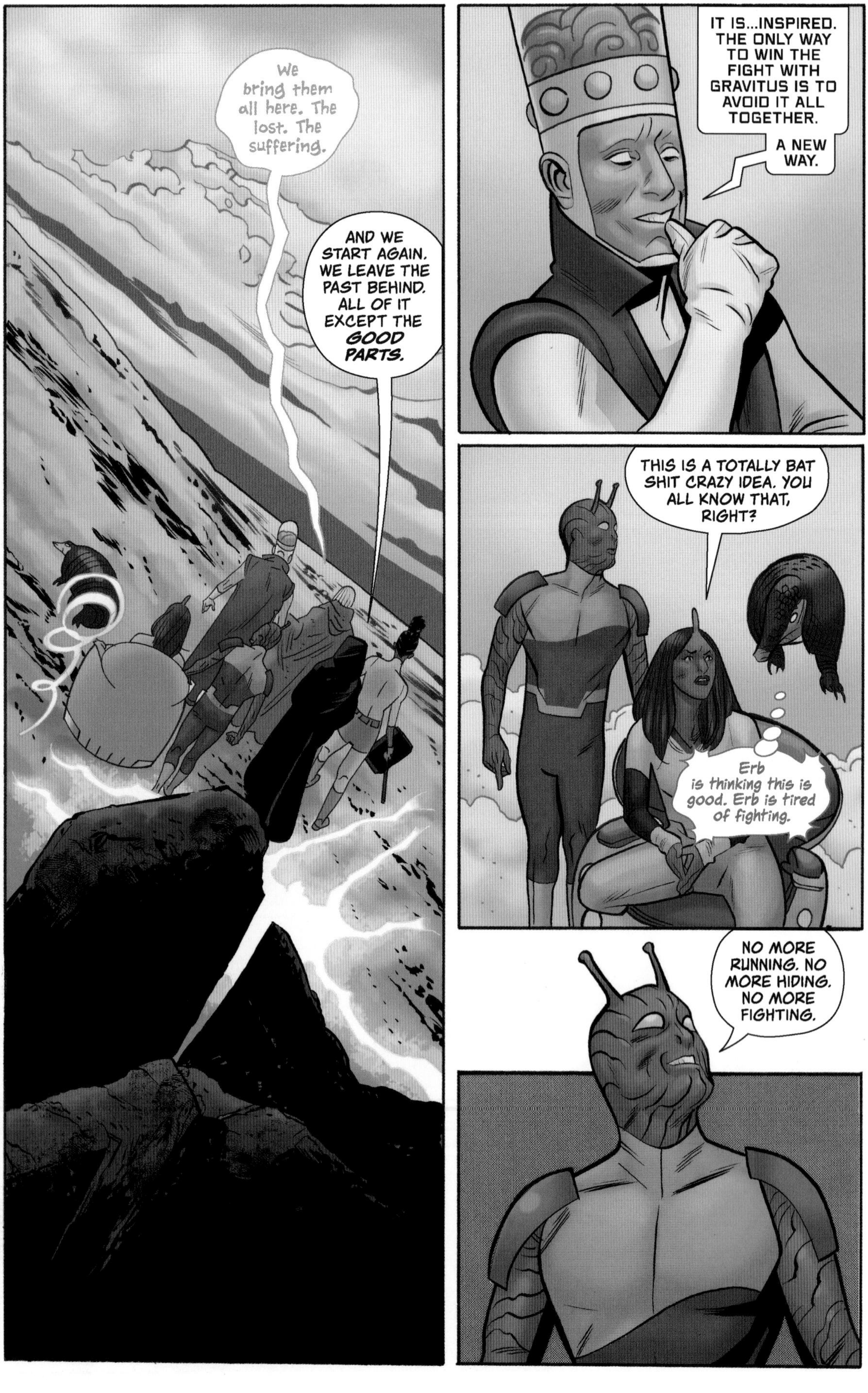
We bring them all here. The lost. The suffering.
AND WE START AGAIN. WE LEAVE THE PAST BEHIND. ALL OF IT EXCEPT THE GOOD PARTS.
IT IS...INSPIRED. THE ONLY WAY TO WIN THE FIGHT WITH GRAVITUS IS TO AVOID IT ALL TOGETHER.
A NEW WAY.
THIS IS A TOTALLY BAT SHIT CRAZY IDEA. YOU ALL KNOW THAT, RIGHT?
Erb is thinking this is good. Erb is tired of fighting.
NO MORE RUNNING. NO MORE HIDING. NO MORE FIGHTING.

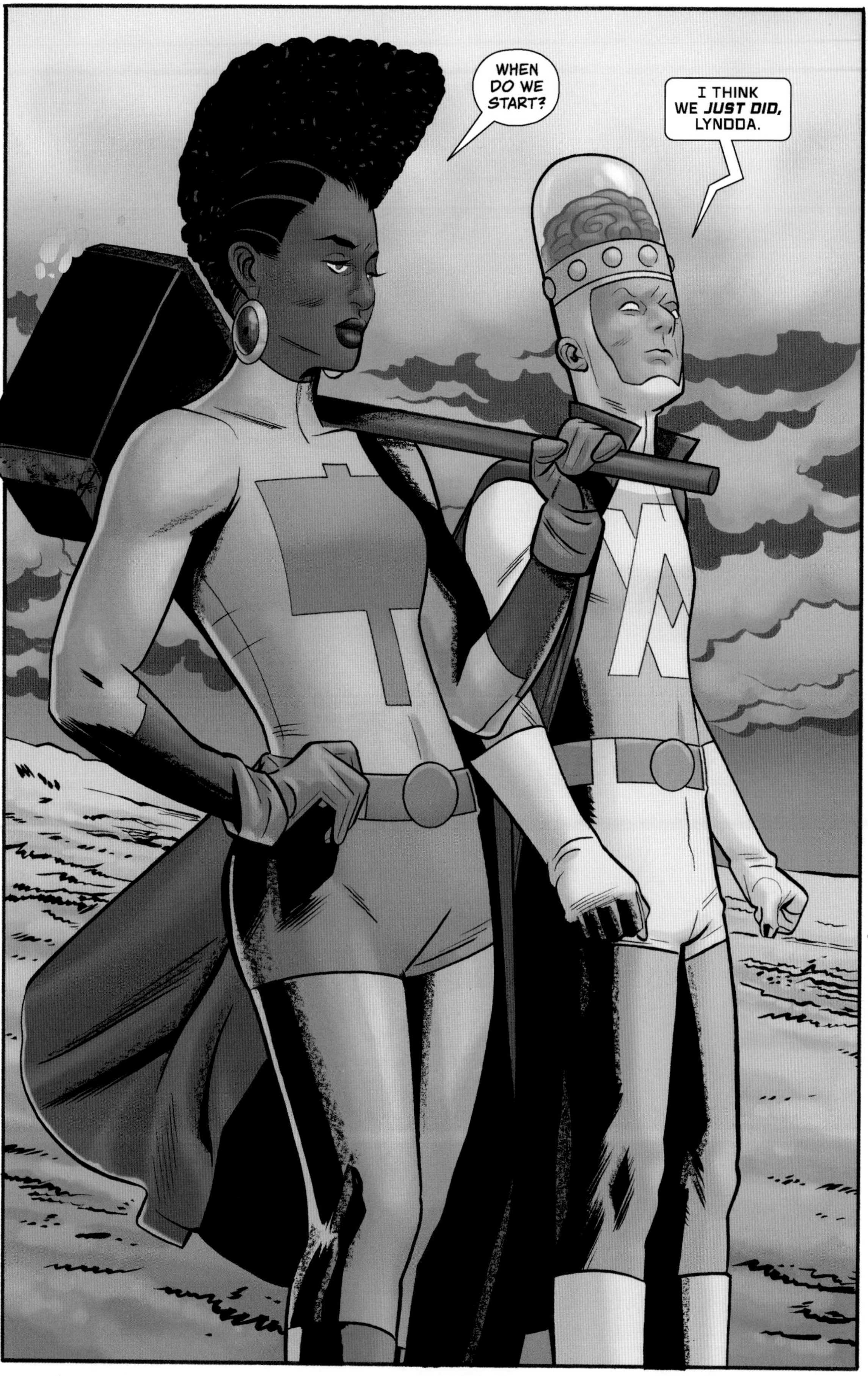
WHEN DO WE START?
I THINK WE *JUST DID,* LYNDDA.

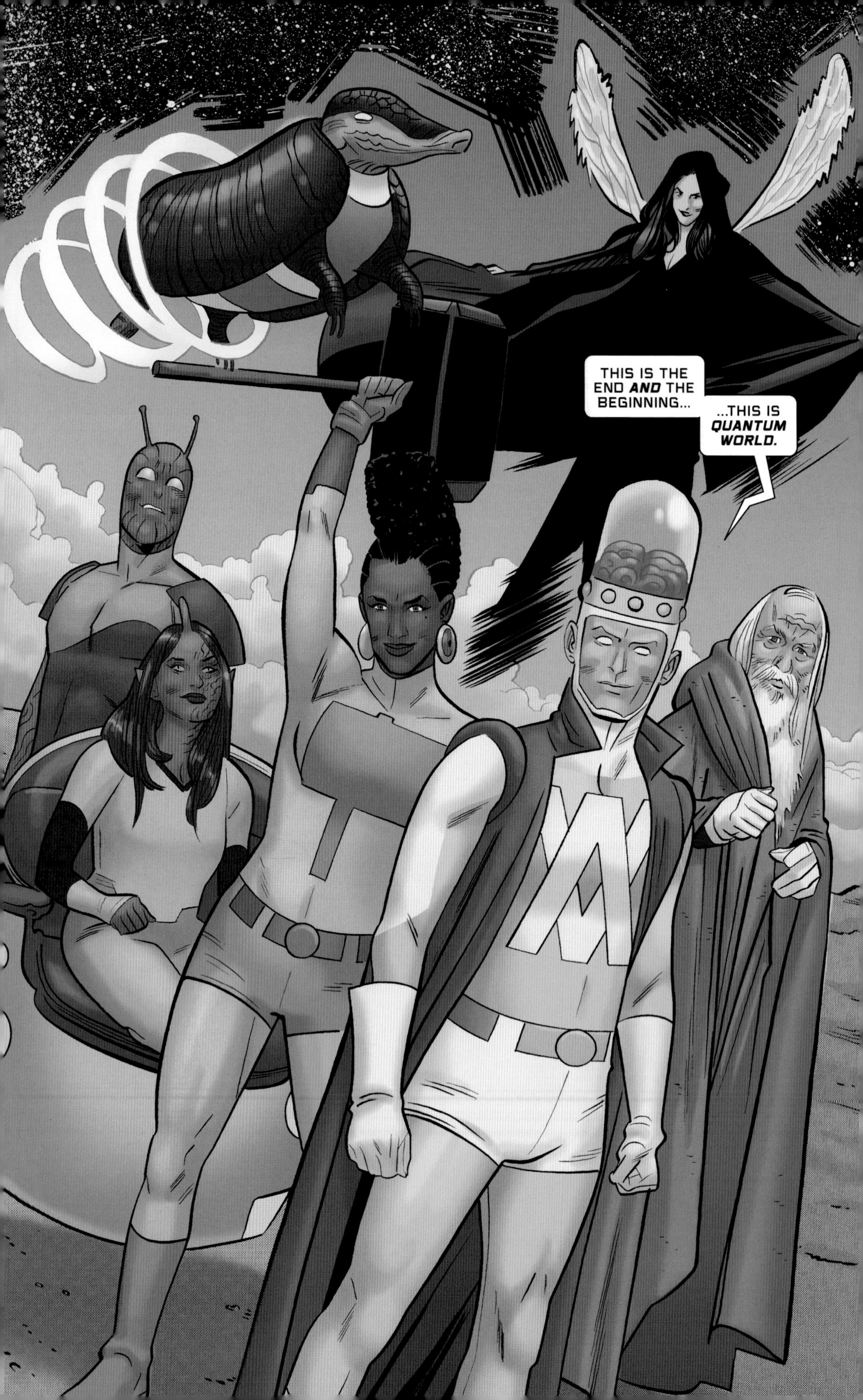
THIS IS THE END AND THE BEGINNING...
...THIS IS QUANTUM WORLD.

SKETCHBOOK

NOTES BY WILFREDO TORRES

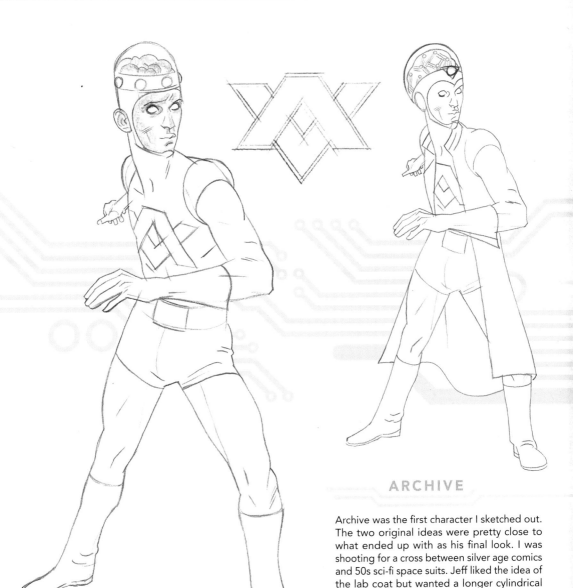

ARCHIVE

Archive was the first character I sketched out.
The two original ideas were pretty close to
what ended up with as his final look. I was
shooting for a cross between silver age comics
and 50s sci-fi space suits. Jeff liked the idea of
the lab coat but wanted a longer cylindrical
shape for his 'brain-dome' and that's where we
ended up on the final.

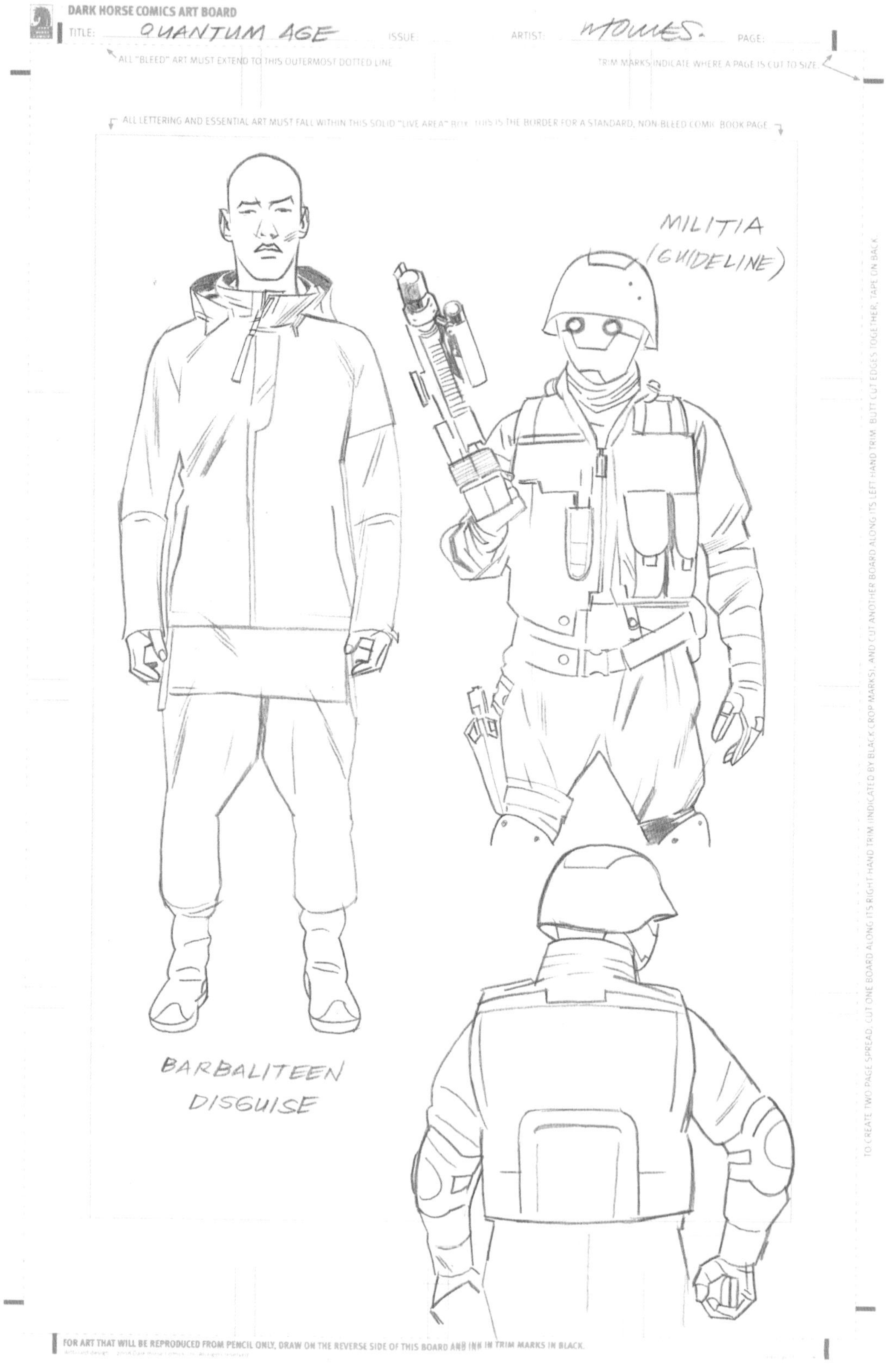
DARK HORSE COMICS ART BOARD
TITLE: QUANTUM AGE
ISSUE:
ARTIST:
PAGE:
ALL "BLEED" ART MUST EXTEND TO THIS OUTERMOST DOTTED LINE
TRIM MARKS INDICATE WHERE A PAGE IS CUT TO SIZE.
ALL LETTERING AND ESSENTIAL ART MUST FALL WITHIN THIS SOLID "LIVE AREA" BOX. THIS IS THE BORDER FOR A STANDARD, NON-BLEED COMIC BOOK PAGE
MILITIA (GUIDELINE)
BARBALITEEN DISGUISE
TO CREATE TWO PAGE SPREAD, CUT ONE BOARD ALONG ITS RIGHT HAND TRIM (INDICATED BY BLACK CROP MARKS), AND CUT ANOTHER BOARD ALONG ITS LEFT HAND TRIM. BUTT CUT EDGES TOGETHER, TAPE ON BACK.
FOR ART THAT WILL BE REPRODUCED FROM PENCIL ONLY, DRAW ON THE REVERSE SIDE OF THIS BOARD AND INK IN TRIM MARKS IN BLACK.

Barbaliteen's disguised human form seemed like something that needed to be very practical and designed to blend in so I kept it pretty basic and utilitarian.

The first draft of the militia soldiers was way too current looking. I wanted the look to be recognizable without being too grounded but also not pushed so far that it seemed so outlandish that it wouldn't be practical for actual street level use.

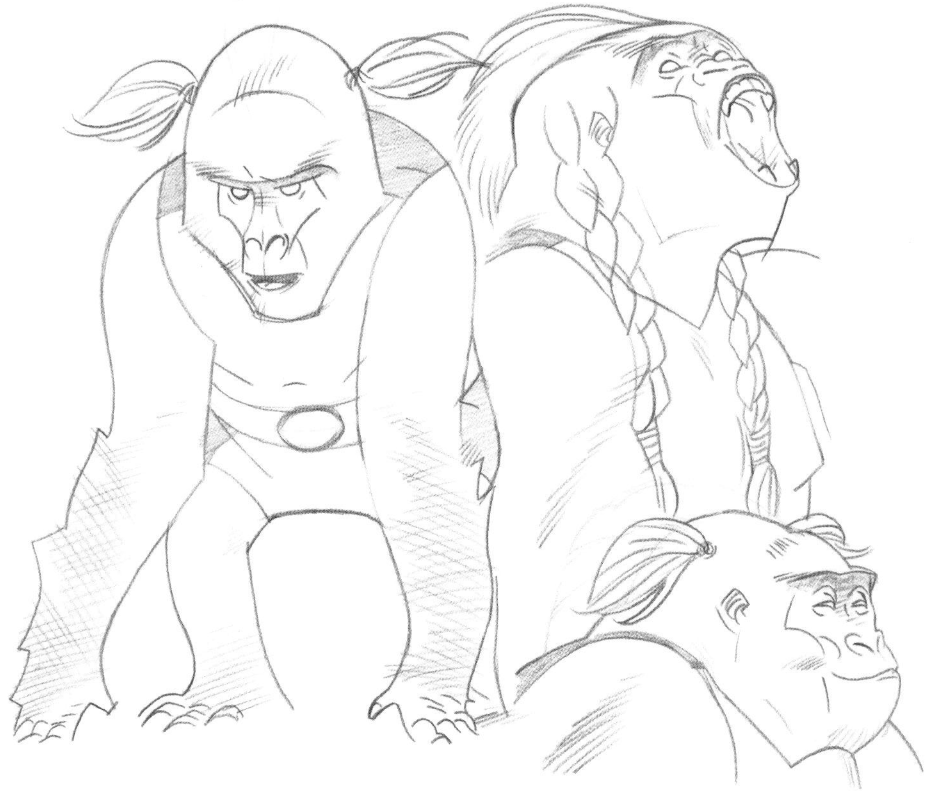

GORILLA GIRL

Very early on Jeff asked what sorts of elements of comics I enjoyed and I told him that I missed comic book gorillas and also dinosaurs. When I got the character list, Jeff had included Gorilla Girl into the Quantum League. I didn't know to what extent she would be included in the script so I even started trying to figure out an older version of the character, kind of a gorilla valkyrie. I also got to draw some dinosaurs.

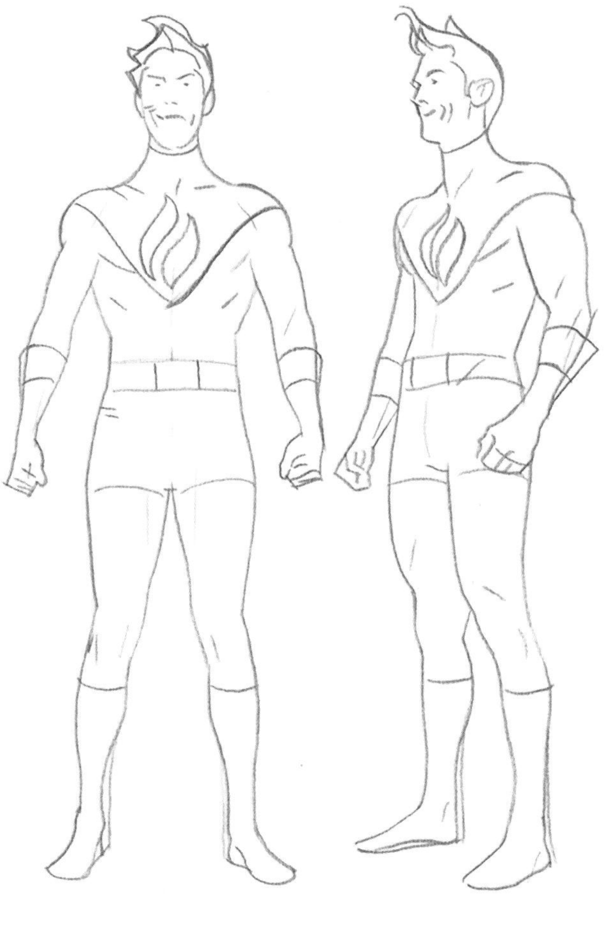

FURNACE LAD

Furnace Lad kinda popped into my head fully formed, a sort of fire elf type guy. The real gag with him had we seen him in action would have been in how his abilities translated visually.

COLONEL WEIRD

By the time we catch up to Colonel Weird in *Quantum* I saw him as someone who was far more powerful than what we'd seen before and much more in control of that power. I tend to overthink everything and when you're working on a guy who can cross time, space, and dimensions there's a lot to exploit there. But my general line of thought was 'How many times has he lived this moment in time?' Is this the first time he's doing this and his reactions are genuine, or is it the hundredth and he's just going through the motions because he knows that no matter what he does the result remains the same?

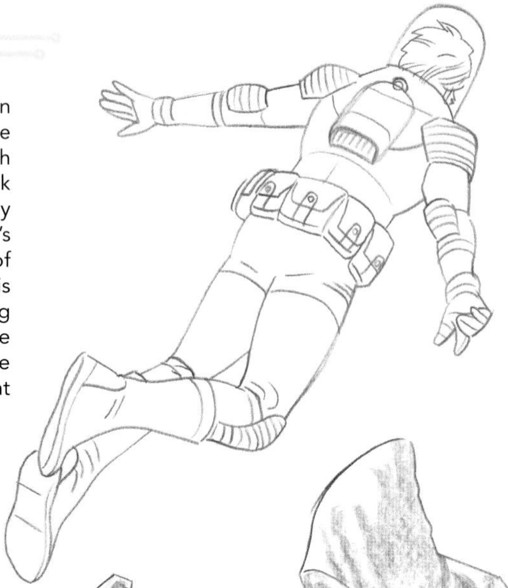

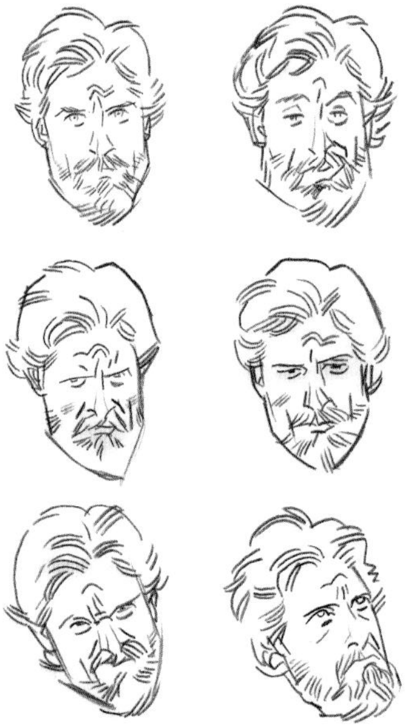

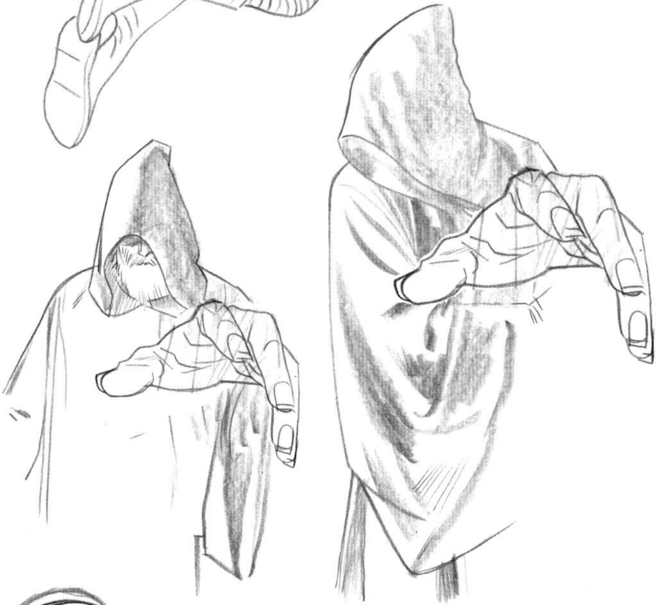

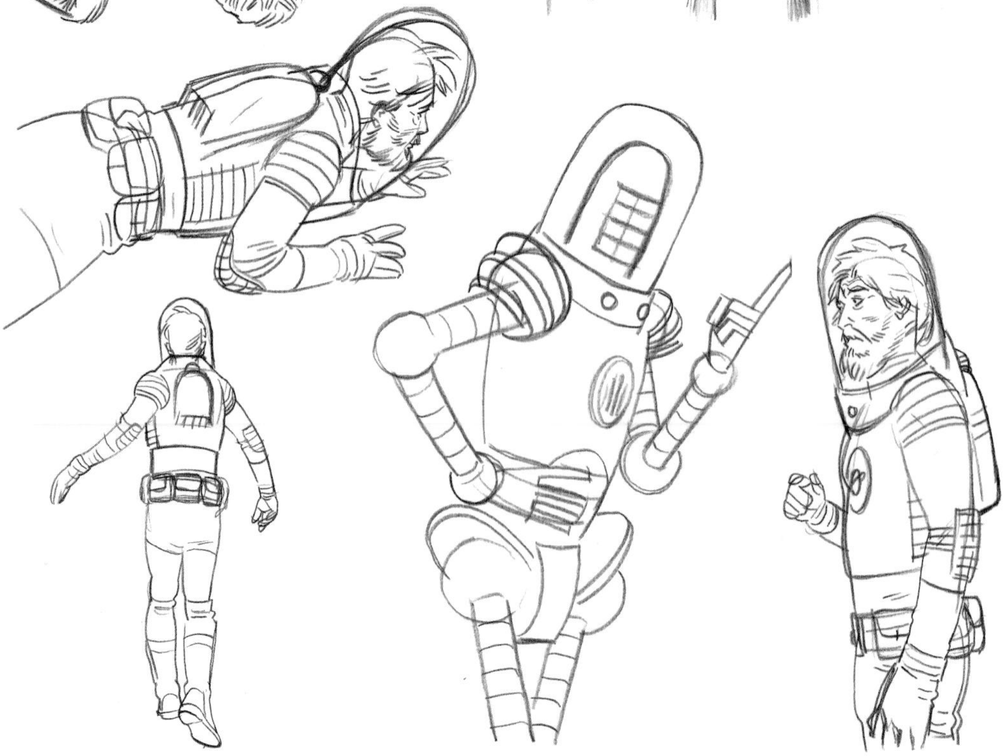

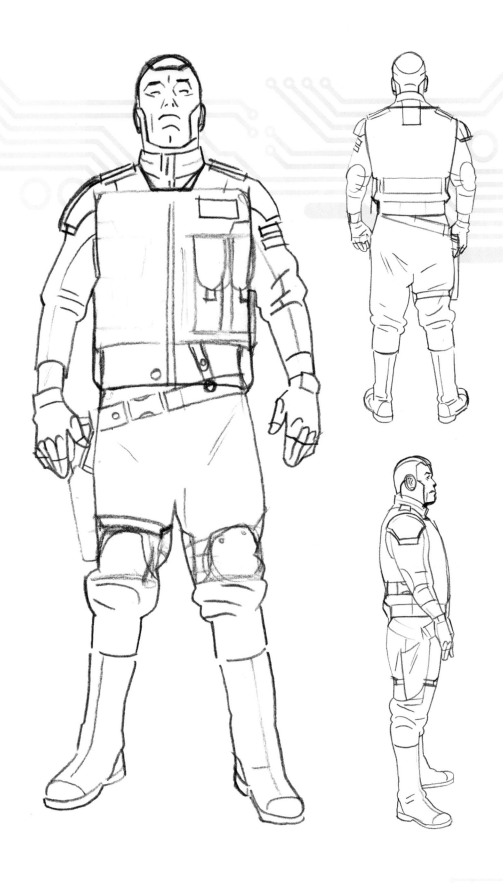

The final take on the human militia guards was a middle ground between what we would see from modern day tactical gear and what we might find in a distant but not unrecognizable future.

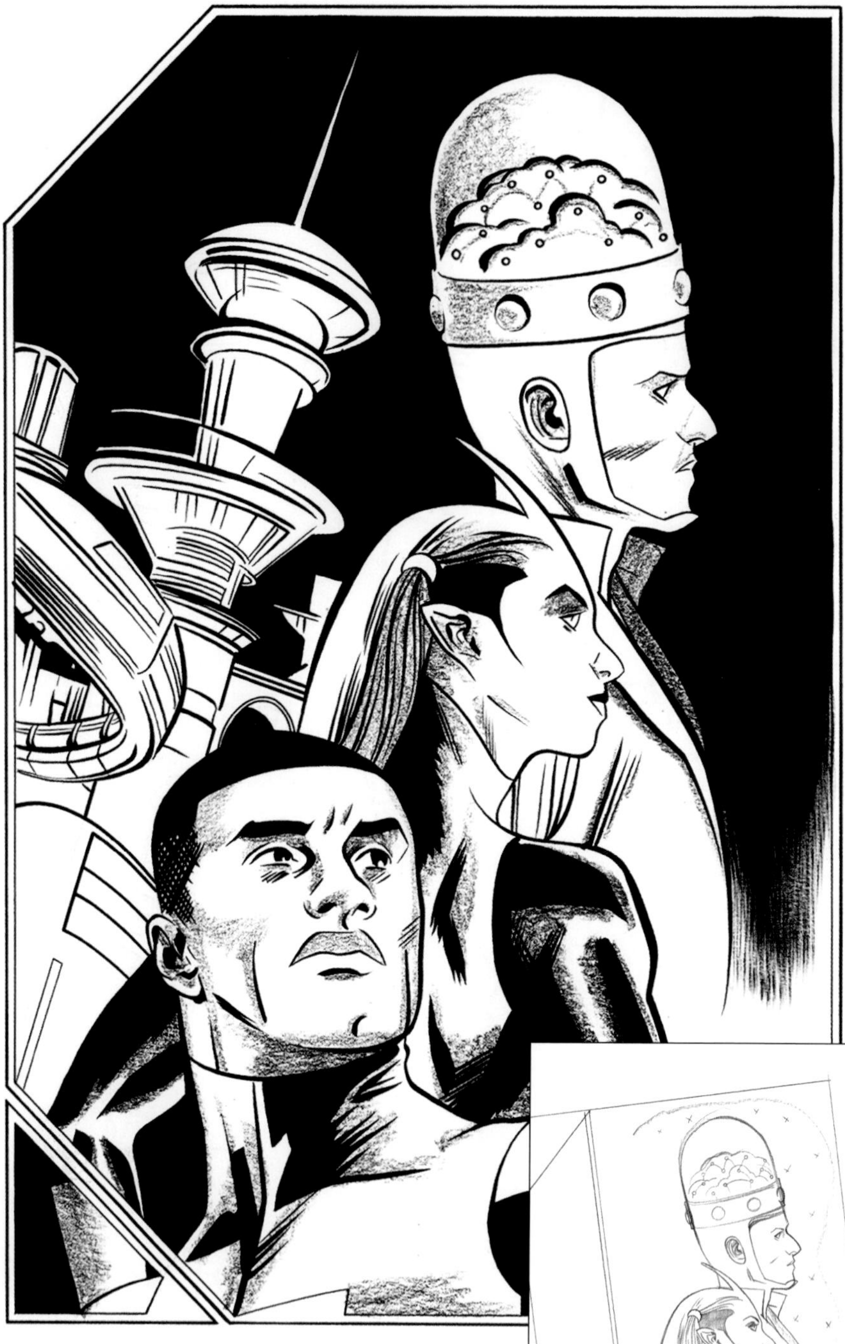

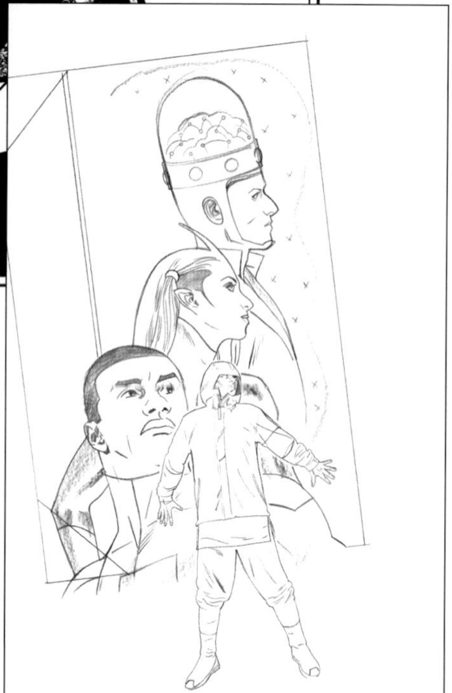

When I was designing the cover for the first issue I wanted to have something that reflected the current state of affairs but that also spoke to what had come before. Barbaliteen is pretty much the reader's guide to this world so it made sense to start right where we first find him, hiding and on the run. In this instance it was very literally backed up by a simplified, almost propagandized idea of what the Quantum League was.

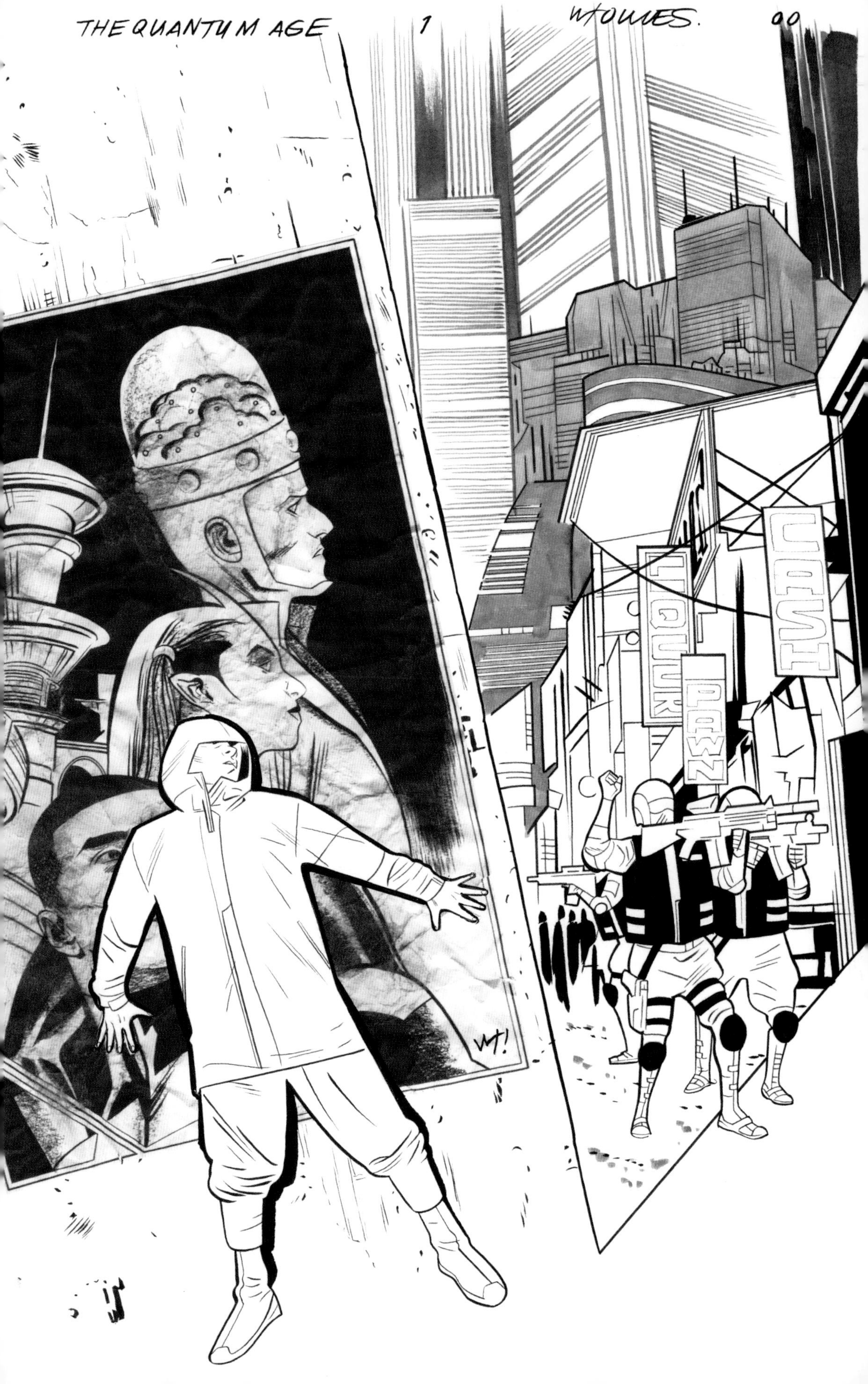
THE QUANTUM AGE
1
WTOWLES
00
LIQUOR
PAWN
CASH

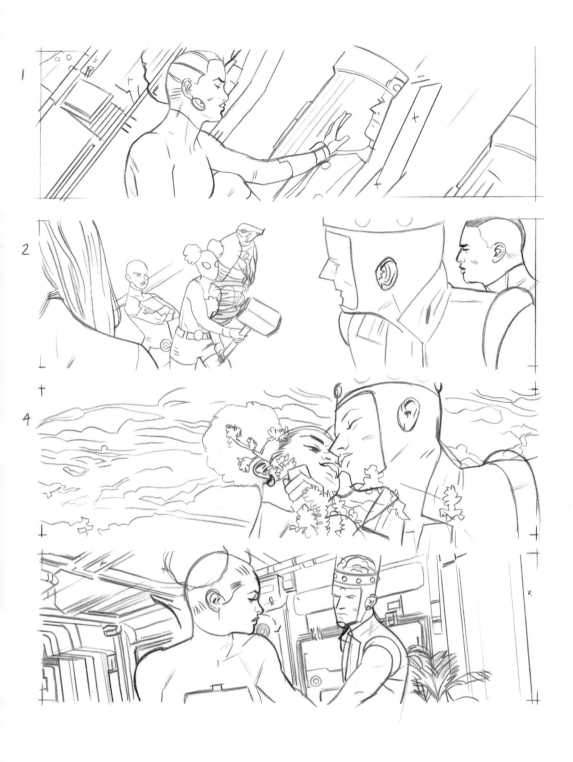

I'll often draw specific elements or panels on a separate sheet so that I can resize or arrange them more easily before moving forward to the final inks on a page. The Hammer Lass/ Archive flashback sequences from Issue #4 were actually the first thing I pencilled on that issue because I had a clear idea of what I wanted them to look like before I even started in on the thumbnails.

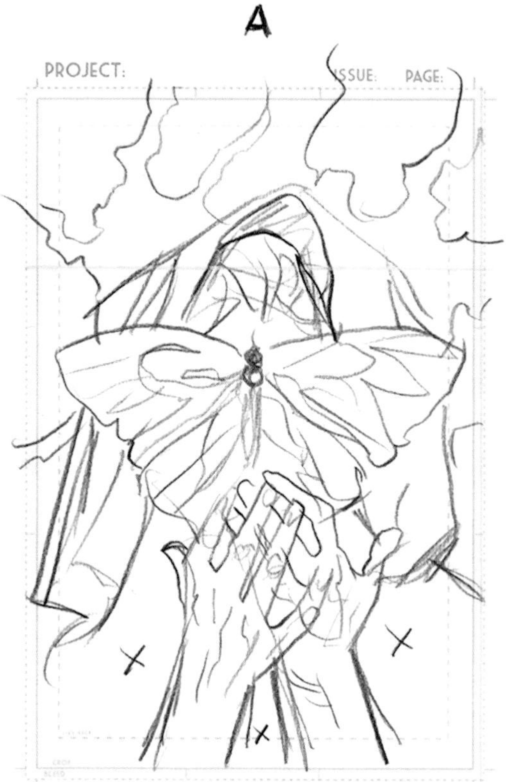
A
PROJECT:
ISSUE:
PAGE:

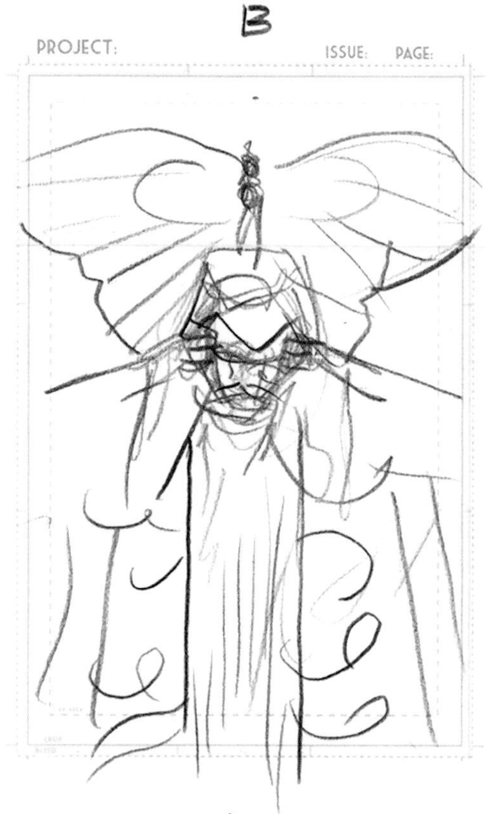
B
PROJECT:
ISSUE:
PAGE:

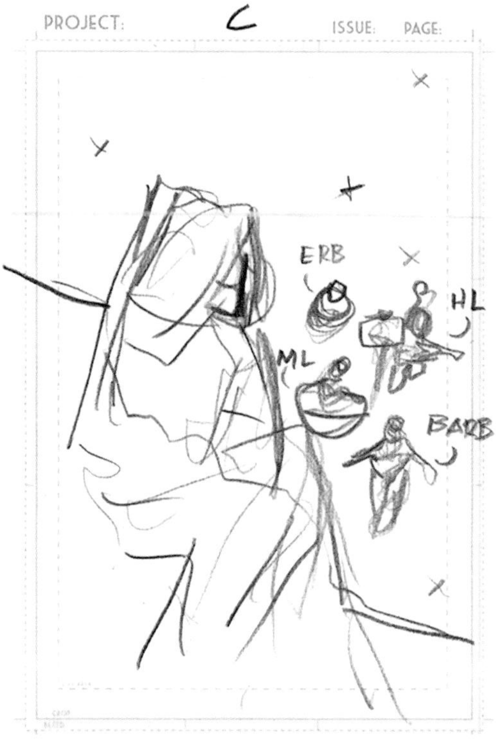
PROJECT:
C
ISSUE:
PAGE:
ERB
HL
ML
BARB

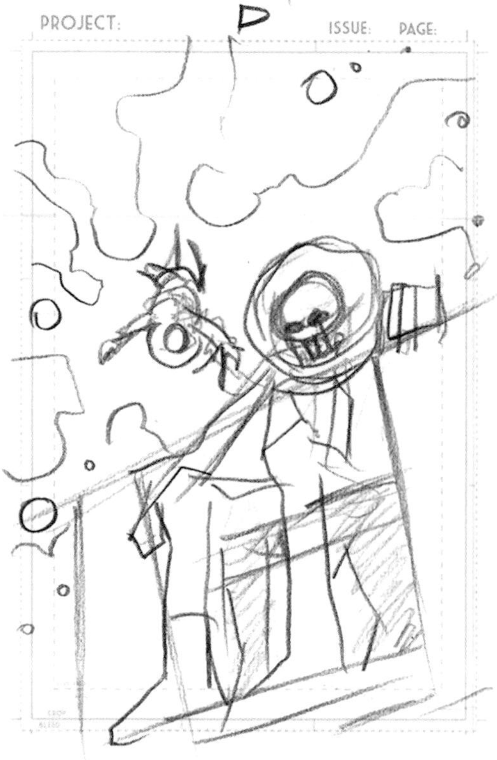
PROJECT:
D
ISSUE:
PAGE:

We wanted to feature Chronokus on the cover to Issue #5 without revealing his identity so all of the preliminary thumbnails were geared in that direction. We also wanted to include a group shot which is how we ended up on the final cover.

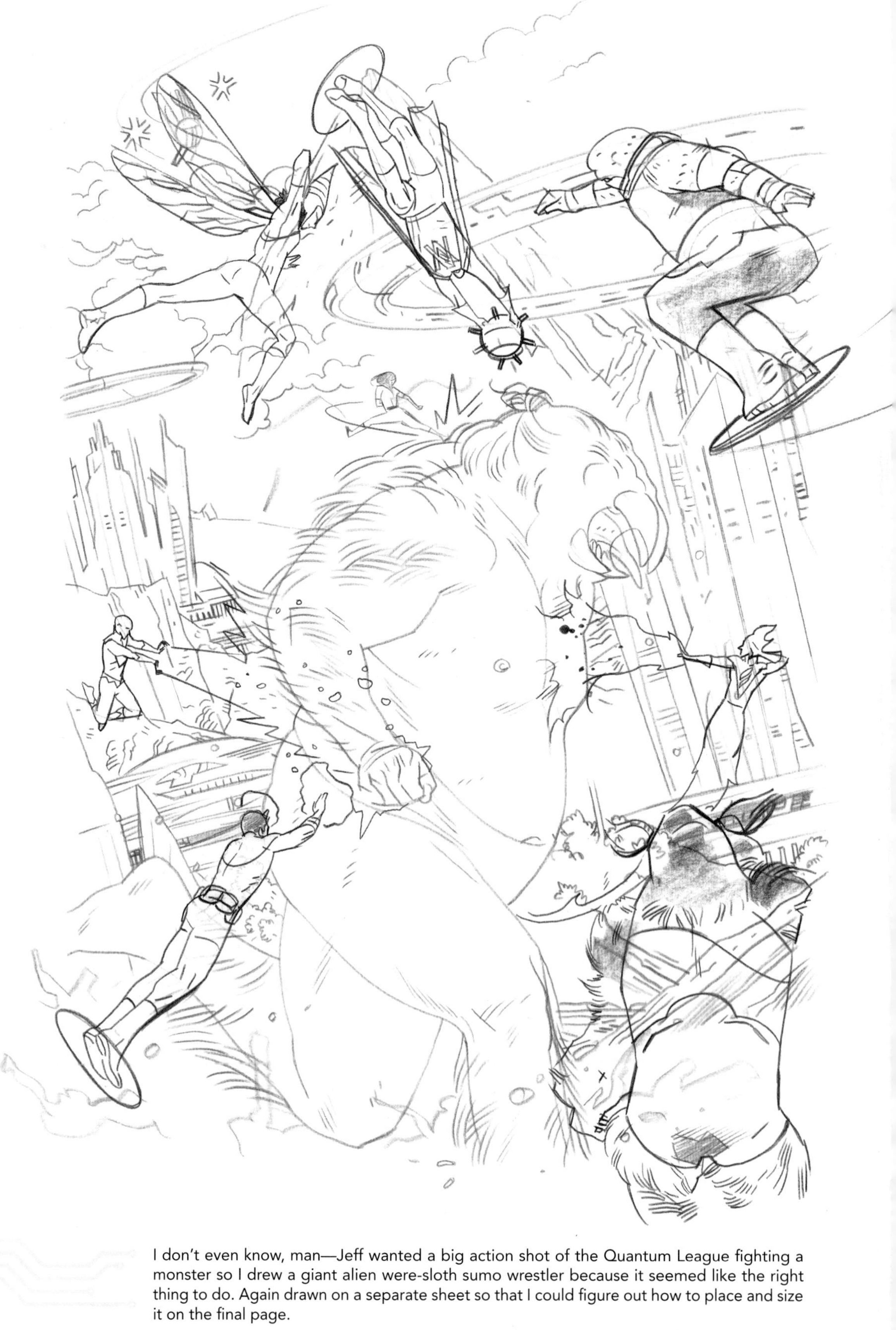

I don't even know, man—Jeff wanted a big action shot of the Quantum League fighting a monster so I drew a giant alien were-sloth sumo wrestler because it seemed like the right thing to do. Again drawn on a separate sheet so that I could figure out how to place and size it on the final page.

Art by Marcos Martín

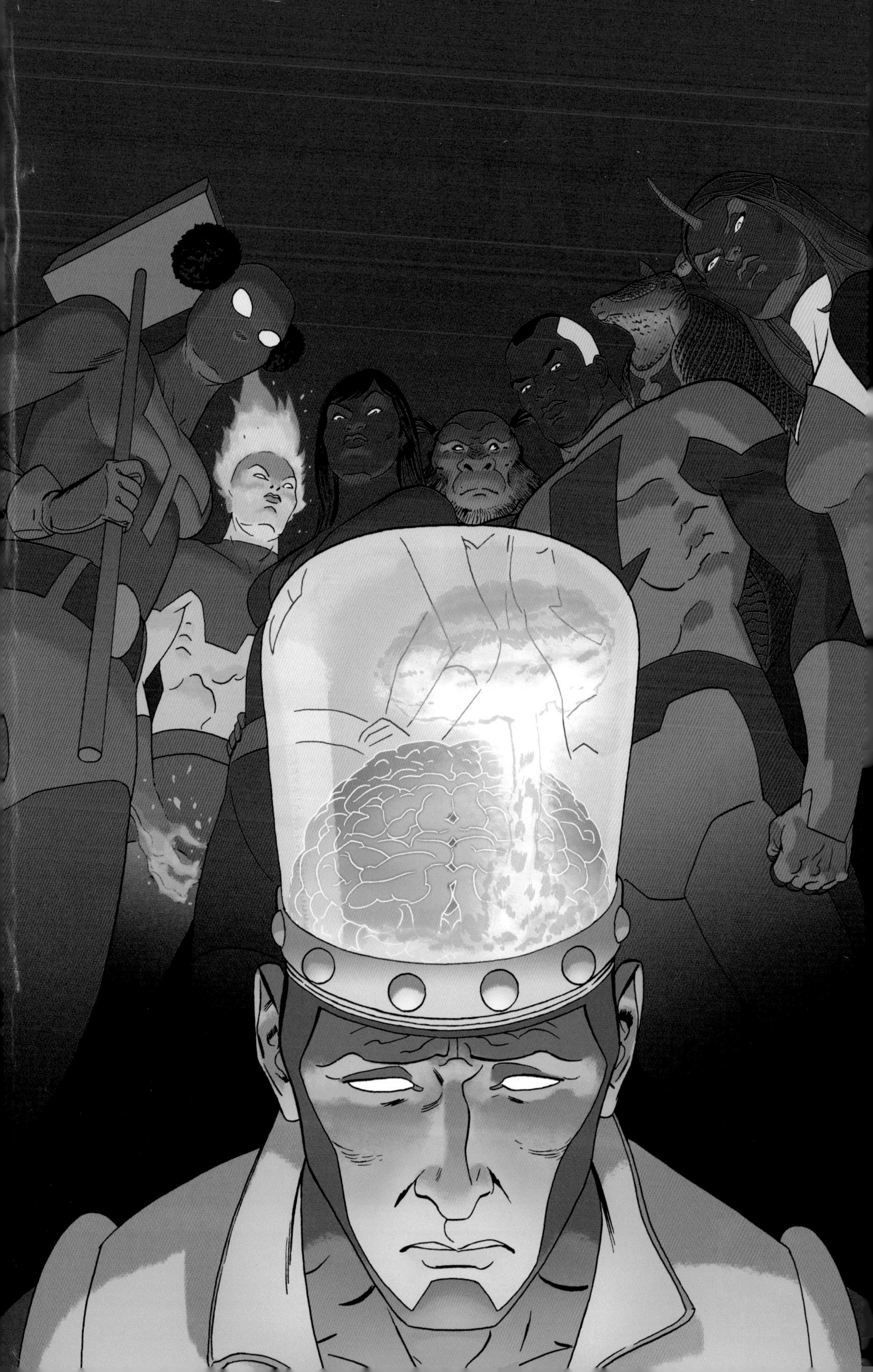

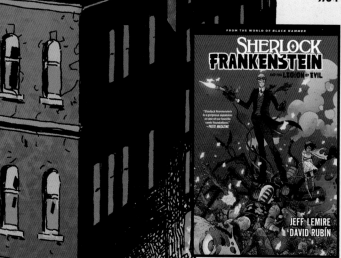